STATISTICAL DECOMPOSITION ANALYSIS

STUDIES
IN MATHEMATICAL AND
MANAGERIAL ECONOMICS

Editor

HENRI THEIL

VOLUME 14

NORTH-HOLLAND PUBLISHING COMPANY – AMSTERDAM · LONDON
AMERICAN ELSEVIER PUBLISHING COMPANY, INC. – NEW YORK

STATISTICAL DECOMPOSITION ANALYSIS

With Applications in the
Social and Administrative Sciences

by

HENRI THEIL

Center for Mathematical Studies in Business and Economics
The University of Chicago

1972

NORTH-HOLLAND PUBLISHING COMPANY – AMSTERDAM · LONDON
AMERICAN ELSEVIER PUBLISHING COMPANY, INC. – NEW YORK

Library of Congress Catalog Card Number: 75–184994
ISBN North-Holland: 0 7204 3314 2
ISBN American Elsevier: 0 444 10378 3

PUBLISHERS:

NORTH-HOLLAND PUBLISHING COMPANY – AMSTERDAM
NORTH-HOLLAND PUBLISHING COMPANY, LTD.–LONDON

SOLE DISTRIBUTORS FOR THE U.S.A. AND CANADA:

AMERICAN ELSEVIER PUBLISHING COMPANY, INC.
52 VANDERBILT AVENUE
NEW YORK, N.Y. 10017

PRINTED IN THE NETHERLANDS

INTRODUCTION TO THE SERIES

This is a series of books concerned with the quantitative approach to problems in the social and administrative sciences. The studies are in particular in the overlapping areas of mathematical economics, econometrics, operational research, and management science. Also, the mathematical and statistical techniques which belong to the apparatus of modern social and administrative sciences have their place in this series. A well-balanced mixture of pure theory and practical applications is envisaged, which ought to be useful for universities and for research workers in business and government.

The Editor hopes that the volumes of this series, all of which relate to such a young and vigorous field of research activity, will contribute to the exchange of scientific information at a truly international level.

THE EDITOR

PREFACE

In the last several years I have been working in the area of decompositions: the division of totals into parts. My first attemps concerned primarily economic applications and were summarized in *Economics and Information Theory* (1967). At a later stage I tried to extend the field of application to other social and administrative sciences. The result is presented in this volume, which covers topics in economics, management science, regional science, sociology, political science, accounting, and other areas. I hope that this book will contribute to breaking down the barriers that presently separate the social and administrative sciences. This objective has induced me to minimize the mathematical requirements. These consist of differential calculus and elementary mathematical statistics; the only exception is Chapter 5 in which matrix algebra is used.

It is a pleasure to acknowledge the help which I received while preparing this book. I received grants from the National Science Foundation, GS-2607 and GS-30084. Also, I was awarded the Henry Schultz Research Professorship of The University of Chicago's Division of Social Sciences in the year 1970. The expansion of the area of application of decomposition analysis was stimulated by my affiliation with the Graduate School of Business in addition to the Division's Department of Economics. The School encompasses many disciplines, which is very conducive to a project of this kind. I published or co-authored articles in a variety of journals, listed below, and I appreciate the willingness of the editors of these journals to permit their use for this volume.

Journal of the American Statistical Association
The Review of Economics and Statistics
International Economic Review
American Journal of Sociology
Journal of Mathematical Sociology
The American Political Science Review
Operations Research
Management Science
The Accounting Review

Several persons assisted me in the preparation and completion of this book. My colleague Duncan MacRae, Jr., gave valuable advice on problems in political science. Professor Edward O. Laumann of the University of Michigan helped me in identifying the occupational groups analyzed in Chapter 5. John Paulus, assisted by Harvey Silverman, was in charge of most of the computations. Harry Dreiser, Editor of Publications of the Graduate School of Business, gave valuable stylistic advice. My former secretary, Mrs. Sharon Roderick Massie, and her successor, Miss Amelia Wright, took professional care of the successive drafts. Mrs. Pat Mackay ably assited me in checking the proofs. It is a privilege for me to express my gratitude to them.

Chicago, Winter 1972   HENRI THEIL

TABLE OF CONTENTS

CHAPTER 1. INFORMATION AND DIVIDEDNESS: RACIAL INTEGRATION, INDUSTRIAL DIVERSITY, AND THE COMBINING OF ASSETS ON BALANCE SHEETS

CHAPTER 2. EXTENSIONS TO SEVERAL DECOMPOSITIONS

CHAPTER 3. MULTIDIMENSIONAL EXTENSIONS

LIST OF TABLES

CHAPTER 4

CHAPTER 5

HINTS FOR SELECTED PROBLEMS

LIST OF FIGURES

CHAPTER 5

TECHNICAL NOTES

The book is divided into chapters; each chapter consists of one or more opening paragraphs and a number of sections. For example, Section 3.2 is the second section of Chapter 3. Most of the sections are divided into an opening paragraph and several (unnumbered) subsections. Some subsections are starred, which indicates that they may be omitted at first reading.

Formulas are indicated by two numbers, the first of which refers to the section and the second to the order of occurrence. Thus, eq. (3.2) is the second equation of the third section of some chapter. Whenever reference is made to eq. (3.2), it is always the equation in the same chapter except when the contrary is stated explicitly.

Tables and figures are indicated by two numbers, the first of which refers to the *chapter* and the second to the order of occurrence: Table 5.1 is the first table in Chapter 5, Figure 4.2 is the second figure in Chapter 4. To facilitate finding a table or figure which is not in the same chapter, the section in which it occurs (or its page number) is usually indicated. The problems are all at the end of the chapters; they are indicated by one number.

Matrix algebra is used only in Chapter 5 and in Problems 10 to 12 of Chapter 2. Matrices are indicated by boldface uppercase letters, column vectors by boldface lowercase letters, and row vectors by boldface lowercase letters with a prime added to indicate that they are the transposes of the corresponding column vectors.

The measures defined in this book are applied to a variety of disciplines. To assist the reader in finding those areas which interest him, lists of entries in the Index are given on page 333 for four groups of disciplines.

CHAPTER 1

INFORMATION AND DIVIDEDNESS:

RACIAL INTEGRATION, INDUSTRIAL DIVERSITY,

AND THE COMBINING OF ASSETS ON BALANCE SHEETS

Many problems in the social and administrative sciences concern the division of some given total into a number of components. The question may then arise: How large is the degree of "dividedness"? The entropy provides an answer to this question. Below it is introduced in simple probabilistic terms, after which the concept is applied to a variety of problems.

1.1. Messages, Information, Entropy, and Uncertainty

Consider an event E with probability p; the nature of the event is irrelevant. At some point in time we receive a reliable message stating that E in fact occurred. The question is: How should one measure the amount of information conveyed by this message?

Information

Since the question is vague, we shall try to answer it in an intuitive manner. Suppose that p is close to 1 (e.g., $p = .95$). Then, one may argue, the message conveys very little information, because it was virtually certain that E would take place. But suppose that $p = .01$, so that it is almost certain E will not occur. If E nevertheless does occur, the message stating this will be unexpected and hence contains a great deal of information.

These intuitive ideas suggest that, if we want to measure the information received from a message in terms of the probability p that prevailed prior to the arrival of the message, we should select a *decreasing* function. The function proposed by SHANNON (1948) is

$$(1.1) \qquad h(p) = \log \frac{1}{p} = -\log p$$

which decreases from ∞ (infinite surprise and hence infinite information when the probability prior to the message is zero) to 0 (zero information when the probability is one). The function is illustrated in Figure 1.1. The unit of information is determined by the base of the logarithm. Frequently 2 is used as a base, which implies that any message concerning a 50-50 event has unit information: $h(\frac{1}{2}) = \log_2 2 = 1$, and information is then said to be measured in binary digits or, for short, *bits*. When natural logarithms are used, the information unit is a *nit*. Both units will be used in this book; they are shown along the two vertical axes of Figure 1.1.

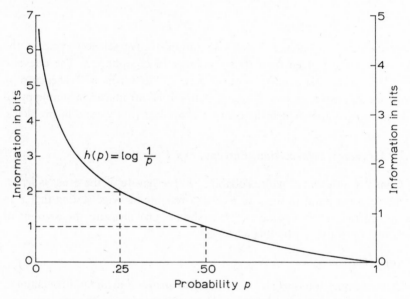

Fig. 1.1. Information measured in bits and in nits

The Additivity of Information

The function (1.1) is one of infinitely many decreasing functions. Its choice is motivated by the very convenient property of additivity, which is indeed important given that we shall add, subtract, and compute weighted averages of information values on a large scale in what follows. The subject is pursued more formally in the next section; here we shall explain what is meant by additivity.

For two events, A and B, consider P[A and B], the chance that both occur; P[A], the chance that A occurs (irrespective of whether B occurs); P[$A|B$], the conditional probability of A given B; and P[B] and P[$B|A$]

defined analogously. These five probabilities satisfy two equations:

(1.2) $P[A \text{ and } B] = P[A]P[B|A] = P[B]P[A|B]$

It is assumed that $P[A]$ and $P[B]$ are both nonzero, so that the two conditional probabilities can be determined from

$$P[B|A] = \frac{P[A \text{ and } B]}{P[A]} \quad \text{and} \quad P[A|B] = \frac{P[A \text{ and } B]}{P[B]}$$

Suppose then that we are first informed that A occurred; hence, using (1.1), we have received an amount of information equal to $\log(1/P[A])$. Given this message, the probability that B will occur is now $P[B|A]$. Assume next that we are informed that B also occurred. The total information received from these two successive messages is

$$\log \frac{1}{P[A]} + \log \frac{1}{P[B|A]} = \log \frac{1}{P[A]P[B|A]}$$

and it follows from (1.2) that this is equal to $\log(1/P[A \text{ and } B])$, the information received from the message stating that both A and B occurred. The content of this message is identical with the combined content of the two earlier messages (first on A, then on B), so that it seems reasonable to require that the total information provided by the messages "A" and "B" be identical with the information provided by the message "A and B". The information definition (1.1) satisfies this condition.

It is easily seen that we obtain the same result when the first message refers to B and the second to A:

$$\log \frac{1}{P[B]} + \log \frac{1}{P[A|B]} = \log \frac{1}{P[B]P[A|B]} = \log \frac{1}{P[A \text{ and } B]}$$

Definition (1.1) thus implies that the total amount of information is independent of the order in which the separate messages arrive. The only thing that matters is the set of probabilities $P[A]$, $P[B]$, $P[A|B]$, and $P[B|A]$.

The Entropy of a Distribution

The information received from the message which states that event E occurred is *not* the same as the information of the message concerning the complementary event (stating that E failed to occur). If p is the probability of E, the information provided by the latter message is

$$h(1-p) = \log \frac{1}{1-p}$$

It should indeed be obvious that the two information values, $h(p)$ and $h(1-p)$, are not the same (unless $p = \frac{1}{2}$), for if $p = .99$ (say), we are not at all surprised to hear later on that E occurred, whereas the opposite message would cause a great deal of surprise.

Therefore, as far as event E is concerned, the information to be received is either $h(p)$ or $h(1-p)$ and we do not know which as long as the message of occurrence or nonoccurrence has not been received. However, we can compute the *expected information content* of this message prior to its arrival.

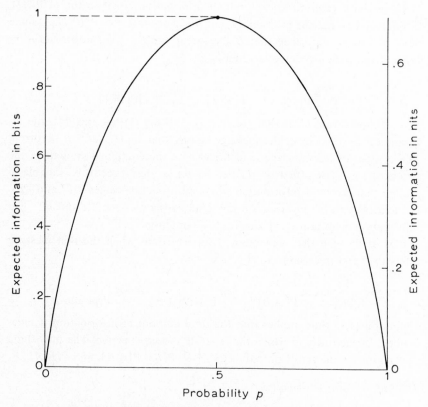

Fig. 1.2.   The entropy function for two alternatives (E and not-E)

Since E will occur with probability p and not-E with probability $1-p$, the information received will be $h(p)$ with the former probability and $h(1-p)$ with the latter. The expected information content is obtained by weighting these information values by their probabilities:

(1.3) $H = p\,h(p) + (1-p)\,h(1-p)$

$$= p \log \frac{1}{p} + (1-p) \log \frac{1}{1-p}$$

This H is also known as the *entropy* of any distribution that assigns probabilities p and $1-p$ to the two different possibilities (E and not-E in this case).[1] It follows directly from (1.3) that the entropy function is symmetric in p and $1-p$ and hence also in E and not-E. The function (1.3) is shown in Figure 1.2; it is nonnegative, it takes the zero value at $p = 0$ and $p = 1$, it reaches a maximum at $p = \frac{1}{2}$, and the value of the maximum is

(1.4) $\frac{1}{2} \log 2 + \frac{1}{2} \log 2 = \log 2 = 1$ bit

The Entropy at Zero or Unit Probability

It was just stated that the entropy vanishes at $p = 0$ and $p = 1$, but note that at $p = 0$, $p \log(1/p)$ is of the form $0 \times \infty$ and is thus undefined. Similarly, at $p = 1$ we have the same problem for the second expression in the second line of (1.3). It is customary to define

(1.5) $x \log \dfrac{1}{x} = 0 \quad \text{if} \quad x = 0$

and we shall follow this custom throughout this book. This definition is in accordance with the limit of $x \log(1/x)$ for x approaching zero, which may be illustrated as follows:

$$\frac{1}{2} \log 2 = \frac{1}{2} \text{ bit}$$
$$\frac{1}{4} \log 4 = \frac{1}{2} \text{ bit}$$
$$\frac{1}{8} \log 8 = \frac{3}{8} \text{ bit}$$
$$\frac{1}{16} \log 16 = \frac{1}{4} \text{ bit}$$
$$\vdots$$
$$\frac{1}{1024} \log 1024 = \frac{10}{1024} \text{ bit}$$

For $x = 1/2^k$, $x \log(1/x) = k/2^k$ bit, which converges to zero as k increases indefinitely. See Problem 2 at the end of this chapter for a formal proof.

---

[1] The term entropy is of physical origin. The concept plays an important role in thermodynamics.

Extension to Several Events

Let there be n events $E_1, \ldots, E_n$ with probabilities $p_1, \ldots, p_n$. It is assumed to be certain that exactly one of these events will occur; hence the p's add up to 1. If E_i occurs, the message which states this has information content $h(p_i)$. Since the probability of E_i is p_i, the expected information of the message on the occurrence of one of these events (or equivalently the entropy of the distribution with probabilities $p_1, \ldots, p_n$) is

$$(1.6) \qquad H = \sum_{i=1}^{n} p_i h(p_i) = \sum_{i=1}^{n} p_i \log \frac{1}{p_i}$$

which includes (1.3) as a special case for $n = 2$.

The entropy (1.6) is nonnegative, because it is obtained by weighting the nonnegative information values $h(p_i)$ with the nonnegative p_i's. It takes the zero value when one of the events has unit probability and (hence) all others zero probability. This is verified by substituting in (1.6) $p_i = 1$ for some i and $p_j = 0$ for all $j \neq i$, and it is in accordance with Figure 1.2 for the case $n = 2$. Hence no information is to be expected from the message when it is known before that one of the events has unit probability. This is as one would expect it to be.

It was stated above that for $n = 2$ the entropy is at its maximum when the two probabilities are equal and that the value of the maximum is $\log 2$ $= 1$ bit. It will be shown later in this section that in the more general case the entropy is maximized when all n probabilities are equal to $1/n$. The maximum value is thus

$$(1.7) \qquad \frac{1}{n} \log n + \ldots + \frac{1}{n} \log n = \log n$$

which is a generalization of (1.4). Note that this maximum increases when we imagine that the number of possible outcomes (n) increases.

These results are intuitively understandable. When there are three possibilities with probabilities $(.98, .01, .01)$, there is little doubt about what will happen and hence little information to be expected from the message which states what actually happened. But when the probabilities are $(\frac{1}{3}, \frac{1}{3}, \frac{1}{3})$, there is a great deal of doubt and hence much information to be expected. When we have ten possibilities rather than three, each of which has probability .1, there is even more uncertainty and hence more information to be expected.

Entropy as a Measure of Uncertainty

The examples discussed in the previous paragraph show that uncertainty and expected information are two sides of the same coin.

Uncertainty prevails prior to the message, and information is received when the message arrives. The more uncertainty prior to the message, the larger is the amount of information conveyed by it, at least on the average. Therefore, the entropy (1.6), originally introduced here as the expected information of the message that states which of the n possible outcomes is realized, may also be regarded as a measure of the uncertainty associated with a distribution whose probabilities are $p_1, \ldots, p_n$. In this regard it is comparable with the variance (or the standard deviation) of a random variable whose values are real numbers; such a variance, too, is a measure of the uncertainty of the outcome. The main difference is that the entropy can and the variance cannot be applied to nominal variables: those which take "qualitative" rather than quantitative values, such as black and white, or Catholic, Protestant, and Jew, or current assets and fixed assets on a balance sheet. This is so because the entropy in contrast to the variance depends exclusively on the probabilities with which these possible outcomes are realized, not on the (numerical or nonnumerical) values of these outcomes.

When we stated at the beginning of the previous paragraph that more uncertainty prior to the message implies a larger amount of information conveyed by the message, we added "at least on the average". This restriction is important. Let E have probability .01 and hence not-E probability .99. There is then little uncertainty but, nevertheless, an amount of information as high as

$$(1.8) \qquad \log \frac{1}{.01} = 6.64 \text{ bits}$$

when E occurs. The point is that this happens only 1 out of 100 times, and that in the other 99 cases the information is as low as

$$(1.9) \qquad \log \frac{1}{.99} = .0145 \text{ bit}$$

The average information received (the entropy) is

$$(1.10) \qquad .01(6.64) + .99(.0145) = .081 \text{ bit}$$

which is a small value in accordance with the low degree of uncertainty.

The variance uses the squared deviation from the mean as the basic ingredient for the measurement of uncertainty, and the entropy uses information for this purpose. But the variance is not equal to such a squared deviation, nor is the entropy equal to any particular information value. The variance is the expectation of the squared deviation from the mean and the entropy is the expectation of information.

Proof of the Entropy Maximum

The objective is to maximize the entropy function (1.6) or, equivalently, to minimize $-H = \sum_i p_i \log p_i$ for variations in the p_i's subject to the constraints $\sum p_i = 1$, $p_i \geq 0$ for $i = 1, \ldots, n$. The Lagrangian technique is the simplest procedure, and it is outlined in the next paragraph for readers who are familiar with it. For those who are not, a proof based on elementary calculus is given in the next subsection.

Consider the expression

$$(1.11) \qquad \sum_{i=1}^{n} p_i \log p_i - \mu \left(\sum_{i=1}^{n} p_i - 1 \right)$$

where μ is a Lagrangian multiplier. Differentiate this expression with respect to p_i and put the derivative equal to zero. If log stands for natural logarithm,[1] this gives $1 + \log p_i - \mu = 0$ or $\log p_i = \mu - 1$, which shows that p_i is independent of i. Hence all p's must be equal and thus equal to $1/n$. Note that we have not imposed the inequality constraints $p_i \geq 0$, $i = 1, \ldots, n$ but that the solution $p_1 = \ldots = p_n = 1/n$ does satisfy the constraint. This means that this is indeed the solution, for it is never possible to obtain a better value of a criterion function by imposing additional constraints (here: the nonnegativity constraints).

Alternative Proof

For a second proof, consider

$$\log n - H = \sum_{i=1}^{n} p_i (\log n + \log p_i) = \sum_{i=1}^{n} p_i \log n p_i$$

When $p_i = 1/n$ for each i, the third member becomes $\sum_i p_i \log 1 = 0$, which confirms $H = \log n$ in the equiprobability case. To prove that this is the

---

[1] When another logarithmic base is used, the entropy is multiplied by a positive constant which is independent of the p's. This does not affect the result.

unique maximum of H it is evidently sufficient to show that

$$(1.12) \qquad \sum_{i=1}^{n} p_i \log np_i > 0$$

when the p_i's are *not* all equal to $1/n$.

Next define:

$$(1.13) \qquad x_i = n\left(p_i - \frac{1}{n}\right) \quad \text{or} \quad p_i = \frac{1}{n}(1+x_i)$$

This x_i is simply n times the deviation of p_i from the equiprobability value $1/n$ and it is thus positive (zero, negative) when p_i is larger than (equal to, smaller than) $1/n$. The sum of the x_i's is zero:

$$(1.14) \qquad \sum_{i=1}^{n} x_i = n \sum_{i=1}^{n}\left(p_i - \frac{1}{n}\right) = n(1-1) = 0$$

We proceed to substitute the x's in the left-hand side of (1.12):

$$(1.15) \qquad \sum_{i=1}^{n} p_i \log np_i = \frac{1}{n}\sum_{i=1}^{n}(1+x_i)\log(1+x_i)$$

$$= \frac{1}{n}\sum_{i=1}^{n} f(x_i)$$

where

$$(1.16) \qquad f(x_i) = (1+x_i)\log(1+x_i)$$

A comparison with (1.12) shows that it is sufficient to prove

$$(1.17) \qquad \sum_{i=1}^{n} f(x_i) > 0 \qquad \text{(not all } x_i\text{'s equal to zero)}$$

To prove that this is so we consider the derivative of $f(\ )$, to be denoted by $f'(\ )$, under the assumption that our logs are natural logarithms:

$$(1.18) \qquad f'(x_i) = 1+\log(1+x_i) \begin{cases} > 1 & \text{if} \quad x_i > 0 \\ = 1 & \text{if} \quad x_i = 0 \\ < 1 & \text{if} \quad x_i < 0 \end{cases}$$

The mean value theorem states that $f(x) = f(0)+xf'(\theta x)$, where θ is a number between zero and one. Since $f(0) = 0$ for the function (1.16), we thus have, using (1.18),

(1.19)
$$f(x_i) = \begin{cases} (1+\delta_i)x_i & \text{if } x_i > 0 \\ x_i & \text{if } x_i = 0 \\ (1-\varepsilon_i)x_i & \text{if } x_i < 0 \end{cases}$$

where the δ's and ε's are all positive numbers. Hence:

$$\sum_{i=1}^{n} f(x_i) = \sum_{i=1}^{n} x_i + {\sum}' \delta_i x_i - {\sum}'' \varepsilon_i x_i$$

$$= {\sum}' \delta_i x_i - {\sum}'' \varepsilon_i x_i \qquad \text{[see (1.14)]}$$

where $\sum'$ indicates summation over all values of i for which $x_i > 0$ and $\sum''$ summation over all values for which $x_i < 0$. But $\delta_i x_i > 0$ for $x_i > 0$ because $\delta_i > 0$, and hence $\sum' \delta_i x_i > 0$. Similarly $\varepsilon_i x_i < 0$ for $x_i < 0$ because $\varepsilon_i > 0$, and hence $-\sum'' \varepsilon_i x_i > 0$. This proves (1.17) and thus also (1.12).

The Entropy Estimated from a Random Sample*

In a number of cases the probabilities $p_1, \ldots, p_n$ will be unknown and must be estimated from a random sample. The entropy computed from such estimates is then subject to a sampling error, and the question arises as to what can be said about the size of this error. The amount of work done in this area is limited, but the following result is useful when the available sample is not too small.

Write $\hat{p}_1, \ldots, \hat{p}_n$ for the observed relative frequencies of the n events in the sample. It is assumed to be a random sample of size N drawn from a multinomial population with probabilities $p_1, \ldots, p_n$. The entropy estimator is

(1.20)
$$\hat{H} = \sum_{i=1}^{n} \hat{p}_i \log \frac{1}{\hat{p}_i}$$

It can be shown that, for large N,[1] this estimator $\hat{H}$ is approximately normally distributed with mean H (the true entropy) and the following variance:

(1.21)
$$\frac{1}{N} \sum_{i=1}^{n} p_i \left(\log \frac{1}{p_i} - H \right)^2$$

Note that this variance expression is nothing but a fraction $1/N$ of the "variance of information". This is so because H is (by definition) expected information and

---

[1] More precisely, as $N \to \infty$ the random variable $\sqrt{N}(\hat{H} - H)$ converges in distribution to a normal variate with zero mean and variance (1.22).

$$(1.22) \qquad \sum_{i=1}^{n} p_i \left(\log \frac{1}{p_i} - H \right)^2$$

is thus the expected square of information after the expectation H is sub-tracted from each information value – which is precisely how a variance is computed. The result (1.21) implies (1) that $\hat{H}$ becomes a more accurate estimator of the population entropy as the sample size increases (which is not a surprising result) and (2) that given N the sampling error of $\hat{H}$ tends to be larger when there are larger differences between the probabilities and hence between the information values $\log (1/p_1), \ldots, \log (1/p_n)$.

When the sample is not large, it has been suggested that one add $(n-1)/2N$ to $\hat{H}$ to obtain an entropy estimator with a small bias (of order $1/N^2$). For further details reference may be made to a survey article by LUCE (1960, pp. 45–48).

1.2. An Axiomatic Approach to the Information Concept

The objective of this section is to show that the logarithmic information definition (1.1) is the only possible definition when certain simple axioms are accepted, the most important one being that of additivity. The approach followed here is based largely on KOOPMAN and KIMBALL (1959); reference should also be made to KHINCHIN (1957, pp. 9–13).

Four Axioms

The axioms are all concerned with the information content of a reliable message which states that event E occurred, given that the probability of E prior to the arrival of the message was p. Axiom I states that this infor-mation depends only on p. Hence it can be written as $h(p)$, but this function is not, of course, of the specific logarithmic form (1.1) at this stage. Axiom II states that $h(p)$ is a continuous function of p in the interval $0 < p \leq 1$ which declines monotonically:

$$(2.1) \qquad h(p_1) > h(p_2) \quad \text{if} \quad 0 < p_1 < p_2 \leq 1$$

Axiom III specifies that the message has zero information when the event has unit probability:

$$(2.2) \qquad h(1) = 0$$

Axiom IV is concerned with two events, E_1 and E_2, which are stochastically independent. Hence, if their probabilities are p_1 and p_2, the probability of their joint occurrence is $p_1 p_2$. The axiom states that the information content of the message which states that both occurred is equal to the information of the message dealing with only E_1 plus that which deals with only E_2:

$$(2.3) \qquad\qquad h(p_1 p_2) = h(p_1) + h(p_2) \qquad\qquad 0 < p_1, p_2 \leqq 1$$

This last axiom (the crucial one) is concerned with the additivity. A comparison with the discussion in the second subsection of Section 1.1 shows that the axiom is weaker than the additivity property described there, because it imposes its requirement only in the special case of stochastically independent events. Nevertheless, this axiom in conjunction with the three others insures that $h(\ )$ has to be of the form (1.1), as will be shown in the next subsection.

Outline of the Proof*

Define the following transformations of the probabilities that occur in (2.3):

$$(2.4) \qquad\qquad y_1 = \log \frac{1}{p_1} \qquad y_2 = \log \frac{1}{p_2}$$

where log stands for natural logarithm. Hence $p_i = e^{-y_i}$, $i = 1$ and 2, so that the two functions in the right-hand side of (2.3) can be written as

$$(2.5) \qquad\qquad h(p_i) = h(e^{-y_i}) = g(y_i) \quad \text{say} \qquad\qquad i = 1, 2$$

or equivalently $g(-\log p_i)$. Similarly for the left-hand side of (2.3):

$$h(p_1 p_2) = g(-\log p_1 p_2) = g(-\log p_1 - \log p_2) = g(y_1 + y_2)$$

Combining this with (2.5), we conclude that (2.3) is equivalent to

$$(2.6) \qquad\qquad g(y_1 + y_2) = g(y_1) + g(y_2) \quad \text{for all} \quad y_1, y_2 \geqq 0$$

Furthermore, since y_i is defined as a decreasing function of p_i, Axiom II implies that $g(\ )$ is an increasing function of its argument:

$$(2.7) \qquad\qquad g(y_1) < g(y_2) \quad \text{if} \quad 0 \leqq y_1 < y_2$$

Next substitute $y_1 = y_2 = 0$ in (2.6), which gives $g(0) = 2g(0)$. This implies that $g(0)$ is either zero or infinitely large. The latter possibility is excluded by Axiom III because $g(0) = h(1)$. Define $c = g(1)$, which is positive because (2.7) implies $0 = g(0) < g(1)$. Then apply (2.6) recursively:

$$g(2) = g(1) + g(1) = 2c$$
$$g(3) = g(2) + g(1) = 3c$$
$$\vdots$$
$$g(n) = nc \quad \text{(where } n \text{ is an integer)}$$

This shows that $g(y)$ is proportional to y when y is an integer. We proceed to show that this also holds when y takes rational values. Write $y = m/n$, where m is a nonnegative integer and n a positive integer. Since we have

$$m = \frac{m}{n} + \ldots + \frac{m}{n} \quad (n \text{ terms})$$

we may conclude, by repeated application of (2.6),

$$g(m) = g\left(\frac{m}{n}\right) + \ldots + g\left(\frac{m}{n}\right) = ng\left(\frac{m}{n}\right)$$

But $g(m) = mc$ because m is an integer. Hence:

(2.8) $$g\left(\frac{m}{n}\right) = c\,\frac{m}{n}$$

which shows that $g(y) = cy$, $c > 0$ holds for any nonnegative rational value of y. A limiting process based on the continuity postulated in Axiom II can be used to prove that we have the same result for irrational y. It then follows directly from (2.4) and (2.5) that $g(y) = cy$ implies

(2.9) $$h(p) = c \log \frac{1}{p}$$

which is equivalent to (1.1), the specification of c being a matter of appropriate choice of the logarithmic base.

1.3. Entropy as a General Measure of Dividedness

The entropy was introduced in Section 1.1 in probabilistic terms. Given that we know that exactly one of a number of events is bound to occur, and also the probabilities of occurrence, how much information will we receive when a message arrives stating what actually happened? This amount of information is a random variable and the entropy is its expectation. Also, we concluded that the entropy may be regarded as a measure for the uncertainty regarding the outcome, the argument being that uncertainty prior to the arrival of the message and expected information provided by the message are two sides of the same coin.

We thus have two different interpretations of the entropy concept. There is a much broader interpretation, however, which goes far beyond the narrow area of messages and even that of probabilities. Some examples, which will be considered in more detail later in this chapter, may serve to substantiate this claim.

(1) Students of a school are distinguished by race, a certain proportion (p) being black and the rest $(1-p)$ white. The entropy of this racial distribution as illustrated in Figure 1.2 is a simple measure for the degree to which the school is integrated. Its minimum is zero (only one race is represented, either black or white) and its maximum is $\log 2 = 1$ bit (both races equally represented).

(2) Let $p_1, \ldots, p_n$ be the market shares of the firms of an industry. Then the entropy (1.6) is an inverse measure of concentration: zero when the industry consists of only one firm ($p_i = 1$ for some i, $p_j = 0$ for each $j \neq i$), the maximum value ($\log n$) when all n firms have equal shares, and this maximum increases when the number of firms (n) increases.

(3) Let n be the number of political parties in a country and $p_1, \ldots, p_n$ the proportions of valid votes cast for these parties in an election. Then the entropy (1.6) measures political dividedness at the voters' level. Furthermore, when the proportions of parliament seats obtained by these parties are $p'_1, \ldots, p'_n$, the associated entropy $H' = -\sum p'_i \log p'_i$ measures political dividedness at the legislative level. Finally, when the election leads to a coalition cabinet and $p''_1, \ldots, p''_n$ are the proportions of cabinet posts obtained by the n parties, the corresponding H'' is the entropy at the executive level. Obviously, $H'' = 0$ for a one-party cabinet.

These examples have three things in common. First, they are all concerned with a given total: the student body of a school, the total market of an industry, the votes cast by all voters, a parliament, and a cabinet. Second, in each instance the total is subdivided into components: black and white students, market shares of individual firms, and votes, parliament seats, and cabinet posts obtained by separate political parties. Third, the entropy is in each case used as a measure for the extent to which the given total is subdivided into parts, with a large entropy value when the components are small and numerous, and a small value when there is one dominant component. It may be added that the probabilistic interpretation of the entropy concept set forth in Section 1.1 also shares these three features. The given total is the set of all events ($E_1, \ldots, E_n$) and our 100 per cent confidence that one of these events will occur. The separate E_i's are the components of this given total, and the corresponding p_i's are proportions that measure our confidence that they will occur. The entropy (1.6) measures the extent to which our total confidence is subdivided into parts. The larger the degree of subdivision, the greater is our uncertainty as to which event will occur.

These considerations show that the entropy can be regarded as a measure in the broad field of *decomposition mathematics*. In fact, in this book the entropy (and related concepts to be described in later chapters) will be employed mostly for this general purpose, rather than in the much narrower interpretation of the expected information of a message. The reason we introduced the concept within the latter framework in Section 1.1 is partly historical (Shannon's article in 1948), partly didactic. It is simpler to develop a concept in terms of the specifics of events, probabilities, and messages than in terms of the generality of decompositions of given totals into components of nonnegative size. However, there is one aspect described in Section 1.1 that is truly essential, and this is the additivity of the measure. It accounts for the superiority of the entropy over many competing measures, a point which will become clear below when specific applications are discussed.

It should also be stressed that the information concept developed in the two previous sections is, in a sense, a primitive one. It is supposed to depend only on the probability p of event E and is thus completely independent of the importance of the event. This means that, when an application is concerned with "information" in the conventional sense and when "importance" is indeed an issue, we shall have to make a special effort to take this importance into consideration. However, in most applications we will be concerned with decompositions that have little to do with "information" in the usual sense of the word.

1.4. The Racial Entropy of Chicago's Public Schools

This section describes an application of the entropy concept to the measurement of racial integration and segregation of schools. The discussion of this subject, based on work done by THEIL and FINIZZA (1967, 1971), will be continued in Sections 2.2 and 3.2.

Description of the Data

In the autumn of each year a racial headcount of students is organized among the principals and teachers of Chicago's public schools. The period considered below is 1963 to 1969. The classification was not constant during this period. In the first four years there were three groups: Caucasian, Negroid, and Other, but in the last three years a Puerto Rican category was formed from the Other category. To obtain comparability we have combined the Puerto Rican and Other groups with the Caucasian, so that only two groups remain: Negro and not-Negro. For simplicity we shall refer to them as black and white.

The total number of schools varied over the years but it was of the order of 500, and the average number of students per school a little below 1000. According to the 1966 districting, shown in Figure 1.3, the schools were combined into 27 geographic-administrative school districts. The first three

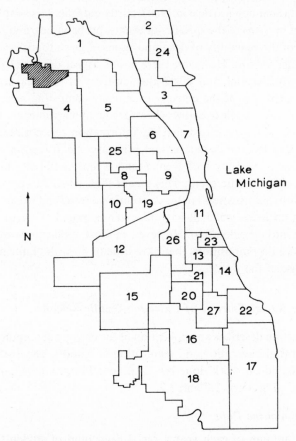

Fig. 1.3.   The public school districts of Chicago according to the 1966 districting

columns of Table 1.1 contain some district data for 1969: the number of schools in each district, the size of the district measured by its share of the city's total school population, and the percentage of white students in each district. It is seen that the latter percentage varies from 0 to almost 100. The percentage of white students in the set of all public schools in the city declined gradually, from 49 in 1963 to 44 in 1969. All data refer to elementary schools.

RACIAL DATA ON THE PUBLIC SCHOOL DISTRICTS OF CHICAGO

District	Number of schools	Number of students (% of city total)	Perc. of white students	Average racial entropy of schools						
				1963	1964	1965	1966	1967	1968	1969
1	27	3.40	99.9	.1	.2	.6	.8	.6	.9	1.0
2	11	1.73	99.7	.3	.3	.1	.1	.5	1.3	2.5
3	17	3.89	99.7	.6	2.4	2.7	2.5	2.0	3.2	2.6
4	23	4.30	64.3	6.7	8.8	14.0	20.7	19.7	35.5	35.5
5	25	4.83	99.8	.1	.1	.0	.2	.3	.3	1.5
6	25	5.32	94.0	17.8	18.6	18.4	19.1	20.9	22.7	25.1
7	20	3.84	43.1	32.7	32.0	29.7	30.0	29.7	27.1	28.2
8	18	4.48	1.7	28.5	23.6	17.7	12.8	11.6	9.6	7.9
9	25	4.27	10.6	26.9	26.1	23.6	20.2	17.8	16.7	14.6
10	16	4.31	19.2	10.7	7.0	6.2	7.1	7.3	8.1	8.9
11	19	3.61	4.3	13.3	9.9	10.0	8.4	9.5	9.5	11.2
12	26	3.44	91.6	12.7	12.4	12.1	11.6	10.3	10.4	9.1
13	18	4.19	.0	.3	.5	.5	.2	.2	.3	.3
14	17	2.84	9.4	30.2	28.4	24.9	22.6	20.8	21.6	20.9
15	24	4.03	73.2	20.8	18.5	14.2	13.1	13.7	15.2	25.8
16	23	5.06	6.4	30.6	28.1	28.1	24.6	21.8	20.5	-14.5
17	20	3.12	74.9	14.1	18.3	20.6	24.1	25.8	30.0	36.4
18	35	5.55	45.0	6.7	7.2	11.4	16.1	20.4	22.6	22.6
19	20	4.34	44.2	10.6	11.1	11.1	11.0	12.1	11.9	11.6
20	15	3.96	.1	4.0	5.4	3.8	2.9	2.5	1.8	.9
21	13	3.05	.3	2.6	1.7	1.6	1.4	1.9	1.5	2.1
22	9	1.98	23.1	37.7	46.8	46.6	44.2	48.2	48.8	42.5
23	16	2.64	.1	1.6	1.2	1.5	.9	1.0	1.0	.7
24	16	2.57	96.7	3.3	3.7	5.1	7.7	8.1	12.5	17.6
25	16	3.87	32.9	22.9	27.4	26.2	24.3	23.0	24.7	20.1
26	13	3.03	58.4	15.2	15.9	18.9	20.9	23.5	23.3	18.1
27	11	2.33	.7	22.7	20.8	16.3	12.2	9.6	7.9	5.8
City average	518*	100*	44.2	14.0	13.7	13.2	12.9	13.1	14.1	14.4

* City total

Average Racial Entropies

We return to example (1) of Section 1.3 and write p_j for the proportion of black students in the jth school and $1-p_j$ for the proportion of white students. The entropy of this racial distribution, to be called the racial entropy of the student body of the jth school, is

$$(4.1) \qquad H_j = p_j \log \frac{1}{p_j} + (1-p_j) \log \frac{1}{1-p_j}$$

which varies from zero (one race only) to a maximum of 1 bit (50–50 black and white).

One can compute these entropies for all N schools of the city and for all years, but since N is so large a complete display of all these numbers in each of the seven years defeats its own purpose. Instead, we shall consider the average racial entropy of all schools in each of the 27 districts. This raises the question of what kind of average is to be used. Recall that entropy is an additive measure; this suggests that the arithmetic average or a weighted average is appropriate, which in turn raises the question of which weights are to be used. Suppose then that we select a student at random from the total student population of a district and ask: How large is the chance that the student selected is in one particular school of this district? The answer is obviously that the chance is equal to this school's proportion of the district's student body, and we shall thus weight accordingly.

Specifically, write w_j for the size of the student body of the jth school, measured as a fraction of the city total. Hence $w_1 + \ldots + w_N = 1$. Write W_r for the size of the student body of the rth district (to be written D_r) also measured as a fraction of the city total. This W_r is obtained by adding the w_j's of the schools that belong to the district:[1]

$$(4.2) \qquad W_r = \sum_{j \in D_r} w_j \qquad\qquad r = 1, \ldots, 27$$

Then the ratio $w_j/W_r, j \in D_r$ is the student body of the jth school measured as a proportion of the total student body of the district to which it belongs. Hence the average racial entropy of the schools of district D_r is

$$(4.3) \quad \bar{H}_r = \sum_{j \in D_r} \frac{w_j}{W_r} H_j = \sum_{j \in D_r} \frac{w_j}{W_r} \left[p_j \log \frac{1}{p_j} + (1-p_j) \log \frac{1}{1-p_j} \right]$$

In the same way, the average racial entropy of all N schools in the city

---

[1] The third column of Table 1.1 specifies these W_r's for 1969 in percentage form.

as a whole is obtained by weighting the H_j's with the w_j's (the student population proportions that refer to the city total):

$$(4.4) \qquad \bar{H} = \sum_{j=1}^{N} w_j H_j = \sum_{j=1}^{N} w_j \left[p_j \log \frac{1}{p_j} + (1-p_j) \log \frac{1}{1-p_j} \right]$$

Note that $\bar{H}$ and $\bar{H}_r$ have the important property of *aggregation consistency*. The city average $\bar{H}$ of the school racial entropies is identical with the weighted average of the district averages $\bar{H}_1, \ldots, \bar{H}_{27}$ with weights proportional to the numbers of students in the districts:

$$(4.5) \qquad \sum_{r=1}^{27} W_r \bar{H}_r = \sum_{r=1}^{27} W_r \sum_{j \in D_r} \frac{w_j}{W_r} H_j = \sum_{j=1}^{N} w_j H_j = \bar{H}$$

where the first equality sign is based on (4.3) and the last on (4.4).

The last seven columns of Table 1.1 contain the average racial entropies of the schools of each district and of the city as a whole in each of the seven years. The entropies are expressed as a percentage of one bit and can thus vary from 0 to 100. The table shows that none of the figures exceeds one-half of the upper limit. In fact, the city average $\bar{H}$ is only about one-seventh of this limit. Its behavior during the seven-year period was not monotonically increasing or decreasing; it decreased slightly from 1963 until the middle of this period and it increased slightly thereafter. There are four districts $(D_4, D_{17}, D_{18}, D_{24})$ for which the 1969 average racial entropy exceeded the 1963 figure by more than .1 bit, four others $(D_8, D_9, D_{16}, D_{27})$ which changed by at least the same amount but in the opposite direction, and the 19 that remain have 1969 figures that differ from those of 1963 by less than .1 bit. The conclusion is that the racial entropy of the schools is generally on the low side and that there is little evidence of a uniform change, either upward or downward.

The Measurement of Integration and Segregation

The use of the racial entropy permits the analyst to investigate systematically the extent to which the student population of a school (or any other group of persons) is "racially divided" or "racially integrated". An alternative measure which is frequently used is the percentage of students attending schools where the dominant race has a share of less than 80 per cent of the student population. One objection to this measure is the arbitrariness of the cut-off point. Another is that it makes no distinction between a 50-50 and a 70-30 composition, nor between an 85-15 and a 95-5 composition; what counts is whether the school is above or below the cut-off point, whatever point is selected, and that is it. Figure 1.2 shows that the entropy is a smooth and continuous measure of integration, which is obviously preferable.

Be that as it may, it is important to realize what the racial entropy does not measure. If the student body of a school district has a 50-50 racial composition, the average racial entropy of its schools can be 1 bit. For this to be the case it is sufficient (and necessary) that all schools of this district have a 50-50 composition. But when a district has a total student body consisting of 20 per cent blacks and 80 per cent whites or vice versa, it is impossible for the average racial entropy of its schools to be as high as 1 bit. Some schools can be 50-50 but evidently not all, and those whose racial composition deviates from 50-50 have an entropy less than 1 bit, which necessarily reduces the average entropy of all schools of the district below 1 bit. An example is the first district of Table 1.1, which is predominantly white (99.9 per cent in 1969). It should come as no surprise that the average racial entropy of its schools is very low.

These considerations suggest that, for the measurement of segregation rather than integration, it is appropriate to compare the racial composition of a school with that of the district to which it belongs. The present analysis does not perform this; it considers each racial distribution separately, it uses the entropies of such distributions and it works with various averages of these entropies, but it does not relate one racial distribution directly to another. We will continue this discussion in Section 2.2.

1.5. The Entropy Decomposition Theorem

One of the most powerful properties of the entropy concept is its simplicity in handling problems of aggregation and disaggregation. This is ultimately due to its additivity.

Events and Sets of Events

We return to the events $E_1, \ldots, E_n$ and their probabilities $p_1, \ldots, p_n$ of Section 1.1. It is assumed that these events are combined into a smaller number of sets of events, $S_1, \ldots, S_G$ in such a way that each E_i falls under exactly one S_g, where $g = 1, \ldots, G$. For example, for $n = 6$ we may have

$$S_1 = (E_1, E_4, E_5) \qquad S_2 = (E_2, E_3) \qquad S_3 = (E_6) \qquad (G = 3)$$

The probability of the set S_g (that is, the probability that one of the E_i's falling under S_g will occur) is obtained by summation:

$$(5.1) \qquad P_g = \sum_{i \in S_g} p_i \qquad\qquad g = 1, \ldots, G$$

and the entropy at the level of sets of events is therefore

$$(5.2) \qquad H_0 = \sum_{g=1}^{G} P_g \log \frac{1}{P_g}$$

The problem is: What is the relationship between this entropy, to be called the *between-group entropy*, and the entropy H defined in (1.6) at the level of the individual events $E_1, \ldots, E_n$?

Between-Group and Within-Group Entropies

To solve this problem we write the entropy H as follows:

$$
\begin{aligned}
\sum_{i=1}^{n} p_i \log \frac{1}{p_i} &= \sum_{g=1}^{G} \sum_{i \in S_g} p_i \log \frac{1}{p_i} \\
&= \sum_{g=1}^{G} P_g \sum_{i \in S_g} \frac{p_i}{P_g} \left(\log \frac{1}{P_g} + \log \frac{P_g}{p_i} \right) \\
&= \sum_{g=1}^{G} P_g \left(\sum_{i \in S_g} \frac{p_i}{P_g} \right) \log \frac{1}{P_g} + \sum_{g=1}^{G} P_g \left[\sum_{i \in S_g} \frac{p_i}{P_g} \log \frac{P_g}{p_i} \right] \\
&= \sum_{g=1}^{G} P_g \log \frac{1}{P_g} + \sum_{g=1}^{G} P_g \left[\sum_{i \in S_g} \frac{p_i}{P_g} \log \frac{1}{p_i/P_g} \right]
\end{aligned}
$$

The left-hand side of this equation is H and the first right-hand term in the last line is H_0. Hence:

$$(5.3) \qquad H = H_0 + \sum_{g=1}^{G} P_g H_g$$

where

$$(5.4) \qquad H_g = \sum_{i \in S_g} \frac{p_i}{P_g} \log \frac{1}{p_i/P_g} \qquad\qquad g = 1, \ldots, G$$

To interpret H_g note that p_i/P_g, $i \in S_g$ is the conditional probability of E_i, given that we know that one of the events of S_g is bound to occur. Hence H_g is the *entropy within set* S_g and the term $\sum P_g H_g$ in (5.3) is the *average within-group entropy*. Equation (5.3) thus states that the total entropy H is equal to the between-group entropy H_0 plus the average within-group entropy. The following comments serve to clarify this result.

(1) The total entropy is never smaller than the between-group entropy: $H \geq H_0$. This is so because the difference $H - H_0$ is equal to $\sum P_g H_g$ and both the P_g's and the H_g's are nonnegative. The interpretation is that there cannot be more dividedness after grouping than there was before grouping, which is intuitively plausible.

(2) We have $H = H_0$ if and only if $\sum P_g H_g = 0$, that is, if and only if $H_g = 0$ for each set S_g for which $P_g > 0$. But $H_g = 0$ is equivalent to $p_i/P_g = 1$ for some $i \in S_g$ and $p_j/P_g = 0$ for each $j \in S_g, j \neq i$. This means that the total entropy is equal to the between-group entropy if and only if the grouping is such that there is in each set at most one event with nonzero probability.[1]

(3) A simple informational interpretation of the decomposition (5.3) is the following. Consider first the message stating that one of the sets of events, $S_1, \ldots, S_g$ occurred. Its expected information is H_0. Next, under the condition that S_g occurred, consider the subsequent message stating that one of the E_i's of this S_g occurred. Its expected information is H_g. Before the first message arrives we do not know which S_g will occur, but we do know that it has probability P_g. Hence the total expected information of the two successive messages, computed prior to the arrival of the first, is equal to $H_0 + \sum P_g H_g$, and (5.3) states that this is equal to the expected information of the message that states immediately which of the E_i's occurred. Note that this line of argument is completely analogous to that of the second subsection of Section 1.1.

Application to Racial Entropy

The decomposition (5.3) can also be applied when the entropy is used as a general measure of dividedness. An elaborate example follows in the next section; here we confine ourselves to a brief illustration of its use in racial analysis.

Let there be n races (white, black, Puerto Rican, Mexican American, American Indian, etc.) and write $p_1, \ldots, p_n$ for their proportions in the student population of our school; there will be no need for a special school subscript, because the attention will be restricted to only one school. First we consider the white-nonwhite racial entropy:

---

[1] The expression "at most" leaves open the possibility that for some S_g, all events of this set have zero probability. This implies $P_g = 0$, which is clearly not in conflict with an equality of the total and the between-group entropy.

$$(5.5) \qquad H_0 = p_1 \log \frac{1}{p_1} + (1-p_1) \log \frac{1}{1-p_1}$$

where p_1 and $1-p_1$ are the white and nonwhite proportions, respectively. There is no further subdivision of the white group, but the nonwhite group consists of $n-1$ races with proportions $p_2/(1-p_1), \ldots, p_n/(1-p_1)$. Hence the racial entropy of the school's nonwhite students is

$$(5.6) \qquad H_N = \sum_{i=2}^{n} \frac{p_i}{1-p_1} \log \frac{1-p_1}{p_i}$$

and the decomposition (5.3) takes the form

$$(5.7) \qquad H = H_0 + (1-p_1)H_N$$

where H is the school's total racial entropy. It goes without saying that any other grouping of races can be handled analogously.

1.6. The Industrial Diversity of American Cities

In some cities a single industry is dominant; e.g., Flint, Michigan, with its automobile plants, and Washington, D.C., with its government offices. Other cities have highly diversified industrial patterns. The objective of this section is to illustrate the use of the entropy concept for the measurement of industrial diversity of the U.S. Standard Metropolitan Statistical Areas (SMSA's). This measurement will be based on the size of the labor force according to the 1960 census. The discussion will be continued in Sections 2.3 and 3.2.

Description of the Data

Our observational units are the SMSA's for which the 1960 census provides the necessary information on the industrial composition of the labor force.[1] There are 178 such SMSA's but the three located in Puerto Rico will be disregarded. We shall also disregard the atypical SMSA centered in Washington, D.C. Thus, we will consider 174 SMSA's, the total population of which was about 106 million in 1960. In Table 1.2 they are classified according to two criteria. One is population size, with large describing a population exceeding half a million and small a population of less than

---

[1] The relevant publications are the PHC(1) reports of the U.S. Census on Population and Housing in 1960.

TABLE 1.2

SMSA'S CLASSIFIED BY SIZE AND BY REGION

	North East	North Central	South	West	Total
	Number of SMSA's				
Large	14	14	13	11	52
Medium	14	11	13	8	46
Small	17	23	31	5	76
Total	45	48	57	24	174
	Average population (in thousands)				
Large	2122	1593	789	1503	1505
Medium	334	340	338	302	331
Small	155	163	159	134	158

250,000. The other is the region in which the SMSA is located.[1] The last three lines of the table contain the average population size of the SMSA's of each size class in each region. The figures indicate that the average large SMSA has a population of about $1\frac{1}{2}$ million and that the corresponding values for medium and small SMSA's are about 330,000 and 160,000, respectively. The only major exceptions are the large SMSA's in the North East which are on the average substantially larger than the national average and those in the South which are on the average substantially smaller.

Six industry groups will be considered: (1) Construction, (2) Durable manufacturing, (3) Nondurable manufacturing, (4) Transportation and utilities, (5) Trade, and (6) Services. All groups except the first are subdivided into smaller classes, to be called industries, as shown in the first column of Table 1.3.[2] The other columns give the labor force composition for the set of all SMSA's of each region-size class combination. The figures reveal some interesting regional differences. Durable manufacturing employs more than one-quarter of the workers in the North Central region, but only about 10 per cent in the South. Construction and Services have large shares

---

[1] North East: Connecticut, Delaware, District of Columbia, Maine, Maryland, Massachusetts, New Hampshire, New Jersey, New York, Pennsylvania, Rhode Island, Vermont. North Central: Illinois, Indiana, Iowa, Kansas, Michigan, Minnesota, Missouri, Nebraska, North Dakota, Ohio, South Dakota, Wisconsin. South: Alabama, Arkansas, Florida, Georgia, Kentucky, Louisiana, Mississippi, North Carolina, Oklahoma, South Carolina, Tennessee, Texas, Virginia, West Virginia. West: Alaska, Arizona, California, Colorado, Hawaii, Idaho, Montana, Nevada, New Mexico, Oregon, Utah, Washington, Wyoming.
[2] The categories "mining" and "other industries" are deleted from the analysis.

TABLE 1.3

EMPLOYMENT DISTRIBUTIONS OF SMSA GROUPS CLASSIFIED BY SIZE AND BY REGION

	North East			North Central			South			West		
	Large	Medium	Small	Large	Medium	Small	Large	Medium	Small	Large	Medium	Small
Construction	5.6	5.6	5.7	5.4	5.7	5.7	8.2	8.4	8.4	7.5	8.9	9.1
Durable manufacturing	19.3	24.4	21.1	26.9	27.7	26.3	12.0	9.2	9.1	19.4	9.2	12.1
Furniture, lumber, wood products	.7	.7	1.1	.8	1.2	1.0	1.2	1.1	1.7	1.3	1.8	.3
Metal industry	5.3	9.4	5.3	7.8	6.1	8.1	3.1	3.3	2.2	4.9	3.3	7.0
Machinery	6.8	7.6	10.2	9.3	8.0	8.0	3.3	1.9	2.1	5.1	1.9	2.1
Transportation	2.7	2.8	1.3	6.4	10.0	6.9	2.9	1.2	1.8	6.1	.9	1.5
Other durable goods	3.8	3.8	3.3	2.6	2.4	2.1	1.5	1.8	1.4	2.1	1.3	1.2
Nondurable manufacturing	16.9	18.8	23.6	13.1	9.5	11.5	11.0	15.4	15.9	9.9	8.5	5.5
Food and kindred products	3.1	2.9	2.8	3.6	4.4	4.2	3.6	3.3	2.9	3.2	4.1	2.8
Textile and apparel products	5.6	6.8	8.9	1.3	.6	.7	1.6	3.3	5.8	1.5	.5	.2
Printing, publishing, and allied ind.	2.9	1.9	2.3	3.0	2.2	1.9	1.8	1.9	1.5	2.1	1.6	1.6
Other nondurable goods	5.3	7.3	9.5	5.2	2.3	4.8	3.9	7.3	5.7	3.2	2.3	.9
Transportation and utilities	8.7	6.8	7.1	8.6	8.5	7.5	10.3	9.5	7.7	8.4	9.6	8.6
Railroad and railway express services	1.3	1.7	1.8	2.2	2.6	2.0	1.8	1.9	1.5	1.2	2.5	3.0
Other transportation	4.0	2.3	2.4	3.4	2.9	2.5	5.0	3.9	3.1	3.7	3.4	2.1
Communications, utilities, etc.	3.3	2.9	2.8	3.0	3.0	3.1	3.5	3.7	3.1	3.5	3.7	3.5
Trade	20.8	18.5	18.8	20.7	21.9	20.9	25.5	24.1	23.0	22.3	26.0	22.2
Wholesale trade	4.8	3.1	3.1	4.3	4.4	3.5	5.9	5.4	4.2	4.8	5.4	3.2
Eating and drinking places	3.3	2.8	2.7	3.0	3.2	3.3	3.4	3.0	3.1	3.6	3.9	3.9
Other retail trade	12.8	12.6	12.9	13.3	14.3	14.1	16.2	15.7	15.7	13.9	16.7	15.1
Services	28.6	25.8	23.8	25.4	26.7	28.1	33.1	33.3	35.8	32.4	37.7	42.5
Business and repair services	3.5	2.2	2.6	2.9	2.6	2.4	3.4	3.0	2.7	4.0	4.6	3.1
Private households	2.5	2.0	2.1	2.1	2.4	2.5	5.1	5.7	6.4	2.8	3.3	3.2
Other personal services	3.3	2.7	3.2	3.1	3.2	3.0	4.7	4.3	4.5	3.7	4.3	9.2
Hospitals	3.4	3.3	2.9	3.1	3.6	3.7	2.9	3.2	3.4	2.9	3.7	4.0
Educational services	5.2	4.4	4.5	4.9	5.8	7.6	5.3	5.8	7.2	6.4	7.8	7.3
Other professional services	5.3	4.4	4.2	4.5	4.7	4.5	4.9	4.7	4.5	5.5	5.5	4.9
Public administration	5.5	5.6	4.4	4.9	4.4	4.3	6.8	6.7	7.2	7.2	8.5	10.8

in the South and the West compared with the other two regions. For Services this is mainly due to personal services in the South and to educational and other professional services in the West. Nondurable manufacturing is particularly prominent in the North East, and it plays a relatively modest role in the West. Not unexpectedly, wholesale trade tends to be concentrated in the larger SMSA's.

Employment Entropies of Individual SMSA's

There are 23 industries as a whole: Construction (an industry group consisting of only one industry) plus the $5+4+3+3+7$ industries which are part of the other five groups. These industries will be denoted by the subscript i and the SMSA's by the subscript s. We shall write p_{si} for the number of persons living in the sth SMSA and employed in the ith industry, measured as a fraction of the total number of persons in *all* 174 SMSA's and *all* 23 industries. Hence $\sum_s \sum_i p_{si} = 1$, where the summations over s and i are from 1 to 174 and from 1 to 23, respectively. We shall write

$$(6.1) \qquad\qquad p_{s.} = \sum_{i=1}^{23} p_{si} \qquad\qquad s = 1, \ldots, 174$$

for the number of persons employed in the sth SMSA, measured as a fraction of the same total. Hence $p_{si}/p_{s.}$ stands for the proportion of the labor force of the sth SMSA that is employed in the ith industry. The employment distribution $p_{s1}/p_{s.}, \ldots, p_{s,23}/p_{s.}$ has the following entropy value:

$$(6.2) \qquad\qquad H_s = \sum_{i=1}^{23} \frac{p_{si}}{p_{s.}} \log \frac{p_{s.}}{p_{si}}$$

This is the employment entropy of the sth SMSA at the level of the 23 industries, and it is a measure for the industrial diversity of this SMSA: zero when all workers are in only one industry, and a maximum of log 23 when all 23 industries employ the same number of persons.

Employment Entropies of Individual SMSA's for Industry Groups

The employment entropy is of course not independent of the industrial classification chosen. This arbitrariness is a disadvantage, but it is inherent in any method of measuring industrial diversity. It is therefore all the more important to use a measure which enables the analyst to link the diversities corresponding to different classifications. One of the merits of the employment entropy as a measure of industrial diversity is that hierarchies of industries and industry groups can be analyzed straightforwardly. Take our six industry groups, to be denoted by $S_1, \ldots, S_6$. The number of persons employed in S_g and in the sth SMSA, again measured as a fraction of total employment in all industries and all SMSA's, is then

$$(6.3) \qquad\qquad P_{sg} = \sum_{i \in S_g} p_{si} \qquad\qquad g = 1, \ldots, 6$$

and the employment entropy at the level of industry groups is

$$(6.4) \qquad\qquad H_{s0} = \sum_{g=1}^{6} \frac{P_{sg}}{p_{s.}} \log \frac{p_{s.}}{P_{sg}}$$

The entropy decomposition is entirely along the lines of (5.3). By subtracting H_{s0} from H_s we obtain

$$\sum_{i=1}^{23} \frac{p_{si}}{p_{s.}} \log \frac{p_{s.}}{p_{si}} - \sum_{g=1}^{6} \frac{P_{sg}}{p_{s.}} \log \frac{p_{s.}}{P_{sg}}$$

$$= \sum_{g=1}^{6} \frac{P_{sg}}{p_{s.}} \sum_{i \in S_g} \frac{p_{si}}{P_{sg}} \left(\log \frac{p_{s.}}{p_{si}} - \log \frac{p_{s.}}{P_{sg}} \right)$$

$$= \sum_{g=1}^{6} \frac{P_{sg}}{p_{s.}} \sum_{i \in S_g} \frac{p_{si}}{P_{sg}} \log \frac{P_{sg}}{p_{si}}$$

This result can be written as follows:

$$(6.5) \qquad\qquad H_s = H_{s0} + \sum_{g=1}^{6} \frac{P_{sg}}{p_{s.}} H_{sg}$$

where

$$(6.6) \qquad\qquad H_{sg} = \sum_{i \in S_g} \frac{p_{si}}{P_{sg}} \log \frac{P_{sg}}{p_{si}} \qquad\qquad g = 1, \ldots, 6$$

is the employment entropy in the sth SMSA within S_g, p_{si}/P_{sg} being the number of persons working in the ith industry measured as a fraction of the number of those who work in the industry group to which this industry belongs $(i \in S_g)$. This H_{sg} thus measures the industrial diversity of the sth SMSA within that particular industry group.

Average Employment Entropies

A complete display of the components of the decomposition (6.5) for all 174 SMSA's amounts to a considerable number of figures, so that there is some merit – as in the case of Section 1.4 – in representing them by averages. Write C_{ab} for the set of all SMSA's in the ath region and the bth size class, where a takes four values and b three (see Table 1.2). Write q_{abi} for the number of workers in the ith industry in C_{ab}, Q_{abg} for that of industry group S_g, and $q_{ab.}$ for that of all industries, all measured as fractions of the total labor force in all SMSA's:[1]

$$(6.7) \qquad q_{abi} = \sum_{s \in C_{ab}} p_{si} \qquad Q_{abg} = \sum_{s \in C_{ab}} P_{sg} \qquad q_{ab.} = \sum_{s \in C_{ab}} p_{s.}$$

Then multiply both sides of (6.5) by $p_{s.}/q_{ab.}$ (the fraction of the labor force of C_{ab} that resides in its sth SMSA) and sum over $s \in C_{ab}$:

$$\sum_{s \in C_{ab}} \frac{p_{s.}}{q_{ab.}} H_s = \sum_{s \in C_{ab}} \frac{p_{s.}}{q_{ab.}} H_{s0} + \sum_{s \in C_{ab}} \frac{p_{s.}}{q_{ab.}} \sum_{g=1}^{6} \frac{P_{sg}}{p_{s.}} H_{sg}$$

$$= \sum_{s \in C_{ab}} \frac{p_{s.}}{q_{ab.}} H_{s0} + \sum_{g=1}^{6} \frac{Q_{abg}}{q_{ab.}} \sum_{s \in C_{ab}} \frac{P_{sg}}{Q_{abg}} H_{sg}$$

This can be abbreviated as

$$(6.8) \qquad \overline{H}_{ab} = \overline{H}_{ab0} + \sum_{g=1}^{6} \frac{Q_{abg}}{q_{ab.}} \overline{H}_{abg}$$

where $\overline{H}_{ab}$ and $\overline{H}_{ab0}$ are average employment entropies based on the employment fractions $p_{s.}/q_{ab.}$ as weights:

$$(6.9) \qquad \overline{H}_{ab} = \sum_{s \in C_{ab}} \frac{p_{s.}}{q_{ab.}} H_s \qquad \overline{H}_{ab0} = \sum_{s \in C_{ab}} \frac{p_{s.}}{q_{ab.}} H_{s0}$$

while $\overline{H}_{abg}$ is exclusively concerned with industry group S_g and, therefore, uses the fractions P_{sg}/Q_{abg} as weights:

$$(6.10) \qquad \overline{H}_{abg} = \sum_{s \in C_{ab}} \frac{P_{sg}}{Q_{abg}} H_{sg} \qquad\qquad g = 1, \ldots, 6$$

Table 1.4 contains for each C_{ab} all average employment entropies (6.9) and (6.10) with the exception of $\overline{H}_{ab1}$, which is zero for each C_{ab} because S_1 consists of only one industry. The unit of measurement is the bit. The table also contains the second term in the right-hand side of (6.8), indicated briefly by $\overline{H}_{ab} - \overline{H}_{ab0}$, which is the average within-group employment entropy. The results indicate that in each region the average entropies $\overline{H}_{ab}$ and $\overline{H}_{ab0}$ decline when we move from large to medium to small SMSA's. This means that on average small cities are less diversified (more specialized)

---

[1] The figures of Table 1.3 are $q_{abi}/q_{ab.}$ and $Q_{abg}/q_{ab.}$ in percentage form.

TABLE 1.4

AVERAGE EMPLOYMENT ENTROPIES OF SMSA'S BY SIZE AND BY REGION

Region	Large	Medium	Small	Large	Medium	Small
		$\bar{H}_{ab}$			$\bar{H}_{ab0}$	
North East	4.249	4.116	3.984	2.388	2.352	2.312
North Central	4.170	3.979	3.978	2.366	2.288	2.258
South	4.140	4.104	3.947	2.349	2.343	2.248
West	4.212	4.076	3.797	2.352	2.269	2.148
		$\bar{H}_{ab}-\bar{H}_{ab0}$			$\bar{H}_{ab2}$	
North East	1.862	1.765	1.672	1.890	1.839	1.692
North Central	1.803	1.691	1.720	1.778	1.454	1.694
South	1.792	1.761	1.698	1.881	1.980	1.535
West	1.860	1.807	1.649	1.991	1.935	1.262
		$\bar{H}_{ab3}$			$\bar{H}_{ab4}$	
North East	1.857	1.633	1.523	1.413	1.513	1.324
North Central	1.776	1.650	1.461	1.542	1.522	1.470
South	1.793	1.539	1.387	1.426	1.463	1.422
West	1.866	1.591	1.515	1.404	1.539	1.331
		$\bar{H}_{ab5}$			$\bar{H}_{ab6}$	
North East	1.329	1.214	1.187	2.735	2.636	2.685
North Central	1.280	1.266	1.224	2.738	2.719	2.638
South	1.285	1.250	1.206	2.707	2.705	2.650
West	1.326	1.282	1.215	2.695	2.681	2.418

than large cities with regard to their employment pattern. The same holds with few exceptions for industries within their group. There are $4\times 5 = 20$ pairs (a, g) for the within-group entropies $\bar{H}_{abg}$ in Table 1.4; we have $\bar{H}_{a1g} > \bar{H}_{a2g}$ (large versus medium) except for four cases, $\bar{H}_{a2g} > \bar{H}_{a3g}$ (medium versus small) except for two cases, and $\bar{H}_{a1g} > \bar{H}_{a3g}$ (large versus small) with no exception.

The large-medium-small comparison faces some difficulties when it is applied across regions, because we know from Table 1.2 that, for example, the large SMSA's of the North East are on the average almost three times as large as the large SMSA's of the South. A simple way of handling this problem is by plotting the employment entropies of the individual SMSA's of each region against their population size. This is shown in Figure 1.4 for the entropies H_{s0} at the level of the six industry groups. The horizontal variable is the population size, measured logarithmically (base 2). The hori-

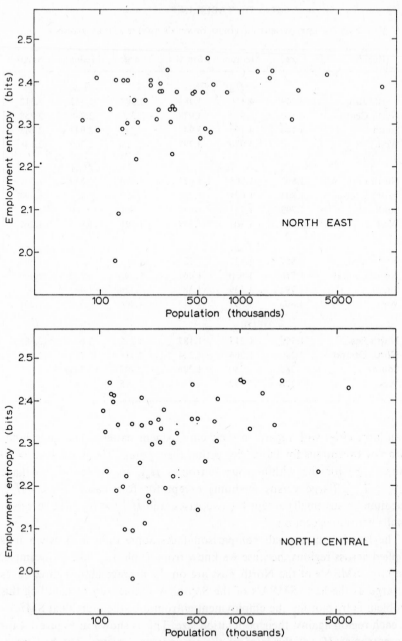

Fig. 1.4.　Scatter diagrams of the employment entropy for six industry groups and population size, for SMSA's in four regions of the United States

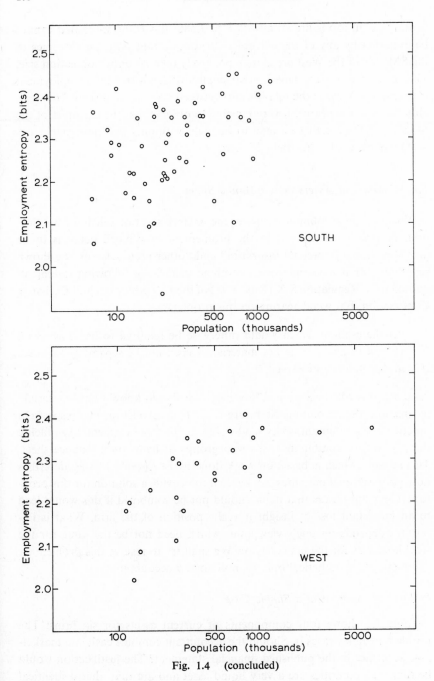

Fig. 1.4   (concluded)

zontal line on top is drawn at $\log_2 6 \approx 2.585$; this is the value that cannot be exceeded by any of the entropies. It appears that only the entropies of the SMSA's of the West are closely positively related to the population size. The other three regions have several small SMSA's with a high employment entropy, which cause the relationship between diversity and size to be weak although still noticeable. It is interesting to observe that the entropies of the SMSA's of the North East tend to be high, with only two (less than 5 per cent) having a value less than 2.2 bits.

1.7. Combining Assets on a Balance Sheet

Whenever an accountant prepares the balance sheet of a firm for publication, he must give thought to the problem of how much detail is to be provided. Should "prepaid insurance" and "other prepaid items" be shown separately, or is it acceptable to combine them? The following statement, quoted from Regulation S-X (Rule 3-02) of the U.S. Securities and Exchange Commission, has some bearing on this problem:

> "If the amount which would otherwise be required to be shown with respect to any item is not material, it need not be separately set forth in the manner prescribed."

To make this rule operational, however, one should know what "material" means, and the accounting literature is far from explicit in this respect. In practice, the accountant is advised to exercise his best judgment when facing the problem of combining items into groups of items on a balance sheet. This section, which is based on work done by LEV (1968, 1970a), describes how informational measures can be used to provide a solution for this problem. The main idea is that items should not be combined if this would lead to an important loss of insight into the position of the firm. What is important depends on one's viewpoint, which need not be the same for the stockholder as for the tax collector. We shall try to resolve this problem by conducting a hypothetical opinion poll among accountants.

Preliminary Analysis of a Simple Case

Table 1.5 shows four components of current assets for six firms. The problem in all six cases is: Should the accountant combine cash and marketable securities in the published financial statement? The justification would be that such securities are a very liquid asset and are thus almost identical

TABLE 1.5

COMPOSITION OF THE CURRENT ASSETS OF SIX FIRMS
(in thousands of dollars)

	(1)	(2)	(3)
Cash	12,500	23,000	24,900
Marketable securities	12,500	2,000	100
Accounts receivable	15,000	15,000	15,000
Inventory	10,000	10,000	10,000
Total	50,000	50,000	50,000
	(4)	(5)	(6)
Cash	2,500	4,600	4,980
Marketable securities	2,500	400	20
Accounts receivable	15,000	15,000	15,000
Inventory	10,000	10,000	10,000
Total	30,000	30,000	30,000

with cash.[1] Notice that the two other items (accounts receivable and inventory) involve identical amounts for all six firms; the differences are confined to cash and marketable securities. The total amount of these two assets is 25 million dollars for each of the first three firms and 5 million for the last three. In each "vertical" comparison, (1) versus (4), (2) versus (5), and (3) versus (6), we have the same percentage composition within the cash-marketable securities group: 50-50 for (1) and (4), 92-8 for (2) and (5), and 99.6-.4 for (3) and (6).

Following the approach of the first subsection of Section 1.1, we shall try to solve the problem along intuitive lines. Consider firm (6). It seems plausible that most accountants would agree that little is lost when cash and marketable securities are combined in this case. There are two main reasons. First, the total amount of these two items – 5 million dollars – consists almost exclusively of only one of the two (cash in this case), so that there are no cogent reasons to show the very small amount of the other item if it is indeed true that the two perform almost identical functions. Second, the total amount of 5 million dollars is a rather small fraction of the total of all current assets (30 million). There is less reason to show detail within a group when that group is a smaller fraction of the total.

---

[1] It is conceivable, however, that a balance sheet user is particularly interested in whether the firm uses its liquid assets to earn money. He would regard cash and marketable securities as inadmissible for aggregation. Here we assume that they are admissible.

The other extreme is firm (1), where both items (cash and marketable securities) are of equal importance and their sum is 50 per cent of all current assets. These considerations would almost certainly lead accountants to segregate the two items. The four other firms are in an intermediate position. In cases (2) and (3), the combined amount of cash and marketable securities is the same as in case (1), but cash dominates in (2), and it dominates even more in (3), which suggests that the accountants' willingness to combine the two will increase in that order. This willingness will also increase in the order (4)–(5)–(6) for the same reason. Finally, in each of the three vertical comparisons we have the same percentage composition within the two-item group, but their combined amount is a lower fraction of the current asset total in the case at the bottom, (4), (5), or (6), so that the combination of the two items in these cases is less objectionable than in the corresponding cases at the top.

In summary, the above paragraphs suggest that the accountants' reluctance to combine two assets is a decreasing function of the degree to which there is a domination by one asset within the pair, and an increasing function of the size of the pair – both assets combined – measured as a fraction of the relevant total (the total amount of all current assets in our examples).

The Information Loss Caused by the Combination of Two Assets

When cash and marketable securities are combined into one item, the only insight lost is their relative sizes. Thus, only proportions matter; we can therefore confine ourselves to the amounts of the four assets measured as fractions of total current assets. For firm (1) we have these proportions:

Cash	.25
Marketable securities	.25
Accounts receivable	.30
Inventory	.20

The entropy of the distribution (.25, .25, .30, .20) is 1.986 bits. When we combine cash and marketable securities, the distribution becomes (.5, .3, .2) with an entropy of 1.486 bits. The combination of the two assets thus leads to an entropy reduction of $\frac{1}{2}$ bit. Recall that entropy is expected information; so, if we hear that aggregation leads to an information reduction, we may be tempted to think that this is an intuitively plausible result. However, recall also the discussion at the end of Section 1.3, where it was stated that our informational measures are based on a primitive information concept. What really counts is whether the entropy reduction of $\frac{1}{2}$ bit is an acceptable description of the accountants' reluctance to combine cash and marketable securities for firm (1), and this has yet to be shown.

More generally, let there be n assets rather than four, the first two of which are candidates for aggregation. Write $p_1, \ldots, p_n$ for their proportions, so that the entropy is H as defined in (1.6). After aggregation the entropy is

$$(7.1) \qquad H' = (p_1 + p_2) \log \frac{1}{p_1 + p_2} + \sum_{i=3}^{n} p_i \log \frac{1}{p_i}$$

and the difference is

$$(7.2) \qquad H - H' = p_1 \log \frac{1}{p_1} + p_2 \log \frac{1}{p_2} - (p_1 + p_2) \log \frac{1}{p_1 + p_2}$$

$$= (p_1 + p_2) \left(\frac{p_1}{p_1 + p_2} \log \frac{p_1 + p_2}{p_1} + \frac{p_2}{p_1 + p_2} \log \frac{p_1 + p_2}{p_2} \right)$$

This can be written in the more convenient form

$$(7.3) \qquad H - H' = P_S H_S$$

where the subscript S on the right indicates the set of items (the pair) whose combination is under consideration, while P_S stands for the share of S:

$$(7.4) \qquad P_S = p_1 + p_2$$

and H_S is the entropy within S:

$$(7.5) \qquad H_S = \frac{p_1}{p_1 + p_2} \log \frac{p_1 + p_2}{p_1} + \frac{p_2}{p_1 + p_2} \log \frac{p_1 + p_2}{p_2}$$

Equation (7.3) states that the entropy reduction is equal to the product of the relative size of the pair and the entropy within the pair. Thus, this reduction is an increasing function of the combined size of the two assets measured as a fraction of the total, and a decreasing function of the degree to which one of these assets is dominated by the other (because a larger H_S implies less domination). This is entirely in agreement with the conclusion reached at the end of the previous subsection, so that we may feel justified in defining the entropy reduction $H - H' = P_S H_S$ as the *information loss* which is caused by combining the assets that are part of S.

For the data of Table 1.5 we have the following information losses (in bits) when cash and marketable securities are combined:

(1) .500	(2) .201	(3) .019
(4) .167	(5) .067	(6) .006

The loss thus declines, as it should, in each row as we move from left to right and also in each column as we move downward. Note that the numerical statements shown here are much stronger than the qualitative statements of the previous subsection. There, we compared only firms with the same size of the pair (P_S) or the same degree of dominance within the pair (H_S), so that firms (2) and (4) were not even related to each other. The present figures state that the former firm's information loss is about 20 per cent larger than that of the latter.

A Third Property of the Information Loss

The information loss as defined above thus has two desirable properties: it increases with P_S and it also increases with H_S. However, the general considerations based on Table 1.5 did not imply that the loss should be of the specific multiplicative form $P_S H_S$. As an additional test, then, take the case in which the accountant considers the combination of an asset of $1000 with two alternative assets, one of $100 and another of $20,000. Both combinations are considered admissible because of the similarity of the functions of the assets. Intuitively, one would regard the combination with the smaller item ($100) as less objectionable than that with the larger item ($20,000), but P_S is smaller and H_S is larger for the former pair than for the latter. The two components of the information loss thus point in different directions, and the question arises as to whether the product $P_S H_S$ leads to an answer which is in agreement with the intuition.

It does, because it is generally true that the combination of a given item with a larger item gives a larger $P_S H_S$ than does that with a smaller item. Take p_1 of (7.2) as the proportion of the given item and p_2 as that of the other item, and imagine that p_2 increases from zero. The proposition is proved when it is shown that $H - H' = P_S H_S$ increases. So we take the derivative with respect to p_2 of the function in the first line of (7.2). Using natural logs, we obtain

$$\frac{\partial}{\partial p_2}\left[p_2 \log \frac{1}{p_2} - (p_1 + p_2) \log \frac{1}{p_1 + p_2}\right] = \log \frac{p_1 + p_2}{p_2}$$

This is positive when $p_1 > 0$, which proves the proposition.

The Additivity of the Information Loss

The most convenient property of the information loss (7.3) as a measure of the undesirability of the aggregation is its additivity. Go back to the discussion of (7.1) to (7.5) and suppose again that the first two items are combined, with information loss (7.3). Next suppose that the pair (1, 2) is subsequently merged with the third item, so that we obtain the set (1, 2, 3). The remaining entropy is

$$H'' = P_{123} \log \frac{1}{P_{123}} + \sum_{i=4}^{n} p_i \log \frac{1}{p_i} \quad \text{where} \quad P_{123} = \sum_{i=1}^{3} p_i$$

The total information loss is

$$H - H'' = \sum_{i=1}^{3} p_i \log \frac{1}{p_i} - P_{123} \log \frac{1}{P_{123}} = P_{123} \sum_{i=1}^{3} \frac{p_i}{P_{123}} \log \frac{P_{123}}{p_i}$$

The third member is of the form $P_S H_S$ with S interpreted as the set (1, 2, 3). This means that we would have obtained the same result if we had combined the three items simultaneously. Also, the fact that the total loss is symmetric in the three items implies that it is immaterial whether we combine items 1 and 2 first and then add the third or proceed in any different order. Thus, one can simply continue the aggregation, step after step, taking one pair at a time, and the total information loss is obtained by adding that of the most recent pair to the previous total.

A Simple Aggregation Procedure

We proceed to describe a systematic aggregation procedure, which will be applied to the 25 assets of the Boston Edison Company as of December 1963, shown in Table 1.6. It is obviously undesirable to combine items that serve highly different functions, such as cash and machinery. We assume, therefore, that the accountant starts by specifying which pairs are admissible for aggregation. Let the admissible pairs in this case be as listed below.

(1, 2)	(5, 6)	(10, 11)	(17, 18)	(23, 24)
(2, 4)	(7, 8)	(13, 14)	(19, 20)	(24, 25)
(3, 4)	(8, 9)	(15, 16)	(21, 22)	

In addition, it is stipulated that the sets (7, 8, 9) and (10, 11, 12) are admissible, but not the pairs (7, 9) and (10, 12). That is, if 7 and 8 or 10 and 11 are combined, the pairs may be further aggregated (the former with 9, the latter with 12).

The simplest procedure is to find the admissible pair with the smallest information loss, which in this case consists of 8 and 9 (special deposits and working funds), next the admissible pair with the second smallest information loss, and so on, each time adding the new loss to the previous total. This is shown in Table 1.7 for the Boston Edison data. The cut-off point is a

TABLE 1.6

ASSETS SIDE OF BOSTON EDISON COMPANY'S BALANCE SHEET OF DECEMBER 31, 1963

Assets and other debits	Published figures	Consolidated up to ½ per cent information loss	Consolidated up to 5 per cent info. loss	Number of item
Plant and investments	364,037,215	364,037,215	364,037,215	
1. Net electric plant in service	327,802,559	327,802,559	327,802,559	1
2. Electric plant, construction in process	21,609,430	21,609,430	21,609,430	2
3. Net steam plant in service	10,520,537	10,700,121	10,700,121	3
4. Steam plant, construction in process	179,584			4
5. Net nonutility property	2,167,063	2,167,063	3,925,105	5
6. Other investments	1,758,042	1,758,042		6
Current and accrued assets	31,149,672	31,149,672	31,149,672	
7. Cash	4,048,773	4,048,773	4,292,434	7
8. Special deposits	1,166	243,661		8
9. Working funds	242,495			9
10. Notes receivable	53,004			10
11. Other accounts receivable (excl. customers accounts)	479,353	532,357	17,981,240	11
12. Customers accounts receivable, net	17,448,883	17,448,883		12
13. Fuel stock	1,218,478	1,218,478	8,395,121	13
14. Plant materials, supplies and merchandise	7,176,643	7,176,643		14
15. Prepaid insurance	369,210	379,238	379,238	15
16. Other prepaid items	10,028			16
17. Rents receivable	40,607	101,639	101,639	17
18. Miscellaneous current and accrued assets	61,032			18
Deferred debits	1,808,299	1,808,299	1,808,299	
19. Unamortized discount series D bonds	41,501	383,376	383,376	19
20. Refunding costs series G bonds	341,875			20
21. Temporary facilities	18,249	100,442	100,442	21
22. Nonutility property additions	82,193			22
23. Deferred debits: Federal income taxes	990,800	990,800	990,800	23
24. Deferred debits: Miscellaneous	321,644	333,681	333,681	24
25. Sewer use tax	12,037			25

TABLE 1.7

CUMULATION OF INFORMATION LOSSES

Step	Aggregated items	Information loss $(10^{-3}$ bits)	Cumulated information loss $(10^{-3}$ bits)
1	8, 9	.03	.03
2	15, 16	.17	.20
3	21, 22	.17	.37
4	24, 25	.19	.56
5	17, 18	.25	.81
6	19, 20	.48	1.29
7	10, 11	.63	1.92
8	3, 4	3.31	5.23
9	(8, 9), 7	3.45	8.68
10	(10, 11), 12	8.37	17.05
11	5, 6	9.81	26.86
12	13, 14	12.64	39.50

matter of choice. The entropy before aggregation is 1.149 bits.[1] If we allow it to decrease by at most $\frac{1}{2}$ per cent (.00575 bit), we can perform the first eight steps shown in Table 1.7. All 12 steps may be performed when we allow a 5 per cent decrease. The last two columns of Table 1.6 show how the assets are combined in these two cases.

Refinements

In the above example we took an available balance sheet as our starting point and we asked how much aggregation can be performed subject to a given maximum total information loss. Clearly, the outcome will depend on this starting point. A preferable procedure is to formulate a general rule according to which the assets of a balance sheet should have a certain minimum entropy value. It goes without saying that this can also be done for the liabilities side. This is a simple way to guarantee that balance sheets will provide a certain minimum of information. It is also possible to formulate minimum entropy values for subcategories, such as current assets and fixed assets. Devices of this kind can be used to insure that the rules are more in accordance with the importance of such subcategories.

---

[1] This is a low entropy value for 25 items; if they were all of equal size, the entropy would be log 25 = 4.644 bits. The low value is largely caused by the domination of the first item (net electric plant in service), which accounts for 83 per cent of the total assets.

The composition of a balance sheet varies over time, so that the computations reported in the previous subsection might have led to different results if they had been based on the balance sheet of a different year. It is clearly undesirable to publish financial statements that contain different asset combinations in successive years. The best procedure is to repeat the computations for a number of successive years in the past and to make the decision on aggregation dependent on the average of the information losses (or entropies). Given the additivity of informational measures, such averages are a natural way to summarize them; we adopt this procedure frequently in what follows.

1.8. Miscellaneous Applications of the Entropy Measure

Industrial Concentration

Consider an industry that consists of n firms and write $p_1, \ldots, p_n$ for the amounts of sales of these firms in any given year, measured as fractions of the total sales of the industry in that year.[1] Then the entropy (1.6) is an inverse measure of concentration (a measure of "unconcentration"). It is zero when one firm accounts for 100 per cent of total sales, it reaches the maximum value of log n when all n firms are of equal size, and this maximum increases as the number of firms increases. Proposals to use the entropy for this purpose have been made independently by HILDENBRAND and PASCHEN (1964), FINKELSTEIN and FRIEDBERG (1967), THEIL (1967), and A. and I. HOROWITZ (1968).

One of the major attractions of the entropy measure for industrial concentration is the decomposition rule (5.3). If we combine the n firms into G sets of firms, the entropies H_0 and H_g measure unconcentration at the level of the sets of firms and within S_g, respectively, where $g = 1, \ldots, G$. Figure 1.5, which is due to TIDEMAN (1967), provides a graphic illustration; it is shown here for industrial concentration, but it is in fact applicable to any entropy decomposition. The figure deals with $n = 21$ automobile makes, five of General Motors (S_1), three of Ford (S_2), four of Chrysler (S_3), and nine Independents (S_4). The underlying data are the shares of the total number of cars produced in the period 1936–1964. Write p_i for the share of the ith make and P_g for the share of S_g. These S_g's have been ranked according to decreasing shares ($P_1 > P_2 > P_3 > P_4$) and the makes within

---

[1] One may also use the number of workers instead of the amount of sales; this is a matter of choice, depending on the problem in which one is interested.

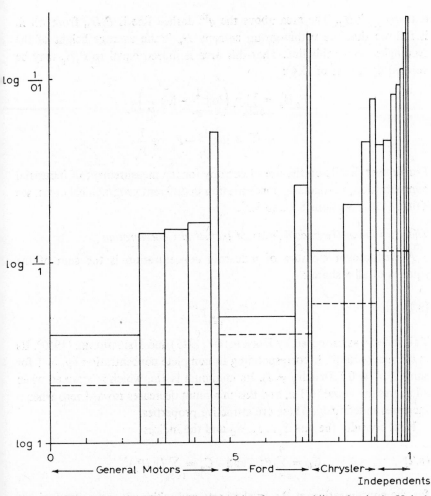

Fig. 1.5. Illustration of the entropy decomposition for automobile makes in the United
States, 1936–1964

each S_g have been ranked in the same way. The successive shares are indicated along the horizontal axis and the logarithm of the reciprocal of the
share is measured vertically. Each rectangle of Figure 1.5 thus has an area
equal to $p_i \log (1/p_i)$ for some i, so that the entropy at the level of automobile makes is equal to the total area shown in the figure. The four dashed
horizontal lines are drawn at the level $\log (1/P_g)$ and hence correspond to
the S_g's. The total area below these dashed lines is therefore the between-
group entropy H_0 and the area above these lines is the average within-group

entropy $\sum P_g H_g$. The area above the gth dashed line is $P_g H_g$, from which it follows that the within-group entropy H_g is the average height of the rectangles above this line. That this area is indeed equal to $P_g H_g$ may be verified by means of (5.4):

$$P_g H_g = \sum_{i \in S_g} p_i \left(\log \frac{1}{p_i} - \log \frac{1}{P_g} \right)$$

$$= \sum_{i \in S_g} p_i \log \frac{1}{p_i} - P_g \log \frac{1}{P_g}$$

For further details on the use of entropy for the measurement of industrial concentration, particularly concentration in different geographical areas, see THEIL (1967, Sections 8.2 and 8.3).

The Hirschman-Herfindahl Index of Industrial Concentration

A well-known measure of industrial concentration is the sum of the squares of all n shares:

$$(8.1) \qquad C = \sum_{i=1}^{n} p_i^2$$

This index was proposed by HIRSCHMAN (1945) and HERFINDAHL (1950). Its maximum value is 1, corresponding to complete concentration ($p_i = 1$ for some i, $p_j = 0$ for each $j \neq i$). Its minimum is $1/n$, which is attained when all shares are equal to $1/n$, and this minimum decreases toward zero when n increases indefinitely. These are attractive properties.

Next consider the sets $S_1, \ldots, S_G$ and the indices

$$(8.2) \qquad C_0 = \sum_{g=1}^{G} P_g^2 \quad \text{and} \quad C_g = \sum_{i \in S_g} (p_i/P_g)^2$$

for the concentration at the level of sets and within S_g, respectively ($g = 1, \ldots, G$). To analyze the relationship between these indices and C we write the latter as follows:

$$C = \sum_{g=1}^{G} \sum_{i \in S_g} p_i^2 = \sum_{g=1}^{G} P_g^2 \sum_{i \in S_g} (p_i/P_g)^2$$

$$= \sum_{g=1}^{G} P_g^2 C_g = C_0 \sum_{g=1}^{G} \frac{P_g^2}{C_0} C_g$$

or, equivalently,

$$(8.3) \qquad C = C_0 \sum_{g=1}^{G} \theta_g C_g$$

where

$$(8.4) \qquad \theta_g = \frac{P_g^2}{C_0} = \frac{P_g^2}{\sum\limits_{h=1}^{G} P_h^2} \qquad\qquad g = 1, \dots, G$$

The decomposition of the Hirschman-Herfindahl index is thus of the multiplicative type, C being equal to the product of the between-group index C_0 and the average within-group index $\sum \theta_g C_g$. A lower index either within or between (or both) leads to a smaller overall index, as one would expect it to do. Notice that the weights of the average (the θ's) are nonnegative and add up to one.

This weighting system has a serious disadvantage, however, which may be illustrated with an example. Consider an industry consisting of three groups of firms with shares $P_1 = .2$, $P_2 = .4$, $P_3 = .4$. The between-group index is then

$$C_0 = (.2)^2 + (.4)^2 + (.4)^2 = .36$$

so that $\theta_1 = P_1^2/C_0 = \frac{1}{9}$. Suppose next that there is a merger of the last two groups, leading to a share of .8 for the new group. This implies a modified value of the between-group index:

$$C_0 = (.2)^2 + (.8)^2 = .68$$

which exceeds the old C_0. This is as it should be, because there is more concentration at the level of groups than there was before. But the weight θ_1 is also affected, the new value being $(.2)^2/(.68) = \frac{1}{17}$, which is almost 50 per cent below the level prior to the merger. This is a very undesirable feature, for it implies the weight θ_g of the within-S_g concentration is not invariant under mergers of other groups, S_h and S_k with $g \neq h$, $g \neq k$, $h \neq k$. When the entropy H is used instead of C, we have H_g with weight P_g for S_g, and this weight is clearly invariant under such mergers.

Market Entropy as a Function of Distances from Factories

Consider n competing firms which serve a given area with a certain product, each having one factory in that area. Consumers in different locations are at different distances from these factories. Since they are charged for the transportation costs, the market share of the ith firm in a location at a distance r_i from its factory is a decreasing function of r_i. Specifically, it is assumed that the ith market share in a location at distances $r_1, \dots, r_n$ from the n factories is of the form

(8.5)
$$p_i(r_1, \ldots, r_n) = \frac{\alpha_i r_i^{-\beta}}{\sum\limits_{k=1}^{n} \alpha_k r_k^{-\beta}} \qquad i = 1, \ldots, n$$

where β is a positive constant which measures the distance effect and α_i is a positive constant which describes the attractiveness of the product of the ith firm. This attractiveness may be due either to high quality or low price.

Equation (8.5) implies that the ith market share at the location of the ith factory ($r_i = 0$, $r_j > 0$ for each $j \neq i$) is equal to one. This is so because $r_i^{-\beta}$ increases indefinitely as $r_i \to 0$.[1] Hence there is a zero market entropy at each of the n factory locations. We shall now consider the change in the market entropy which results from a small change in the distances. That is, we imagine that we start in a location at distances $(r_1, \ldots, r_n)$ from the n factories, get into our car and drive a modest number of miles in some direction, so that we arrive in another location at distances $(r_1 + dr_1, \ldots, r_n + dr_n)$ from the factories. Is the market entropy in the new location larger or smaller than in the old one, and by how much?

To answer this question we consider the derivative of the entropy with respect to the distance r_i, assuming that natural logarithms (nits) are used:

(8.6)
$$\frac{\partial H}{\partial r_i} = -\frac{\partial}{\partial r_i} \sum_{j=1}^{n} p_j \log p_j = -\sum_{j=1}^{n} (1 + \log p_j) \frac{\partial p_j}{\partial r_i} = -\sum_{j=1}^{n} (\log p_j) \frac{\partial p_j}{\partial r_i}$$

The derivative $\partial p_j / \partial r_i$ is obtained from (8.5) with the following result (see Problem 10 for intermediate steps):

(8.7)
$$\frac{\partial p_j}{\partial r_i} = -\beta p_i (1 - p_i)/r_i \quad \text{if} \quad i = j$$
$$\beta p_i p_j / r_i \qquad \text{if} \quad i \neq j$$

This shows that an increase in r_i reduces the ith share and raises all other shares.

Combining (8.6) and (8.7), we find

$$\frac{\partial H}{\partial r_i} r_i = -\beta p_i \sum_{j=1}^{n} p_j \log p_j + \beta p_i \log p_i$$

$$= -\beta p_i \left(\log \frac{1}{p_i} - H \right)$$

---

[1] We have $r_i^{-\beta}$ in the numerator and also the denominator of (8.5), and both increase indefinitely while leaving the $n-1$ other terms of the denominator behind at fixed levels.

The expression on the left can be written as $\partial H/\partial(\log r_i)$. Consequently, the change in the market entropy caused by small relative (logarithmic) distance changes $d(\log r_i), \ldots, d(\log r_n)$ is

$$(8.8) \qquad dH = -\beta \sum_{i=1}^{n} p_i \left(\log \frac{1}{p_i} - H\right) d(\log r_i)$$

To interpret the sum in the right-hand side, go back to (1.22), the variance of information. This comparison shows that the entropy change dH is equal to a negative multiple $(-\beta)$ of the covariance of the "market share information" and the relative distance change. Thus, if the relative distance increase is on the average algebraically larger for factories with large shares, their $\log(1/p_i)$ being small, the market entropy will increase, and the increase will be larger when the distance effect measured by β is larger. This is as one would intuitively expect.

One may object to the idea of a strictly zero entropy at the n factory locations on the ground that there will always be some local customers who prefer a brand produced elsewhere. To take this into consideration one has to modify the market share function (8.5). One possibility is

$$(8.9) \qquad p_i(r_1, \ldots, r_n) = \frac{a_i e^{-br_i}}{\sum\limits_{k=1}^{n} a_k e^{-br_k}} \qquad i = 1, \ldots, n$$

where $a_1, \ldots, a_n$ and b are positive constants. Since $e^{-br_i} = 1$ at $r_i = 0$, and hence finite, all shares are strictly less than one for whatever nonnegative values of the r's. The expression $a_i e^{-br_i}$ may be written as $a_i(e^{r_i})^{-b}$, which shows that the results based on (8.5) are all directly applicable to (8.9), provided that we interpret α_i as a_i, β as b, and r_i as e^{r_i}. The change in the logarithm of r_i thus becomes $d(\log e^{r_i}) = dr_i$, so that (8.8) is modified to

$$(8.10) \qquad dH = -b \sum_{i=1}^{n} p_i \left(\log \frac{1}{p_i} - H\right) dr_i$$

Hence the covariance involves the changes in the distances themselves rather than their logarithmic changes.

See Problem 17 of Chapter 2, the last two subsections of Section 4.7, and Problems 28 to 31 of Chapter 4 for further results on these distance models.

Brand Loyalty and Party Loyalty

The entropy may also be used to measure the brand loyalty of a household. Using panel data, one can determine the expenditure shares $p_1, \ldots, p_n$ of n brands of coffee (say) for this household during a certain period of time. The entropy (1.6) measures the disloyalty of the household with respect to coffee brands. The average of such entropies over a group of households is a plausible summary measure for this group, and the entropy decomposition theorem may be used should one wish to distinguish between sets of brands.

Since the entropy is a measure of dividedness, it can naturally be used to describe the degree of disagreement in a parliamentary roll call.[1] Write N for the number of legislators who vote either yea or nay and N_y for the number of yeas, so that the entropy is

$$(8.11) \qquad \frac{N_y}{N} \log \frac{N}{N_y} + \frac{N-N_y}{N} \log \frac{N}{N-N_y}$$

If N stands for the number of voting legislators of only one party, the entropy (8.11) measures the dividedness of this party at this particular roll call. The average entropy of a number of successive roll calls is a summary measure of the party's dividedness during a certain period of time.

Next consider one particular legislator. Our question is: How loyal is he to the party line? One way of measuring the individual legislator's allegiance to his party is by means of the entropy reduction caused by his vote. If he voted yea at the above roll call, the entropy in the case of his absence would have been

$$(8.12) \qquad \frac{N_y-1}{N-1} \log \frac{N-1}{N_y-1} + \frac{N-N_y}{N-1} \log \frac{N-1}{N-N_y}$$

and if he had voted nay, the entropy in his absence would have been

$$(8.13) \qquad \frac{N_y}{N-1} \log \frac{N-1}{N_y} + \frac{N-N_y-1}{N-1} \log \frac{N-1}{N-N_y-1}$$

The entropy reduction caused by this legislator's vote is then either (8.12) minus (8.11) or (8.13) minus (8.11) depending on how he voted. The reduction is always positive (negative) when the legislator votes with the majority (minority) of his party, and the algebraic average reduction of a series of

---

[1] The use of the entropy in political science was originally suggested by MacRae and applied by Kesselman (1967, pp. 27–34). In his recent monograph (1970, Chapter 6) MacRae discusses Rice's index, to be considered in the next subsection, as well as other indices.

roll calls is a summary measure for his voting behavior in relation to that of the party as a whole.

Rice's Index of Cohesion

RICE (1928) proposed $|1-2p|$ as an "index of cohesion", where p is the proportion of legislators voting yea and $1-p$ the proportion of those voting nay. It is equal to 1 when all legislators agree ($p = 0$ or 1) and 0 when there is a tied vote ($p = .5$). If we subtract this index from 1, we obtain $1-|1-2p|$, which is an index of disagreement. This is shown in Figure 1.6 along with the entropy in bits. The two functions have the same maximum

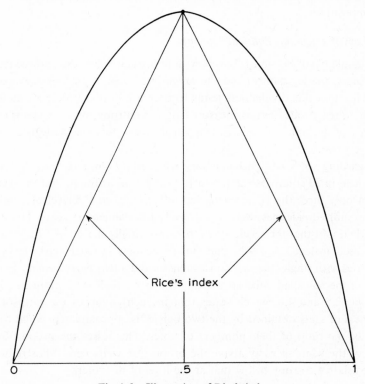

Fig. 1.6.   Illustration of Rice's index

and minima, but Rice's disagreement index has a kink at $p = .5$, whereas the behavior of the entropy is much smoother. This smoothness is a great advantage, particularly when the measure is used to ascertain the loyalty of an individual legislator to his party's position. If the entropy reduction is used for this purpose, as proposed in the previous subsection, we obtain a value very close to zero when the party's votes are about evenly split. One may argue that this is as it should be, because the party as such has no real position in this case. But if Rice's index is used, the legislator is either loyal or disloyal depending on whether he voted with the majority or the minority, and the amount of loyalty or disloyalty is fixed irrespective of the size of the majority or minority. This follows from the linearity of the two segments of Rice's index shown in Figure 1.6, and it is not an attractive property.

Another reason to prefer the entropy to Rice's index is the possibility of decomposition (legislators' positions by parties, states, etc.). The latter index works with absolute values, $|1-2p|$, which are difficult to handle in decompositions.

The Law of Declining Political Entropy

Example (3) of Section 1.3 deals with political dividedness at three levels: the voters, the legislature, and the executive. There are strong reasons for believing that this dividedness tends to decrease in that order; a statement which, when dividedness is measured by the entropy, may be regarded as the law of declining political entropy from the voters via the legislature to the executive.

Regarding votes and parliamentary seats, RAE (1967) analyzed 115 elections held in 20 countries[1] after World War II and he found that in all cases except only three the Hirschman-Herfindahl index at the level of votes indicates more dividedness than at the level of parliamentary seats. There can be little doubt that the result would be substantially the same if the entropy were used instead. The difference in dividedness is particularly large for countries with single-member constituencies and a two-party system. In fact, there is the so-called cube law, about which we shall have more to say in Sections 2.5 and 4.6, which states that in such countries the ratio of the numbers of seats obtained by the two parties is approximately equal to the cube of the ratio of their numbers of votes. This raises the proportion of seats of the winning party above the proportion of its votes, thus reducing the legislative entropy below that at the level of the voters.

But even in countries with a proportional representation system we have this effect, simply because no representation is strictly proportional. For one

---

[1] Australia, Austria, Belgium, Canada, Denmark, Finland, France, Germany (West), Iceland, Ireland, Israel, Italy, Luxembourg, the Netherlands, New Zealand, Norway, Sweden, Switzerland, United Kingdom, and United States.

thing, there are numerous constitutions requiring that a party should have a certain minimum percentage of votes in order to obtain any seat at all. This eliminates the smallest parties, which lowers the legislative entropy. For another, there is the obvious constraint that the number of parliamentary seats assigned to each party be an integer, and the way in which this problem is solved is usually such that the larger parties are favored at the expense of the smaller ones. A prominent example is d'Hondt's method, which may be briefly described as follows. Let there be N seats in the House and suppose that $N' < N$ seats have been assigned. To determine which party should receive the $(N'+1)^{st}$ seat one computes for each of them the ratio of its number of votes to one plus the number of seats already received. This ratio is the number of votes per seat if the party actually obtains the $(N'+1)^{st}$ seat, and d'Hondt's method assigns this seat to the party with the largest ratio, after which it repeats the procedure for the $(N'+2)^{nd}$ seat. The important point is that the addition of 1 to the number of seats already received in the denominator of the ratio has a larger relative effect for small parties than for large ones, thus reducing the ratios of the former relative to those of the latter. This raises the likelihood that large parties obtain additional seats, which tends to lower the legislative entropy.

As to dividedness at the level of parliament seats and cabinet posts, it is typically the case that in a two-party system only one party is represented in the government, so that the executive entropy is then zero, which is necessarily less than the legislative entropy. The executive entropy is positive for a coalition cabinet, but it is usually smaller than the legislative entropy because only a subset of the parties is represented in the cabinet. An example is given in Table 1.8, which deals with France in the period 1947–1958 (the Fourth French Republic). During this period there were three legislatures, each preceded by an election. The legislative entropy varied over time within each legislature owing to deaths, resignations, formation of new and disappearance of old parties, and so on, but since the degree of variation was relatively modest only the three average legislative entropies are shown. They are of the order of $2\frac{1}{2}$ to 3 bits, which is on the high side because 3 bits amounts to as much dividedness as eight proportions of $\frac{1}{8}$ each. In all cabinets except the first a distinction is made between junior and senior posts. The executive entropies of the table are based on the assumption that a junior post is equivalent to a fraction θ of a senior post; the figures shown are the entropies for $\theta = 0, .5,$ and 1. They are all smaller than the legislative entropies but are still substantial.

TABLE 1.8

Prime Minister	Executive entropy for		
	$\theta = 0$	$\theta = .5$	$\theta = 1$
First Legislature, 1947–1951			
(Average legislative entropy 2.64 bits)			
1. Ramadier	1.65	1.65	1.65
2. Schuman	1.30	1.35	1.35
3. Marie	1.32	1.53	1.61
4. Queuille (1)	1.42	1.69	1.77
5. Bidault	1.47	1.59	1.62
6. Pleven (1)	1.54	1.50	1.47
7. Queuille (2)	1.51	1.68	1.73
Second Legislature, 1951–1955			
(Average legislative entropy 3.09 bits)			
8. Pleven (2)	1.48	1.50	1.50
9. Faure (1)	1.53	1.56	1.56
10. Pinay	1.50	1.55	1.56
11. Mayer	1.61	1.62	1.62
12. Laniel	1.83	1.84	1.84
13. Mendès-France	1.72	1.80	1.81
14. Faure (2)	1.84	1.85	1.83
Third Legislature, 1956–1958			
(Average legislative entropy 3.07 bits)			
15. Mollet	1.16	1.10	1.08
16. Bourgès-Mannoury	1.33	1.36	1.36
17. Gaillard	1.68	1.87	1.92

Soccer Matches: *Outcomes and Predictions of Outcomes*

Soccer is Europe's most popular sport. In the Netherlands, as elsewhere, there is much interest in predicting the outcomes of matches, particularly since large prizes are awarded to those who are successful in this respect. What follows is based on JOCHEMS (1962) and THEIL (1966, Section 12.B).

For each match, three possible outcomes will be distinguished: (1) the home team wins, (2) there is a draw, and (3) the visiting team wins. The performance of the two teams in the previous matches of the season will be used as a predictor. Specifically, we count 2 for a match won, 1 for a draw, and 0 for a match lost. The average score of the home team (indicated by the subscript i) in the previous matches will be written w_i, which obviously satisfies $0 \leqq w_i \leqq 2$. The average score of the visiting team will be written w_j, and the score difference $w_i - w_j$ will be used to measure the difference in performance. This difference can vary between -2 and 2; it is positive when the home team has been more successful than the visiting team and negative in the opposite case.

The solid curve in the upper part of Figure 1.7 gives the proportion p_1 of about 1800 matches of the Royal Netherlands Soccer League in 1955–1958 that resulted in a victory for the home team. This proportion is described in the figure as a function of the score difference $w_i - w_j$,[1] and the curve clearly shows that the chances of the home team are better when the score difference is more in its favor. The solid curve in the second diagram gives p_2, the relative frequency of a draw, and that in the third p_3, the relative frequency of a victory for the visiting team. The curves indicate that p_2 does not change very much with the score difference and that p_3 declines rather regularly.

The dashed lines of the figure are based on about 6000 outcome predictions in the years 1955–1957. Sport journalists make forecasts of the outcomes of next Sunday's soccer matches. The dashed curve on top gives the proportion q_1 of cases in which the home team was predicted to win, the second dashed curve gives the proportion q_2 of a predicted draw, and the third gives the proportion q_3 of a predicted victory for the visiting team, all as functions of the score difference $w_i - w_j$. The curves indicate that the predictions vary much more with the score differences than the actual outcomes do.

In fact, it is much easier to predict how the forecasters will predict than how the match will actually end. This is shown at the bottom of the figure, where the entropies of the distributions of forecasts and realizations are displayed. The maximum entropy is $\log 3 = 1.585$ bits, and the entropy of the realizations is less than 10 per cent below this maximum except when the score difference exceeds .4. The entropy of the forecasts has a rather sharp peak for small negative values of the score difference and it declines monotonically for algebraically larger and smaller values. This entropy difference between forecasts and realizations is a phenomenon that occurs

---

[1] The score differences are grouped into intervals of width .2. The line segments are drawn between the midpoints of successive intervals except for the extreme intervals (.8, 2) and $(-2, -.8)$, for which .9 and $-.9$, respectively, are used.

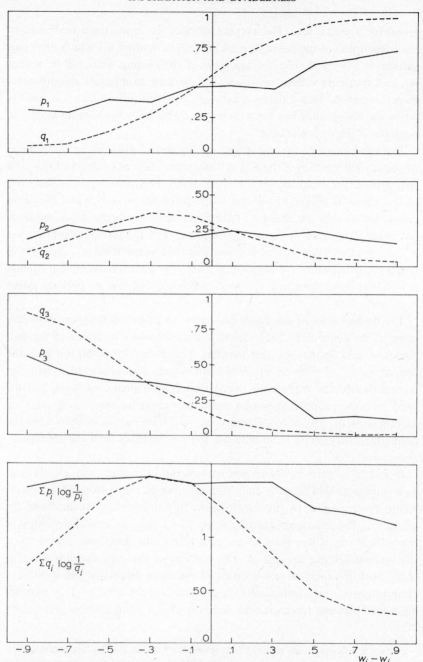

Fig. 1.7.   Outcomes of soccer matches and predictions of outcomes as functions of the score difference

more frequently. The outcome typically has some components that were more certain before the event than other components, and forecasters concentrate on the former rather than the latter. The result is that on the average forecasts show more regularity and less uncertainty than the events themselves. See also Problem 14.

PROBLEMS

1 Prove that the slope of the information function shown in Figure 1.1 increases monotonically from $-\infty$ at $p = 0$ to -1 at $p = 1$ when natural logarithms (nits) are used. Prove also that the slope of the entropy function shown in Figure 1.2 decreases monotonically from ∞ at $p = 0$ to $-\infty$ at $p = 1$.

2 Use L'Hôpital's rule to prove that $x \log(1/x)$ converges to zero when x decreases toward zero.

3 Compute the entropy of the distribution with probabilities (.98, .01, .01). Next determine the distribution with two possible outcomes (probabilities p and $1-p$) which has the same entropy value. Why is it that the larger probability of the second distribution is smaller than .98?

4 For $N = 1000$, $n = 3$, $p_1 = .5$, $p_2 = .3$, $p_3 = .2$, compute the entropy (1.6) and the asymptotic variance (1.21). Draw your own conclusions as to the distribution of the entropy estimator (1.20) and state the qualifications that must be made.

5 Consider Table 1.1 in Section 1.4, in particular the fourth district with the increasing average racial entropy of its schools. Compare this with the percentage of white students in 1969 and state what, in your view, happened in this district. See also Problem 5 of Chapter 2.

6 In Table 1.4, $\bar{H}_{ab4}$ presents three exceptions to the rule that the average employment entropy of large SMSA's exceeds that of medium-sized SMSA's, and hence only one case which agrees with this rule. For all other $\bar{H}_{abg}$'s ($g = 2, 3, 5, 6$) there is only one exception. Can you explain this difference?

7 Let there be five assets on a balance sheet with proportions $p_1 = .2$, $p_2 = .1$, $p_3 = .15$, $p_4 = .25$, $p_5 = .3$. The pairs which are admissible for aggregation are (1, 2), (3, 4), (3, 5), and (4, 5). How far can one aggregate if the assets side of the balance sheet is required to have an entropy of 2 bits?

8 Consider the Hirschman-Herfindahl index C defined in (8.1). Prove

that it can be written in the form

$$C = \frac{1}{n} + \sum_{i=1}^{n} \left(p_i - \frac{1}{n}\right)^2$$

Use this expression to prove that $C \geq 1/n$ and that the minimum is attained if and only if all n shares are equal to $1/n$.

9   (*Continuation*)   Let p_1 be the largest of the n shares and suppose that it increases by a positive amount Δp_1 at the expense of the share p_2. Prove that the new value of the Hirschman-Herfindahl index is

$$\sum_{i=1}^{n} p_i^2 + 2(p_1 - p_2)\Delta p_1 + 2(\Delta p_1)^2$$

Use this result to prove that the maximum value of the Hirschman-Herfindahl index is 1 and that this maximum is attained if and only if one of the n shares is 1 and all others 0.

10   To verify the derivatives (8.7), write

$$p_j(r_1, \ldots, r_n) = \frac{A_j(r_j)}{\sum_{k=1}^{n} A_k(r_k)} \quad \text{where} \quad A_k(r_k) = \alpha_k \, r_k^{-\beta}$$

Prove $\partial A_k / \partial r_i = -\beta A_i / r_i$ for $k = i$, 0 for $k \neq i$, and use this to prove (8.7).

11   The covariance of two random variables is commonly defined as the expectation of their product with the understanding that both variables are measured as deviations from their means. But in the discussion of eq. (8.8), the term covariance is used for an expression in which only one of the two variables, $\log (1/p_i)$ with expectation H, is measured as a deviation from the mean. Can you reconcile the difference?

12   When N, N_y and $N - N_y$ are all sufficiently large, the entropy reductions discussed below eq. (8.13) may be approximated by a linear Taylor expansion of the entropy around $(N_y, N - N_y)$. Prove that when natural logarithms are used, these approximate entropy reductions are of the form

$$\pm \frac{1}{N} \log \frac{N_y}{N - N_y}$$

Indicate when $+$ and when $-$ is applicable.

13   In Figure 1.7 the entropy of the realizations is about equal to the entropy of the forecasts at a score difference of $-.3$. This is also true at

a score difference of $-.1$. Does this mean that the distributions of forecasts and realizations are identical at each of these score differences?

14 Suppose that a journalist knows nothing about the relative strength of two teams that will meet next Sunday except $p_1(w_i - w_j)$, $p_2(w_i - w_j)$ and $p_3(w_i - w_j)$. His strategy is to predict the outcome at random with probabilities q_1, q_2, q_3 which he selects in such a way that the chance of a correct prediction is maximized. Prove that this is equivalent to maximizing $p_1 q_1 + p_2 q_2 + p_3 q_3$ subject to $q_1 + q_2 + q_3 = 1$ and $q_1 \geq 0$, $q_2 \geq 0$, $q_3 \geq 0$. Prove also that the solution amounts to always predicting the outcome with the largest p, so that the entropy of the predictions is zero. Compare this with the actual predictions displayed in Figure 1.7 to conclude that their position is between this journalist's predictions and the actual outcomes.

CHAPTER 2

EXTENSION TO SEVERAL DECOMPOSITIONS

In the previous chapter we confined ourselves to a single distribution with proportions or probabilities $p_1, , ..., p_n$. In this chapter we consider several distributions, first viewing them within a probabilistic framework, then applying them to a number of problems outside the probabilistic area.

2.1. A Generalized Form of Message and Its Expected Information

We return to the event E with probability p of Section 1.1. It is now assumed that a message arrives which – contrary to the messages considered in Section 1.1 – does *not* state with certainty whether or not E occurred. Rather, it states that the odds in favor of E have changed such that the new probability of E is q, some number between zero and one. This is a generalization of the situation discussed in Section 1.1, because the message considered there stated with certainty that E occurred and hence $q = 1$. The problem is the same as before: How can we measure the amount of information provided by the message – this time the message which states that E's probability has changed from p to q?

Prior and Posterior Probabilities and Information

We shall use the term prior probability for the original probability p of E (before the message arrived) and posterior probability for the value q which is stated by the message. The problem is thus that of measuring the information content of the message which transforms prior p into posterior q.

The approach of Section 1.1 can be applied straightforwardly when we proceed *under the condition that E ultimately does occur*. The starting point is the prior probability p, the endpoint is the certainty that E occurred, and between these two points two alternative routes will be considered: one in which, as explained above, a message is received that transforms p into q followed by a second message that transforms q into 1 (certainty), and a second route in which p is directly transformed into 1 with no intermediate step. Since the initial situation (probability p) and the eventual situation

56

(certainty) are the same for the two routes, we shall require that they have the same total amount of information; this is completely in line with the discussion in the second subsection of Section 1.1 (pages 2-3). The information provided by the second (direct) route consists of the single value $h(p)$ $= -\log p$. The total information provided by the first route is equal to the information of the message that transforms p into q, plus $h(q)$. Hence the information content of the message which transforms prior p into posterior q is, if event E ultimately occurs, equal to

$$(1.1) \qquad h(p) - h(q) = \log \frac{q}{p}$$

This information value is zero for $p = q$, as it should be, because $p = q$ implies that the odds favoring E are unchanged. The value is $-\log p$ for $q = 1$ and thus includes, as it also should, the special case of the message which states with certainty that E occurred. We obtain a negative value when $q < p$, which may seem surprising. Note, however, that E is supposed to occur at the end; a message which states that E has become less probable than before $(q < p)$ then has a negative information value, which is not unreasonable.

Expected Information

The information definition (1.1) thus applies only when it ultimately turns out that E occurs. If it appears that E fails to occur at the end, we can apply the same line of argument to not-E, which amounts to replacing p by $1-p$, q by $1-q$, and (1.1) by

$$(1.2) \qquad h(1-p) - h(1-q) = \log \frac{1-q}{1-p}$$

The information received is thus either (1.1) or (1.2) and we do not know which until it has finally become certain that E has or has not occurred. Recall that we had precisely the same situation in the third subsection of Section 1.1 (pages 3–5). Recall also that we concluded there that it is still possible to compute the expected information. Here we may draw exactly the same conclusion. The information received is (1.1) when E occurs and the probability of this happening is q, and the information is (1.2) when E does not occur and this holds with probability $1-q$. [Note that the relevant probabilities are q and $1-q$, not p and $1-p$, because the latter are declared outmoded by the message whose expected information we are deriving here.] Hence the expectation of the information provided by the message that transforms the prior probabilities $(p, 1-p)$ into the posterior probabilities $(q, 1-q)$ is

$$(1.3) \qquad I = q \log \frac{q}{p} + (1-q) \log \frac{1-q}{1-p}$$

The value of this function is zero when $p = q$; it will be proved later in this section that it is positive whenever $p \neq q$. Contour lines of the function are shown in Figure 2.1.

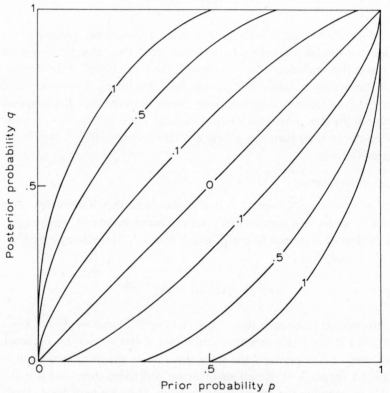

Fig. 2.1. Contour lines of constant expected information (in bits) of the posterior probabilities $(q, 1-q)$, given the prior probabilities $(p, 1-p)$

Extension to Several Events

The approach can be extended easily to a complete system of n mutually exclusive events with its prior and posterior probabilities displayed below.

Events	E_1	E_2	...	E_n
Prior probabilities	p_1	p_2	...	p_n
Posterior probabilities	q_1	q_2	...	q_n

If it turns out that E_i ultimately occurs, the information provided by the message that transforms the p's into the q's is, in view of (1.1), equal to $\log (q_i/p_i)$. Since this message states that the probability of E_i is q_i, its expected information is

$$(1.4) \qquad I(q : p) = \sum_{i=1}^{n} q_i \log \frac{q_i}{p_i}$$

where q and p on the left stand for the sets of probabilities $q_1, \ldots, q_n$ and $p_1, \ldots, p_n$, respectively.

The function (1.4) vanishes when the two sets of probabilities are pairwise equal: $p_i = q_i$ for $i = 1, \ldots, n$. We shall show in the next subsection that it takes positive values when there are pairwise differences. When one of the events, say E_i, has unit posterior probability, the function (1.4) becomes $-\log p_i$ in accordance with the basic information definition. In the case of prior equiprobability, $p_i = 1/n$ for each i, we have

$$(1.5) \qquad I(q : p) = \sum_{i=1}^{n} q_i \log \frac{q_i}{1/n} = \log n - \sum_{i=1}^{n} q_i \log \frac{1}{q_i}$$

Recall that $\log n$ is the entropy of the equiprobability case and that it is also the maximum entropy value. Hence the third member is the difference between the prior and the posterior entropies, so that in the case of prior equiprobability the information expectation (1.4) is equal to the amount by which the entropy is reduced below the original (maximum) value.

Proof of the Nonnegativity of the Information Expectation

To analyze the sign of the information expectation (1.4) we introduce

$$(1.6) \qquad a_i = \frac{p_i - q_i}{q_i} \qquad\qquad i = 1, \ldots, n$$

which is the difference between corresponding prior and posterior probabilities measured as a fraction of the latter.[1] The weighted average of these ratios with the q's as weights vanishes:

---

[1] The definition (1.6) presupposes that q_i does not vanish. If it does, the ith component of the right-hand sum in (1.4) is zero, so that the component need not be considered.

(1.7) $$\sum_{i=1}^{n} q_i a_i = \sum_{i=1}^{n} (p_i - q_i) = 1 - 1 = 0$$

Then substitute a's for the p's in (1.4):

(1.8) $$I(q:p) = -\sum_{i=1}^{n} q_i \log \frac{p_i}{q_i} = -\sum_{i=1}^{n} q_i \log (1 + a_i)$$

Applying (1.7), we can write this as

(1.9) $$I(q:p) = \sum_{i=1}^{n} q_i [a_i - \log (1 + a_i)] = \sum_{i=1}^{n} q_i f(a_i)$$

where

(1.10) $$f(x) = x - \log (1 + x)$$

For the derivative of $f(\ )$ we have, assuming that log stands for natural logarithm,

(1.11) $$f'(x) = 1 - \frac{1}{1+x} = \frac{x}{1+x} > 0 \quad \text{if} \quad x > 0$$
$$< 0 \quad \text{if} \quad -1 \leqq x < 0$$

Since $f(0) = 0$, we may conclude from the positive derivative for $x > 0$ that $f(x) > 0$ for $x > 0$ and from the negative derivative for $x < 0$ that $f(x) > 0$ for $x < 0$.[1] Hence $f(\ )$ is strictly positive except when its argument vanishes, in which case the function also takes the zero value. It then follows from (1.9) that $I(q:p) > 0$ except when all a's vanish, and this exception refers to the case of pairwise equality of the prior and posterior probabilities that was discussed earlier.

Note that the information expectation (1.4) has no finite upper limit. This is verified by specifying $q_i > p_i = 0$ for some i. The prior probabilities specify in that case that E_i has zero chance, and the message states that this is raised to a positive level. That is, the probability has been raised by a factor "infinity", and we are thus "infinitely surprised" by the message.

A Quadratic Approximation to the Information Expectation

We can obtain more insight into the behavior of the function (1.4) for moderate discrepancies between corresponding prior and posterior prob-

---

[1] The restriction $x \geqq -1$ in (1.11) is not essential, because $a_i \geqq -1$ follows from the definition (1.6).

abilities by expanding the logarithm according to a Taylor series. Consider $\log (1+a_i)$ in (1.8):

$$\log (1+a_i) = a_i - \tfrac{1}{2} a_i^2 + \ldots$$

Substitution of the right-hand side in (1.8) gives

$$I(q : p) = -\sum_{i=1}^{n} q_i(a_i - \tfrac{1}{2}a_i^2 + \ldots) = \tfrac{1}{2}\sum_{i=1}^{n} q_i a_i^2 + \ldots$$

where use is made of (1.7) in the second step. This result can be written as

(1.12) $$I(q : p) \approx \tfrac{1}{2}\sum_{i=1}^{n} q_i \left(\frac{p_i - q_i}{q_i}\right)^2 = \tfrac{1}{2}\sum_{i=1}^{n} \frac{(p_i - q_i)^2}{q_i}$$

The expression in the middle indicates that, as a first approximation, the information expectation is equal to one-half of the weighted average of the squared relative discrepancies between corresponding prior and posterior probabilities, with weights equal to the latter probabilities. The third member of (1.12) indicates that $I(q:p)$ is also approximately proportional to a chi-square with the q's regarded as the theoretical probabilities and the p's as the observed relative frequencies.

Remarks:

(1) The expansion of the logarithm is based on the assumption that natural logarithms are used. It is therefore to be understood that $I(q:p)$ in (1.12) is measured in nits. When bits are used, the factors $\tfrac{1}{2}$ in the two other members of (1.12) are to be replaced by $\tfrac{1}{2}\log_2 e \approx .721$.

(2) The convergence of the expansions presupposes $|a_i| < 1$ for each i or, equivalently, $0 < p_i < 2q_i$. There is no particular reason to expect that these inequalities are satisfied in the context of messages, but in many applications the two sets of proportions are close, and the approximation (1.12) is then usually sufficiently accurate.

(3) It was stated above that $I(q:p)$ is approximately proportional to a chi-square. Note that such a chi-square is of the form $\sum (o_i - e_i)^2/e_i$, where o_i and e_i are observed and expected *absolute* frequencies, whereas p_i and q_i are probabilities and thus correspond to relative rather than absolute frequencies. Hence, given fixed relative proportions, $I(q:p)$ is also fixed but the chi-square is not; it increases proportionally with the number of observations on which it is based.

Decomposition of the Information Expectation

The entropy decomposition theorem of Section 1.5 can be extended straightforwardly to the information expectation (1.4). Combine the events $E_1, \ldots, E_n$ into G sets of events, $S_1, \ldots, S_G$ in such a way that each E_i falls under exactly one S_g, where $g = 1, \ldots, G$. Define prior and posterior probabilities at the level of sets:

$$(1.13) \qquad P_g = \sum_{i \in S_g} p_i \qquad Q_g = \sum_{i \in S_g} q_i \qquad\qquad g = 1, \ldots, G$$

The information expectation (1.4) after the aggregation of events to sets of events is thus

$$(1.14) \qquad I_0(q : p) = \sum_{g=1}^{G} Q_g \log \frac{Q_g}{P_g}$$

Next consider:

$$\sum_{i=1}^{n} q_i \log \frac{q_i}{p_i} = \sum_{g=1}^{G} Q_g \sum_{i \in S_g} \frac{q_i}{Q_g} \left(\log \frac{Q_g}{P_g} + \log \frac{q_i/Q_g}{p_i/P_g} \right)$$

$$= \sum_{g=1}^{G} Q_g \log \frac{Q_g}{P_g} + \sum_{g=1}^{G} Q_g \sum_{i \in S_g} \frac{q_i}{Q_g} \log \frac{q_i/Q_g}{p_i/P_g}$$

or

$$(1.15) \qquad I(q : p) = I_0(q : p) + \sum_{g=1}^{G} Q_g I_g(q : p)$$

where

$$(1.16) \qquad I_g(q : p) = \sum_{i \in S_g} \frac{q_i}{Q_g} \log \frac{q_i/Q_g}{p_i/P_g} \qquad\qquad g = 1, \ldots, G$$

Since p_i/P_g and q_i/Q_g, $i \in S_g$ are conditional probabilities of E_i given S_g, the interpretation of $I_g(q:p)$ is that of the expected information of our message under the condition that one of the events of S_g will ultimately occur. We have $I_g(q:p) = 0$ if and only if the message changes the probabilities of all events of S_g in the same proportion ($q_i/Q_g = p_i/P_g$ or, equivalently, $q_i/p_i = Q_g/P_g$ for each $i \in S_g$). In that special case the effect of the message, as far as S_g is concerned, is confined to the set rather than the constituent events, and the effect on the sets is taken care of by the first term of the decomposition (1.15).

As in the case of the entropy decomposition in eq. (5.3) of Section 1.5, the present decomposition has a simple informational interpretation in two stages. Let the first message state that the prior probabilities $P_1, \ldots, P_G$ of the sets are modified to $Q_1, \ldots, Q_G$, so that the expected information is $I_0(q:p)$. Then, under the condition that one of the events of S_G will occur, consider the subsequent message stating that the prior conditional probabilities p_i/P_g are modified to q_i/Q_g, $i \in S_g$. Its expected information is $I_g(q:p)$. Since the probability of S_g is Q_g according to the first message, the total expected information is equal to the right-hand side of (1.15), and this equation thus states that this total is equal to the expected information of the message which states immediately how the probabilities of all n events have changed.

2.2. Further Results on the Racial Composition of Chicago's Public Schools

It was stated at the end of Section 1.4 that the measurement of segregation requires a comparison of the racial composition of the school's student population with that of the district to which it belongs. This is the subject of the present section. The discussion will be continued in Section 3.2.

The Racial Entropy of a School District

Recall the basic notation employed in Section 1.4: p_j for the proportion of black students in the jth school, w_j for this school's student population measured as a fraction of the city total, and $W_r = \sum_j w_j \, (j \in D_r)$ for the student population of district D_r, measured in the same way. The proportion of black students in that district is then

$$(2.1) \qquad P_r = \sum_{j \in D_r} \frac{w_j}{W_r} p_j \qquad\qquad r = 1, \ldots, 27$$

and the proportion of white students in D_r is $1-P_r$. Hence the racial entropy of the student population of this district is

$$(2.2) \qquad K_r = P_r \log \frac{1}{P_r} + (1-P_r) \log \frac{1}{1-P_r}$$

where the symbol K on the left is used to distinguish the district's racial entropy from that of the separate schools.

Table 2.1 presents Chicago's district racial entropies for all 27 districts in each of the years 1963 to 1969. As in the case of Table 1.1 in Section 1.4, they are expressed as a percentage of 1 bit and can thus vary from 0 to 100. Recall that we concluded from the latter table that none of the average racial entropies of the schools in any district exceeded one-half of the upper limit and that the city average was only about one-seventh of this limit. The

TABLE 2.1

ADDITIONAL RACIAL DATA ON THE PUBLIC SCHOOL DISTRICTS OF CHICAGO

District	Racial entropy of school districts							Segregation: $100(K_r - H_t)$						
	1963	1964	1965	1966	1967	1968	1969	1963	1964	1965	1966	1967	1968	1969
1	.1	.3	.9	1.0	.8	1.1	1.2	.0	.1	.3	.2	.2	.2	.2
2	.3	.3	.2	.2	.6	1.6	2.9	.1	.1	.0	.0	.1	.2	.4
3	.8	3.0	3.4	3.1	2.5	3.9	3.0	.1	.7	.7	.6	.5	.7	.4
4	10.7	15.9	22.9	46.9	68.2	82.8	94.0	4.0	7.1	8.9	26.2	48.5	47.2	58.5
5	.2	.1	.0	.3	.4	.4	1.8	.0	.0	.0	.1	.1	.1	.3
6	24.0	24.8	25.0	24.6	26.8	29.6	32.6	6.1	6.2	6.6	5.5	5.9	6.9	7.5
7	99.9	99.9	100.0	100.0	99.9	99.4	98.6	67.2	67.9	70.2	70.0	70.1	72.3	70.4
8	42.7	33.6	22.9	16.3	15.3	13.4	12.3	14.3	10.0	5.1	3.5	3.8	3.8	4.4
9	68.4	63.1	58.5	53.9	53.3	48.9	48.8	41.5	37.0	35.0	33.7	35.5	32.2	34.2
10	53.9	55.8	55.4	57.7	61.2	65.8	70.5	43.2	48.8	49.2	50.6	53.8	57.7	61.6
11	25.7	23.6	24.6	20.9	21.9	22.7	25.6	12.4	13.7	14.6	12.5	12.4	13.3	14.4
12	39.7	39.1	39.6	38.3	39.7	39.6	41.8	27.1	26.7	27.5	26.7	29.4	29.3	32.6
13	.4	.6	.7	.2	.3	.4	.4	.1	.1	.1	.1	.1	.1	.1
14	53.8	52.1	50.0	49.0	46.6	47.1	45.1	23.6	23.7	25.1	26.4	25.8	25.5	24.2
15	63.8	71.3	75.4	78.9	77.5	78.0	83.8	43.0	52.9	61.2	65.8	63.8	62.8	58.0
16	93.5	85.9	77.3	66.2	55.9	43.0	34.4	62.9	57.8	49.2	41.6	34.1	22.5	19.9
17	35.3	38.0	41.6	48.9	58.1	68.4	81.2	21.1	19.7	21.0	24.8	32.3	38.3	44.9
18	93.2	96.3	97.5	98.3	99.4	100.0	99.3	86.5	89.1	86.1	82.2	78.9	77.4	76.7
19	95.3	95.7	96.1	96.3	97.1	97.8	99.0	84.7	84.6	85.0	85.4	85.0	85.9	87.4
20	4.1	6.1	4.2	3.0	2.8	2.1	1.1	.1	.7	.3	.1	.2	.2	.1
21	2.8	1.9	1.8	1.5	2.2	1.7	2.7	.2	.2	.2	.1	.3	.2	.6
22	79.2	95.3	99.6	99.7	98.0	91.1	77.8	41.6	48.5	53.0	55.5	49.9	42.3	35.4
23	1.8	1.4	1.8	1.1	1.3	1.2	.9	.2	.2	.3	.2	.3	.2	.2
24	4.0	4.7	6.3	9.2	10.1	14.5	20.9	.7	1.0	1.2	1.5	2.0	2.0	3.3
25	100.0	99.0	97.5	96.5	95.4	93.8	91.4	77.1	71.6	71.3	72.1	72.4	69.1	71.3
26	88.2	87.0	86.5	88.0	90.9	96.3	98.0	73.0	71.1	67.6	67.1	67.4	73.0	79.9
27	35.3	28.3	22.0	15.3	11.7	9.0	6.3	12.6	7.5	5.8	3.1	2.0	1.1	.5
City average	42.7	42.7	42.2	42.3	43.1	44.0	45.5	28.8	29.0	29.0	29.3	30.0	29.9	31.1

present figures are much higher. About one-half of the districts have K_r's exceeding $\frac{1}{2}$ bit in at least one year. The city average of the district entropies,

$$(2.3) \qquad \bar{K} = \sum_{r=1}^{27} W_r K_r$$

is between .4 and .5 bit in every year and is thus about three times as large as the city average of the school entropies. This $\bar{K}$ decreased slightly from 1963 until the middle of the seven-year period, and it increased thereafter. Recall that in Section 1.4 we observed the same kind of development for the city average of the racial entropies of the schools.

A Measure of Segregation

It is easily shown that the district's racial entropy K_r can never be smaller than the average racial entropy $\bar{H}_r$ of the schools that fall under D_r. Consider the difference $K_r - \bar{H}_r$, using the definition of $\bar{H}_r$ given in eq. (4.3) of Section 1.4:

$$
\begin{aligned}
K_r - \bar{H}_r &= P_r \log \frac{1}{P_r} + (1-P_r) \log \frac{1}{1-P_r} \\
&\quad - \sum_{j \in D_r} \frac{w_j}{W_r} \left[p_j \log \frac{1}{p_j} + (1-p_j) \log \frac{1}{1-p_j} \right] \\
&= \sum_{j \in D_r} \frac{w_j}{W_r} p_j \left(\log \frac{1}{P_r} - \log \frac{1}{p_j} \right) \\
&\quad + \sum_{j \in D_r} \frac{w_j}{W_r} (1-p_j) \left(\log \frac{1}{1-P_r} - \log \frac{1}{1-p_j} \right)
\end{aligned}
$$

where the second equality sign is based on (2.1). The result can be simplified to

$$(2.4) \qquad K_r - \bar{H}_r = \sum_{j \in D_r} \frac{w_j}{W_r} \left[p_j \log \frac{p_j}{P_r} + (1-p_j) \log \frac{1-p_j}{1-P_r} \right]$$

Consider in particular the expression in brackets:

$$(2.5) \qquad I_j = p_j \log \frac{p_j}{P_r} + (1-p_j) \log \frac{1-p_j}{1-P_r} \qquad j \in D_r$$

A comparison with (1.3) shows that this I_j is the expected information of the message which transforms the prior probabilities $(P_r, 1-P_r)$ into the posterior probabilities $(p_j, 1-p_j)$. The present analysis is not formulated in probabilistic terms; we thus regard I_j simply as a measure for the extent to which the district's racial composition $(P_r, 1-P_r)$ differs from that of its jth school, $(p_j, 1-p_j)$. We have $I_j = 0$ if and only if the two compositions are identical, and otherwise $I_j > 0$. If the school is all black $(p_j = 1)$, then $I_j = -\log P_r$; if it is all white, $I_j = -\log(1-P_r)$. Thus, when a district is predominantly black $(P_r$ close to 1$)$, the presence of an all-black school implies a low value $I_j = -\log P_r$ but that of an all-white school a large value $I_j = -\log(1-P_r)$.

In (2.4), the I_j's are weighted proportionally to the size of the schools. These weights are all positive, so that $K_r - \bar{H}_r$ is positive unless all schools of D_r have the same racial composition as that of their district, in which case $K_r - \bar{H}_r = 0$. Hence the average racial entropy $\bar{H}_r$ of the schools of D_r is at most equal to the racial entropy K_r of the district as a whole, and $\bar{H}_r < K_r$ holds as soon as there are differences between the racial compositions of these schools. The extent to which $\bar{H}_r$ is reduced below the maximum permitted by the racial composition of D_r – that is, the difference $K_r - \bar{H}_r$ – is a simple measure for the degree of segregation that prevails in the schools of this district.[1]

The entropy difference $K_r - \bar{H}_r$, measured as a percentage of 1 bit, is shown in the last seven columns of Table 2.1. The values are substantial for several districts, particularly those that have large K_r's. The city average of these entropy differences,

$$(2.6) \qquad \sum_{r=1}^{27} W_r(K_r - \bar{H}_r) = \bar{K} - \bar{H}$$

is shown in the last line. It increased slowly but almost uninterruptedly, from less than .29 bit in 1963 to a little over .31 bit in 1969. Thus, insofar as there is any evidence of change in the city as a whole, it is in the direction of more segregation.

Segregation as a Function of the District's Racial Entropy

Table 2.2 contains $K_r - \bar{H}_r$ as a percentage of the corresponding K_r for each district and each year. This amounts to the relative reduction of the average racial entropy of the schools below the entropy of their district. The

---

[1] An additional justification of this definition is provided by the examples given at the end of the previous paragraph. If a district is predominantly black, an all-white school implies a large I_j and thus (given w_j/W_r) a substantial contribution to $K_r - \bar{H}_r$ in (2.4), as it should. But an all-black school is much closer to its district as far as racial composition is concerned, which is in agreement with its small I_j and, hence, with its small contribution to $K_r - \bar{H}_r$.

TABLE 2.2

RELATIVE SEGREGATION MEASURES: $100(K_r - \bar{H}_r)/K_r$

District	1963	1964	1965	1966	1967	1968	1969
1	26	22	34	24	21	20	16
2	24	24	21	22	17	15	13
3	17	22	21	20	19	17	14
4	37	45	39	56	71	57	62
5	23	34	*	29	27	26	18
6	26	25	26	22	22	23	23
7	67	68	70	70	70	73	71
8	33	30	22	22	24	29	36
9	61	59	60	63	67	66	70
10	80	88	89	88	88	88	87
11	48	58	59	60	57	58	56
12	68	68	69	70	74	74	78
13	16	15	20	28	23	26	24
14	44	46	50	54	55	54	54
15	67	74	81	83	82	81	69
16	67	67	64	63	61	52	58
17	60	52	50	51	56	56	55
18	93	92	88	84	79	77	77
19	89	88	88	89	87	88	88
20	3	11	8	4	8	11	13
21	8	8	9	8	13	11	23
22	52	51	53	56	51	46	45
23	12	16	18	17	24	19	19
24	18	21	20	16	20	14	16
25	77	72	73	75	76	74	78
26	83	82	78	76	74	76	82
27	36	27	26	20	17	12	8
Districts with:				*Medians*			
small K_r	17	21	20	20	20	17	16
medium K_r	44	46	50	54	56	54	56
large K_r	67	72	73	76	76	74	71

* Of the form 0/0.

figures vary widely from one district to the other, but they do exhibit regularity as is shown in the last three lines of the table. In each year, the 27 districts are divided into three groups consisting of nine districts each, one with the smallest racial entropies K_r, one with the largest, and one with "medium" entropies. The figures for each year are the median ratios

$(K_r - \bar{H}_r)/K_r$ in percentage form. They show that on the average (in the median sense), the reduction of the average racial entropies of the schools below the attainable maximum is about 20 per cent for districts with low racial entropies, about 50 per cent for districts with "medium" entropies, and about 70 per cent for those with large racial entropies. This indicates a higher degree of segregation in those districts in which the racial entropy of the total student population is large – that is, those districts in which the racial entropies of the schools would be large if there were no segregation.

It would be interesting to verify whether, for individual districts, a change in the entropy K_r over time has led to a corresponding change in the degree of segregation. However, there are only seven observations for each district; more will be needed to attack this problem.

The Dissimilarity Index

Various other measures of segregation have been recommended; several of them are described in a survey article by DUNCAN and DUNCAN (1955). We refer to that article for a more complete summary of such measures and confine ourselves here to the so-called dissimilarity index because of its frequent use in the sociological literature. This index is based on a comparison of the number of black students in each school, measured as a fraction of the total number of black students in the district, and the analogous proportion of white students in the same school. The index is defined as one-half of the sum over all schools of the absolute differences of these proportions.

To translate this into our notation we note that $w_j p_j$ is the number of black students in the jth school measured as a fraction of the city's total student body. Since $W_r P_r$ is the analogous fraction for the rth district, the ratio $w_j p_j / W_r P_r$ stands for the black students in the jth school as a proportion of the district's black student population $(j \in D_r)$. The analogous proportion for whites is the ratio of $w_j(1-p_j)$ to $W_r(1-P_r)$, so that the dissimilarity index of D_r is

$$(2.7) \quad d_r = \tfrac{1}{2} \sum_{j \in D_r} \left| \frac{w_j p_j}{W_r P_r} - \frac{w_j(1-p_j)}{W_r(1-P_r)} \right| = \tfrac{1}{2} \sum_{j \in D_r} \frac{w_j}{W_r} \left| \frac{p_j}{P_r} - \frac{1-p_j}{1-P_r} \right|$$

Since we have

$$\left| \frac{p_j}{P_r} - \frac{1-p_j}{1-P_r} \right| = \frac{|p_j(1-P_r)-(1-p_j)P_r|}{P_r(1-P_r)} = \frac{|p_j-P_r|}{P_r(1-P_r)}$$

we can simplify (2.7) to

$$(2.8) \qquad d_r = \frac{\sum\limits_{j \in D_r} \frac{w_j}{W_r} |p_j - P_r|}{2P_r(1 - P_r)}$$

It is immediately apparent that $d_r = 0$ (the minimum) when all schools of D_r have the same racial composition. We proceed to prove that $d_r = 1$ (the maximum) when all schools of D_r are either all black or all white. Write D_{r1} for the set of all-black schools of D_r, and D_{r2} for the set of all-white schools, so that $p_j = 1$ for $j \in D_{r1}$ and $p_j = 0$ for $j \in D_{r2}$. The right-hand numerator of (2.8) then becomes

$$(2.9) \qquad (1 - P_r) \sum\limits_{j \in D_{r1}} \frac{w_j}{W_r} + P_r \sum\limits_{j \in D_{r2}} \frac{w_j}{W_r}$$

But $\sum_j (w_j/W_r)$ equals P_r for $j \in D_{r1}$ and $1 - P_r$ for $j \in D_{r2}$, because in the former case we count all black students in the district and in the latter all white students. It follows immediately that the expression (2.9) is equal to the right-hand denominator of (2.8), and hence $d_r = 1$.

Aggregation Problems of the Dissimilarity Index

So far so good. Difficulties arise, however, when one wants to relate the dissimilarity indexes of the districts to that of the city. To clarify this point, define P as the proportion of black students in the city as a whole:

$$(2.10) \qquad P = \sum\limits_{j=1}^{N} w_j p_j$$

and consider first the average segregation value of the 27 districts as defined in (2.6) and (2.4):

$$(2.11) \qquad \bar{K} - \bar{H} = \sum\limits_{r=1}^{27} \sum\limits_{j \in D_r} w_j \left[p_j \log \frac{p_j}{P_r} + (1 - p_j) \log \frac{1 - p_j}{1 - P_r} \right]$$

Since the expression in brackets can be written as

$$p_j \log \frac{p_j}{P} + (1 - p_j) \log \frac{1 - p_j}{1 - P} - \left[p_j \log \frac{P_r}{P} + (1 - p_j) \log \frac{1 - P_r}{1 - P} \right]$$

we can rewrite (2.11), using (2.1), as

$$(2.12) \qquad \bar{K} - \bar{H} = \sum\limits_{j=1}^{N} w_j \left[p_j \log \frac{p_j}{P} + (1 - p_j) \log \frac{1 - p_j}{1 - P} \right]$$
$$- \sum\limits_{r=1}^{27} W_r \left[P_r \log \frac{P_r}{P} + (1 - P_r) \log \frac{1 - P_r}{1 - P} \right]$$

This shows that the city average of the segregation values of the districts is equal to the difference of two other segregation values, $A - B$, where A is the value obtained when the racial compositions of all N schools are compared with that of the city (without any reference to school districts) and B is the value obtained when the racial compositions of the 27 school districts are compared with that of the city (without any reference to any of the separate schools).

We now turn to the dissimilarity index and apply the same line of argument as that of the previous subsection to the racial compositions of schools and of school districts in relation to that of the city. This gives

$$(2.13) \qquad \frac{\sum_{j=1}^{N} w_j |p_j - P|}{2P(1-P)} \quad \text{and} \quad \frac{\sum_{r=1}^{27} W_r |P_r - P|}{2P(1-P)}$$

These expressions are the dissimilarity index analogues of the two terms in the right-hand side of (2.12). The left-hand term of that equation corresponds to

$$(2.14) \qquad \sum_{r=1}^{27} W_r d_r = \sum_{r=1}^{27} \frac{\sum_{j \in D_r} w_j |p_j - P_r|}{2P_r(1-P_r)}.$$

A comparison of the expressions in (2.13) and (2.14) shows that there exists no relation that expresses one in terms of the other two, which is a serious disadvantage of the use of the dissimilarity index. The use of absolute differences is a major obstacle for simple decompositions such as (2.12).

Also, note that the dissimilarity index is confined to two races, whereas the entropy measure (2.4) can be easily extended to a larger number as is shown in Problems 6 and 7 at the end of this chapter.

2.3. Further Results on the Industrial Diversity of American Cities

This section describes an extension of the results of Section 1.6, leading to the subject of industrial diversity *between* rather than *within* cities. The mathematical approach is the same as that of Section 2.2. The discussion will be continued in Section 3.2.

The Employment Entropy of a Group of SMSA's

Our starting point in the previous section was the racial entropy of a school district, rather than that of a school. Our starting point here is the employment entropy of a group of SMSA's, rather than that of a single SMSA, and we will define such a group as the set C_{ab} of SMSA's in the ath region and the bth size class, where a takes four values and b three. Recall eq. (6.7) of Section 1.6, which defines

q_{abi}　as the number of workers in the ith industry in C_{ab}

Q_{abg}　as the number of workers in industry group S_g in C_{ab}

$q_{ab.}$　as the total number of workers in C_{ab},

all measured as fractions of the total labor force in all SMSA's. The employment entropy of C_{ab} at the level of the 23 industries is thus

$$(3.1) \qquad K_{ab} = \sum_{i=1}^{23} \frac{q_{abi}}{q_{ab.}} \log \frac{q_{ab.}}{q_{abi}}$$

and at the level of the six industry groups:

$$(3.2) \qquad K_{ab0} = \sum_{g=1}^{6} \frac{Q_{abg}}{q_{ab.}} \log \frac{q_{ab.}}{Q_{abg}}$$

Within S_g, the ith industry $(i \in S_g)$ has an employment share q_{abi}/Q_{abg} in C_{ab}. Hence the employment entropy in C_{ab} within S_g is

$$(3.3) \qquad K_{abg} = \sum_{i \in S_g} \frac{q_{abi}}{Q_{abg}} \log \frac{Q_{abg}}{q_{abi}} \qquad\qquad g = 1, \ldots, 6$$

It is readily verified that these entropies are related by

$$(3.4) \qquad K_{ab} = K_{ab0} + \sum_{g=1}^{6} \frac{Q_{abg}}{q_{ab.}} K_{abg}$$

where the weight $Q_{abg}/q_{ab.}$ of K_{abg} is the employment share of industry group S_g in C_{ab}.

The Industrial Diversity Between SMSA's

The above K's are of some interest, but their excess over the corresponding average entropy of the individual SMSA's is even more interesting. Consider $\bar{H}_{ab}$, the average employment entropy of the SMSA's of C_{ab} defined in eq. (6.9) of Section 1.6, and subtract it from K_{ab}:

$$\sum_{i=1}^{23} \frac{q_{abi}}{q_{ab.}} \log \frac{q_{ab.}}{q_{abi}} - \sum_{s \in C_{ab}} \frac{p_{s.}}{q_{ab.}} \sum_{i=1}^{23} \frac{p_{si}}{p_{s.}} \log \frac{p_{s.}}{p_{si}}$$

$$= \sum_{s \in C_{ab}} \frac{p_{s.}}{q_{ab.}} \sum_{i=1}^{23} \frac{p_{si}}{p_{s.}} \left(\log \frac{q_{ab.}}{q_{abi}} - \log \frac{p_{s.}}{p_{si}} \right)$$

or, equivalently,

$$(3.5) \qquad K_{ab} - \overline{H}_{ab} = \sum_{s \in C_{ab}} \frac{p_{s.}}{q_{ab.}} \left[\sum_{i=1}^{23} \frac{p_{si}}{p_{s.}} \log \frac{p_{si}/p_{s.}}{q_{abi}/q_{ab.}} \right]$$

A comparison with (2.4) shows that the two results are of the same form. In the present expression in brackets we have $q_{abi}/q_{ab.}$, the employment distribution in C_{ab}, which plays the role of the prior distribution, and $p_{si}/p_{s.}$, the employment distribution of the sth SMSA, which takes on the role of the posterior distribution. This expression vanishes if and only if the employment distribution of C_{ab} is identical with that of its sth SMSA; otherwise it is positive. In (3.5) it is weighted proportionally to the number of workers in the SMSA. We may conclude that $K_{ab} - \overline{H}_{ab}$ measures the extent to which the employment distribution of C_{ab} deviates on average from the distributions of its constituent SMSA's or, equivalently, the extent to which the labor compositions of these SMSA's differ *from each other*,

At the level of industry groups we have an analogous result:

$$(3.6) \qquad K_{ab0} - \overline{H}_{ab0} = \sum_{s \in C_{ab}} \frac{p_{s.}}{q_{ab.}} \left[\sum_{g=1}^{6} \frac{P_{sg}}{p_{s.}} \log \frac{P_{sg}/p_{s.}}{Q_{abg}/q_{ab.}} \right]$$

and similarly for the industries within each S_g $(g = 1, \ldots, 6)$:

$$(3.7) \qquad K_{abg} - \overline{H}_{abg} = \sum_{s \in C_{ab}} \frac{P_{sg}}{Q_{abg}} \left[\sum_{i \in S_g} \frac{p_{si}}{P_{sg}} \log \frac{p_{si}/P_{sg}}{q_{abi}/Q_{abg}} \right]$$

Equation (3.6) enables us to analyze the differences between the SMSA's of C_{ab} at the level of the six industry groups, and (3.7) performs the same role for the industries within S_g. The left-hand sides of (3.5) through (3.7) are connected by

$$(3.8) \qquad K_{ab} - \overline{H}_{ab} = K_{ab0} - \overline{H}_{ab0} + \sum_{g=1}^{6} \frac{Q_{abg}}{q_{ab.}} (K_{abg} - \overline{H}_{abg})$$

which follows from (3.4) and eq. (6.8) of Section 1.6.

Table 2.3 presents the entropy differences (3.5) through (3.7) for each C_{ab}. Its format is the same as that of Table 1.4 in Section 1.6; in fact, by adding the corresponding elements of the two tables we obtain the employment entropy $(K_{ab}$ or K_{abg}, $g = 0, 1, \ldots, 6)$ for the set of all SMSA's in C_{ab}. The results show that within each region, the smaller SMSA's have employment distributions that tend to be more different from one another than those of the larger SMSA's. The within-group results show interesting differences, too. The values of $K_{ab2} - \overline{H}_{ab2}$ $(S_2$, durable manufacturing) are

TABLE 2.3

INDUSTRIAL DIVERSITY BETWEEN SMSA'S, BY SIZE AND BY REGION

Region	Large	Medium	Small	Large	Medium	Small
	$K_{ab}-\bar{H}_{ab}$			$K_{ab0}-\bar{H}_{ab0}$		
North East	.093	.140	.237	.032	.051	.104
North Central	.111	.259	.255	.030	.075	.111
South	.109	.125	.270	.032	.038	.092
West	.077	.077	.259	.028	.022	.075
	$K_{ab}-\bar{H}_{ab}-(K_{ab0}-\bar{H}_{ab0})$			$K_{ab2}-\bar{H}_{ab2}$		
North East	.061	.088	.133	.187	.145	.198
North Central	.081	.184	.144	.244	.580	.332
South	.077	.087	.178	.338	.226	.772
West	.049	.055	.184	.146	.253	.464
	$K_{ab3}-\bar{H}_{ab3}$			$K_{ab4}-\bar{H}_{ab4}$		
North East	.082	.175	.233	.042	.041	.236
North Central	.078	.104	.264	.021	.061	.093
South	.108	.276	.444	.050	.058	.095
West	.068	.123	.130	.047	.026	.225
	$K_{ab5}-\bar{H}_{ab5}$			$K_{ab6}-\bar{H}_{ab6}$		
North East	.008	.004	.015	.018	.064	.073
North Central	.005	.008	.012	.011	.024	.059
South	.007	.006	.008	.054	.049	.076
West	.004	.009	.007	.028	.042	.234

very large on the average, and those of S_5 (trade) are very small. This indicates that the three industries of the trade group (wholesale, eating and drinking places, and other retail) have nearly constant shares of the total employment in trade in each C_{ab}, whereas these shares differ substantially from one SMSA to the other in the case of the five industries that fall under durable manufacturing. All these results seem intuitively plausible.

2.4. Evaluating the Accuracy of Decomposition Forecasts

One particular application of the information expectation (1.4) concerns the situation in which a decomposition is predicted, either once or several times, and in which the analyst wishes to measure the accuracy of such predictions. The approach implies that the predicted decomposition takes the role of a set of prior probabilities and the observed decomposition that of a set of posterior probabilities. The procedure is outlined below for the particular case of a consumer buying intention survey analyzed by THEIL and KOSOBUD (1968), after which it is extended and applied to other types of decompositions.

Description of a Consumer Buying Intention Survey

The Quarterly Survey of Intentions is the source of our data. In the period to be considered here – January 1960 through July 1965 – there were 19 surveys conducted by the U.S. Bureau of the Census around the middle of the first month of every quarter. One of the questions asked was: "In the next six months, does any member of this family expect to buy a car?" There were six possible answers: No, Don't know, Maybe (depends on old car), Maybe (other reasons), Yes (probably), and Yes (definitely). In what follows we shall regard any of the last four answers as indicative of a buying intention to some degree.

Twelve months following each survey there was a reinterview as part of the normal survey held at that time. This reinterview enables the analyst to determine whether or not the family bought a car during the past twelve months. The survey thus reveals two possible types of intention and also two possible types of behavior. Table 2.4 summarizes the outcomes for all

TABLE 2.4

BUYING INTENTIONS AND PURCHASES OF CARS, 1960–1965

Intention	Behavior		Total
	No purchase	Purchase	
Don't intend	.849	.068	.917
Intend	.051	.032	.083
Total	.900	.100	1

19 surveys combined; the proportions shown are the averages of the 19 proportions in each cell. The figures indicate that there was a substantial fraction of persons who intended to buy a car but who nevertheless did not buy. This result is not surprising, given our liberal interpretation of the word "intention".

The Information Inaccuracy of a Decomposition Prediction

The objective of the survey is to predict how many people will actually buy a car. Write p for the prediction of the proportion of car buyers and (hence) $1-p$ for the predicted proportion of nonbuyers. Write q for the corresponding observed proportion of buyers, and consider the information expectation (1.3):

$$(4.1) \qquad I = q \log \frac{q}{p} + (1-q) \log \frac{1-q}{1-p}$$

We thus take the predicted proportions as prior probabilities and the observed proportions as posterior probabilities. The larger the information expectation (4.1), the larger are the pairwise differences of the two sets of proportions, and hence the more inaccurate are the predictions as approximations of the observed proportions. This means that the function (4.1) can be interpreted as the *information inaccuracy* of the decomposition prediction $(p, 1-p)$; the larger the expected information of the posterior probabilities $(q, 1-q)$ for given prior probabilities $(p, 1-p)$, the more inaccurate is the decomposition prediction $(p, 1-p)$ relative to a given observed decomposition $(q, 1-q)$. When there are n possible outcomes rather than 2, and when the predicted and observed proportions are $p_1, \ldots, p_n$ and $q_1, \ldots, q_n$, respectively, we simply extend (4.1) to

$$(4.2) \qquad I(q : p) = \sum_{i=1}^{n} q_i \log \frac{q_i}{p_i}$$

Application to the Buying Intention Survey

Returning to the survey described in the first subsection, we may wish to predict the proportion of car purchasers during any 12-month period by the fraction of those who intend to buy at the beginning of that period (for short, the crude intention fraction). This is the simplest use of the surveys; it leads to 19 information inaccuracy values, one for each survey, and the arithmetic average is a summary measure for the performance of this particular prediction method. Its value (.00234 nit) is shown in the first line of Table 2.5. We use nits rather than bits here because of the convenience of the former unit in relation to the quadratic approximation (1.12).

The crude intention fraction is a very poor predictor. This becomes clear when we go back to Table 2.4, which shows that two-thirds of the actual purchases are made by those who declare initially that they do not intend to buy. This may suggest the surveys are worthless, but that is a premature conclusion. In fact, the table indicates that there is a large difference between the behavior of the intenders and that of the nonintenders. For all 19 surveys

TABLE 2.5

AVERAGE INFORMATION INACCURACY VALUES (IN 10^{-2} NIT) OF ALTERNATIVE PREDICTIONS
OF CAR PURCHASE RATES

Prediction method	All 19 surveys	Last 15 surveys
Crude intention fraction (x_t)	.2341	
Method (4.3)	.0764	.0652
Mean purchase rate	.2868	
After one quarter: (4.5)		.0475
After two quarters: (4.6)		.0371
After three quarters: (4.7)		.0243

combined, a fraction .032/.083 or about 40 per cent of the intenders do buy
a car, whereas for the group of nonintenders this is .068/.917 or only about
$7\frac{1}{2}$ per cent. If these two percentages (40 and $7\frac{1}{2}$) are constants in the sense
that they apply to each and every survey, we can obtain a perfect prediction
of the purchase rate. Write x_t for the fraction of intenders at the tth survey,
and hence $1 - x_t$ for the fraction of nonintenders. Then, under the condition
just mentioned, the corresponding purchase rate is equal to

$$(4.3) \qquad .4x_t + .075(1 - x_t) = .075 + .325x_t$$

The condition is obviously unlikely to be fulfilled, but it is quite possible
that the two percentages fluctuate within a rather narrow range around 40
and $7\frac{1}{2}$, respectively, in which case the procedure (4.3) may be used as an
approximation to the purchase rate. The average information inaccuracy of
this prediction method is shown in the second line of Table 2.5. The improvement over the crude intention fraction is evidently substantial.

It is quite possible, however, that the predictions thus modified are still
worthless. Suppose we predict that the purchase rate is 10 per cent for each
of the 19 periods, in accordance with the mean purchase rate shown in the
last line of Table 2.4. If the average information inaccuracy corresponding
to this method were less than or equal to that of the procedure (4.3), we
would indeed have to conclude that the latter method is worthless because
it fails to catch the changes in the purchase rate over time. The third line
of Table 2.5 shows that this is not the case. Note, however, that the performance of the crude intention fraction is only marginally better than that
of the mean purchase rate.

The Information Improvement of a Prediction Revision

Suppose that the decomposition $(q_1, \ldots, q_n)$ is first predicted to be $(p_1, \ldots, p_n)$ and that at some later stage (but before the data on realizations become available) the prediction is revised to a new set of proportions, $p'_1, \ldots, p'_n$. The original information inaccuracy is $I(q:p)$ as defined in (4.2) and the new value is $I(q:p')$, which is identical with the right-hand side of (4.2) except that each p_i is replaced by p'_i. If the new forecast is more accurate than its predecessor, $I(q:p')$ should be less than $I(q:p)$. Hence the difference,

$$(4.4) \qquad I(q:p) - I(q:p') = \sum_{i=1}^{n} q_i \log \frac{q_i}{p_i} - \sum_{i=1}^{n} q_i \log \frac{q_i}{p'_i}$$

$$= \sum_{i=1}^{n} q_i \log \frac{p'_i}{p_i}$$

may be called the *information improvement* of the prediction revision. It vanishes when $p_i = p'_i$ holds for each i, but this is obviously only a sufficient, not a necessary, condition. The maximum value of the information improvement is $I(q:p)$, corresponding to a perfect prediction revision. The improvement may be negative, which indicates that the revision amounts to a deterioration rather than an improvement.

We return again to the surveys on car purchases and recall that these quarterly surveys refer to overlapping 12-month periods. The t-th survey provides us with the intention rate x_t. The observed purchase rate for the corresponding period, to be written y_t, is provided by the $(t+4)$-th survey. One quarter after the t-th survey we have the $(t+1)$-st which provides y_{t-3}. This y_{t-3} has a one-quarter overlap with y_t, so that we may wish to use y_{t-3} to improve on the forecast (4.3) of the future purchase rate y_t. We use a weighted average:

$$(4.5) \qquad \tfrac{1}{4} y_{t-3} + \tfrac{3}{4} (.075 + .325 x_t)$$

where the weight of $\tfrac{1}{4}$ is motivated by the consideration that y_{t-3} and y_t have one quarter out of four in common.

In the same way, two quarters later we may wish to use y_{t-2} rather than y_{t-3}. Since y_{t-2} and y_t have two quarters in common, we raise the weight to $\tfrac{1}{2}$:

$$(4.6) \qquad \tfrac{1}{2} y_{t-2} + \tfrac{1}{2} (.075 + .325 x_t)$$

Three quarters later (one quarter before y_t becomes available) we have y_{t-1}

which we give a weight of $\frac{3}{4}$:

(4.7) $\frac{3}{4} y_{t-1} + \frac{1}{4}(.075 + .325x_t)$

The average information inaccuracies of the procedures (4.5) to (4.7) are shown in the last column of Table 2.5. [Only the last 15 surveys are used because of the occurrence of lagged values; the figure in the second row (.0652) is given to provide the appropriate comparison with the method (4.3).] The results indicate that the successive purchase rates y_{t-3}, y_{t-2} and y_{t-1} are indeed informative with respect to y_t. The average values of the information improvement (4.4) are obtained by taking the successive differences of the figures in the last column:

$$
\begin{array}{lll}
\text{After one quarter} & 10^{-6}(652-475) = & .000177 \\
\text{After two quarters} & 10^{-6}(475-371) = & .000104 \\
\text{After three quarters} & 10^{-6}(371-243) = & .000128
\end{array}
$$

Average Information Inaccuracies and Root-Mean-Square Prediction Errors

When we have only two possible outcomes and when the prediction errors are not too large, we can use eq. (1.12) to obtain an approximation to the mean square error of the proportion predictions. It is readily verified that for $n = 2$ the approximation (1.12) can be simplified to

(4.8) $$I \approx \frac{(p-q)^2}{2q(1-q)}$$

Both the numerator (the squared prediction error) and the denominator vary from one survey to the other, but the numerator is much more variable than the denominator. If we make the simplifying assumption that the variability of the denominator can be ignored and use the average proportions shown in the last row of Table 2.4, the denominator becomes $2(.1)(.9) = .18$, so that (4.8) implies $(p-q)^2 \approx .18I$. If we then average over the surveys, $(p-q)^2$ on the left becomes the mean square prediction error and the right-hand side becomes $.18\bar{I}$, where $\bar{I}$ is the average information inaccuracy. By taking square roots of both sides we obtain the root-mean-square (RMS) prediction error, which is thus equal (approximately) to $\sqrt{.18\bar{I}}$. For the figures in the last column of Table 2.5 we obtain the RMS prediction errors shown below.

$$
\begin{array}{ll}
\text{At beginning of 12-month period} & \sqrt{(.18)(.000652)} \approx .0108 \\
\text{After one quarter} & \sqrt{(.18)(.000475)} \approx .0092 \\
\text{After two quarters} & \sqrt{(.18)(.000371)} \approx .0082 \\
\text{After three quarters} & \sqrt{(.18)(.000243)} \approx .0066
\end{array}
$$

According to Table 2.4, purchase rates are of the order of .1. The results obtained here thus indicate that the RMS prediction error is initially about 10 per cent of this figure and that it declines slowly but gradually in the successive quarters of the year.

Evaluating the Fit of Decomposition Models

The information inaccuracy is a useful tool for a comparative analysis of the fit of alternative decomposition models, of which the following is an example. The classical theory of consumer demand is concerned with the quantities bought, $x_1, \ldots, x_n$, of each of n commodities during a certain period of time (a quarter or a year, say). Its objective is to describe each x_i as a function of the consumer's total expenditure (m) in that period and the prices of the commodities $(\pi_1, \ldots, \pi_n)$ prevailing during the period:

$$(4.9) \qquad x_i = f_i(m, \pi_1, \ldots, \pi_n) \qquad\qquad i = 1, \ldots, n$$

Such a function $f_i(\ )$ is known as a *demand function*. For what follows it is important to note that, once total expenditure and the n prices are given, the demand functions determine the expenditure share, $\pi_i x_i / m$, of each commodity:

$$(4.10) \qquad \frac{\pi_i x_i}{m} = \frac{\pi_i f_i(m, \pi_1, \ldots, \pi_n)}{m} \qquad\qquad i = 1, \ldots, n$$

The theory postulates that the consumer takes m and $\pi_1, \ldots, \pi_n$ as given and that he adjusts the quantities bought by maximizing a utility function, $u = u(x_1, \ldots, x_n)$, subject to the budget constraint $\sum \pi_i x_i = m$. The utility function measures the level of the consumer's satisfaction when he consumes x_1 units of the first commodity, x_2 units of the second, and so on. The form of the demand functions depends on the form of the utility function, and this leads to several possibilities. In principle, one can compare alternative forms of demand equations by adjusting them to the same body of data. An important criterion for the problem of which functional form is to be preferred is the closeness of fit.

This procedure was applied by PARKS (1969) in order to compare four different demand models, to be denoted by A, B, C and D. [A description of these models is beyond the scope of this book.] He adjusted these models to annual Swedish data of the period 1862–1955 for $n = 8$ commodity groups and computed for each year the expenditure share estimates that are implied by each of the adjusted models. Write $p_1, \ldots, p_8$ for such a set of estimates and $q_1, \ldots, q_8$ for the corresponding observed shares in the same year; then

TABLE 2.6

AVERAGE INFORMATION INACCURACY VALUES (IN 10^{-2} NIT) OF EXPENDITURE SHARE ESTIMATES
OF ALTERNATIVE DEMAND MODELS

	Model A	Model B	Model C	Model D	No-change extrapolation
All years	.199	.260	.308	.260	.310
1863–1901	.224	.243	.309	.295	.233
1902–1914	.103	.122	.170	.148	.198
1920–1940	.175	.284	.250	.253	.367
1941–1955	.220	.329	.310	.326	.390

the sum over i ($= 1, \ldots, 8$) of $q_i \log (q_i/p_i)$ is the information inaccuracy
for that year. Table 2.6 contains average information inaccuracies for each
of the models, both for the entire period and for subperiods; the last column
refers to the no-change extrapolation method, which simply predicts that
each share is equal to its value one year ago. The results indicate that Model
A has a better fit than all other models in each of the subperiods, and that it
is also the only model that beats no-change extrapolation in all subperiods.
None of the models B, C or D dominates the two others.

Comparison with Multiple Correlation Coefficients

An alternative way of evaluating the fit of demand equations according
to different models is by means of multiple correlation coefficients computed
for each equation separately. There is no fundamental objection to this
approach,[1] but is should be recognized that it may lead to different verdicts
for different equations. For example, there may be five commodities for
which Model A produces demand equations with a larger correlation coefficient than Model B does, but three commodities for which the converse
is true. It is not self-evident how this result should be interpreted from the
standpoint of the comparative performance of the two competing models,
particularly when the latter three commodities have a combined expenditure
share exceeding that of the first five. One of the advantages of the information inaccuracy is that it gives an appraisal of the fit of each model *as a whole*.
On the other hand, it is quite possible that the analyst is interested in the

---

[1] One should, however, be careful when different models have different left-hand variables
in their equations (such as x_i and $\log x_i$). The multiple correlation coefficients are then
not directly comparable; see THEIL (1971a; Section 11.1).

prediction for one particular commodity. This can also be handled easily by the information inaccuracy concept as will be shown in the next subsection.

Another advantage of the information inaccuracy is that it can be computed for each individual observation (for each year in the case of Table 2.6), which enables the analyst to investigate for which observations his model went wrong by producing large prediction errors. The multiple correlation coefficient computed for each demand equation is always based on more observations than one. Also, the use of the information inaccuracy recognizes the fact that classical demand theory is basically an allocation theory. It takes total expenditure as given and asks "What is the proportion of this total that is allocated to the ith commodity, given the level of total expenditure and the prices of the n commodities?" When the model is concerned with a set of nonnegative proportions that add up to one, there is something to be said in favor of the idea that the evaluation of the fit of the model take this mathematical fact into account.

It is customary to correct multiple correlation coefficients for the loss of degrees of freedom which is caused by the adjustment of a number of unknown parameters. This is also possible for the average information inaccuracy. For details, see THEIL (1971a, Section 12.7).

Decomposition of the Information Inaccuracy and the Information Improvement

The decomposition (1.15) is obviously also valid when the information expectation $I(q:p)$ is interpreted as an information inaccuracy of, say, the prediction of n expenditure shares. The decomposition is then concerned with the combination of n commodities into G commodity groups, and $I_0(q:p)$ is the information inaccuracy at the level of groups, while $I_g(q:p)$ measures the inaccuracy within the gth group $(g = 1, \ldots, G)$. We have $I_g(q:p) = 0$ if and only if there is perfect prediction of the expenditure of each commodity of the gth group when this expenditure is measured as a fraction of the total expenditure of the group. Note that the weight of $I_g(q:p)$ in the decomposition is Q_g, the observed expenditure share of the group.

The information improvement (4.4) can be handled similarly. At the level of commodity groups it is

$$(4.11) \quad I_0(q:p) - I_0(q:p') = \sum_{g=1}^{G} Q_g \log \frac{P_g'}{P_g} \quad \text{where} \quad P_g' = \sum_{i \in S_g} p_i'$$

and within the gth group it is

$$(4.12) \qquad I_g(q : p) - I_g(q : p') = \sum_{i \in S_g} \frac{q_i}{Q_g} \log \frac{p_i'/P_g'}{p_i/P_g} \qquad g = 1, \ldots, G$$

It may be verified that by adding to (4.11) a weighted average of the G expressions (4.12) with weights $Q_1, \ldots, Q_G$ one obtains $I(q:p) - I(q:p')$, the information improvement defined in (4.4).

TABLE 2.7

AVERAGE INFORMATION INACCURACY VALUES (IN 10^{-2} NIT) OF EXPENDITURE SHARE
ESTIMATES OF A DUTCH DEMAND MODEL

	Demand model			No-change extrapolation		
	All obser- vations	Prewar	Postwar	All obser- vations	Prewar	Postwar
All commodity groups	.0145	.0149	.0141	.0406	.0370	.0451
Food	.0059	.0054	.0065	.0126	.0103	.0153
Beverages and tobacco	.0023	.0021	.0025	.0033	.0022	.0046
Durables	.0071	.0068	.0075	.0268	.0222	.0323
Remainder	.0047	.0064	.0026	.0136	.0170	.0094

An example for expenditure shares, taken from THEIL (1971a, Section 12.7), is shown in Table 2.7. It is concerned with the expenditure shares of four commodity groups in the Netherlands for 17 annual observations prior to World War II and 14 observations after the war. The first line of the table shows the average information inaccuracies of a particular demand model and of the no-change extrapolation method. The second line shows the inaccuracies obtained when only two commodities are considered, food and nonfood, the latter being a combination of beverages and tobacco, durables, and remainder. The figures of the second line are averages of $I_0(q:p)$, the between-group information inaccuracies corresponding to the food-nonfood distinction; the within-group information inaccuracies are not shown in the table. Thus these figures are measures of badness of fit which are relevant when the analyst is only interested in the performance of the demand equation for food. The other lines of the table play the same role for the other three commodities. Note that the fit is better, and in many cases substantially better, than that of the no-change extrapolation method. Note also that in each column the figure on top is the largest. In fact, it is a mathematical impossibility for any figure not in the first line to exceed the corresponding figure on top, because the former is a between-group information inaccuracy for some grouping, and $I_0(q:p) \leqq I(q:p)$.[1]

Analyzing the Constancy of Shares

There are economic theories which are concerned with the shares of production factors of total revenue, such as labor's share of national income. Some of these theories declare such shares to be constant, which raises the question, How constant is constant? The information expectation $I(q:p)$ is a convenient tool to handle this problem analytically and empirically. This is largely unexplored territory, but the following example, based on Leontief's input-output analysis, provides an empirical evaluation of share constancy.

Description of Input-Output Analysis

Input-output analysis allocates each firm of an economy to one of a number of sectors; for example, agriculture, manufacturing, and services. It uses an accounting identity which states that the total amount of goods and services bought by the firms of a sector (the total input of the sector) is equal to the total amount of goods and services sold by the sector (total output). The objective of input-output analysis is to predict the *output* of each sector under certain conditions, and the crucial assumption underlying the prediction procedure is the constancy of certain *input proportions*. Specifically, consider the flow of goods and services that goes from sector i to sector j in a certain year, to be written x_{ij} (measured in dollars per year). By summing x_{ij} over i we obtain the total *sector input* of sector j. This is not the total input of this sector, because it also buys goods and services from economic agents other than the nation's firms, such as workers (wages) and foreign firms (imports). The latter are the so-called *primary inputs*.

The total input of a sector is equal to its total sector input plus its total primary input. The basic assumption of input-output analysis in its simplest form is that the input composition is constant over time. Thus, the ratio of x_{ij} to the total input ($\equiv$ total output) of sector j is a constant, which means

---

[1] This is also one of the reasons why the figures of Table 2.6 are so much larger than those of the first line of Table 2.7. The former table is based on eight commodity groups; if these were combined into four larger groups, the information inaccuracies would be smaller.

that to produce one dollar of output, sector j needs a fixed amount of goods and services from sector i. This assumption applies also to the primary inputs; hence the wage bill of sector j is supposed to be a constant fraction of the sector's total output. In the analysis which follows, which is based on THEIL (1966, pp. 267–282), we shall use three primary inputs: wages, imports, and gross profits.[1] The data refer to annual Dutch input-output tables in the period 1948–1957, which contain 35 sectors. Hence there are 35 sector inputs x_{ij} for each j, but since many of them are zero or very small, we shall consider for every j only the four sectors with the largest average sector input ratios in the ten-year period and combine all sector inputs into a fifth (remainder) sector. For example, for the sector Agriculture, forestry and fishing these five sector input ratios have the following averages in 1948–1957:

$$(4.13) \qquad .163 \qquad .124 \qquad .040 \qquad .017 \qquad .076$$

The first figure (.163) refers in this case to deliveries by other firms of the same sector. It indicates that, on the average, a one dollar output of Agriculture, forestry and fishing requires almost one-sixth of a dollar input from other firms of this sector. The second figure refers to Food manufacturing (nonanimal products), the third to Chemicals and petroleum refineries (mainly fertilizers), the fourth to Wholesale trade (gross profit margins), and the fifth to all other sectors.[2] In addition to the five average sector input ratios (4.13), there are three average primary input ratios: .036 for imports, .113 for wages, and .431 for gross profits. By adding these three to the ratios of (4.13) we obtain 1, as we should.

Evaluating the Constancy of Input Ratios

Input-output analysis is not concerned with average ratios but with ratios obtained for individual years. Thus we write $a_{ij}(t)$ for the flow from i to j in year t divided by the total output of j in that year, where $i = 1, \ldots, 5$ refers to sector inputs and $i = 6, 7, 8$ to primary inputs. To evaluate the constancy of this decomposition we compute

---

[1] Wages include employers' social insurance fees. Gross profits consist of depreciation on fixed assets, indirect taxes minus subsidies, and other income such as profits and interest. This specification guarantees that the accounting identity mentioned in the previous paragraph is satisfied.

[2] It need hardly be stressed that the four sectors with the largest average sector input ratios are not the same for all sectors. For example, the sector with the largest input ratio for Metal products and machinery is Basic metal industries.

$$(4.14) \qquad \sum_{i=1}^{8} a_{ij}(t+\tau) \log \frac{a_{ij}(t+\tau)}{a_{ij}(t)}$$

where $t+\tau$ stands for a later year. The information inaccuracies (in 10^{-5} bit) are shown in the upper triangle of Table 2.8 for the sector Agriculture, forestry and fishing. The figures indicate that the inaccuracy is of the order of 10^{-3} to 10^{-2} bit for prediction one year ahead and that it increases rather regularly for forecasts over a longer time span until it becomes almost one-tenth of a bit for prediction nine years ahead.

Next define $A_{1j}(t)$ and $A_{2j}(t)$ as the total sector and primary input proportions, respectively, in year t:

$$(4.15) \qquad A_{1j}(t) = \sum_{i=1}^{5} a_{ij}(t) \qquad A_{2j}(t) = \sum_{i=6}^{8} a_{ij}(t)$$

Then the sector input information inaccuracy is

$$(4.16) \qquad \sum_{i=1}^{5} \frac{a_{ij}(t+\tau)}{A_{1j}(t+\tau)} \log \frac{a_{ij}(t+\tau)/A_{1j}(t+\tau)}{a_{ij}(t)/A_{1j}(t)}$$

and the primary input information inaccuracy:

$$(4.17) \qquad \sum_{i=6}^{8} \frac{a_{ij}(t+\tau)}{A_{2j}(t+\tau)} \log \frac{a_{ij}(t+\tau)/A_{2j}(t+\tau)}{a_{ij}(t)/A_{2j}(t)}$$

while

$$(4.18) \qquad \sum_{h=1}^{2} A_{hj}(t+\tau) \log \frac{A_{hj}(t+\tau)}{A_{hj}(t)}$$

is the between-group information inaccuracy which separates total sector input from total primary input. The inaccuracies (4.16) to (4.18) are also given in Table 2.8 for Agriculture, forestry and fishing. The results show that for this sector the sector input figures increase much faster with the time span of prediction than the primary input figures, while the between-group inaccuracies take relatively modest values.

Table 2.8 deals with only one sector, and a summary measure is called for when we want to present similar results for many sectors. Figure 2.2 gives a graphic description for 15 sectors whose input structure is analyzed in the same way. The nine information inaccuracies for prediction one year ahead are represented by their arithmetic average; the same is done for the eight inaccuracy values for prediction two years ahead, and so on. There are only five predictions five years ahead in each case, and four for six years

EXTENSION TO SEVERAL DECOMPOSITIONS

TABLE 2.8

INFORMATION TABLEAU FOR THE INPUTS OF AGRICULTURE, FORESTRY AND FISHING

Base year(t)	Year to be predicted ($t+\tau$)								
	1949	1950	1951	1952	1953	1954	1955	1956	1957
	Total information inaccuracy								
1948	365	1519	2304	3643	3523	4603	5862	7109	8391
1949		547	1269	2092	2113	2946	3899	4957	5914
1950			765	846	1293	1677	2572	3562	4205
1951				547	845	1382	1643	2885	3833
1952					369	431	795	1687	2197
1953						131	359	800	1404
1954							256	550	945
1955								252	599
1956									175
	Sector input information inaccuracy								
1948	321	1195	1979	4867	6308	8719	9916	13265	16245
1949		494	1611	3486	4447	6432	7402	10001	12429
1950			740	1681	2390	3740	4421	6498	8563
1951				848	1726	2992	3716	6326	8856
1952					177	676	1042	2652	4469
1953						221	455	1571	3014
1954							46	717	1826
1955								431	1365
1956									268
	Primary input information inaccuracy								
1948	390	1678	2266	2807	1292	1629	2246	1550	2076
1949		491	801	1131	271	445	806	396	698
1950			193	232	56	11	279	103	215
1951				48	181	137	13	74	9
1952					319	203	97	206	100
1953						26	214	29	152
1954							195	48	139
1955								92	6
1956									51
	Information inaccuracy between groups								
1948	3	32	161	0	100	26	267	378	193
1949		55	120	5	68	11	213	313	148
1950			337	26	245	115	485	631	383
1951				175	7	58	13	45	1
1952					111	32	285	400	209
1953						24	40	89	15
1954							127	206	78
1955								10	6
1956									30

Note. All information values are expressed in 10^{-5} bit.

ahead; these are combined into one group, labeled five and one-half years ahead for convenience. Similarly, the six predictions that cover a time span of seven years or more are also combined and labeled eight years ahead. Figure 2.2 uses a double-log scale; it shows that the inaccuracies – both total and between and within – tend to increase with increasing τ (the time span of prediction) for most of the sectors.

2.5. The Desired Political Entropy

Taking the Square of the Number of Votes

In an article published in the December 30, 1967 issue of the Dutch weekly magazine *Vrij Nederland*, F. GROSFELD proposed the following modification of the procedure for parliamentary representation of political parties. Instead of the familiar proportional representation method, which assigns to each party a number of representatives proportional to the number of votes obtained by the party, he suggested that the number of representatives be proportional to the square of the number of votes. Thus, when there are n parties and when $p_1, \ldots, p_n$ are the proportions of the total number of valid votes obtained by these parties, he would allocate to the ith party a fraction q_i of the total number of representatives which is determined by

$$(5.1) \qquad q_i = \frac{p_i^2}{\sum\limits_{j=1}^{n} p_j^2} \qquad\qquad i = 1, \ldots, n$$

GROSFELD made this proposal for the Dutch political situation on the grounds that the country's number of political parties is large and that even the largest p_i belongs to a minority party, so that several months of political negotiations were often necessary to obtain a coalition cabinet. By squaring the p_i's one obtains much larger differences between the larger and the smaller parties, so that the largest party (or this party combined with a politically related party) has a far better chance of obtaining a majority in parliament. Also, the representation system (5.1) provides an incentive for parties to merge, contributing to a reduction of political dividedness.

A Class of Representation Systems

The representation system (5.1) is the special case for $\alpha = 2$ of the following class of systems:

$$(5.2) \qquad q_i = \frac{p_i^\alpha}{\sum\limits_{j=1}^{n} p_j^\alpha} \qquad\qquad i = 1, \ldots, n$$

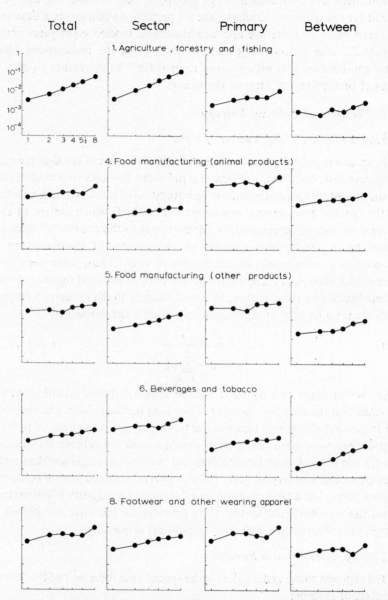

Fig. 2.2.   The average information inaccuracy and its components as functions of the
time span τ for the input structure of 15 sectors

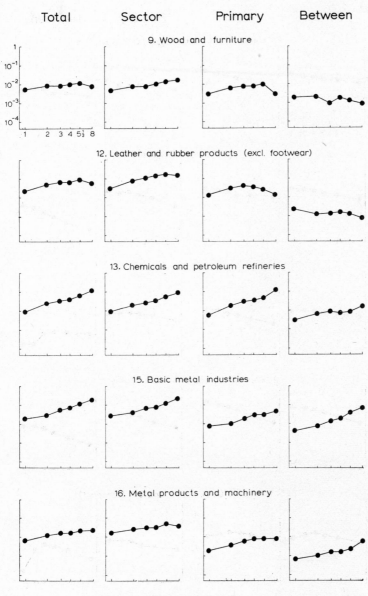

Fig. 2.2 (continued)

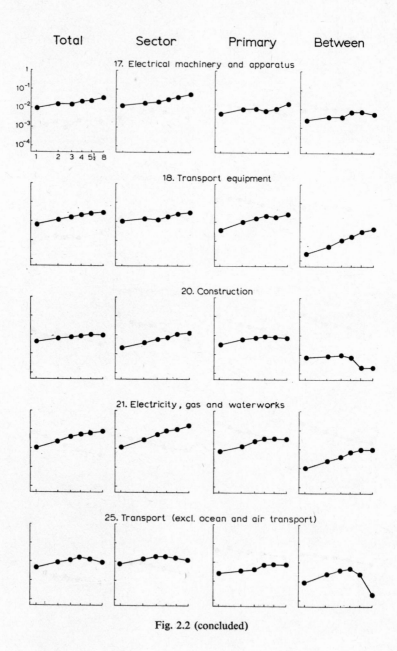

Fig. 2.2 (concluded)

There are several other members of this class:

(1) The so-called *cube law* is an empirical regularity which states that in a two-party system with single-member constituencies, the ratio of the number of representatives of the two parties elected is approximately proportional to the cube of the ratio of the number of votes. This falls under (5.2) with $\alpha = 3$, $n = 2$. This law will be examined in more detail in Section 4.6.

(2) The International Federation of Operational Research Societies (IFORS) faces the problem that the national member societies are of very unequal size, so that the Federation could be dominated by the societies of one or two countries if proportional representation based on national membership were applied. The desire is thus to reduce the representation of the larger groups, which is precisely the opposite of the objective considered in the previous subsection. The solution chosen by IFORS is that each member society has a number of votes which is proportional to the square root of the number of its members. This falls under (5.2) when n is interpreted as the number of member societies, p_i as the ith society's share of the total membership, q_i as its share in the IFORS voting procedure, and $\alpha = \frac{1}{2}$. Thus, if the ith society has four times as many members as the jth, the number of its votes is only twice as large.

(3) The U.S. Senate gives equal representation to all 50 states; each state is entitled to elect two Senators. Hence, if p_i stands for the number of voters of the ith state measured as a fraction of the national total and $q_i = \frac{1}{50}$ for the proportion of Senators allocated to this state, then the class (5.2) applies to this situation when we specify $\alpha = 0$.

The apparent popularity of this class of representation systems provides a justification to study it in further detail. The account which follows is based on THEIL (1969*d*, 1971*b*).

The Entropy of the Representation System

The developments of the two previous subsections suggest that, at the level of the numbers of representatives, we reduce their entropy by selecting an α larger than 1 and we raise the entropy by choosing an α smaller than 1. This is indeed correct. Consider the legislative entropy:

$$(5.3) \qquad H_q = \sum_{i=1}^{n} q_i \log \frac{1}{q_i}$$

and assume that the q's are determined by the p's as indicated in (5.2). For fixed $p_1, \ldots, p_n$, each q_i and hence H_q are functions of α. It is shown in the next paragraph that for $\alpha > 0$, the logarithmic derivative of H_q (natural logs) with respect to α has the following simple form:

$$(5.4) \qquad \frac{\partial H_q}{\partial(\log \alpha)} = -\sum_{i=1}^{n} q_i \left(\log \frac{1}{q_i} - H_q\right)^2$$

The sum in the right-hand side is of the same form as the expression (1.22) of Section 1.1, which we identified there as the variance of information. The conclusion to be drawn from (5.4) is that the entropy H_q is a monotonically decreasing function of α unless all q's are equal. It follows from (5.2) that equality of all q's requires all p's to be equal. In that special case each p_i and q_i is equal to $1/n$, and raising the p's to whatever power has no effect.

To prove eq. (5.4) we substitute (5.2) in (5.3):

$$H_q = -\sum_{i=1}^{n} q_i \log q_i$$

$$= \frac{-\sum_{i=1}^{n} p_i^{\alpha} \left(\log p_i^{\alpha} - \log \sum_{j=1}^{n} p_j^{\alpha}\right)}{\sum_{j=1}^{n} p_j^{\alpha}}$$

which can be simplified to

$$(5.5) \qquad H_q = \log \sum_{i=1}^{n} p_i^{\alpha} - \frac{\alpha \sum_{i=1}^{n} p_i^{\alpha} \log p_i}{\sum_{i=1}^{n} p_i^{\alpha}}$$

The derivative of the first right-hand term with respect to α is

$$\frac{\partial}{\partial \alpha} \log \sum_{i=1}^{n} p_i^{\alpha} = \frac{1}{\sum_{i=1}^{n} p_i^{\alpha}} \frac{\partial}{\partial \alpha} \sum_{i=1}^{n} p_i^{\alpha} = \frac{\sum_{i=1}^{n} p_i^{\alpha} \log p_i}{\sum_{i=1}^{n} p_i^{\alpha}}$$

and that of the second right-hand term:

$$\frac{\partial}{\partial \alpha} \left[\alpha \left(\sum_{i=1}^{n} p_i^{\alpha} \log p_i\right)\left(\sum_{i=1}^{n} p_i^{\alpha}\right)^{-1}\right]$$

$$= \frac{\sum_{i=1}^{n} p_i^{\alpha} \log p_i}{\sum_{i=1}^{n} p_i^{\alpha}} + \frac{\alpha}{\sum_{i=1}^{n} p_i^{\alpha}} \sum_{i=1}^{n} p_i^{\alpha}(\log p_i)^2 - \frac{\alpha \sum_{i=1}^{n} p_i^{\alpha} \log p_i}{(\sum_{i=1}^{n} p_i^{\alpha})^2} \sum_{i=1}^{n} p_i^{\alpha} \log p_i$$

Combining these two results, we obtain

$$
(5.6) \qquad \frac{\partial H_q}{\partial \alpha} = -\alpha \frac{\sum\limits_{i=1}^{n} p_i^\alpha (\log p_i)^2}{\sum\limits_{i=1}^{n} p_i^\alpha} + \alpha \frac{\left(\sum\limits_{i=1}^{n} p_i^\alpha \log p_i\right)^2}{\left(\sum\limits_{i=1}^{n} p_i^\alpha\right)^2}
$$

$$
= -\alpha \sum_{i=1}^{n} q_i (\log p_i)^2 + \alpha \left(\sum_{i=1}^{n} q_i \log p_i\right)^2
$$

$$
= -\alpha \sum_{i=1}^{n} q_i \left(\log p_i - \sum_{j=1}^{n} q_j \log p_j\right)^2
$$

The expression in the second line is a multiple $-\alpha$ of the excess of the weighted second moment of $\log p_1, \ldots, \log p_n$ with weights $q_1, \ldots, q_n$ over the square of the corresponding weighted first moment. This excess is equal to the weighted variance which is shown in the third line. Next write (for $\alpha > 0$):

$$
\log p_i - \sum_{j=1}^{n} q_j \log p_j = \frac{1}{\alpha}\left(\log q_i - \sum_{j=1}^{n} q_j \log q_j\right) = -\frac{1}{\alpha}\left(\log \frac{1}{q_i} - H_q\right)
$$

By combining this with (5.6) we obtain

$$
\frac{\partial H_q}{\partial \alpha} = -\frac{1}{\alpha} \sum_{i=1}^{n} q_i \left(\log \frac{1}{q_i} - H_q\right)^2
$$

which is equivalent to (5.4).

An Informational Justification of the Class of Representation Systems

There can be no doubt that the proportional representation system $q_i = p_i$ (corresponding to $\alpha = 1$) is the simplest and most straightforward, and the reason for choosing a different system is basically the same for Grosfeld's proposal, for IFORS, and for the U.S. Senate. In all these cases there exists a dissatisfaction with the degree to which the total representation would be divided if proportional representation were adopted. The dividedness is either regarded as too large, in which case an $\alpha > 1$ is proposed, or as too small, with an $\alpha < 1$ suggested. We shall prove below that the class of representation systems (5.2) has an optimal property in terms of informational concepts. It will be shown thereafter that, when certain simple axioms are accepted, the class (5.2) is the only acceptable class.

We shall indicate the entropy of the p's by H_p:

$$(5.7) \qquad\qquad H_p = \sum_{i=1}^{n} p_i \log \frac{1}{p_i}$$

This will be our measure of dividedness at the level of the p's. It will be assumed that H_p is neither equal to its lower limit (zero) nor to its upper limit ($\log n$):

$$(5.8) \qquad\qquad 0 < H_p < \log n$$

If $H_p = 0$, then some $p_i = 1$ and $p_j = 0$ for each $j \neq i$. Clearly there exists no nonarbitrary way of assigning parliament seats to parties which received no vote at all, so this case must be excluded. If $H_p = \log n$, all n parties receive exactly the same number of votes, and there is no reasonable way to assign parliament seats to these parties on other than an equal basis.

Obviously, the constraint (5.8) will usually be satisfied, in which case one can conceive of a set of parliamentary fractions $q_1, \ldots, q_n$ whose entropy H_q as defined in (5.3) differs from H_p. Imagine then that we fix the parliamentary entropy H_q at a pre-assigned level. There is then still freedom as to the choice of $q_1, \ldots, q_n$ as long as $n \geq 2$,[1] which we may use to choose these q's as close to the p's as is possible. Our measure of closeness is the expected information of the message that transforms the p's into the q's:

$$(5.9) \qquad\qquad I(q : p) = \sum_{i=1}^{n} q_i \log \frac{q_i}{p_i}$$

It will be shown in the next subsection that under condition (5.8), the parliamentary representation $q_1, \ldots, q_n$ which minimizes (5.9) subject to the entropy constraint is of the form (5.2) for some particular value of α, and that this α can be determined uniquely for any pre-assigned value of the entropy H_q in the interval from zero to $\log n$ when exactly one party has the largest number of votes.

Derivation of the Constrained Minimum

Write the information expectation (5.9) as follows:

$$(5.10) \qquad\qquad I(q : p) = -H_q - \sum_{i=1}^{n} q_i \log p_i$$

---

[1] Even for $n = 2$ the entropy does not determine the q's uniquely, because $(\theta, 1-\theta)$ and $(1-\theta, \theta)$ have the same entropy for any θ in the interval from zero to one. There are thus two solutions for $n = 2$, but there is actually little freedom because it is obvious to assign the larger q_i to the party with the larger p_i. Basically, the present discussion is interesting only for the case $n > 2$.

Since H_q is now a fixed number, our task is thus to maximize the function $\sum q_i \log p_i$ for variations in the q's subject to the constraints (5.3) and $\sum q_i = 1$. So we construct the Lagrangian expression

$$(5.11) \qquad \sum_{i=1}^{n} q_i \log p_i - \lambda(-\sum_{i=1}^{n} q_i \log q_i - H_q) - \mu(\sum_{i=1}^{n} q_i - 1)$$

where λ and μ are Lagrangian multipliers. We differentiate (5.11) with respect to q_i and equate the result to zero:

$$(5.12) \qquad \log p_i + \lambda(1 + \log q_i) - \mu = 0 \qquad\qquad i = 1, \ldots, n$$

If $\lambda = 0$, this equation amounts to $\log p_i = \mu$, which implies that all p_i's must be equal to $1/n$ and hence $H_p = \log n$. This, however, is excluded by (5.8), so that $\lambda \neq 0$. We may thus conclude from (5.12):

$$(5.13) \qquad \log q_i = -1 + \frac{\mu}{\lambda} - \frac{1}{\lambda} \log p_i$$

or, equivalently,

$$(5.14) \qquad q_i = \frac{p_i^{-1/\lambda}}{C} \quad \text{where} \quad C = e^{1 - \mu/\lambda}$$

We now write $\alpha = -1/\lambda$, so that $q_i = p_i^{\alpha}/C$ in accordance with (5.2), and C obviously satisfies

$$(5.15) \qquad C = \sum_{i=1}^{n} p_i^{\alpha}$$

in view of the constraint $\sum q_i = 1$.

We have thus proved that constrained minimization of (5.9) leads to the class (5.2) for some value of α, and we must now show how this particular value can be derived. For this purpose we return to (5.5), which is a nonlinear equation in α when $H_q, p_1, \ldots, p_n$ are fixed. The right-hand side of (5.5) is $\log n$ for $\alpha = 0$ and it converges to zero when α increases indefinitely, provided that one party has the largest p_i.[1] It follows from (5.6) that H_q is a monotonically decreasing function of α in the interval $(0, \infty)$ when the p's are not all equal, and this condition is fulfilled because (5.8) excludes $H_p = \log n$. This establishes the existence of a unique nonnegative solution

[1] Proof: write p_1 for the largest p_i, then q_1 converges to 1 as $\alpha \to \infty$, so that $H_q = 0$ in the limit.

of α for any pre-assigned nonnegative value of H_q that does not exceed $\log n$.[1]

An Axiomatic Justification of the Class of Representation Systems

In the system of proportional representation the proportion of parliament seats allocated to each party is determined uniquely by the proportion of votes which it obtained on the basis of the simple rule $q_i = p_i$, $i = 1, \ldots, n$. Other systems, such as (5.2) for $\alpha \neq 1$, do not have this property, but a weaker variant – which may be called *weak proportionality* – certainly seems reasonable. Consider any two parties i and j; then the number of parliament seats allocated to i divided by the number of seats allocated to j should be determined uniquely by the ratio of the number of votes cast for i to that cast for j, and the underlying relationship should be nondecreasing and it should be the same for all pairs (i, j):

$$(5.16) \qquad \frac{q_i}{q_j} = f\left(\frac{p_i}{p_j}\right) \qquad i, j = 1, \ldots, n$$

The axiom of weak proportionality states that (5.16) holds with the specification that $f(\ )$ is nondecreasing and that it takes positive values for positive values of the argument. In addition, we shall require $f(\ )$ to be continuous. It will be shown in the next paragraph that if these axioms are accepted, the representation $q_1, \ldots, q_n$ is necessarily of the form (5.2) for some nonnegative value of α.

Consider any triple of parties (i, j, k), for which we obviously have

$$\frac{p_i}{p_k} = \frac{p_i}{p_j} \frac{p_j}{p_k} \quad \text{and} \quad \frac{q_i}{q_k} = \frac{q_i}{q_j} \frac{q_j}{q_k}$$

This implies $f(p_i/p_k) = f(p_i/p_j)f(p_j/p_k)$. Since this equation holds for all positive values of the arguments, we may write it in the general form

$$(5.17) \qquad f(xy) \equiv f(x)f(y) \qquad x, y > 0$$

Next introduce $\xi = \log x$ and $\eta = \log y$, so that

$$(5.18) \qquad \log f(x) \equiv \log f(e^\xi) \equiv \phi(\xi) \quad \text{say}$$

---

[1] If $p_1 = p_2$ and if all other p_i's are smaller, then $q_1 = q_2 = \frac{1}{2}$ in the limit for $\alpha \to \infty$, so that H_q converges to a positive value. In the case of a k-fold multiple maximum, $p_1 = \ldots = p_k > p_{k+1} \geqq \ldots \geqq p_n$, the interval of H_q that allows a nonnegative solution of α is reduced to $(\log k, \log n)$.

Taking logarithms of both sides of (5.17), we obtain on the left $\phi(\log xy)$
$\equiv \phi(\xi+\eta)$ and on the right $\phi(\xi)+\phi(\eta)$:

(5.19) $$\phi(\xi+\eta) \equiv \phi(\xi)+\phi(\eta) \qquad -\infty < \xi, \eta < \infty$$

We may now return to the analogous developments in Section 1.2 [eq. (2.6)
and ff.] to conclude that, if $f(\ )$ and hence $\phi(\ )$ are continuous nondecreasing
functions, $\phi(\xi)$ must be of the form $\alpha\xi$ for some nonnegative constant α.
Hence:

$$f(x) = e^{\phi(\xi)} = (e^\xi)^\alpha = x^\alpha$$

which gives $q_i/q_j = (p_i/p_j)^\alpha$ for each pair (i,j). This condition determines
the ratios of all q's. Since they add up to one, they are thus individually
determined and it is immediately obvious that they are of the form (5.2)
for some $\alpha \geq 0$.

The Special Case of the Square-Root Representation System

Two different justifications have been provided for the class of representation systems (5.2), but the second provides no clue at all regarding the
choice of α, while the first defers this choice to that of a pre-assigned entropy
H_q. The question which we shall address here is this: Consider a nation or
federation which is characterized by racial, ethnic, or linguistic differences.
Supposing that its unity is not questioned, how should political power be
divided among the groups in such a way that social tension (appropriately
measured) is minimized? It seems plausible that this requires that more
power be allocated to minority groups than accords with their population
shares. The IFORS voting rule described in the second subsection provides
an example; it allocates a vote to each group which is proportional to the
square root of the size of the group, thus favoring minority groups at the
expense of the larger groups, and it is this particular representation system
that we shall focus upon in this subsection.[1]

Write $p_1, \ldots, p_n$ for the population shares and $q_1, \ldots, q_n$ for the power
shares of the n groups. If one wants a concrete interpretation, the latter
shares may be viewed as the proportions of the representatives of the various
groups. Suppose that each representative favors the members of his group
only; for a generalization of this assumption see Problems 9 to 12. Thus, if
any member of the ith group expresses a desire, the probability is q_i that he
will meet a willing ear. For example, if $q = .2$, he will have a success rate

---

[1] For an alternative justification of the square-root system, see PENROSE (1946, 1952).

of 20 per cent in a long series of experiments of this sort. Conversely, in such a series there are $1/q_i = 5$ efforts for each successful effort, and hence $1/q_i - 1 = 4$ unsuccessful ones. This number of unsuccessful efforts per successful effort is a plausible measure of frustration.

Suppose that the goal is to minimize the aggregate frustration in the society as a whole – a simple measure of the tension of the system. We thus sum frustration over all individuals without regard to their affiliation with a particular group. Since the ith group contains a proportion p_i of the population, aggregate frustration is thus proportional to

$$(5.20) \qquad \sum_{i=1}^{n} p_i \left(\frac{1}{q_i} - 1 \right) = \sum_{i=1}^{n} \frac{p_i}{q_i} - 1$$

This expression indicates that p_i/q_i may be regarded as the incremental contribution of the ith group to the tension of the system. In the case of proportional representation the value of the criterion function (5.20) is $n-1$ and thus increases linearly with the number of groups. Note further that this function is completely symmetric both with respect to individuals and also with respect to groups. For individuals this follows directly from the way in which the function is derived. For groups it follows from the fact that (5.20) is a symmetric function of $q_1/p_1, \ldots, q_n/p_n$, which measure per capita power of the n groups.

To minimize (5.20) for variations in the q's subject to $\sum q_i = 1$ we form the Lagrangian expression

$$(5.21) \qquad \sum_{i=1}^{n} \frac{p_i}{q_i} - 1 - \lambda \left(\sum_{i=1}^{n} q_i - 1 \right)$$

where λ is a Lagrangian multiplier. We differentiate (5.21) with respect to q_i and equate the result to zero, which gives $-p_i/q_i^2 = \lambda$. This shows that q_i must be proportional to the square root of p_i, which amounts to the system (5.2) for $\alpha = \frac{1}{2}$. The square-root representation system can thus be justified on the basis of the simple criterion function $\sum (p_i/q_i)$.

The Problem of Non-Integer Solutions

When the q's are proportions of parliament seats, we face the problem that the solutions obtained from the above procedures may fail to produce integer values. [Recall that we met this problem in Section 1.8 (pages 48–49) when we discussed the relationship between political dividedness at the voters' and the legislative levels.] It is now possible to attack this problem. Write N for the total number of parliament seats, so that each of the values

$Nq_1, \ldots, Nq_n$ should be nonnegative integers in order that the solution can be implemented. In the case of (5.20), one may minimize this criterion function subject to $\sum q_i = 1$ and the additional constraint that $Nq_1, \ldots, Nq_n$ are nonnegative integers. Since the number of integer solutions is finite, a minimizing solution can always be found.

In the approach of minimizing (5.9) subject to $\sum q_i = 1$ and a pre-assigned H_q one may proceed as follows. Write $q_1, \ldots, q_n$ for the solution that is obtained when the integer constraint is disregarded. Then choose as the solution for implementation the fractions $q'_1, \ldots, q'_n$ which minimize the information expectation,

$$(5.22) \qquad I(q' : q) = \sum_{i=1}^{n} q'_i \log \frac{q'_i}{q_i}$$

subject to $\sum q'_i = 1$ and the integer constraint. Again, such a solution can always be found because the number of integer solutions is finite. Note, however, that this solution $q'_1, \ldots, q'_n$ will not, in general, have an entropy which is exactly equal to the pre-assigned value H_q. Actually, the mere fact that there is only a finite number of integer solutions implies that there is also only a finite number of possible values of the legislative entropy.

The approach of minimizing (5.22) for variations in $q'_1, \ldots, q'_n$ subject to $\sum q'_i = 1$ and the integer constraint can, of course, also be applied to proportional representation ($q_i \equiv p_i$). The existence of a well-defined criterion function is an advantage over such procedures as d'Hondt's.

2.6. The Measurement of Income Inequality

A simple measure of income inequality is the expected information of the message which transforms population shares into income shares. It was proposed by THEIL (1967, Chapter 4); a brief summary follows in this section.

Inequality Among Individual Income Earners

Consider a society consisting of n income earners with incomes $z_1, \ldots, z_n$. It is assumed that these z's are nonnegative and that at least some of them are positive, so that total personal income, $\sum z_i$, and per capita personal income, $\bar{z} = (1/n) \sum z_i$, are both positive. The income share of the ith individual is his share of total personal income:

$$(6.1) \qquad q_i = \frac{z_i}{\sum_{j=1}^{n} z_j} = \frac{z_i}{n\bar{z}} \qquad\qquad i = 1, \ldots, n$$

His population share is his share of the total population, which is simply $1/n$ for each individual. We have pairwise equality of all income and population shares if and only if all z_i's are equal. There are differences between corresponding income and population shares as soon as the z_i's differ. Consequently, the expected information of the message which transforms the population shares into the income shares,

$$(6.2) \qquad \sum_{i=1}^{n} q_i \log \frac{q_i}{1/n} = \frac{1}{n} \sum_{i=1}^{n} \frac{z_i}{\bar{z}} \log \frac{z_i}{\bar{z}}$$

is a measure of income inequality. The right-hand side of (6.2) indicates that this measure is equal to the mean product of income and its own logarithm with the understanding that per capita income is used as the income unit.[1]

Note that this mean product vanishes when all incomes are equal and that its value does not change when all incomes are multiplied by the same positive factor k. These are two obvious requirements for a good measure of income inequality. Another desirable property has to do with aggregation of income earners to groups and will be examined now.

Between-Group and Within-Group Inequality

Imagine that each of the n income earners belongs to one of G groups $S_1, \ldots, S_G$. Let S_g consist of n_g individuals ($\sum n_g = n$) and write Q_g for the income share of S_g:

$$(6.3) \qquad Q_g = \sum_{i \in S_g} q_i \qquad\qquad g = 1, \ldots, G$$

Then go back to the decomposition (1.15) of the information expectation $I(q:p)$ and note that in this case the prior probabilities of the groups, $P_1, \ldots, P_G$, are their population shares $n_1/n, \ldots, n_G/n$. The decomposition thus takes the following form:

$$(6.4) \qquad \sum_{i=1}^{n} q_i \log \frac{q_i}{1/n} = \sum_{g=1}^{G} Q_g \log \frac{Q_g}{n_g/n} + \sum_{g=1}^{G} Q_g \sum_{i \in S_g} \frac{q_i}{Q_g} \log \frac{q_i/Q_g}{1/n_g}$$

To interpret this result we start with the second term on the right, which is a weighted average (with the group income shares $Q_1, \ldots, Q_G$ as weights) of the G expressions

---

[1] Also notice that the left-hand side of (6.2) is the expected information corresponding to prior equiprobability which was considered in (1.5).

$$(6.5) \qquad \sum_{i \in S_g} \frac{q_i}{Q_g} \log \frac{q_i/Q_g}{1/n_g} \qquad\qquad g = 1, \ldots, G$$

Since q_i/Q_g is the income share of the ith individual in his group and $1/n_g$ his population share in this group, the expression (6.5) is of the same form as the general inequality measure (6.2) but it confines itself to the individuals of S_g. Hence (6.5) measures the income inequality within S_g and the second term in the right-hand side of (6.4) is the average within-group inequality.

The first right-hand term in (6.4) is also an expected information which deals with population and income shares, but it does so at the aggregative rather than the individual level. To interpret this term, consider

$$Q_g = \frac{\text{total income of } S_g}{\text{total income of all individuals}}$$

$$= \frac{n_g \times \text{per capita income of } S_g}{n \times \text{overall per capita income}}$$

This clearly shows that $Q_g = n_g/n$ holds for each g if and only if all G per capita incomes are equal. In that case the first right-hand term in (6.4) vanishes. Therefore, this term is the between-group income inequality and it is concerned with the extent to which the groups have different per capita incomes.

Application to Incomes of White and of Nonwhite Families in the U.S.

Table 2.9 applies the above inequality measures to income data for white and nonwhite families in the U.S. during the period 1947–1963. The data are obtained from the *Current Population Reports* of the Bureau of the Census. The first two columns of the table contain the per capita incomes of the two groups. The third column specifies the income inequality (in nits) for all families, the fourth and fifth are the within-group measures (6.5) for the two groups, and the last provides the between-group comparison. The behavior of the inequality values over time is a little erratic, which is at least partly due to the sampling errors of the survey. The main conclusions are that total inequality is of the order of almost one-quarter of a nit, that the inequality among nonwhites is consistently higher than that among whites, and that there is no clear evidence of a narrowing gap between the two population groups during the period considered here.

It should be stressed that Table 2.9 is based on published income distributions which specify only the numbers of income recipients within certain income intervals. To obtain numerical results for the q_i's and Q_g's of (6.4),

TABLE 2.9

AVERAGE INCOME AND INCOME INEQUALITY FOR WHITE AND NONWHITE FAMILIES, 1947–1963

Year	Average income ($)		Inequality (in nits)			
	White	Nonwhite	Total	White	Nonwhite	Between groups
1947	3760	2033	.249	.236	.286	.010
1948	3892	2113	.244	.231	.280	.010
1949	3740	1952	.250	.236	.287	.012
1950	3982	2141	.249	.236	.282	.011
1951	4419	2359	.237	.223	.277	.011
1952	4741	2411	.258	.241	.329	.013
1954	4986	2784	.255	.243	.281	.010
1955	5257	2906	.241	.229	.252	.010
1956	5712	3087	.239	.226	.263	.011
1957	5805	3258	.226	.213	.270	.010
1958	6041	3363	.233	.219	.291	.010
1959	6449	3525	.240	.225	.288	.011
1960	6756	3954	.245	.232	.291	.009
1961	7030	4091	.256	.243	.310	.009
1962	7255	4055	.238	.224	.273	.011
1963	7541	4460	.226	.213	.266	.009

it was assumed that all income recipients of a given income bracket have incomes equal to the midpoint of the bracket.[1] This procedure under-estimates the level of inequality, because it declares the within-bracket in-equalities to be zero whereas they are actually positive. The other extreme is the case in which all income recipients of each income bracket have an income equal to either the lower limit or the upper limit of the bracket. For the data of Table 2.9 this alternative assumption leads to inequality values (total, within-white, and within-nonwhite) that are about .025 nit higher in the earlier years, and about .015 nit after 1950. This suggests that the figures of the three relevant columns of this table should be increased by an amount of the order of 1 per cent of a nit.

Application to Total Personal Incomes of the States of the U.S.

We now leave the area of family incomes and consider the total personal

---

[1] For the open-ended income brackets (such as $25,000 or more) the average income was used, obtained by means of a Pareto approximation of the upper tail of the income distribution.

income of each state of the United States. Alaska and Hawaii will not be included, but the District of Columbia will be; hence there are $n = 49$ regional units. Write p_i and q_i for the ith state's share of the national population and of the national personal income, respectively. It is then readily verified that q_i/p_i is equal to the ratio of the per capita income of the ith state to national per capita income. The information expectation $I(q:p) = \sum q_i \log (q_i/p_i)$ is our measure of income inequality among states; it vanishes

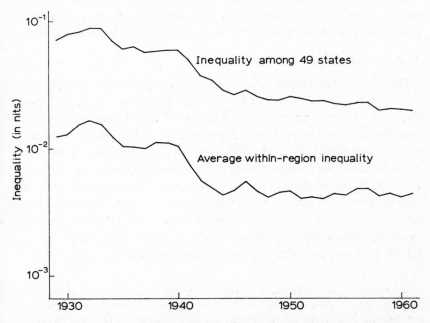

Fig. 2.3.   Income inequality among the states of the United States, 1929–1961

when all 49 per capita incomes are equal, and is positive otherwise. Figure 2.3 gives a picture of the development of this income inequality from 1929 to 1961. Its vertical axis has a logarithmic scale, and the curve on top measures the inequality among all 49 states individually. It shows that inequality rose until 1932 and declined thereafter. The inequality was of the order of .02 nit around 1960, which is less than one-quarter of the peak level of 1932. The curve at the bottom refers to eight regions: New England, Mideast, Great Lakes, Plains, Southeast, Southwest, Rocky Mountain, and

Far West.[1] It is concerned with the decomposition

$$(6.6) \qquad \sum_{i=1}^{49} q_i \log \frac{q_i}{p_i} = \sum_{g=1}^{8} Q_g \log \frac{Q_g}{P_g} + \sum_{g=1}^{8} Q_g \sum_{i \in S_g} \frac{q_i}{Q_g} \log \frac{q_i/Q_g}{p_i/P_g}$$

where $S_1, \ldots, S_8$ are the eight regions and P_g and Q_g are the population share and the income share, respectively, of region S_g. The curve at the bottom in Figure 2.3 describes the development of the second term on the right, which is the average within-region inequality. Its behavior is similar to the curve on top, but it is much lower and the vertical distance between the two curves does not change much. This means that the per capita income differences of the states were and continued to be of a mainly regional nature.

An International Income Comparison

Table 2.10 is concerned with the income inequality of 54 countries, grouped into six areas: North America and Northwest Europe, Southern Europe, Near East, Africa, Asia, and Latin America.[2] Data on these countries have been published by DOSSER (1963), DOSSER and PEACOCK (1964), and ROSEN-STEIN-RODAN (1961) for 1949, 1957, and 1976. The 1976 figures are conditional forecasts, the condition being that the developed countries will donate all the economic aid that the less-developed countries can absorb. Such forecasts are necessarily rough; the resulting figures on income inequality should merely be regarded as an approximation to the lower limit of the actual inequality that should be expected in 1976, given the presumption that less aid will lead to more inequality between rich and poor countries.

---

[1] *New England*: Connecticut, Maine, Massachusetts, New Hampshire, Rhode Island, and Vermont. *Mideast*: Delaware, District of Columbia, Maryland, New Jersey, New York, and Pennsylvania. *Great Lakes*: Illinois, Indiana, Michigan, Ohio, and Wisconsin. *Plains*: Iowa, Kansas, Minnesota, Missouri, Nebraska, North Dakota, and South Dakota. *Southeast*: Alabama, Arkansas, Florida, Georgia, Kentucky, Louisiana, Mississippi, North Carolina, South Carolina, Tennessee, Virginia, and West Virginia. *Southwest*: Arizona, New Mexico, Oklahoma, and Texas. *Rocky Mountain*: Colorado, Idaho, Montana, Utah, and Wyoming. *Far West*: California, Nevada, Oregon, and Washington.
[2] *North America and Northwest Europe*: Belgium, Canada, Denmark, Finland, France, Germany, Luxembourg, Netherlands, Norway, Sweden, Switzerland, United Kingdom, and United States. *Southern Europe*: Greece, Italy, Portugal, and Spain. *Near East*: Egypt, Iraq, Israel, Lebanon, Syria, and Turkey. *Africa*: Congo (formerly Belgian Congo), Ghana, Kenya, Nigeria, and Uganda. *Asia*: Burma, Ceylon, India, Malaya, Pakistan, Philippines, South Korea, and Thailand. *Latin America*: Argentina, Bolivia, Brazil, Chile, Colombia, Costa Rica, Cuba, Dominican Republic, Ecuador, Guatemala, Honduras, Jamaica, Mexico, Panama, Paraguay, Peru, Puerto Rico, and Venezuela.

TABLE 2.10

INCOME INEQUALITY AMONG 54 COUNTRIES: 1949, 1957, 1976

	1949	1957	1976
Total inequality	.530	.526	.576
Between-region inequality	.456	.462	.545
Average within-region inequality	.074	.064	.031
	With fixed population shares of 1949		
Total inequality	.530	.522	.540
Between-region inequality	.456	.458	.509
Average within-region inequality	.074	.064	.030

The relevant inequality values are shown in the first three lines of Table 2.10; the last three will be discussed in the next subsection. It appears that the total inequality is much higher than any of the figures shown in Table 2.9 and Figure 2.3. Also, inequality in 1976 is expected to exceed the level of 1957 by about 10 per cent, even under the favorable assumptions on foreign aid. This is in sharp contrast to the case of Figure 2.3, which shows that within the United States the income differences among states have been declining since 1932. Finally, the second and third lines of the table show that inequality among countries is largely a regional matter and that this may be expected to become even more pronounced in the future.

Income Inequality and Population Changes

The income inequality among countries is obviously not determined exclusively by the ratios of their per capita incomes, since their relative magnitudes must also play a role. Write z_{it} for the per capita income of the ith country in year t and p_{it} for its share of the world's population in that year. Its share of world income is then

$$(6.7) \qquad q_{it} = \frac{p_{it} z_{it}}{\sum_{j=1}^{n} p_{jt} z_{jt}}$$

The figures in the first three lines of Table 2.10 are therefore of the form $\sum_i q_{it} \log (q_{it}/p_{it})$ for three values of t. Imagine that we want to separate the effect on income inequality of the changing per capita incomes and that of the changing population shares. One way of doing this is by fixing the population shares at the level of a certain year and retaining the original development of the per capita incomes. This leads to hypothetical income shares,

$$(6.8) \qquad q_{it}^* = \frac{p_i z_{it}}{\sum\limits_{j=1}^{n} p_j z_{jt}}$$

where $p_1, \ldots, p_n$ are the fixed population shares of the base year. In the lower half of Table 2.10, the population distribution of 1949 is taken for this purpose. The figures shown in the first line are

$$(6.9) \qquad \sum_{i=1}^{n} q_{it}^* \log \frac{q_{it}^*}{p_i}$$

which may be interpreted as the income inequality values among countries that would have materialized if (1) the population distribution had been constant since 1949 and (2) the development of the per capita incomes were identical with that of the upper half of the table. The results show that under these conditions the inequality increase that is expected to occur from 1957 to 1976 is barely over one-third of the figure that corresponds to the situation of changing population shares. The last two lines of the table indicate that this population effect is regional in nature.

It is not entirely satisfactory to conclude from this result that the development of inequality would have been as shown in the lower part of Table 2.10 if the population distribution had been constant, because it is possible that a different development of the population affects the per capita incomes. Also, differences between per capita incomes may affect the distribution of the population; for example, by migration. Figure 2.4 illustrates this for the states of the U.S. in two decades. The horizontal variable is state per capita income in the middle year of the decade (1935 or 1945), measured according to a logarithmic scale with the national per capita income in the origin. The vertical variable is net migration (total immigration minus total emigration) during the decade, expressed as a percentage of the average population of the state in the first and the last year of the decade. The results show that there is a clear positive association between net migration and the relative income position of the state, particularly in the second decade. Note also that the horizontal dispersion of the points is less in the lower figure than in the upper. This indicates that there is less income inequality among the states in 1945 than in 1935, as we already know from earlier results.

Alternative Measures of Income Inequality

A rather popular measure of income inequality is Gini's *concentration*

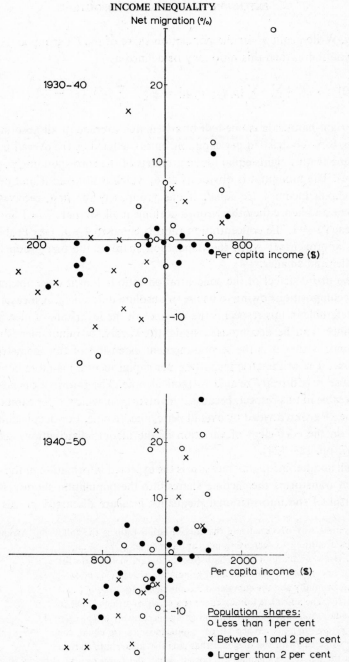

Fig. 2.4. The relationship between net migration per state and state per capita income, 1930–40 and 1940–50. [States are indicated by different types of dots depending on their share of the national population.]

ratio. Write again p_i for the population share of the ith group and q_i for its income share, then this ratio may be defined as

$$(6.10) \qquad \tfrac{1}{2}\sum_{i=1}^{n}\sum_{j=1}^{n}|p_i q_j - p_j q_i| = \tfrac{1}{2}\sum_{i=1}^{n}\sum_{j=1}^{n}p_i p_j\left|\frac{q_i}{p_i} - \frac{q_j}{p_j}\right|$$

The right-hand side is one-half of a weighted average of all absolute differences between deflated per capita incomes (deflated by the overall per capita income) with weights equal to the products of the corresponding population shares. The minimum is obviously zero, which is attained if and only if all per capita incomes are equal. If one group, say the first, receives all the income and hence the other groups nothing at all, so that $q_1 = 1$ and $q_j = 0$ for each $j \neq 1$, the concentration ratio is equal to $1 - p_1$ (see Problem 16). This approaches 1 when the population share of the first group becomes smaller and smaller.[1]

The major defect of the concentration ratio is that it does not lend itself to decompositions owing to its use of absolute differences. A measure which is preferable in this respect is the variance of the logarithm of income, since variances can be decomposed straightforwardly. A minor blemish of this variance is that it is the second-moment extension of the geometric mean income. The arithmetic mean (the per capita income) is more convenient, because it is directly related to total income. The information measure is preferable in this respect, because it involves q_i/p_i which is per capita income of the ith group divided by overall per capita income. For details on this and also on the coefficient of variation of the income distribution, see THEIL (1967, pp. 123–124).

Still another inequality measure is the expected information of the message which transforms the income shares into the population shares – that is, a reversal of the informational inequality measure discussed in this section

---

[1] A simple way of visualizing the concentration ratio is the following. Arrange the n groups according to increasing per capita income: $q_1/p_1 \leqq \ldots \leqq q_n/p_n$. Draw a square of unit length (see the figure on the right for $n = 3$) and measure the cumulated population shares ($p_1, p_1 + p_2$, ...) horizontally and the cumulated income shares ($q_1, q_1 + q_2, \ldots$) vertically. The so-called Lorenz curve is a series of straight lines in this square, starting at the origin and going successively to (p_1, q_1), ($p_1 + p_2, q_1 + q_2$), ... When all per capita incomes are equal, the curve coincides with the diagonal that cuts the square into halves.

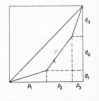

When the per capita incomes are not all equal, the Lorenz curve is below the diagonal and it can be shown that the concentration ratio is equal to twice the area between the curve and the diagonal.

which uses the population shares as prior probabilities and the income shares as posterior probabilities. This alternative may not seem obvious, but it does have its merits for those analysts who would prefer population shares to income shares as weights of the within-region term in a decomposition such as (6.6). It should be noted, however, that when this informational inequality measure is applied at the individual level, it becomes infinitely large as soon as there is one person with zero income.

PROBLEMS

1 Prove that the information expectation (1.3), when measured in nits, has the following derivatives:

$$\frac{\partial I}{\partial p} = \frac{p-q}{p(1-p)}$$

$$\frac{\partial I}{\partial q} = \log \frac{q}{1-q} - \log \frac{p}{1-p}$$

2 A state contains n congressional districts with population proportions $v_1, \ldots, v_n$ ($\sum v_j = 1$). A Federal Judge orders redistricting whenever the expected information of the message that transforms the perfect-equality proportions $1/n, \ldots, 1/n$ into the observed proportions exceeds c bits, where c is a positive number selected by the Judge. Prove that this ruling is equivalent to stating that the entropy of the distribution of the population over districts is not allowed to be more than c bits below the maximum possible.

3 Compute the information expectation of the message that transforms the prior probabilities (.3, .3, .4) into the posterior probabilities (.31, .29, .4). Do so in nits and compare the outcome with that of the quadratic approximation (1.12). Do the same for the prior probabilities (.05, .35, .6) and the posterior probabilities (.1, .3, .6), and draw your conclusions.

4 In Section 2.1, at the end of the subsection containing the proof of the nonnegativity of the information expectation, it is stated that this expectation has no finite upper limit. Does this also apply to the information expectation (2.5)? Explain your answer.

5 Consider the data on the fourth school district given in Tables 2.1 and 2.2. Compare them with Problem 5 of Chapter 1 and give further details on what, in your view, happened in this district.

6 Suppose that students belong to one of n races, with proportions $p_{j1}, \ldots, p_{jn}$ in the jth school. Prove that the average racial entropy of the schools of district D_r is

$$\bar{H}_r = \sum_{j \in D_r} \frac{w_j}{W_r} \sum_{i=1}^n p_{ji} \log \frac{1}{p_{ji}}$$

Derive similarly the average racial entropy of the schools of the city and prove that when n races instead of two are considered, we still have the property of aggregation consistency mentioned below eq. (4.4) of Section 1.4.

7 (*Continuation*) Prove that the proportion of students of the ith race in district D_r is $P_{ri} = \sum w_j p_{ji}/W_r$, where the summation is over $j \in D_r$. Next show that the extension of the segregation measure (2.4) is

$$K_r - \bar{H}_r = \sum_{j \in D_r} \frac{w_j}{W_r} \sum_{i=1}^n p_{ji} \log \frac{p_{ji}}{P_{ri}}$$

Finally, derive the generalizations of eqs. (2.10) to (2.12).

8 Consider the following set of predictions (p_i), revised predictions (p_i'), and observed proportions (q_i):

	$i = 1$	$i = 2$	$i = 3$
p_i	.3	.2	.5
p_i'	.35	.25	.4
q_i	.4	.2	.4

Compute the information inaccuracies and the information improvement. Next, form the sets $S_1 = (1, 3)$ and $S_2 = (2)$ and compute the decompositions of these informational measures.

9 The criterion function (5.20) is based on the assumption that each representative favors the members of his group only. Generalize this by assuming that each member of the ith group is favored by any representative of the jth group with probability r_{ij}. Prove that the function (5.20) is then replaced by

(1)
$$\sum_{i=1}^n \frac{p_i}{\sum_j r_{ij} q_j} - 1$$

10 (*Continuation*) To minimize (1) for variations in the q's subject to $\sum q_i = 1$, form the Lagrangian expression

$$\frac{p_1}{\sum\limits_{j=1}^{n} r_{1j}q_j} + \ldots + \frac{p_n}{\sum\limits_{j=1}^{n} r_{nj}q_j} - 1 - \lambda(\sum\limits_{i=1}^{n} q_i - 1)$$

Differentiate this expression with respect to $q_1, \ldots, q_n$, equate these derivatives to zero, and prove that this leads to n equations which can be written in vector form as follows:

$$(2) \qquad \left[\frac{p_1}{x_1^2} \cdots \frac{p_n}{x_n^2}\right] \mathbf{R} = -\lambda \iota'$$

where $\mathbf{R} = [r_{ij}]$, ι' is a row vector consisting of n unit elements, and

$$(3) \qquad x_i = \sum_{j=1}^{n} r_{ij}q_j \qquad\qquad i = 1, \ldots, n$$

Assume that $\mathbf{R}$ is nonsingular and write $\mathbf{R}^{-1} = [r^{ij}]$. Then prove $p_i/x_i^2 = -\lambda s_i$, where

$$(4) \qquad s_i = \sum_{k=1}^{n} r^{ki} \qquad\qquad i = 1, \ldots, n$$

Conclude that x_i is proportional to $\sqrt{p_i/s_i}$, and from (3) that x_i is the ith element of $\mathbf{Rq}$, where $\mathbf{q} = [q_1 \ldots q_n]'$. Hence,

$$\mathbf{Rq} = c \begin{bmatrix} \sqrt{p_1/s_1} \\ \vdots \\ \sqrt{p_n/s_n} \end{bmatrix}$$

where c is a scalar. Multiply both sides by $\mathbf{R}^{-1}$ and prove that the solution for q_i is

$$(5) \qquad q_i = \frac{\sum\limits_{j=1}^{n} r^{ij}\sqrt{p_j/s_j}}{\sum\limits_{j=1}^{n} \sqrt{p_j s_j}} \qquad\qquad i = 1, \ldots, n$$

Verify that this includes the system (5.2) with $\alpha = \frac{1}{2}$ as a special case; which case?

11 (*Continuation*) Take $n = 2$ and $r_{11} = r_{22} = 1$. Write p and q for the population share and the share of representatives, respectively, of the first group. Prove that the solution (5) implies the following ratio of the shares of representatives:

(6)
$$\frac{q}{1-q} = \frac{\left(\dfrac{p}{1-r_{21}}\right)^{\frac{1}{2}} - r_{12}\left(\dfrac{1-p}{1-r_{12}}\right)^{\frac{1}{2}}}{-r_{21}\left(\dfrac{p}{1-r_{21}}\right)^{\frac{1}{2}} + \left(\dfrac{1-p}{1-r_{12}}\right)^{\frac{1}{2}}}$$

Prove that this is equivalent to the square-root representation system in the case $r_{12} = r_{21} = 0$. Prove also that when r_{21} increases, so that the first group becomes more generous in its dealings with members of the second group, the share of representatives of the former group is increased. Is the ratio (6) always nonnegative? Draw your conclusion as to the general validity of the solution (5).

12 (*Continuation*) For general n, consider the special case in which r_{ij} equals 1 for $i = j$ and equals $r < 1$ for all $i \neq j$. Prove that **R** can then be written

$$\mathbf{R} = (1-r)\mathbf{I} + r\mathbf{u}\mathbf{u}'$$

with inverse

$$\mathbf{R}^{-1} = \frac{1}{1-r}\left[\mathbf{I} - \frac{r}{1+r(n-1)}\mathbf{u}\mathbf{u}'\right]$$

where **I** is the $n \times n$ unit matrix and $\mathbf{u}$ the n-element column vector whose elements are all equal to 1. Prove that the solution (5) takes the form

(7)
$$q_i = \left(1 + \frac{rn}{1-r}\right)\frac{\sqrt{p_i}}{\sum\limits_{j=1}^{n}\sqrt{p_j}} - \frac{r}{1-r} \qquad i = 1, \ldots, n$$

Next write $q_i(r)$ for the solution (7) when r takes a particular value, so that $q_i(0)$ stands for the ith share of representatives under the square-root representation system. Prove that (7) can then be written as

(8)
$$q_i(r) - q_i(0) = \frac{rn}{1-r}\left[q_i(0) - \frac{1}{n}\right] \qquad i = 1, \ldots, n$$

and state the implications of this result for groups for which the square-root system produces shares $q_i(0)$ larger than and smaller than $1/n$. Does the solution (7) satisfy the axiom of weak proportionality?

13 Prove that $\sum_i p_i q_i^{(\alpha-1)/\alpha}$ is a criterion function which, when minimized for variations in the q's subject to $\sum q_i = 1$, leads to the class of representation systems (5.2).

14 Consider a continuous income distribution with density function $f(\ )$. Assume that the density is zero for all nonpositive values of the argument. Prove that the extension of the inequality measure (6.2) for this continuous case is

(9) $$\mathscr{E}\left(\frac{z}{\mathscr{E}z}\log\frac{z}{\mathscr{E}z}\right) = \int_0^\infty \left(\frac{z}{m}\log\frac{z}{m}\right)f(z)dz$$

where m is the mean of the income distribution:

$$m = \int_0^\infty zf(z)dz$$

In particular, assume that the natural logarithm of income is normally distributed with mean μ and variance σ^2. Prove that the inequality measure (9) is $\frac{1}{2}\sigma^2$ (in nits). Why is the outcome independent of μ?

15 To analyze the effect of varying population shares on the income inequality between groups, given fixed ratios of their per capita incomes, consider a country consisting of two groups of people with population shares p and $1-p$. Their per capita incomes are θ and 1, respectively, where $0 < \theta < 1$. Prove that the inequality between the groups [the first right-hand term of (6.4) for $G = 2$] is

$$I = \frac{p\theta\log\theta}{1-p(1-\theta)} - \log\left[1-p(1-\theta)\right]$$

and that its derivative with respect to p is

$$\frac{\partial I}{\partial p} = \frac{1}{1-p(1-\theta)}\left[1-\theta+\frac{\theta\log\theta}{1-p(1-\theta)}\right]$$

Prove next that I has a unique maximum at

$$\bar{p} = \frac{1}{1-\theta}\left(1+\frac{\theta\log\theta}{1-\theta}\right)$$

Tabulate $\bar{p}$ as a function of θ for $\theta = 0, .1, .2, \ldots, 1$ to conclude that (1) the largest inequality level is always attained at a population share $\bar{p}$ of the poor group which exceeds $\frac{1}{2}$ and (2) this $\bar{p}$ is larger the poorer this group is relative to the other group.

16 Arrange the n groups in (6.10) according to decreasing per capita incomes: $q_1/p_1 \geqq q_2/p_2 \geqq \cdots \geqq q_n/p_n$. Prove that the concentration ratio can then be written as

(10) $$\sum_{i=1}^{n} \sum_{j>i} p_i p_j \left(\frac{q_i}{p_i} - \frac{q_j}{p_j} \right)$$

Use this expression to prove that the inequality increases as the richest group (the first) becomes richer relative to the others, q_1 converging to 1 and q_j to 0 for each $j \neq 1$. Prove that in the limit the value of (10) is $1 - p_1$.

17 Consider Section 1.8, eq. (8.5) and ff., in particular the trip by car from a location at distances $(r_1, \ldots, r_n)$ from the n factories to a location at distances $(r_1 + dr_1, \ldots, r_n + dr_n)$. Prove that under condition (8.5) the expected information of the message that transforms the market shares of the former location into those of the latter is

(11) $$\tfrac{1}{2} \beta^2 \sum_{i=1}^{n} p_i [d(\log r_i) - \sum_{j=1}^{n} p_j d(\log r_j)]^2$$

Give a statistical interpretation of the sum that occurs in (11), and indicate how (11) is to be modified under condition (8.9) of Section 1.8.

CHAPTER 3

MULTIDIMENSIONAL EXTENSIONS

This chapter deals with classifications in several dimensions, such as the sales of a firm by area and product type, or voters by race, sex, and age group. The first section concerns the bivariate case (two dimensions) and it is formulated in terms of messages of a particular kind. The later sections provide extensions and a wide variety of substantive interpretations of the concepts introduced.

3.1. Joint, Marginal, and Conditional Entropies

Messages Sent and Messages Received

Our starting point is a set of $m+n$ messages. The first m, to be indicated by $X_1, \ldots, X_m$, are the messages sent and the last n, indicated by $Y_1, \ldots, Y_n$, are the messages received. We write p_{ij} for the probability that X_i is the message sent and Y_j the message received.

Note that these messages differ in nature from those considered in Sections 1.1 and 2.1. The latter messages stated either that some event had occurred, the probability of which was p before the message arrived, or that this probability p had changed to some value q. Here we consider pairs of messages (X_i, Y_j) and we attach the probability p_{ij} to the occurrence of such a pair. This means that such message pairs and their probabilities should be compared with the events and their probabilities of Sections 1.1 and 2.1. It should be stressed that the interpretation in terms of messages sent and received only serves to make the exposition more specific. The basic objective is to analyze the informational measures that are based on the array $[p_{ij}]$ of the bivariate probabilities.

Joint and Marginal Entropies

Define $p_{i.}$ and $p_{.j}$ as the probabilities of the two marginal distributions:

$$p_{i.} = \sum_{j=1}^{n} p_{ij} \qquad\qquad (i = 1, \ldots, m)$$

(1.1)

$$p_{.j} = \sum_{i=1}^{m} p_{ij} \qquad\qquad (j = 1, \ldots, n)$$

The entropies of the two marginal distributions (to be abbreviated as the marginal entropies) are

(1.2) $$H(X) = \sum_{i=1}^{m} p_{i.} \log \frac{1}{p_{i.}} \qquad H(Y) = \sum_{j=1}^{n} p_{.j} \log \frac{1}{p_{.j}}$$

where X and Y to the left of the equality signs stand for the sets of messages sent and of messages received, respectively. The entropy $H(X)$ measures the uncertainty of the message sent (irrespective of the message received) and $H(Y)$ performs the same role for the message received.

The joint entropy is the entropy of the joint distribution of the messages sent and received:

(1.3) $$H(X, Y) = \sum_{i=1}^{m} \sum_{j=1}^{n} p_{ij} \log \frac{1}{p_{ij}}$$

This $H(X, Y)$ measures the uncertainty of the messages sent and received simultaneously. Since the number of possible outcomes is mn in the joint distribution, the maximum value of $H(X, Y)$ is $\log mn = \log m + \log n$, which is the maximum of $H(X)$ plus the maximum of $H(Y)$. The relationship between these three entropies will be pursued further in the subsections that follow.

Conditional Distributions and Conditional Entropies

Consider $p_{ij}/p_{i.}$, the conditional probability that Y_j is the message received when it is given that X_i is the message sent. Take a fixed X_i and let Y_j vary over the set of messages received. This leads to the conditional distribution of the messages received, given that X_i is sent, with probabilities $p_{i1}/p_{i.}, \ldots, p_{in}/p_{i.}$. The entropy of this distribution is

(1.4) $$H_{X_i}(Y) = \sum_{j=1}^{n} \frac{p_{ij}}{p_{i.}} \log \frac{p_{i.}}{p_{ij}} \qquad\qquad i = 1, \ldots, m$$

This is the conditional entropy of Y given $X = X_i$. It measures the uncertainty of the message received under the condition that X_i is the message sent.

Similarly, consider $p_{ij}/p_{.j}$, the conditional probability that X_i is the message sent given that Y_j is the message received. The associated entropy is

$$(1.5) \qquad H_{Y_j}(X) = \sum_{i=1}^{m} \frac{p_{ij}}{p_{.j}} \log \frac{p_{.j}}{p_{ij}} \qquad j = 1, \ldots, n$$

which is the conditional entropy of the message sent (X), given that the message received is Y_j.

Average Conditional Entropies

The conditional entropy (1.4) measures the uncertainty of Y only under the condition $X = X_i$. We know that this condition is satisfied with probability $p_{i.}$. Therefore we define the *average* conditional entropy of Y given X as

$$(1.6) \qquad H_X(Y) = \sum_{i=1}^{m} p_{i.} H_{X_i}(Y) = \sum_{i=1}^{m} \sum_{j=1}^{n} p_{ij} \log \frac{p_{i.}}{p_{ij}}$$

This $H_X(Y)$ does not measure the uncertainty of the message received given a *particular* message sent. Such uncertainties vary, in general, with the messages sent, and $H_X(Y)$ measures the average uncertainty of the message received given the message sent, averaged over all m messages sent.

In the same way we have the average conditional entropy of X given Y, based on (1.5):

$$(1.7) \qquad H_Y(X) = \sum_{j=1}^{n} p_{.j} H_{Y_j}(X) = \sum_{i=1}^{m} \sum_{j=1}^{n} p_{ij} \log \frac{p_{.j}}{p_{ij}}$$

which measures the uncertainty of the message sent that prevails, on the average, when it is known which is the message received.

Since $H_X(Y)$ and $H_Y(X)$ are both obtained by averaging nonnegative conditional entropies with nonnegative weights, they must also be nonnegative. We have $H_X(Y) = 0$ if and only if $H_{X_i}(Y) = 0$ holds for each X_i for which $p_{i.} > 0$. That is, there is a zero average conditional entropy of Y given X if and only if it is certain (unit probability) what value Y will take when the X value is given, for whatever X value that has nonzero probability. The interpretation of the case $H_Y(X) = 0$ is analogous. Note that we may have $H_Y(X) = 0$ but $H_X(Y) > 0$, or vice versa. An example $(m = 2, n = 3)$ is shown below, with no uncertainty of X given Y but with uncertainty of Y given $X = X_1$.

	$Y = Y_1$	$Y = Y_2$	$Y = Y_3$
$X = X_1$	$p_{11} = .1$	$p_{12} = 0$	$p_{13} = .7$
$X = X_2$	$p_{21} = 0$	$p_{22} = .2$	$p_{23} = 0$

*An Average Conditional Entropy Never Exceeds the Corresponding Uncondi-
tional Entropy* . . .

The lower limit of $H_X(Y)$ and $H_Y(X)$ is thus zero, which is attained when
there is certainty of Y and of X, respectively, for every value of the conditioning factor. We proceed to prove that the corresponding unconditional
(marginal) entropies are the upper limits:

$$(1.8) \qquad H_X(Y) \leqq H(Y) \qquad H_Y(X) \leqq H(X)$$

and that these limits are attained if and only if the messages sent and the
messages received are stochastically independent.

We confine ourselves to the first inequality in (1.8); the proof of the second
is entirely analogous. Consider the difference of the two sides of the inequality:

$$(1.9) \qquad H(Y) - H_X(Y) = \sum_{j=1}^{n} p_{.j} \log \frac{1}{p_{.j}} - \sum_{i=1}^{m} \sum_{j=1}^{n} p_{ij} \log \frac{p_{i.}}{p_{ij}}$$

$$= \sum_{i=1}^{m} \sum_{j=1}^{n} p_{ij} \left(\log \frac{1}{p_{.j}} + \log \frac{p_{ij}}{p_{i.}} \right)$$

$$= \sum_{i=1}^{m} \sum_{j=1}^{n} p_{ij} \log \frac{p_{ij}}{p_{i.} p_{.j}}$$

The expression in the last line is nonnegative, because it may be interpreted
as the expected information of the message (a message in the sense of Section 2.1!) which transforms the mn prior probabilities $p_{i.} p_{.j}$:

$$p_1.p_{.1}, \cdots, p_1.p_{.n}, p_2.p_{.1}, \cdots, p_2.p_{.n} \cdot \cdots, p_m.p_{.1}, \cdots, p_m.p_{.n}$$

into the mn posterior probabilities p_{ij}:

$$p_{11}, \cdots, p_{1n}, p_{21}, \cdots, p_{2n}, \cdots, p_{m1}, \cdots, p_{mn}$$

The expression in the third line of (1.9) is identical with the right-hand side
of eq. (1.4) of Section 2.1 when we interpret the present probabilities $p_{i.} p_{.j}$
and p_{ij} as p_i and q_i, respectively.[1] Our conclusion is that the entropy differ-

---

[1] Whenever it is claimed that an expression of the form

$$(1) \qquad \sum_i A_i \log \frac{A_i}{B_i}$$

can be regarded as the expected information of the message that transforms the B's into
the A's, it is important to verify (i) that both the A's and the B's are nonnegative and (ii)
that the A's (and similarly the B's) add up to unity when summed in accordance with the
summation sign in (1). Condition (i) is obviously satisfied by the expression in the last
line of (1.9). For condition (ii) we note that there is a summation both over i and over j
in (1.9), and when this is applied to $p_{i.} p_{.j}$ and to p_{ij}, we obtain 1 in both cases.

ence (1.9) is positive except when

$$(1.10) \qquad p_{ij} = p_{i.}p_{.j} \quad \text{for each pair} \quad (i,j)$$

in which case the equality sign applies in (1.8). Condition (1.10) is equivalent to stochastic independence of the set of messages sent and that of the messages received.

... but an Individual Conditional Entropy May Exceed the Unconditional Entropy

The above result implies that knowledge of X reduces the uncertainty of Y, on the average, below the level of uncertainty that prevailed prior to the knowledge of X (except when X and Y are stochastically independent, in which case this knowledge is of no use for Y). This is intuitively plausible. Note, however, that this holds only *on the average*; the uncertainty of Y given a particular value of X may well be larger than the unconditional entropy of Y.[1] To illustrate this we consider the following 2×2 example:

	$Y = Y_1$	$Y = Y_2$	
$X = X_1$	$p_{11} = .25$	$p_{12} = .25$	$p_{1.} = .5$
$X = X_2$	$p_{21} = .5$	$p_{22} = 0$	$p_{2.} = .5$
	$p_{.1} = .75$	$p_{.2} = .25$	

The unconditional entropy of Y is

$$H(Y) = \tfrac{3}{4} \log \tfrac{4}{3} + \tfrac{1}{4} \log 4 \approx .81 \text{ bit}$$

The conditional entropies of Y given $X = X_1$ and $X = X_2$ are 1 bit and zero, respectively, so that $H_X(Y) = \tfrac{1}{2}(1) + \tfrac{1}{2}(0) = \tfrac{1}{2}$ bit. This is indeed smaller than $H(Y) \approx .81$ bit, as it should be. However, the conditional entropy of Y given $X = X_1$ is 1 bit and is thus larger than the unconditional entropy. Knowledge of X therefore raises the uncertainty of Y when this knowledge amounts to $X = X_1$; there is a reduction of uncertainty in the case $X = X_2$, and the uncertainty reduction $H(Y) - H_X(Y) \approx .31$ bit is only an *average* uncertainty reduction.

Average Conditional Entropies and the Joint Entropy

The third member of eq. (1.6) can be written as

$$\sum_{i=1}^{m} \sum_{j=1}^{n} p_{ij} \log \frac{1}{p_{ij}} - \sum_{i=1}^{m} \sum_{j=1}^{n} p_{ij} \log \frac{1}{p_{i.}} = \sum_{i=1}^{m} \sum_{j=1}^{n} p_{ij} \log \frac{1}{p_{ij}} - \sum_{i=1}^{m} p_{i.} \log \frac{1}{p_{i.}}$$

---

[1] Basically, the point made here is the same as that made in the discussion of eqs. (1.8) to (1.10) of Section 1.1.

This proves

(1.11) $$H_X(Y) = H(X, Y) - H(X)$$

A similar derivation based on (1.7) gives

(1.12) $$H_Y(X) = H(X, Y) - H(Y)$$

and these two results can also be written in the following form:

(1.13) $$H(X, Y) = H(X) + H_X(Y) = H(Y) + H_Y(X)$$

The first equality sign in (1.13) states that when we are first informed which message was sent and next which message was received, the sum of the two information expectations is equal to the expectation of the information received when it is stated immediately which message was sent and which message was received. The second equality sign implies that it is immaterial whether we hear first about the message sent and later about the message received or conversely.

Note that (1.13) in conjunction with (1.8) implies

(1.14) $$H(X, Y) \leqq H(X) + H(Y)$$

with the equal sign applying if and only if X and Y are stochastically independent. Thus, the joint entropy of a bivariate distribution is always smaller than the sum of the marginal entropies except when there is stochastic independence. This is an intuitively plausible result. When X and Y are dependent, knowledge of X implies some degree of knowledge of Y (and vice versa), so that the uncertainty of the random pair (X, Y) is less than the sum of the uncertainties of X and Y separately.

Equations (1.11) and (1.12) provide a simple way to compute an average conditional entropy from unconditional entropies. Note that the probabilities of the distributions whose entropies occur in the right-hand side of (1.11) are of the form p_{ij} and $p_{i.}$, and that by taking their ratio we obtain $p_{ij}/p_{i.}$ which is a probability of one of the distributions whose average entropy occurs on the left. In (1.11) we subtract rather than divide, which is in accordance with the additivity of the logarithmic information concept.

Decomposition of the Joint Entropy

The decomposition of bivariate information measures is straightforward. We shall illustrate this here for the joint entropy; see Problem 2 at the end of this chapter for the expected information of a message which transforms prior to posterior probabilities in the bivariate case.

Let us combine the messages sent $X_1, \ldots, X_m$ to groups $S_1, \ldots, S_G$ and the messages received $Y_1, \ldots, Y_n$ to groups $T_1, \ldots, T_H$ in such a way that each X_i falls under exactly one S_g and each Y_j under exactly one T_h, where $g = 1, \ldots, G$ and $h = 1, \ldots, H$. Define P_{gh} as the joint probability of a message sent which is part of S_g and a message received which is part of T_h:

$$(1.15) \qquad P_{gh} = \sum_{i \in S_g} \sum_{j \in T_h} p_{ij} \qquad \begin{array}{l} g = 1, \ldots, G \\ h = 1, \ldots, H \end{array}$$

The bivariate entropy at the level of message groups is thus

$$(1.16) \qquad \sum_{g=1}^{G} \sum_{h=1}^{G} P_{gh} \log \frac{1}{P_{gh}}$$

To establish the link between this entropy and the corresponding entropy (1.3) at the level of individual messages, we write the latter as follows:

$$(1.17) \quad H(X, Y) = \sum_{g=1}^{G} \sum_{h=1}^{H} P_{gh} \sum_{i \in S_g} \sum_{j \in T_h} \frac{p_{ij}}{P_{gh}} \left(\log \frac{1}{P_{gh}} + \log \frac{P_{gh}}{p_{ij}} \right)$$

$$= \sum_{g=1}^{G} \sum_{h=1}^{H} P_{gh} \log \frac{1}{P_{gh}}$$

$$+ \sum_{g=1}^{G} \sum_{h=1}^{H} P_{gh} \left[\sum_{i \in S_g} \sum_{j \in T_h} \frac{p_{ij}}{P_{gh}} \log \frac{P_{gh}}{p_{ij}} \right]$$

This means that the joint entropy $H(X, Y)$ of the messages sent and received is equal to the expression (1.16), the joint entropy at the level of message groups, plus a weighted average of the GH expressions in brackets in the last line, one for each pair (S_g, T_h). Each such expression is a conditional joint entropy of messages sent and received, the condition being that the message sent belongs to S_g and the message received to T_h. This result implies that $H(X, Y)$ is never smaller, and usually larger, than the joint entropy (1.16), which is intuitively plausible given that $H(X, Y)$ measures the uncertainty at a more detailed level than does the latter entropy. The two entropies are equal if and only if for each pair (S_g, T_h), at most one p_{ij} with $i \in S_g$ and $j \in T_h$ is nonzero.

3.2. Application to Chicago's Public Schools and to Industrial Diversity

The objective of this section is to show that the informational measures of racial integration, racial segregation, and industrial diversity that were developed in the two previous chapters have a simple interpretation in terms of average conditional entropies.

The Average Racial Entropy of the Schools

In Section 1.4 we divided the student body of each school into groups according to race, which suggests that the problem considered there is one-dimensional. However, it may also be argued that we actually considered a two-dimensional classification of the student population: according to the school which the student attends and the race to which he belongs. Recall that w_j stands for the share of the jth school of the city's student population and p_j for the proportion of black students in that school. The bivariate array of proportions p_{ij} is then as shown below.

	Black	White
First school	$w_1 p_1$	$w_1(1-p_1)$
Second school	$w_2 p_2$	$w_2(1-p_2)$
.	.	.
.	.	.
.	.	.
N^{th} school	$w_N p_N$	$w_N(1-p_N)$

Write L for the school, which takes N values $(L_1, \ldots, L_N)$, and R for race, which takes two values (black and white). Consider then the joint entropy of these two variables as defined in (1.3) with p_{ij} interpreted in accordance with the above array of proportions:

$$(2.1) \quad H(L, R) = \sum_{j=1}^{N} w_j p_j \log \frac{1}{w_j p_j} + \sum_{j=1}^{N} w_j(1-p_j) \log \frac{1}{w_j(1-p_j)}$$

$$= \sum_{j=1}^{N} w_j \left[p_j \log \frac{1}{p_j} + (1-p_j) \log \frac{1}{1-p_j} \right]$$

$$+ \sum_{j=1}^{N} w_j(p_j + 1 - p_j) \log \frac{1}{w_j}$$

The expression in the second line is nothing but $\bar{H}$, the city average of the racial entropies of the schools defined in eq. (4.4) of Section 1.4. The expression in the last line can be simplified to $-\sum w_j \log w_j = H(L)$, the school entropy. Hence we have proved:

$$(2.2) \qquad\qquad \bar{H} = H(L, R) - H(L) = H_L(R)$$

which means that the city average of the racial entropies of the schools is simply the average conditional entropy of race, given the schools. The latter entropy measures how much uncertainty there is as to the race of a randomly selected student, on the average, when we know which school he attends. Clearly, the larger this uncertainty, the more the schools are integrated.

The analogous average racial entropy of the schools of a district can similarly be described as the average conditional entropy of race, given the schools of this district (see Problem 3). It is interesting in this connection to go back to the paragraph between eqs. (4.1) and (4.2) of Section 1.4, where we discussed what kind of average is appropriate for the average racial entropy of the schools. The result obtained here provides an additional justification of the choice made.

The City Average of the Segregation Values

Consider $\overline{K} - \overline{H}$, the city average of the differences between the racial entropies of the school districts and the average racial entropies of the corresponding schools, which was used in Section 2.2 as a measure for the segregation in the city as a whole. Using eqs. (2.3) and (2.2) of that section for $\overline{K}$, we can write this expression as

$$(2.3) \qquad \overline{K} - \overline{H} = \sum_{r=1}^{27} W_r \left[P_r \log \frac{1}{P_r} + (1 - P_r) \log \frac{1}{1 - P_r} \right] - H_L(R)$$

where use is made of the result $\overline{H} = H_L(R)$ proved in the previous subsection. The first term in the right-hand side is concerned with the bivariate array of proportions that refer to school district and race:

	Black	White
First district	$W_1 P_1$	$W_1(1 - P_1)$
Second district	$W_2 P_2$	$W_2(1 - P_2)$
.	.	.
.	.	.
.	.	.
27th district	$W_{27} P_{27}$	$W_{27}(1 - P_{27})$

Since the first right-hand term of (2.3) is of precisely the same form as the expression in the second line of (2.1), the only difference being that it refers to districts rather than schools, we may conclude from the developments of the previous subsection that this term is equal to

$$H(D, R) - H(D) = H_D(R)$$

where D stands for the district variable (which takes the values $D_1, \ldots, D_{27}$). So we can simplify (2.3) to

$$(2.4) \qquad \overline{K} - \overline{H} = H_D(R) - H_L(R)$$

with the following interpretation. There is zero segregation in the city as a whole when its student body has an average conditional entropy of race given the districts which is equal to the average conditional entropy of race given the schools. There is a positive level of segregation when the former average conditional entropy exceeds the latter, as is usually the case. The reason is that the condition "given the schools" is more specific than "given the districts", so that there is on the average less uncertainty as to the race of a randomly selected student when the school is given than when the school district is given. This conclusion is incorrect if and only if all schools of each district have the same racial composition; this is the case of zero segregation. Otherwise the value is positive, and it is larger when the difference between the two average conditional entropies is larger.

Industrial Diversity

We return to the set C_{ab} of SMSA's and write C ("city") for the SMSA variable and I for the industry variable. Recall that p_{si} stands for the number of workers in the sth SMSA and the ith industry and $q_{ab.}$ for the total number of those in C_{ab}, both measured as a proportion of the total number of workers in all SMSA's and all 23 industries. Hence $p_{si}/q_{ab.}$ is the share of the sth SMSA and the ith industry of the total of C_{ab}. The joint entropy of C and I in C_{ab} is thus

$$(2.5) \qquad H_{ab}(C, I) = \sum_{s \in C_{ab}} \sum_{i=1}^{23} \frac{p_{si}}{q_{ab.}} \log \frac{q_{ab.}}{p_{si}}$$

and the marginal entropy of C in the same set of SMSA's:

$$(2.6) \qquad H_{ab}(C) = \sum_{s \in C_{ab}} \frac{p_{s.}}{q_{ab.}} \log \frac{q_{ab.}}{p_{s.}}$$

where $p_{s.}$ is the sum over i of p_{si}. By subtracting $H_{ab}(C)$ from $H_{ab}(C, I)$ we obtain the average conditional entropy of employment given the SMSA's:

$$H_{ab}(C, I) - H_{ab}(C) = \sum_{s \in C_{ab}} \frac{p_{s.}}{q_{ab.}} \sum_{i=1}^{23} \frac{p_{si}}{p_{s.}} \left(\log \frac{q_{ab.}}{p_{si}} - \log \frac{q_{ab.}}{p_{s.}} \right)$$

$$= \sum_{s \in C_{ab}} \frac{p_{si.}}{q_{ab.}} \sum_{i=1}^{23} \frac{p_{si}}{p_{s.}} \log \frac{p_{s.}}{p_{si}}$$

The expression in the last line is, in view of eqs. (6.9) and (6.2) of Section 1.6, nothing but the average employment entropy of the SMSA's of C_{ab}.

This proves

$$(2.7) \qquad \overline{H}_{ab} = H_{ab}(C, I) - H_{ab}(C)$$

The interpretation is again straightforward. The expression in the right-hand side is the average conditional entropy of employment, given the SMSA's of C_{ab}, and it thus measures how much uncertainty there is, on the average, as to the industry of a randomly selected worker when it is known in which SMSA he is living. Clearly, the less this uncertainty, the more these SMSA's are specialized.

As a measure of the industrial diversity *between* the SMSA's of C_{ab} we used the expression $K_{ab} - \overline{H}_{ab}$ defined in eq. (3.5) of Section 2.3, where K_{ab} is the employment entropy of C_{ab}. It is readily verified that K_{ab} is nothing but $H_{ab}(I)$, the marginal entropy of employment in C_{ab}. Combining this result with (2.7), we conclude that $K_{ab} - \overline{H}_{ab}$ is equal to the excess of the unconditional employment entropy of C_{ab} over the average conditional employment entropy given the SMSA's. When this excess is small, knowledge of the worker's domicile is of little value for the answer to the question in which industry he is employed. Evidently, this means that there is little difference between the employment distributions of the SMSA's of C_{ab}.

The above two paragraphs are confined to the 23 industries. For analogous developments at the level of the six industry groups and of the industries within each group, see Problem 4.

3.3. The Expected Mutual Information

Mutual Information and Expected Mutual Information

We return to the messages sent $X_1, \ldots, X_m$ and the messages received $Y_1, \ldots, Y_n$ and consider

$$(3.1) \qquad \log \frac{p_{ij}}{p_{i.} p_{.j}} \qquad \begin{array}{l} i = 1, \ldots, m \\ j = 1, \ldots, n \end{array}$$

This logarithm is known as the *mutual information* of the message sent X_i and the message received Y_j. Its value is zero when the two sets of messages are stochastically independent. It is positive when Y_j is more frequently the message received, given that X_i is the message sent, than the independence pattern implies, and it is negative in the opposite case.

When we average all mn mutual information values with the corresponding probabilities p_{ij} as weights, we obtain

$$(3.2) \qquad J(X, Y) = \sum_{i=1}^{m} \sum_{j=1}^{n} p_{ij} \log \frac{p_{ij}}{p_{i.} p_{.j}}$$

which is the *expected mutual information*. The right-hand side is identical with the expression in the last line of (1.9), and it follows from the discussion below that equation that $J(X, Y) = 0$ when X and Y are independent, and $J(X, Y) > 0$ otherwise. We may also conclude from (1.9):

$$(3.3) \qquad J(X, Y) = H(Y) - H_X(Y) = H(X) - H_Y(X)$$

The second equality sign in (3.3) follows from the fact that $J(X, Y)$ as defined in (3.2) is symmetric in X and Y. The first equality sign may be interpreted in the sense that $J(X, Y)$ measures the average reduction of the uncertainty of Y when X becomes known. Given the symmetry just mentioned, this is identical with the average reduction of the uncertainty of X when Y becomes known.

By combining (1.13) and (3.3) we obtain

$$(3.4) \qquad H(X, Y) = H(X) + H(Y) - J(X, Y)$$

This means that the expected mutual information is the amount to be subtracted from the total marginal entropy, $H(X) + H(Y)$, in order to obtain the joint entropy. This amount is zero when X and Y are independent, and positive otherwise.

The Expected Mutual Information as a Measure of Dependence

In fact, $J(X, Y)$ can be used as a measure for the degree to which the probability array $[p_{ij}]$ is characterized by dependence rather than independence. It is comparable in this respect with the product-moment correlation coefficient in the same way that the entropy is comparable with the variance in that both are measures of the uncertainty of the random outcome. The correlation coefficient and the variance can only be used when the underlying random variables take real values, but the expected mutual information and the entropy can also be applied to random variables that take qualitative values, because they depend exclusively on probabilities.

The simplest way to assess the sensitivity of $J(X, Y)$ for departures from stochastic independence is by means of the quadratic approximation given in eq. (1.12) of Section 2.1:

$$(3.5) \quad J(X, Y) \approx \tfrac{1}{2} \sum_{i=1}^{m} \sum_{j=1}^{n} p_{ij} \left(\frac{p_{ij} - p_{i.} p_{.j}}{p_{ij}} \right)^2 = \tfrac{1}{2} \sum_{i=1}^{m} \sum_{j=1}^{n} \frac{(p_{ij} - p_{i.} p_{.j})^2}{p_{ij}}$$

The expression in the middle indicates that a given *relative* discrepancy of p_{ij} from the independence value $p_{i.}p_{.j}$ has a small weight when p_{ij} is small. The third member implies that a given *absolute* discrepancy of p_{ij} from that value has a large weight when p_{ij} is small. Note that the approximation (3.5) is accurate only when such discrepancies are not too large. Note also that it is understood that natural logarithms (nits) are used.

Application to Federal Grants to The University of Chicago

It is frequently argued that one of the felicitous aspects of American higher education is the fact that grants do not come from one source but from several, so that undesirable pressures by one donor can be avoided by recourse to another. Bivariate informational measures provide a convenient tool for the analysis of the financial ties of donors and recipients. This will be illustrated by means of data on current annual levels of Federal grants to The University of Chicago, shown in Table 3.1 and obtained from the Office of the Vice-President for Programs and Projects of the University. Seven major sources will be considered:

HEW   (Department of Health, Education, and Welfare)
NSF   (National Science Foundation)
DoD   (Department of Defense)
AEC   (Atomic Energy Commission)
NASA   (National Aeronautics and Space Administration)
DoC   (Department of Commerce)
OEO   (Office of Economic Opportunity)

and also seven major recipients:

  – Four graduate divisions (of Biological Sciences, Physical
    Sciences, Social Sciences, and Humanities)
  – Two professional schools (Social Service Administration
    and Education)
  – The Office of Admissions and Aid.

Table 3.1 shows that the total amounts increased from about 30 to almost 40 million dollars per year from 1965 to 1969. These amounts are between 13 and 15 per cent less than the total of all Federal grants to the University, because grants from minor donors and to minor recipients are disregarded.

The individual conditional entropies (in nits) are displayed in Table 3.2. The top row of this table contains the conditioning factor, indicated by a number in parentheses; this number refers to the source or the destination

TABLE 3.1

FEDERAL GRANTS TO THE UNIVERSITY OF CHICAGO, BY SOURCE AND BY DESTINATION

(Current annual levels in thousands of dollars per year)

Source	Graduate Divisions				Professional Schools		Admissions and Aid	Total
	Biological Sciences	Physical Sciences	Social Sciences	Humanities	Social Service Admin.	Education		
1965								
HEW	10833	301	2064	281	1162	403	496	15540
NSF	585	2616	71	71	0	0	597	3940
DoD	747	3719	69	0	0	0	105	4640
AEC	149	1306	6	0	0	0	0	1455
NASA	195	3125	0	0	0	0	311	3631
DoC	0	199	0	0	0	0	0	199
OEO	0	0	51	0	0	86	0	137
Total	12509	11266	2255	352	1162	489	1509	29542
1966								
HEW	12227	264	2579	302	999	760	878	18009
NSF	385	3001	538	107	0	87	823	4941
DoD	735	3699	109	0	0	0	87	4630
AEC	88	1379	0	0	0	0	0	1467
NASA	200	2505	0	0	0	0	311	3016
DoC	0	195	129	0	0	0	0	324
OEO	0	0	47	0	0	133	0	180

NSF	552	4619	904	108	0	213	864	7260
DoD	690	2561	142	0	0	79	86	3558
AEC	33	1640	0	0	0	0	0	1673
NASA	200	1886	109	0	0	0	186	2272
DoC	0	210	0	0	0	0	0	319
OEO	156	0	0	0	0	212	0	368
Total	15662	11233	3340	450	1224	1686	2435	36030

1968

HEW	14969	290	2319	347	1368	1092	1427	21812
NSF	680	5034	964	109	0	156	877	7820
DoD	616	2282	58	0	0	80	11	3047
AEC	42	1677	0	0	0	0	0	1719
NASA	200	2260	0	0	0	0	165	2625
DoC	0	208	211	0	0	0	0	419
OEO	99	0	0	0	68	145	0	312
Total	16606	11751	3552	456	1436	1473	2480	37754

1969

HEW	14770	362	3234	343	1536	1211	1882	23338
NSF	752	4822	671	92	0	0	760	7097
DoD	567	2177	0	0	0	0	0	2744
AEC	99	1666	0	0	0	0	0	1765
NASA	235	2735	0	0	0	0	62	3032
DoC	0	139	111	0	0	0	0	250
OEO	204	0	0	0	0	0	0	204
Total	16627	11901	4016	435	1536	1211	2704	38430

TABLE 3.2

CONDITIONAL ENTROPIES OF GRANTS, GIVEN SOURCES OR DESTINATIONS
(in nits)

	(1)	(2)	(3)	(4)	(5)	(6)	(7)
	Conditional entropy of the destination, given the source						
1965	1.07	.99	.62	.33	.50	0	.66
1966	1.11	1.20	.63	.23	.57	.67	.57
1967	1.14	1.16	.86	.10	.57	.64	.68
1968	1.12	1.14	.73	.11	.50	.69	1.05
1969	1.23	1.02	.51	.22	.37	.69	0
	Conditional entropy of the source, given the destination						
1965	.55	1.48	.38	.50	0	.47	1.24
1966	.45	1.48	.80	.57	0	.68	1.15
1967	.47	1.46	.88	.55	0	.91	1.02
1968	.45	1.44	.87	.55	.19	.85	.89
1969	.51	1.45	.57	.52	0	0	.70

that corresponds to the successive rows or columns, respectively, of Table 3.1. The results indicate that only HEW and NSF have destination entropies that are consistently of the order of 1 nit or higher. The lower part of the table shows that the Division of Biological Sciences (the largest recipient) has a donor entropy which is only about one-third of that of the Division of Physical Sciences (the second largest recipient). This is obviously due to the heavy reliance of the former Division on HEW and the much more diversified sources of the latter (NSF, DoD, and NASA). Note also the decline of the source entropy of student financial aid (last column). An inspection of Table 3.1 reveals that this is in large measure due to the increasing role of HEW.

Table 3.3 contains the five unconditional and average conditional entropies as well as the expected mutual information. The figures indicate that the unconditional entropy of the source, indicated by X in the table, declined steadily during the five years, and that this is also true for $H_Y(X)$, the corresponding average conditional entropy given the destination (Y). This means that the financial diversity that was alluded to in the beginning of this subsection was subject to a decreasing trend, at least with respect to Federal sources. [A more exhaustive analysis would have to take Foundation and other private grants also into consideration.] The expected mutual informa-

TABLE 3.3

UNCONDITIONAL AND AVERAGE CONDITIONAL ENTROPIES OF GRANTS
(in nits)

	$H(X, Y)$	$H(X)$	$H_Y(X)$	$H(Y)$	$H_X(Y)$	$J(X, Y)$
1965	2.232	1.362	.905	1.328	.871	.457
1966	2.285	1.326	.874	1.411	.960	.451
1967	2.299	1.277	.858	1.441	1.022	.419
1968	2.261	1.262	.831	1.430	.999	.431
1969	2.218	1.206	.782	1.437	1.013	.424

tion was a little over .4 nit during this period. To understand the implications of this figure, note that $J(X, Y)$ is at most equal to the smaller of the two marginal entropies:

$$(3.6) \qquad J(X, Y) \leqq \text{Min } [H(X), H(Y)]$$

This follows from (3.4) combined with $H(X, Y) - H(X) = H_X(Y) \geqq 0$ and $H(X, Y) - H(Y) = H_Y(X) \geqq 0$. Hence the equality sign applies in (3.6) when either each donor has only one recipient or each recipient has only one donor. Table 3.3 shows that the smaller of $H(X)$ and $H(Y)$ is about three times as large as $J(X, Y)$ in each of the five years, which may be interpreted in the sense that the source-destination pattern analyzed here is about three times closer to source-destination independence than to the other extreme of one-recipient-only or one-donor-only.

3.4. The Analysis and Prediction of Changes in Two-dimensional Decompositions

The upper half of Table 3.4 contains the numbers of workers in seven non-agricultural industry groups and nine regions of the United States in 1960 and 1966,[1] In this section we consider the problem of how changes in such

---

[1] The data are from the *Statistical Abstract of the United States* (1961 and 1967); the mining category has been combined with services and miscellaneous. The geographical division is the following. *North-East*: Connecticut, Maine, Massachusetts, New Hampshire, Rhode Island, Vermont. *Middle Atlantic*: New Jersey, New York, Pennsylvania. *East North Central*: Indiana, Illinois, Michigan, Ohio, Wisconsin. *West North Central*: Iowa, Kansas, Minnesota, Missouri, Nebraska, North Dakota, South Dakota. *South Atlantic*: Delaware, District of Columbia, Florida, Georgia, Maryland, North Carolina, South Carolina, Virginia, West Virginia. *East South Central*: Alabama, Kentucky, Mississippi, Tennessee. *West South Central*: Arkansas, Louisiana, Oklahoma, Texas. *Mountain*: Arizona, Colorado, Idaho, Montana, Nevada, New Mexico, Utah, Wyoming. *Pacific*: California, Oregon, Washington. Alaska and Hawaii are deleted in both years.

TABLE 3.4

EMPLOYMENT BY REGIONS AND INDUSTRY GROUPS IN THE UNITED STATES, 1960 AND 1966

Region	Contract construction	Manufacturing	Transportation and public utilities	Wholesale and retail trade	Finance, insurance and real estate	Service and miscellaneous	Government
Numbers of workers (in thousands) in 1960							
North East	163	1445	202	709	186	524	469
Middle Atlantic	524	4128	911	2325	726	1792	1508
East North Central	529	4460	796	2311	480	1420	1493
West North Central	238	996	375	1012	206	615	716
South Atlantic	456	2030	504	1511	329	1011	1347
East South Central	145	840	182	568	109	394	503
West South Central	275	820	386	1047	194	745	777
Mountain	140	262	166	435	81	372	415
Pacific	383	1689	466	1384	307	882	1131
Numbers of workers (in thousands) in 1966							
North East	187	1548	204	812	210	672	553
Middle Atlanctic	551	4334	912	2576	777	2136	1869
East North Central	584	5152	799	2699	556	1827	1909
West North Central	254	1174	362	1147	239	776	904
South Atlantic	587	2494	556	1852	413	1332	1788
East South Central	200	1105	195	663	135	492	647
West South Central	361	1049	403	1214	253	948	1000
Mountain	134	316	167	511	102	477	566
Pacific	393	1952	520	1679	395	1262	1528
Mutual informations (in nits) in 1960							
North East	−.190	.227	−.310	−.096	.028	−.022	−.208
Middle Atlantic	−.192	.107	.026	−.078	.220	.038	−.210
East North Central	−.146	.221	−.072	−.048	−.157	−.159	−.183
West North Central	.072	−.262	.191	.142	.013	.021	.098
South Atlantic	.174	−.097	−.060	−.004	−.066	−.029	.183
East South Central	−.007	−.016	−.115	−.018	−.207	−.008	.162
West South Central	.196	−.477	.200	.156	−.067	.192	.159
Mountain	.340	−.799	.175	.097	−.122	.317	.351
Pacific	.141	−.140	.002	.049	.006	−.025	.149
Mutual informations (in nits) in 1966							
North East	−.138	.204	−.287	−.067	.032	.026	−.251
Middle Atlantic	−.202	.088	.065	−.058	.196	.037	−.178
East North Central	−.172	.233	−.095	−.039	−.167	−.147	−.185
West North Central	.020	−.221	.138	.130	.013	.021	.092
South Atlantic	.238	−.087	−.052	−.010	−.059	−.058	.155
East South Central	.127	.064	−.135	−.073	−.212	−.089	.103
West South Central	.298	−.407	.171	.113	−.004	.147	.119
Mountain	.140	−.774	.123	.081	−.079	.294	.383
Pacific	−.008	−.177	.035	.046	.051	.043	.152

two-dimensional decompositions can be approximated by means of the marginal distributions, and also the problem of predicting these changes.

Changes in Mutual Informations

The table enables us to find out by how much the total number of workers increased from 1960 to 1966. Once we know this, the next important feature is the change in the proportions of workers in the various regions and industry groups. We shall indicate these proportions by p_{ij} for the first year (1960) and by q_{ij} for the last (1966), where $i = 1, \ldots, m \ (=9)$ refers to the region and $j = 1, \ldots, n \ (=7)$ to the industry group. The proportions of the marginal distributions are indicated in the usual way:

$$
\begin{aligned}
p_{i.} = \sum_{j=1}^{n} p_{ij} \qquad q_{i.} = \sum_{j=1}^{n} q_{ij} \qquad & i = 1, \ldots, m \\
p_{.j} = \sum_{i=1}^{m} p_{ij} \qquad q_{.j} = \sum_{i=1}^{m} q_{ij} \qquad & j = 1, \ldots, n
\end{aligned}
$$

(4.1)

For the analysis of the changes from the array $[p_{ij}]$ to the later array $[q_{ij}]$ it is important to note two things. First, such arrays are usually not characterized by stochastic independence, because certain industrial activities are more concentrated in some regions than in others. Second, this concentration pattern will typically change rather slowly over time. One way of measuring this region-industry dependence and its change is by means of the mutual information given in (3.1). These information values are shown in the lower half of Table 3.4; a positive (negative) sign indicates that the region's share of the industry is larger (smaller) than is in accordance with the region's size: $p_{ij}/p_{.j} \gtrless p_{i.}$.

Figure 3.1 is a scatter diagram with the 1960 mutual informations measured horizontally and those of 1966 measured vertically. The figure shows that most of the $9 \times 7 = 63$ points are located close to the line that makes an angle of 45 degrees with both axes. This suggests that the deviations from the independence pattern that prevailed in 1960 can be used to predict the corresponding deviations in 1966.

A Multiplicative Adjustment Procedure Based on Marginal Constraints

A simple way of exploiting the regularity revealed by Figure 3.1 is by approximating the 1966 array so that its mn mutual informations become equal to the corresponding information values of 1960. However, this is, in general, impossible when we also require that the approximation preserve

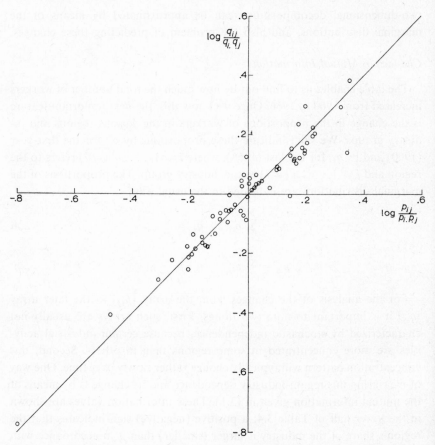

Fig. 3.1.   Mutual information values of employment by regions and industry groups in 1960 and in 1966

the observed marginal distributions, $q_{i.}$ and $q_{.j}$.[1] To prove this, write q'_{ij} for the adjusted value of the $(i, j)^{\text{th}}$ proportion in 1966, based on unchanged mutual information values and the observed marginal proportions $q_{i.}$ and $q_{.j}$,

$$\log \frac{q'_{ij}}{q_{i.} \, q_{.j}} = \log \frac{p_{ij}}{p_{i.} \, p_{.j}}$$

_____

[1] It is possible, however, to further adjust the approximations so that the marginal constraints are satisfied; see THEIL (1967, Sections 10.1 and 10.2).

Taking antilogs, we find that this amounts to the following adjustment rule:

$$(4.2) \qquad q'_{ij} = \frac{q_{i.}\, q_{.j}}{p_{i.}\, p_{.j}}\, p_{ij}$$

Summation of q'_{ij} over $j = 1, \ldots, n$ does not give $q_{i.}$, nor does summation over $i = 1, \ldots, m$ give $q_{.j}$. Hence there is indeed a conflict between (4.2) and the observed proportions of the marginal distributions, $q_{i.}$ and $q_{.j}$.

The constant-mutual-information approach imposes too many restrictions. An alternative approach which is preferable in this respect is the multiplicative adjustment procedure,

$$(4.3) \qquad \hat{q}_{ij} = r_i s_j p_{ij} \qquad \begin{array}{l} i = 1, \ldots, m \\ j = 1, \ldots, n \end{array}$$

where $r_1, \ldots, r_m, s_1, \ldots, s_n$ are coefficients which are fitted by imposing the marginal constraints:

$$(4.4) \qquad \sum_{j=1}^{n} \hat{q}_{ij} = q_{i.} \quad \text{or} \quad r_i \sum_{j=1}^{n} s_j p_{ij} = q_{i.} \qquad i = 1, \ldots, m$$

$$(4.5) \qquad \sum_{i=1}^{m} \hat{q}_{ij} = q_{.j} \quad \text{or} \quad s_j \sum_{i=1}^{m} r_i p_{ij} = q_{.j} \qquad j = 1, \ldots, n$$

This approach was applied by STONE and BROWN (1964) to the adjustment of input coefficients in input-output analysis.[1] An r_i larger than one indicates that the ith region has increased relative to the nation as a whole, and an $r_i < 1$ that it has declined in relative importance. The s_j's refer to industry groups and have an analogous interpretation. The method (4.3) adjusts the 1960 proportions in a multiplicative manner, and does so uniformly for each region and each industry group. It thus denies the possibility of a change in the region-industry interaction and this is, of course, the reason why $\hat{q}_{ij}$ is only an approximation to the observed (i, j)th proportion in 1966.

Application to the Employment Data

The number of parameters r_i, s_j is $m+n$, but there is one multiplicative degree of freedom due to the fact that each r_i may be multiplied by $c > 0$ and each s_j by $1/c$ without affecting $\hat{q}_{ij}$ for any pair (i, j). Hence there are

---

[1] Actually, methods of this kind date back to DEMING and STEPHAN (1940). See also MOSTELLER (1968) and FIENBERG (1970) as well as the references quoted in these articles.

only $m+n-1$ parameters to be adjusted. They are subject to m constraints (4.4) and n constraints (4.5). One of these constraints is redundant, however, because summation of the m equations (4.4) leads to an equation which states that the sum of all mn adjusted proportions is equal to one, and summation of the n equations (4.5) gives the same result. Hence there are $m+n-1$ parameters to be adjusted subject to the same number of constraints. This number is much smaller than the total number of proportions (mn) unless m and n are very small. Therefore, the adjustment procedure (4.3) implies an important reduction of the number of unknowns.

The following iterative procedure is efficient for the solution of the r_i's and s_j's. First, put $s_1 = \ldots = s_n = 1$ in (4.4), so that this equation gives a first solution of r_i. These solutions are substituted in (4.5) to give new values of the s_j's, which are in turn substituted in (4.4) to give new r_i's, and so on. The values after convergence are shown below.

$$
\begin{array}{llll}
r_1 = .9573 & r_6 = 1.0554 & s_1 = .9564 & s_6 = 1.0804 \\
r_2 = .9347 & r_7 = 1.0357 & s_2 = .9735 & s_7 = 1.0800 \\
r_3 = .9989 & r_8 = 1.0148 & s_3 = .8718 & \\
r_4 = .9856 & r_9 = 1.0434 & s_4 = .9808 & \\
r_5 = 1.0567 & & s_5 = .9983 &
\end{array}
$$

(4.6)

These figures indicate that the first four regions have all declined in importance relative to the last five, and that the third industry group (Transportation and public utilities) has declined rather considerably relative to the other six.

Given the r_i's and s_j's, one can compute the adjusted proportions from (4.3). Table 3.5 contains the observed proportions of 1960 on top, those of 1966 in the middle, and the $\hat{q}_{ij}$'s at the bottom. In a considerable majority of the $9 \times 7 = 63$ cases, $\hat{q}_{ij}$ is closer to q_{ij} than p_{ij} is, as one would expect. A more systematic comparison will be discussed later in this section.

The Mutual Information Changes Implied by the Adjustment Procedure

Since the relative constancy of the mutual information values was our point of departure, it is appropriate to ask what changes in these values are implied by the adjustment procedure. For this purpose we write (4.3) as follows:

$$
\frac{\hat{q}_{ij}}{q_{i.}q_{.j}} = \frac{p_{ij}}{p_{i.}p_{.j}} \frac{cr_i p_{i.}}{q_{i.}} \frac{s_j p_{.j}}{cq_{.j}}
$$

TABLE 3.5

OBSERVED AND ADJUSTED DISTRIBUTIONS OF WORKERS IN 1960 AND 1966, BY REGIONS AND
INDUSTRY GROUPS

Region	Contract construction	Manufacturing	Transportation and public utilities	Wholesale and retail trade	Finance, insurance and real estate	Service and miscellaneous	Government
Observed percentage distribution in 1960 ($100p_{ij}$)							
North East	.30	2.70	.38	1.32	.35	.98	.88
Middle Atlantic	.98	7.71	1.70	4.34	1.36	3.35	2.82
East North Central	.99	8.33	1.49	4.32	.90	2.65	2.79
West North Central	.44	1.86	.70	1.89	.38	1.15	1.34
South Atlantic	.85	3.79	.94	2.82	.61	1.89	2.52
East South Central	.27	1.57	.34	1.06	.20	.74	.94
West South Central	.51	1.53	.72	1.96	.36	1.39	1.45
Mountain	.26	.49	.31	.81	.15	.69	.78
Pacific	.72	3.15	.87	2.58	.57	1.65	2.11
Observed percentage distribution in 1966 ($100q_{ij}$)							
North East	.29	2.44	.32	1.28	.33	1.06	.87
Middle Atlantic	.87	6.83	1.44	4.06	1.23	3.37	2.95
East North Central	.92	8.12	1.26	4.26	.88	2.88	3.01
West North Central	.40	1.85	.57	1.81	.38	1.22	1.43
South Atlantic	.93	3.93	.88	2.92	.65	2.10	2.82
East South Central	.32	1.74	.31	1.05	.21	.78	1.02
West South Central	.57	1.65	.64	1.91	.40	1.49	1.58
Mountain	.21	.50	.26	.81	.16	.75	.89
Pacific	.62	3.08	.82	2.65	.62	1.99	2.41
Adjusted percentage distribution in 1966 ($100\hat{q}_{ij}$)							
North East	.28	2.51	.31	1.24	.33	1.01	.91
Middle Atlantic	.87	7.02	1.39	3.98	1.27	3.38	2.84
East North Central	.94	8.10	1.29	4.23	.89	2.86	3.01
West North Central	.42	1.78	.60	1.83	.38	1.22	1.42
South Atlantic	.86	3.90	.87	2.92	.65	2.16	2.87
East South Central	.27	1.61	.31	1.10	.21	.84	1.07
West South Central	.51	1.54	.65	1.99	.37	1.56	1.62
Mountain	.25	.48	.27	.81	.15	.76	.85
Pacific	.71	3.20	.79	2.65	.60	1.86	2.38

where c is an arbitrary positive number. Taking logarithms of both sides, we obtain

$$\log \frac{\hat{q}_{ij}}{q_{i.}\,q_{.j}} = \log \frac{p_{ij}}{p_{i.}\,p_{.j}} + \log \frac{cr_i\,p_{i.}}{q_{i.}} + \log \frac{s_j\,p_{.j}}{cq_{.j}}$$

or, equivalently,

(4.7) $$\log \frac{\hat{q}_{ij}}{q_{i.}\,q_{.j}} - \log \frac{p_{ij}}{p_{i.}\,p_{.j}} = \alpha_i + \beta_j \qquad \begin{array}{l} i = 1, \ldots, m \\ j = 1, \ldots, n \end{array}$$

where

(4.8)
$$\alpha_i = \log \frac{r_i\,p_{i.}}{q_{i.}} + \log c \qquad i = 1, \ldots, m$$

$$\beta_j = \log \frac{s_j\,p_{.j}}{q_{.j}} - \log c \qquad j = 1, \ldots, n$$

The left-hand side of (4.7) is the change in the $(i,j)^{\text{th}}$ mutual information value which is implied by the adjustment procedure. The equation thus states that this change is equal to a regional effect (α_i) plus an industry effect (β_j). Equation (4.8) indicates that these $m+n$ regional and industry effects are subject to an additive degree of freedom $(\log c)$. One way of obtaining unique values is by imposing the rule that the average of the α's be equal to the average of the β's:

(4.9) $$\frac{1}{m}\sum_{i=1}^{m}\alpha_i = \frac{1}{n}\sum_{j=1}^{n}\beta_j$$

This implies that $\log c$ is to be specified as

(4.10) $$\log c = -\frac{1}{2m}\sum_{i=1}^{m}\log\frac{r_i\,p_{i.}}{q_{i.}} + \frac{1}{2n}\sum_{j=1}^{n}\log\frac{s_j\,p_{.j}}{q_{.j}}$$

which in conjunction with (4.8) leads to unique values of the α_i's and β_j's once the r_i's and s_j's are known.

In our application we have the nine α_i's and seven β_j's listed below.

(4.11)

$\alpha_1 = .0020$	$\alpha_6 = -.0028$	$\beta_1 = -.0065$	$\beta_6 = -.0004$
$\alpha_2 = .0030$	$\alpha_7 = -.0039$	$\beta_2 = .0045$	$\beta_7 = -.0072$
$\alpha_3 = .0053$	$\alpha_8 = -.0103$	$\beta_3 = -.0007$	
$\alpha_4 = -.0000$	$\alpha_9 = -.0016$	$\beta_4 = -.0024$	
$\alpha_5 = -.0025$		$\beta_5 = .0044$	

The averages of the α's and of the β's are both equal to $-.0012$. The figures shown in (4.11) are typically between 10^{-3} and 10^{-2} in absolute value, so that $\alpha_i + \beta_j$, the change in the $(i, j)^{\text{th}}$ mutual information value implied by the adjustment procedure, is of the same low order of magnitude. A comparison with the 1960 mutual informations given in Table 3.4 indicates that for the data considered here, the adjustment (4.3) implies substantially unchanged mutual information values.

The Accuracy of the Adjustment Procedure

A simple measure for the fit of the adjustment is the two-dimensional information inaccuracy,

$$(4.12) \qquad I(q : \hat{q}) = \sum_{i=1}^{m} \sum_{j=1}^{n} q_{ij} \log \frac{q_{ij}}{\hat{q}_{ij}}$$

where q and $\hat{q}$ on the left stand for the arrays $[q_{ij}]$ and $[\hat{q}_{ij}]$, respectively. Then write (4.7) as follows:

$$\log \hat{q}_{ij} = \log p_{ij} + \log \frac{q_{i.}}{p_{i.}} + \log \frac{q_{.j}}{p_{.j}} + (\alpha_i + \beta_j)$$

and substitute the right-hand side for $\log \hat{q}_{ij}$ in (4.12):

$$I(q : \hat{q}) = \sum_{i=1}^{m} \sum_{j=1}^{n} q_{ij} \log \frac{q_{ij}}{p_{ij}} - \sum_{i=1}^{m} \sum_{j=1}^{n} q_{ij} \log \frac{q_{i.}}{p_{i.}}$$
$$- \sum_{i=1}^{m} \sum_{j=1}^{n} q_{ij} \log \frac{q_{.j}}{p_{.j}} - \sum_{i=1}^{m} \sum_{j=1}^{n} q_{ij}(\alpha_i + \beta_j)$$

This can be simplified to

$$(4.13) \qquad I(q : \hat{q}) = I(q : p) - \sum_{i=1}^{m} q_{i.} \log \frac{q_{i.}}{p_{i.}} - \sum_{j=1}^{n} q_{.j} \log \frac{q_{.j}}{p_{.j}}$$
$$- \left(\sum_{i=1}^{m} q_{i.} \alpha_i + \sum_{j=1}^{n} q_{.j} \beta_j \right)$$

where

$$(4.14) \qquad I(q : p) = \sum_{i=1}^{m} \sum_{j=1}^{n} q_{ij} \log \frac{q_{ij}}{p_{ij}}$$

is the information inaccuracy attained when the 1960 proportions are used without any modification. One may call $I(q:p)$ the inaccuracy that corresponds to no-change extrapolation.

Equation (4.13) states that the information inaccuracy of the adjustment procedure (4.3) is equal to that of no-change extrapolation minus the sum of three terms. The first two of these three are nonnegative; they are the one-dimensional information inaccuracies corresponding to the marginal distributions of 1960 used as predictors of the corresponding distributions of 1966. The last term refers to the α's and β's and thus represents the effect on $I(q:\hat{q})$ of the changes in the mutual information values implied by the adjustment procedure. We shall therefore call it the mutual information effect on $I(q:\hat{q})$; it may be of either sign.

In our application we have the following numerical values (in nits) for the decomposition (4.13):

$$(4.15) \qquad .00063 = .00353 - .00112 - .00190 + .00012$$

This shows that $I(q:\hat{q})$ is less than 20 per cent of $I(q:p)$ or, equivalently, that the two marginal distributions of 1966 jointly account for more than 80 per cent of the change in the bivariate distribution from 1960 to 1966. The second and third terms in the right-hand side are, apart from sign, the individual contributions of the two marginal distributions to the inaccuracy reduction. The mutual information effect cannot be allocated to either of these marginal distributions separately.[1] Its value is close to zero, as could be expected.

Predictions of Two-dimensional Decompositions Based on Predicted Marginal Distributions

An extension of the adjustment procedure (4.3) may be used to predict bivariate arrays on the basis of predicted marginal distributions. Specifically, consider a firm whose management wants a prediction of next year's sales by areas and product types. Let $[p_{ij}]$ be the observed array of proportions the year before, where i refers to the area and j to the product type. The array to be predicted is $[q_{ij}]$, and it is assumed that the firm's staff has provided predictions of the marginal proportions $q_{i.}$ and $q_{.j}$, to be denoted by $\hat{q}_{i.}$ and $\hat{q}_{.j}$. The problem is to obtain predictions $\hat{q}_{ij}$ of the bivariate proportions which satisfy the marginal constraints as predicted by the firm's staff.

The following prediction procedure, proposed by Lev (1970b), is a simple extension of the adjustment method described above. Consider eq. (4.3), where the r_i's and s_j's are determined from (4.4) and (4.5) except that $q_{i.}$

---

[1] One may think it worthwhile to separate the mutual information effect in terms of a regional effect ($\Sigma\, q_{i.}\, \alpha_i$) and an industry effect ($\Sigma\, q_{.j}\, \beta_j$), but this is essentially arbitrary because the result depends on the normalization rule chosen. The sum of the two is independent of this rule (see Problem 6).

and $q_{.j}$ in the right-hand sides are replaced by their predicted values. This modification leads to the following changes. First, the left-hand side of (4.7) becomes

$$\log \frac{\hat{q}_{ij}}{\hat{q}_{i.}\hat{q}_{.j}} - \log \frac{p_{ij}}{p_{i.}p_{.j}}$$

which is the predicted change in the mutual information. Second, $q_{i.}$ and $q_{.j}$ in (4.8) and (4.10) are replaced by $\hat{q}_{i.}$ and $\hat{q}_{.j}$, respectively. The predicted change in the mutual information is thus equal to an area effect (α_i) and a product effect (β_j), but the definition of the α's and β's is now in terms of $\hat{q}_{i.}$ and $\hat{q}_{.j}$.

Third, the modification of (4.7) implies that $I(q:\hat{q})$ of (4.12) becomes

$$I(q:\hat{q}) = \sum_{i=1}^{m}\sum_{j=1}^{n} q_{ij}\log \frac{q_{ij}}{p_{ij}} - \sum_{i=1}^{m}\sum_{j=1}^{n} q_{ij}\log \frac{\hat{q}_{i.}}{p_{i.}}$$

$$-\sum_{i=1}^{m}\sum_{j=1}^{n} q_{ij}\log \frac{\hat{q}_{.j}}{p_{.j}} - \sum_{i=1}^{m}\sum_{j=1}^{n} q_{ij}(\alpha_i + \beta_j)$$

which can be simplified to

(4.16) $$I(q:\hat{q}) = I(q:p) - \sum_{i=1}^{m} q_{i.}\log \frac{\hat{q}_{i.}}{p_{i.}} - \sum_{j=1}^{n} q_{.j}\log \frac{\hat{q}_{.j}}{p_{.j}}$$

$$-\left(\sum_{i=1}^{m} q_{i.}\alpha_i + \sum_{j=1}^{n} q_{.j}\beta_j\right)$$

A comparison with (4.13) shows that the second and third terms on the right are different. The present second term can be written as minus the following difference:

$$\sum_{i=1}^{m} q_{i.}\log \frac{q_{i.}}{p_{i.}} - \sum_{i=1}^{m} q_{i.}\log \frac{q_{i.}}{\hat{q}_{i.}}$$

which is simply the information improvement of the prediction $\hat{q}_{1.}, \ldots, \hat{q}_{m.}$ over the no-change extrapolation $p_{1.}, \ldots, p_{m.}$; see eq. (4.4) of Section 2.4. In contrast to the corresponding term in (4.13), this expression has no definite sign because the prediction may be worse than the no-change extrapolation.

Applications to Forecasts of Firms

The prediction procedure described in the previous subsection was applied by LEV to data obtained from several major Midwestern firms. Here we shall discuss briefly his results for three firms: a state-wide public utility, a manufacturer of agricultural tools, and a steel products manufacturer. The data on the first firm are annual, those on the other two quarterly. The number of regions (m) varies between 3 and 20, and that of the product types (n) between 2 and 14.

TABLE 3.6

DECOMPOSITION PREDICTIONS OF SALES OF THREE FIRMS, BY REGIONS AND PRODUCT TYPES
(in 10^{-2} nit)

Data used*	Firm's forecast	$I(q : \hat{q})$	$I(q : p)$	Regional effect	Product effect	Mutual information effect
		Public utility, annual data ($m = 3$, $n = 2$)				
C	.056	.034	.026	.004	.006	−.002
L	.056	.049	.063	−.015	.001	−.001
		Agricultural tools manufacturer, quarterly data ($m = 4$, $n = 11$)				
C	1.99	1.63	1.37	.10	.16	−.01
L	1.99	1.95	1.95	−.02	.04	−.02
		Steel products manufacturer, quarterly data ($m = 20$, $n = 14$)				
C	3.63	3.08	3.22	.09	−.27	.04
L	3.63	3.92	5.05	−.03	−1.20	.11

* C = current, L = lagged (see text).

The results are summarized in Table 3.6. All three firms prepare forecasts of the complete bivariate array, not only of the marginal distributions, and this enables us to compare each firm's performance with that of the prediction procedure described here. The figures of the table are all average information values (in 10^{-2} nit) over the relevant set of available observations. The first column contains the average information inaccuracy of the bivariate predictions made by the firm's staff and the second gives the average of $I(q:\hat{q})$ defined in (4.16). The first line of the table shows that in the case of the public utility the latter is below the former. This means that the application of the prediction rule (4.3) to the firm's marginal predictions leads to a result which is on the average better than that of the firm's own bivariate predictions.

However, this statement requires certain qualifications, which can be explained by means of the other figures of the first row. These figures are the average values of the four successive terms in the right-hand side of (4.16), the sum of which is the average of $I(q:\hat{q})$. In the first row, $I(q:p)$ appears to be less on the average than $I(q:\hat{q})$, and the regional and product effects are positive, which means that the information improvements tend to be negative.[1] This suggests that it is better to disregard the firm's marginal predictions altogether by relying completely on the current year's array, $[p_{ij}]$, but that is not realistic. The point is that forecasts for next year are made before the end of this year, so that $[p_{ij}]$ is not really available when needed. The result $I(q:p) < I(q:\hat{q})$ simply indicates that the firm's staff does not succeed in preparing marginal predictions which are better than the not-yet-available no-change extrapolations. A more realistic procedure is then to extrapolate from the year before the current one. This amounts to interpreting $[p_{ij}]$ in (4.3) and (4.16) as the observed bivariate array of this earlier year. One would expect that this raises the average values of both $I(q:\hat{q})$ and $I(q:p)$, because a more outmoded array is used in the prediction procedure. The results are shown in the second line of the table, and they confirm the expectations. Note that the average inaccuracy $I(q:\hat{q})$ is still smaller, although not much, than that of the firm's own forecasts. The no-change extrapolations have a higher inaccuracy; the regional proportion predictions $(\hat{q}_{1.}, \hat{q}_{2.}, \hat{q}_{3.})$ contribute to the accuracy of the prediction procedure, but those of the product type $(\hat{q}_{.1}, \hat{q}_{.2})$ do not.

The analogous results for the two other firms are given in the lower lines of the table. The information inaccuracies are larger than those of the first firm due to the larger values of m and n. In the case of the second firm the procedure (4.3) when based on $[p_{ij}]$ of one quarter earlier leads to an average inaccuracy barely below that of the firm's own forecasts, and about equal to that of no-change extrapolation; for the third firm we obtain an average inaccuracy exceeding that of the firm's forecasts (last line of the table). It is interesting to see that some of the regional and product effects for our three firms are positive, even when the lagged array $[p_{ij}]$ is used. This suggests that these firms would be wise to devote more resources to their marginal predictions $\hat{q}_{i.}$ and $\hat{q}_{.j}$, which would contribute to a better performance of the prediction procedure (4.3).

---

[1] Note that the regional and product effects of Table 3.6 include the minus signs before the second and third terms in the right-hand side of (4.16), whereas the information improvements do not include these minus signs.

3.5. The Information Balance Sheet

Below are shown the balance sheets of F. W. Woolworth Company as of December 31, 1963 and 1964, in thousands of dollars. For both assets and liabilities, items are combined into two groups, current and fixed. The fixed (long-term) liabilities include stockholders' equity.

	Assets		Liabilities		Total	
	1963	1964	1963	1964	1963	1964
Current	325,782	347,287	99,924	111,773	425,706	459,060
Fixed	503,471	509,693	729,329	745,207	1,232,800	1,254,900
Total	829,253	856,980	829,253	856,980	1,658,506	1,713,960

These figures indicate that total assets and total liabilities increased from a little over \$ 829 million to almost \$ 857 million. The next interesting problem is how the components of this total changed. In this section, which is based on THEIL (1969c) and LEV (1969), we shall attack this problem by means of informational concepts.

Assets and Liabilities Information

By dividing each of the four items of 1963 (assets as well as liabilities, current as well as fixed) by their sum (twice \$ 829 million), we obtain four ratios which will be denoted by p_{ij}, where i takes the values 1 (current) and 2 (fixed), while j takes the same values but with different interpretations: 1, assets, and 2, liabilities. The analogous proportions of 1964 will be written q_{ij}, and the marginal proportions are indicated in the usual way: $p_{i.}, p_{.j}, q_{i.}$ and $q_{.j}$. Note that we have

$$(5.1) \qquad p_{.j} = q_{.j} = \tfrac{1}{2} \quad \text{for} \quad j = 1 \text{ and } 2$$

because total assets and total liabilities are identical.

Considering assets first, note that the proportion of current assets in 1963 is $p_{11}/p_{.1} = 2p_{11}$ and in 1964 $q_{11}/q_{.1} = 2q_{11}$. For fixed assets the two proportions are $2p_{21}$ and $2q_{21}$. The expected information of the message that transforms the 1963 proportions into those of 1964,

$$(5.2) \qquad I_A(q:p) = \sum_{i=1}^{2} (2q_{i1}) \log \frac{2q_{i1}}{2p_{i1}} = 2 \sum_{i=1}^{2} q_{i1} \log \frac{q_{i1}}{p_{i1}}$$

is a measure for the extent to which the ratio of current to fixed assets of 1964 differs from that of 1963. It is called the *assets information* of 1964, given the data of the preceding year. The analogous *liabilities information* is based on the proportions of short-term liabilities, $2p_{12}$ and $2q_{12}$, and those of the long-term liabilities, $2p_{22}$ and $2q_{22}$:

$$(5.3) \qquad I_L(q:p) = 2 \sum_{i=1}^{2} q_{i2} \log \frac{q_{i2}}{p_{i2}}$$

This is a measure of the difference between the ratios of short-term to long-term liabilities in the two years. For the balance sheets shown in the opening paragraph of this section we have the following values (in nits):

$$(5.4) \qquad I_A = .00032 \qquad I_L = .00046$$

which indicates that the change in the liabilities composition exceeds that in the assets composition by almost 50 per cent.

The Balance Sheet Information

The notation (p_{ij} and q_{ij}) indicates that we regard a balance sheet as a bivariate array. This suggests that it is appropriate to consider the expected information that corresponds to the four bivariate proportions,

$$(5.5) \qquad I(q:p) = \sum_{i=1}^{2} \sum_{j=1}^{2} q_{ij} \log \frac{q_{ij}}{p_{ij}}$$

which is known as the *balance sheet information* of 1964, given the data of the preceding year. This terminology indicates that $I(q:p)$ is concerned with the changes in all four proportions of the balance sheet.

To analyze the relationship between $I(q:p)$ and the assets and liabilities informations we write (5.5) as follows:

$$(5.6) \qquad I(q:p) = \sum_{j=1}^{2} q_{.j} \sum_{i=1}^{2} \frac{q_{ij}}{q_{.j}} \left[\log \frac{q_{ij}/q_{.j}}{p_{ij}/p_{.j}} + \log \frac{q_{.j}}{p_{.j}} \right]$$

$$= \sum_{j=1}^{2} q_{.j} \sum_{i=1}^{2} \frac{q_{ij}}{q_{.j}} \log \frac{q_{ij}/q_{.j}}{p_{ij}/p_{.j}} + \sum_{j=1}^{2} q_{.j} \log \frac{q_{.j}}{p_{.j}}$$

Using (5.1), we find that the last term in the second line vanishes and that the first term can be written as

$$\sum_{i=1}^{2} q_{i1} \log \frac{q_{i1}}{p_{i1}} + \sum_{i=1}^{2} q_{i2} \log \frac{q_{i2}}{p_{i2}}$$

Combining this with (5.2) and (5.3), we conclude that (5.6) can be simplified to

$$(5.7) \qquad I(q:p) = \frac{I_A(q:p) + I_L(q:p)}{2}$$

or in words: The balance sheet information is equal to the arithmetic average of the assets information and the liabilities information.

The Time Horizon Decomposition of the Balance Sheet Information

The result (5.7) is the assets-and-liabilities decomposition of the balance sheet information. An alternative decomposition is obtained by writing $I(q:p)$ in the following form:

$$(5.8) \qquad I(q:p) = \sum_{i=1}^{2} q_{i.} \sum_{j=1}^{2} \frac{q_{ij}}{q_{i.}} \left[\log \frac{q_{ij}/q_{i.}}{p_{ij}/p_{i.}} + \log \frac{q_{i.}}{p_{i.}} \right]$$

$$= \sum_{i=1}^{2} q_{i.} \left[\sum_{j=1}^{2} \frac{q_{ij}}{q_{i.}} \log \frac{q_{ij}/q_{i.}}{p_{ij}/p_{i.}} \right] + \sum_{i=1}^{2} q_{i.} \log \frac{q_{i.}}{p_{i.}}$$

We start by considering the last term in the second line,

$$(5.9) \qquad I_T(q:p) = \sum_{i=1}^{2} q_{i.} \log \frac{q_{i.}}{p_{i.}}$$

This is the expected information of the message which transforms the proportions $(p_{1.}, p_{2.})$ into the values $(q_{1.}, q_{2.})$. Since $p_{1.}$ and $q_{1.}$ are the ratios of all current items (assets and liabilities combined) and, similarly, $p_{2.}$ and $q_{2.}$ refer to all fixed items, this information expectation is a measure of the extent to which the company's assets plus liabilities have become "more current" or "less current" as a whole. Therefore, $I_T(q:p)$ is called the *time horizon information*.

Whereas $I_T(q:p)$ combines assets and liabilities, the first term in the second line of (5.8) does make a distinction between the two. This term can be regarded as a weighted average, with weights $q_{1.}$ and $q_{2.}$, of

$$(5.10) \qquad I_C(q:p) = \sum_{j=1}^{2} \frac{q_{1j}}{q_{1.}} \log \frac{q_{1j}/q_{1.}}{p_{1j}/p_{1.}}$$

$$(5.11) \qquad I_F(q:p) = \sum_{j=1}^{2} \frac{q_{2j}}{q_{2.}} \log \frac{q_{2j}/q_{2.}}{p_{2j}/p_{2.}}$$

The ratio $q_{11}/q_{1.}$ is the amount of current assets expressed as a fraction of current assets plus current liabilities (that is, as a fraction of all current items). Similarly, $q_{12}/q_{1.}$ is current liabilities expressed in the same way, and $p_{11}/p_{1.}$ and $p_{12}/p_{1.}$ are the analogous fractions for the earlier year. Thus $I_C(q:p)$ is an information expectation which measures the degree to which the ratio of current assets to current liabilities has changed during two consecutive years, and it is therefore called the *current items information*. In the same way, $I_F(q:p)$ concerns the ratio of fixed assets to long-term liabilities and it is called the *fixed items information*.

We may thus write (5.8) as

$$(5.12) \qquad I(q:p) = q_1.I_C(q:p) + q_2.I_F(q:p) + I_T(q:p)$$

which is known as the time horizon decomposition of the balance sheet information. The right-hand side is the weighted average of the current items information and the fixed items information, with weights equal to the proportions of these items in the second year (1964), plus the time horizon information.

The Information Balance Sheet

The two decompositions can be summarized conveniently in tabular form, known as the information balance sheet, which is shown in Table 3.7 for the Woolworth data presented in the opening paragraph of this section. It appears that in this case the fixed items information is very small compared

TABLE 3.7

INFORMATION BALANCE SHEET OF F. W. WOOLWORTH CO., 1963–1964
(in 10^{-2} nit)

Assets and liabilities decomposition		Time horizon decomposition	
I_A Assets information	.032	I_C Current items information	.021
I_L Liabilities information	.046	I_F Fixed items information	.001
Arithmetic mean	.039	Weighted mean	.007
I Balance sheet information	.039	I_T Time horizon information	.032
		I Balance sheet information	.039

with the current items information. Since the 1964 dollar value of the former items is more than twice as large as that of the latter, the weighted mean of the two information values is also small, so that the time horizon information accounts for a considerable proportion of the balance sheet information.

An adequate evaluation of a particular information balance sheet requires knowledge of the "normal" order of magnitude of these various information values. The results to be discussed in the next subsection will provide some guidance in this respect.

Application to U.S. Corporate Balance Sheets, 1947–1966

The simplest way to obtain an idea of the order of magnitude of the items of information balance sheets is by computing averages over time for reasonably homogeneous groups of companies. LEV (1969) made a step in this direction using the balance sheets of all firms on the Standard and Poor Compustat tape. This is a magnetic tape library containing annual financial statement data for about 900 companies represented on the major (New York, American, over-the-counter, and regional) stock exchanges.

Lev's most interesting findings are summarized in Table 3.8. The Compustat firms are divided into groups according to two criteria, one of which is the nature of their products (durable or nondurable, with services regarded as nondurable) and the other the size of the firm, with "large" indicating that the assets exceed the median value (\$67.7 million) in 1956. The figures

TABLE 3.8

AVERAGE INFORMATION BALANCE SHEETS OF COMPUSTAT FIRMS, 1947–1966
(in 10^{-2} nit)

Nondurable large				Nondurable small			
I_A	.35	I_C	.32	I_A	.58	I_C	.53
I_L	.42	I_F	.10	I_L	.74	I_F	.20
I	.39	average	.17	I	.66	average	.30
		I_T	.22			I_T	.36
		I	.39			I	.66
Durable large				Durable small			
I_A	.49	I_C	.46	I_A	.60	I_C	.75
I_L	.77	I_F	.15	I_L	1.36	I_F	.32
I	.63	average	.25	I	.98	average	.48
		I_T	.38			I_T	.50
		I	.63			I	.98

shown are averages over the relevant set of firms and over the 20 years, 1947–1966. They are consistently larger for small firms than for large firms, and for firms producing durable goods than for those which produce non-durables. This reflects the fact that small firms and firms producing durable goods are subject to relatively large year-to-year fluctuations. In all four cases the assets information is below the liability information. Also, the current items information is about two or three times larger than the fixed items information, and their weighted average is consistently closer to the latter because the fixed items tend to be larger than the current items. A comparison with Table 3.7 shows that the change in the balance sheet composition of Woolworth from 1963 to 1964 was very modest.

LEV also computed average information balance sheets for nonsuccessive years. It appears that these averages increase with the time span, but less than proportionally. See further Problems 10 and 11, which apply analogous measures to cross-sectional balance sheet data.

3.6. How to Worry About Increased Expenditures

Imagine that you are the president of a large company. As usual, a budget of planned expenditures was made before the start of this year, but it appears that many of the actual expenditure figures exceed those of the budget rather substantially. The immediate question is: What are the causes of the increases, and where in particular are they very large? Table 3.9 shows that the company consists of five divisions; for each of them, a distinction is

TABLE 3.9

BUDGET AND ACTUAL EXPENDITURE AT THE DIVISIONAL LEVEL
(in millions of dollars per year)

	Budget			Actual expenditure		
	wages	other	total	wages	other	total
Division A	150	200	350	200	220	420
Division B	50	150	200	70	140	210
Division C	150	50	200	210	60	270
Division D	50	100	150	60	90	150
Division E	80	20	100	120	30	150
Total	480	520	1000	660	540	1200

made between the wage and the nonwage components of budgeted and actual expenditures. In this section, which is an extension of THEIL (1969a), we will design a systematic comparison of what was planned and what actually happened.

Raw Budget Scores

Table 3.9 shows that total actual expenditure exceeds the total budget by 20 per cent. If this relative discrepancy applied to every item, very little more could be said, but such is not the case here. Let us indicate by p_{ij} the proportion of the budget corresponding to the ith division and the jth expenditure category, where i takes five values ($i = 1, \ldots, 5$) and j two values (1, wages and 2, nonwage expenditures). The analogous proportions for actual expenditures will be written q_{ij}, and the marginal proportions in the usual way ($p_{i.}, p_{.j}, q_{i.}, q_{.j}$).

We start by disregarding the wage-nonwage distinction. The budget proportion of the ith division is then $p_{i.}$ and that of actual expenditure is $q_{i.}$. The information expectation,

$$(6.1) \qquad I_1 = \sum_{i=1}^{5} q_{i.} \log \frac{q_{i.}}{p_{i.}}$$

is a measure for the extent to which the divisions have different expenditure/ budget ratios. Consider now the components of this expectation:

$$(6.2) \qquad q_{i.} \log \frac{q_{i.}}{p_{i.}} \qquad\qquad i = 1, \ldots, 5$$

The ratio $q_{i.}/p_{i.}$ is larger than unity when the ith division has a larger share of the actual expenditure than of the budget; or, equivalently, when the degree to which it exceeded the budget is larger than the corresponding figure for the company as a whole. If $q_{i.}/p_{i.}$ is larger (smaller) than one, its logarithm is positive (negative); hence the value of the expression (6.2) is positive for all divisions with larger than average expenditure excesses, and negative for those with smaller than average excesses. The degree to which such an excess affects the company is, of course, larger when the division is larger. The expression (6.2) takes this into account by multiplying the logarithm by the division's share $q_{i.}$ of realized expenditure.

These considerations suggest that we may regard the expression (6.2) as the *raw budget score* of the manager of the ith division; the adjective "raw" serves to emphasize that only total expenditure of each division is considered. [The wage and nonwage components will be analyzed in the next

TABLE 3.10

RAW AND PARTIAL BUDGET SCORES

Budget score	Divisions					Total
	A	B	C	D	E	
Raw	.000	−.023	.027	−.023	.028	.0082
Partial:						
wages	−.009	.002	.006	−.012	.016	.0018
other	.023	−.028	.016	−.024	.020	.0084

subsection.] The manager's score is thus positive (negative) when his division exceeds its budget by a larger (smaller) percentage than the company as a whole exceeds the budget, and the absolute value of the score is larger when the relative excess differs more from that of the company ($q_{i.}/p_{i.}$ being farther away from 1 in either upward or downward direction) and also when the division's share of expenditure is larger. In addition, the sum of all division scores is equal to the information expectation I_1 given in (6.1), which measures the extent to which the divisions differ with respect to the relative excess of actual over budgeted expenditure.

The first line of Table 3.10 contains the raw budget scores of the five divisions of Table 3.9, with their total (the information expectation I_1) in the last column. It appears that Division A has a zero score, its relative excess being equal to that of the company, and that B and D have negative and C and E positive scores. This suggests that praise should be heaped on B and D, and that a further investigation of C and E is indicated. However, before drawing this conclusion we should pay special attention to the developments of wages and of nonwage expenditures, particularly since it is known that sizeable wage increases were given early in the year.

A Two-dimensional Analysis

Since the arrays of the budget and of actual expenditure shown in Table 3.9 are two-dimensional, it is appropriate to consider the information expectation

$$(6.3) \qquad I = \sum_{i=1}^{5} \sum_{j=1}^{2} q_{ij} \log \frac{q_{ij}}{p_{ij}}$$

To establish the relationship between I and I_1 we write the former as follows:

(6.4)
$$I = \sum_{i=1}^{5} q_{i.} \sum_{j=1}^{2} \frac{q_{ij}}{q_{i.}} \left[\log \frac{q_{ij}/q_{i.}}{p_{ij}/p_{i.}} + \log \frac{q_{i.}}{p_{i.}} \right]$$

$$= I_1 + \sum_{i=1}^{5} q_{i.} \sum_{j=1}^{2} \frac{q_{ij}}{q_{i.}} \log \frac{q_{ij}/q_{i.}}{p_{ij}/p_{i.}}$$

This shows that I exceeds I_1, and that the excess is equal to a weighted average of five information expectations, each of which describes for some division the extent to which the actual wage/nonwage ratio differs from that of the budget. For the figures of Table 3.9 we have the following numerical values (in nits) for the decomposition in the second line of (6.4):

(6.5) $.0146 = .0082 + (.350)(.0046) + (.175)(.0174) + (.225)(.0021)$
$$+ (.125)(.0097) + (.125)(.0000)$$

In this case we have a rather substantial excess $I - I_1$, which is due to the considerable discrepancies between the budgeted and the actual wage/nonwage ratios, particularly for divisions B and D.

As in the case of the information balance sheet of the previous section, the two-dimensional information expectation (6.3) can be decomposed in two ways. The second is

$$I = \sum_{j=1}^{2} q_{.j} \sum_{i=1}^{5} \frac{q_{ij}}{q_{.j}} \left[\log \frac{q_{ij}/q_{.j}}{p_{ij}/p_{.j}} + \log \frac{q_{.j}}{p_{.j}} \right]$$

$$= \sum_{j=1}^{2} q_{.j} \log \frac{q_{.j}}{p_{.j}} + \sum_{j=1}^{2} q_{.j} \sum_{i=1}^{5} \frac{q_{ij}}{q_{.j}} \log \frac{q_{ij}/q_{.j}}{p_{ij}/p_{.j}}$$

which may be abbreviated as

(6.6) $$I = I_2 + q_{.1} I_{.1} + q_{.2} I_{.2}$$

where

(6.7) $$I_2 = \sum_{j=1}^{2} q_{.j} \log \frac{q_{.j}}{p_{.j}}$$

is the information expectation which concerns the company's budgeted and actual wage and nonwage proportions. Furthermore,

(6.8) $$I_{.j} = \sum_{i=1}^{5} \frac{q_{ij}}{q_{.j}} \log \frac{q_{ij}/q_{.j}}{p_{ij}/p_{.j}} \qquad j = 1, 2$$

is another information expectation which describes the extent to which the expenditure ratios $q_{ij}/q_{.j}$ differ from the corresponding budget ratios $p_{ij}/p_{.j}$ ($i = 1, \ldots, 5$). For $j = 1$ this $I_{.j}$ vanishes if and only if the actual amounts spent on wages by all divisions exceed the corresponding budget figures by the same percentage, and it takes larger positive values when these relative excesses are more different. For $j = 2$ we have an analogous result concerning nonwage expenditure.

For the data of Table 3.9 we have the following numerical values (in nits) corresponding to the decomposition (6.6):

$$(6.9) \qquad .0146 = .0098 + (.55)(.0018) + (.45)(.0084)$$

A comparison with (6.5) shows that I_2 accounts for a larger proportion of I than I_1 does, which is mainly due to the low value of $I_{.1}$. This low value implies that wage expenditures have risen almost proportionately in the five divisions. Since the company's wage policy is not really controlled by the divisions managers, it may be argued that I_2 of (6.6) should be regarded as top management's responsibility and that $I_{.1}$ and $I_{.2}$ are measures which can be used for the evaluation of division managers.

Partial Budget Scores

In (6.2) we considered the component of the information expectation (6.1) that corresponds to the ith division. We may similarly consider the ith component of the information expectation (6.8),

$$(6.10) \qquad \frac{q_{ij}}{q_{.j}} \log \frac{q_{ij}/q_{.j}}{p_{ij}/p_{.j}} \qquad \begin{aligned} i &= 1, \ldots, 5 \\ j &= 1, 2 \end{aligned}$$

which will be called the *partial budget score* of the manager of the ith division with respect to the jth expenditure category. For $j = 1$ this score is positive (negative) when the actual wage bill of the ith division exceeds the budget by more (less) than the company's actual wage bill exceeds its budget. The logarithm in (6.10) is multiplied by the division's share of the company's wage bill, which gives an appropriate weighting. Again, for $j = 2$ (nonwage expenditure) we have a similar result. The partial budget scores thus measure the performance of individual managers after the overall company effect is eliminated [this effect is measured by I_2 in (6.6)], and there are separate measures for the two expenditure categories. Note that the sums of the two sets of partial scores, the information expectations $I_{.1}$ and $I_{.2}$, are weighted proportionally to their total amounts in the decomposition (6.6).

The partial budget scores corresponding to the data of Table 3.9 are shown in Table 3.10 below the raw scores. The partial scores for wages are mostly close to zero; only in the case of Division E is further investigation clearly indicated. The partial scores for nonwage expenditure are all farther from zero than the corresponding wage scores. Division A, for example, has a large positive score for nonwage expenditure whereas it has a zero raw score. This suggests that more detailed attention be given to that division's purchase policies. Similar conclusions for other divisions are left to the reader.

Budget Scores for Departments Within Divisions

The procedure can be continued at a lower level of the company's hierarchy. Suppose, for example, that Division A consists of five departments, A1, ..., A5, the managers of which all report directly to the Division Head. Let the departmental budgets and actual expenditures be as shown in Table 3.11. This table is entirely comparable with Table 3.9. Consequently, if we redefine p_{ij} and q_{ij} as the budgeted expenditure and the actual expenditure, respectively, of the ith department and the jth expenditure category, both measured as a fraction of the relevant divisional total (350 or 420 million dollars per year), then the decomposition (6.6) and the partial budget scores (6.10) may be applied to the departments within the division. Such a score is positive when the actual expenditure of the ith department on the jth category exceeds the budget by more than the division's expenditure on this category exceeds its budget, negative in the opposite case, and so on. This extension of the procedure may be applied at still lower levels of the hierarchy (subdepartments), but this is so straightforward that it is unnecessary to provide further details.

TABLE 3.11

BUDGET AND ACTUAL EXPENDITURE AT THE DEPARTMENTAL LEVEL
(in millions of dollars per year)

	Budget			Actual expenditure		
	wages	other	total	wages	other	total
Department A1	50	50	100	70	50	120
Department A2	10	60	70	10	50	60
Department A3	30	10	40	40	20	60
Department A4	40	20	60	55	35	90
Department A5	20	60	80	25	65	90
Division A	150	200	350	200	220	420

3.7. Generalizations for More than Two Dimensions

The previous sections are all concerned with the bivariate case, but generalizations are straightforward as is shown in Problems 7 to 9 for the adjustment procedure (4.3). [See also Problem 14 for a three-variate interpretation of cross-sectional balance sheets based on concepts developed below.] In this section we shall extend the analysis of Section 3.1 on joint, marginal, and average conditional entropies. Of course, the interpretation of messages sent and received is no longer applicable when there are more than two variables, but this is not a matter of great concern, because the developments of Section 3.2 to 3.6 have shown that the concepts of Section 3.1 can be used in many other areas.

Roll Calls in the American House of Representatives

We shall illustrate the generalization to three variables by means of 275 roll calls taken in the House of Representatives in the years 1949–1950 (the 81st Congress). Following FRIEDMAN (1971), we write Q_{psv} for the number of congressmen of party p from state s who take position v at any given roll call, measured as a fraction of the total number of votes cast. We disregard those who abstain from voting, so that v takes only two values, 1 ("yea") and 2 ("nay"). There are two parties, $p = 1$ (Republicans) and $p = 2$ (Democrats), and there are 48 states. Proportions of marginal distributions will be indicated by dots used as subscripts.

The objective is to find out how much uncertainty there is, on the average, as to the vote of a randomly selected legislator, and by how much this uncertainty is reduced when we know to which party he belongs and from which state he comes. A natural measure for the uncertainty that prevails before any such knowledge is available is the (one-dimensional) marginal entropy of the votes,

$$(7.1) \qquad H(V) = \sum_{v=1}^{2} Q_{..v} \log \frac{1}{Q_{..v}}$$

Since there are two possible positions, this entropy varies between zero and one bit. Its actual value can be computed for each of the 275 roll calls, and the arithmetic average is a simple measure for the 81st Congress as a whole:

$$(7.2) \qquad \text{average } H(V) = .75 \text{ bit}$$

This is the upper limit for the average uncertainty; when we know the party affiliation of the legislator and/or the state from which he comes, this average uncertainty will be reduced, and the problem is simply by how much.

The Contribution of the Legislator's Party Affiliation

When it is known that the legislator belongs to the pth party (but not from which state he comes), the chance that he takes the vth position is no longer $Q_{..v}$ but $Q_{p.v}/Q_{p..}$. The uncertainty as to his vote is then the conditional entropy of V given the pth party affiliation. By weighting this entropy with the probability of the condition $(Q_{p..})$ we obtain the average conditional entropy of the votes given the party affiliation,

$$(7.3) \qquad H_P(V) = \sum_{p=1}^{2} Q_{p..} \sum_{v=1}^{2} \frac{Q_{p.v}}{Q_{p..}} \log \frac{Q_{p..}}{Q_{p.v}}$$

It is readily verified along the lines of (1.11) that this average conditional entropy is equal to the difference of two unconditional entropies:

$$(7.4) \qquad H_P(V) = H(P, V) - H(P)$$

where

$$(7.5) \quad H(P, V) = \sum_{p=1}^{2} \sum_{v=1}^{2} Q_{p.v} \log \frac{1}{Q_{p.v}} \quad \text{and} \quad H(P) = \sum_{p=1}^{2} Q_{p..} \log \frac{1}{Q_{p..}}$$

Again, these unconditional and average conditional entropies can be computed for each roll call, and their averages for the 81st Congress are as shown below.

$$(7.6) \qquad \begin{aligned} \text{average } H(P, V) &= 1.51 \text{ bits} \\ \text{average } H(P) &= .96 \text{ bit} \\ \text{average } H_P(V) &= .55 \text{ bit} \end{aligned}$$

Note in particular that the average $H_P(V)$ is below the value shown in (7.2), and that the difference is .20 bit. This difference measures the average contribution of knowledge of the legislator's party affiliation to a decrease of the uncertainty of his vote.

The Contribution of the Legislator's State

Suppose now that it is known that the legislator comes from the sth state, his party affiliation being unknown. The same line of reasoning leads to the average conditional entropy of the votes given the states,

$$(7.7) \qquad H_S(V) = \sum_{s=1}^{48} Q_{.s.} \sum_{v=1}^{2} \frac{Q_{.sv}}{Q_{.s.}} \log \frac{Q_{.s.}}{Q_{.sv}}$$

which measures the vote uncertainty that prevails, on the average, when the legislator's state is known. This average conditional entropy can be determined from the unconditional entropies $H(S, V)$ and $H(S)$, and the average values of these three entropies in the 81st Congress are as follows:

$$\text{average } H(S, V) = 5.53 \text{ bits}$$

(7.8) $$\text{average } H(S) = 5.03 \text{ bits}$$

$$\text{average } H_S(V) = .50 \text{ bit}$$

The average $H_S(V)$ is lower than the average $H_P(V)$ given in (7.6), which means that knowledge of the state is on the average more valuable for determining the legislator's vote than knowledge of his party. This may seem a surprising result. Note, however, that since there are 48 states and only two parties, knowledge of the state implies more detailed information than knowledge of the party.

The Joint Contribution of the Legislator's Party Affiliation and State

Next suppose that it is known that the legislator belongs to the pth party and also that he comes from the sth state. The probability that he takes the vth position is now $Q_{psv}/Q_{ps.}$, and this leads to a three-dimensional extension of the concepts used in the preceding subsections. We measure the uncertainty of the vote by its conditional entropy, given the pth party and the sth state:

$$\sum_{v=1}^{2} \frac{Q_{psv}}{Q_{ps.}} \log \frac{Q_{ps.}}{Q_{psv}}$$

The probability that the legislator belongs to the pth party and that he comes from the sth state is $Q_{ps.}$. By weighting the above conditional entropy with this probability we obtain the average conditional entropy of the vote given the party and the state,

(7.9) $$H_{PS}(V) = \sum_{p=1}^{2} \sum_{s=1}^{48} Q_{ps.} \sum_{v=1}^{2} \frac{Q_{psv}}{Q_{ps.}} \log \frac{Q_{ps.}}{Q_{psv}}$$

$$= \sum_{p=1}^{2} \sum_{s=1}^{48} \sum_{v=1}^{2} Q_{psv} \log \frac{Q_{ps.}}{Q_{psv}}$$

This is a measure of the average uncertainty as to the vote which prevails when both party and state are known. It can be determined as the excess of the three-dimensional entropy $H(P, S, V)$ over the two-dimensional entropy $H(P, S)$ of the conditioning factors,

$$(7.10) \qquad H_{PS}(V) = H(P, S, V) - H(P, S)$$

which may be verified as follows:

$$H(P, S, V) - H(P, S)$$

$$= \sum_{p=1}^{2} \sum_{s=1}^{48} \sum_{v=1}^{2} Q_{psv} \log \frac{1}{Q_{psv}} - \sum_{p=1}^{2} \sum_{s=1}^{48} Q_{ps.} \log \frac{1}{Q_{ps.}}$$

$$= \sum_{p=1}^{2} \sum_{s=1}^{48} \sum_{v=1}^{2} Q_{psv} \left(\log \frac{1}{Q_{psv}} - \log \frac{1}{Q_{ps.}} \right) = H_{PS}(V)$$

For the 81st Congress we have the average values shown below.

$$(7.11) \qquad \begin{aligned} \text{average } H(P, S, V) &= 5.91 \text{ bits} \\ \text{average } H(P, S) &= 5.62 \text{ bits} \\ \text{average } H_{PS}(V) &= .29 \text{ bit} \end{aligned}$$

The average $H_{PS}(V)$ is less than both the average $H_P(V)$ and the average $H_S(V)$, thus indicating that knowledge of the legislator's state is informative with respect to his vote when his party is already known, and also vice versa (with state and party interchanged).

For further details, including variations of the entropies over time and differences between the two parties, the reader should consult Friedman's thesis (1971). See also Problem 15.

Partial Entropy Reductions

It is of considerable interest to analyze more explicitly the reduction of the average conditional entropy which results from the introduction of an additional conditional factor. For this purpose consider $H_P(V)$ and $H_{PS}(V)$ defined in (7.3) and (7.9), respectively. Their difference is the incremental reduction of the average vote uncertainty due to knowledge of the state, given that the legislator's party is already known. So consider this difference, to be called the *partial entropy reduction* of V due to S given P:

$$(7.12) \quad H_P(V) - H_{PS}(V) = \sum_{p=1}^{2} \sum_{v=1}^{2} Q_{p.v} \log \frac{Q_{p..}}{Q_{p.v}} - \sum_{p=1}^{2} \sum_{s=1}^{48} \sum_{v=1}^{2} Q_{psv} \log \frac{Q_{ps.}}{Q_{psv}}$$

$$= \sum_{p=1}^{2} \sum_{s=1}^{48} \sum_{v=1}^{2} Q_{psv} \left(\log \frac{Q_{p..}}{Q_{p.v}} - \log \frac{Q_{ps.}}{Q_{psv}} \right)$$

$$= \sum_{p=1}^{2} \sum_{s=1}^{48} \sum_{v=1}^{2} Q_{psv} \log \frac{Q_{psv}}{Q_{p.v} Q_{ps.}/Q_{p..}}$$

The expression in the third line may be regarded as the information expectation of the message which transforms prior probabilities of the form $Q_{p.v}Q_{ps.}/Q_{p..}$ to the corresponding posterior probabilities Q_{psv}, where $p = 1$ and 2, $s = 1, \ldots, 48$, and $v = 1$ and 2. Note that these prior probabilities do indeed add up to one when summed over p, s and v!

Since information expectations are nonnegative, we have thus proved

$$(7.13) \qquad\qquad H_{PS}(V) \leqq H_P(V)$$

The equality sign applies if and only if the logarithm in the third line of (7.12) is equal to $\log 1 = 0$ for each triple (p, s, v). This amounts to

$$(7.14) \qquad\qquad \frac{Q_{psv}}{Q_{ps.}} = \frac{Q_{p.v}}{Q_{p..}} \quad \text{for all triples } (p, s, v)$$

The left-hand side is the conditional probability of the vth position in the roll call, given that the legislator belongs to the pth party and comes from the sth state. Equation (7.14) states that this conditional probability is completely independent of the state from which the legislator comes. If this is true, knowledge of the state is completely uninformative with respect to the legislator's vote once his party is known, and it stands to reason that $H_{PS}(V)$ equals $H_P(V)$ in that case. The analogous result $H_{PS}(V) \leqq H_S(V)$ can be proved and interpreted similarly. Extensions to four dimensions are discussed in Section 4.5.

A Comparison with Partial and Multiple Correlation Coefficients

It was stated in Section 3.3 that the expected mutual information is comparable with the product moment correlation coefficient in the sense that both are measures of stochastic dependence, and also that the entropy is comparable with the variance in the sense that both are measures of the uncertainty of the random outcome. We have a similar result for average conditional entropies and their differences in relation to partial and multiple correlation coefficients. To show this, assume that P, S and V are all real-valued variables (which is, of course, not true under the interpretation of these variables in the previous subsections) and imagine that we run a linear regression of V on P and S. Write $R_{V.PS}$ for the multiple correlation coefficient corresponding to this regression and consider the following identity from correlation theory:

$$(7.15) \qquad\qquad 1 - R_{V.PS}^2 = (1 - r_{VP}^2)(1 - r_{VS.P}^2)$$

where r_{VP} is the correlation coefficient of V and P, and $r_{VS.P}$ is the partial correlation coefficient of V and S given P. The left-hand side of this equation may be regarded as a measure of the uncertainty of V given knowledge of both P and S. Hence it performs the same role as $H_{PS}(V)$. The first factor on the right, $1 - r_{VP}^2$, measures the uncertainty of V given P only and thus corresponds to $H_P(V)$. The equation implies that this factor is equal to the left-hand side if and only if the partial correlation of V and S given P is zero, i.e., if and only if S contributes nothing to a reduction of the residual variance when P is used as an explanatory variable in the regression. In exactly the same way, the entropy $H_{PS}(V)$ which corresponds to the left-hand side of (7.15) is equal to the entropy $H_P(V)$ corresponding to the first right-hand factor if and only if condition (7.14) is true, and this condition implies that knowledge of S does not reduce the uncertainty of V when P is known.

Therefore, the partial entropy reduction $H_P(V) - H_{PS}(V)$ plays essentially the same role as the second factor in (7.15), but it is applicable to variables that are not real-valued. Note finally that the entropy reduction is additive in character whereas the right-hand side of (7.15) is the product of two factors. This distinction is due to the additivity of the information concept.

PROBLEMS

1 Prove the second inequality in (1.8).

2 Consider eqs. (1.15) to (1.17) and regard the probabilities p_{ij} and P_{gh} as prior probabilities which are subsequently modified to new values (posterior probabilities) q_{ij} and Q_{gh}. Consider the expected information of this message and prove that it satisfies the following decomposition:

$$\sum_{i=1}^{m} \sum_{j=1}^{n} q_{ij} \log \frac{q_{ij}}{p_{ij}} = \sum_{g=1}^{G} \sum_{h=1}^{H} Q_{gh} \log \frac{Q_{gh}}{P_{gh}} + \sum_{g=1}^{G} \sum_{h=1}^{H} Q_{gh} I_{gh}$$

where

$$I_{gh} = \sum_{i \in S_g} \sum_{j \in T_h} \frac{q_{ij}}{Q_{gh}} \log \frac{q_{ij}/Q_{gh}}{p_{ij}/P_{gh}} \qquad \begin{array}{l} g = 1, \ldots, G \\ h = 1, \ldots, H \end{array}$$

Interpret this result.

3 Prove that the joint school-race entropy of the students of the r th district is

$$\sum_{j \in D_r} \frac{w_j p_j}{W_r} \log \frac{W_r}{w_j p_j} + \sum_{j \in D_r} \frac{w_j(1 - p_j)}{W_r} \log \frac{W_r}{w_j(1 - p_j)}$$

and prove also that this expression can be written as

$$\sum_{j \in D_r} \frac{w_j}{W_r} \left[p_j \log \frac{1}{p_j} + (1 - p_j) \log \frac{1}{1 - p_j} \right] + \sum_{j \in D_r} \frac{w_j}{W_r} \log \frac{W_r}{w_j}$$

Then go back to the average racial entropy of the schools of D_r, $\bar{H}_r$ defined in eq. (4.3) of Section 1.4, to prove that this $\bar{H}_r$ is equal to the average conditional entropy of race, given the schools of D_r. Conclude that the segregation value $K_r - \bar{H}_r$ of D_r, defined in eq. (2.4) of Section 2.2, is equal to the excess of this district's unconditional racial entropy over this average conditional entropy, and prove that this excess is equal to the expected mutual information of school and race in D_r as defined in Section 3.3.

4 Prove that the average employment entropy in C_{ab} at the level of industry groups, $\bar{H}_{ab0}$ defined in eq. (6.9) of Section 1.6, is equal to the average conditional entropy of employment by industry groups, given the SMSA's of C_{ab}. State and prove an analogous result for $\bar{H}_{abg}$ defined in eq. (6.10) of Section 1.6. Also, extend the result on industrial diversity between SMSA's, discussed at the end of Section 3.2, to industry groups and to industries within each group, and include the expected mutual information of the two variables in your discussion.

5 Prove that in the iteration described above eq. (4.6), the first solution of r_i is equal to $q_{i.}/p_{i.}$.

6 Apply the specification (4.8) of α_i and β_j to prove that the mutual information effect on $I(q:\hat{q})$ as given in (4.13) is independent of c.

7 Consider the three-dimensional arrays $[p_{ijk}]$ and $[q_{ijk}]$, where $i = 1, \ldots, m$ and $j = 1, \ldots, n$ and $k = 1, \ldots, p$. Extend the adjustment procedure (4.3) as follows:

$$\hat{q}_{ijk} = r_i s_j t_k p_{ijk}$$

where the r_i's, s_j's and t_k's are coefficients fitted by imposing the marginal constraints:

$$r_i \sum_{j=1}^{n} \sum_{k=1}^{p} s_j t_k p_{ijk} = q_{i..} \qquad i = 1, \ldots, m$$

$$s_j \sum_{i=1}^{m} \sum_{k=1}^{p} r_i t_k p_{ijk} = q_{.j.} \qquad j = 1, \ldots, n$$

$$t_k \sum_{i=1}^{m} \sum_{j=1}^{n} r_i s_j p_{ijk} = q_{..k} \qquad k = 1, \ldots, p$$

Prove that there are $m + n + p - 2$ free coefficients to be adjusted subject to the same number of independent constraints, and suggest an iterative procedure for obtaining numerical values of these coefficients.

8 (*Continuation*)   Consider the logarithmic ratio:

$$\log \frac{p_{ijk}}{p_{i..}\, p_{.j.}\, p_{..k}}$$

and discuss its sign under various conditions of dependence and independence. Prove that the adjustment procedure of Problem 7 implies changes in these log-ratios equal to the sum of three terms,

$$\log \frac{\hat{q}_{ijk}}{q_{i..}\, q_{.j.}\, q_{..k}} - \log \frac{p_{ijk}}{p_{i..}\, p_{.j.}\, p_{..k}} = \alpha_i + \beta_j + \gamma_k$$

where α_i, β_j and γ_k are to be defined. How many additive degrees of freedom do these α's, β's and γ's have?

9 (*Continuation*)   Prove that in the three-dimensional case, eq. (4.13) becomes

$$I(q:\hat{q}) = I(q:p) - \sum_{i=1}^{m} q_{i..} \log \frac{q_{i..}}{p_{i..}} - \sum_{j=1}^{n} q_{.j.} \log \frac{q_{.j.}}{p_{.j.}}$$

$$- \sum_{k=1}^{p} q_{..k} \log \frac{q_{..k}}{p_{..k}} - \left(\sum_{i=1}^{m} q_{i..}\, \alpha_i + \sum_{j=1}^{n} q_{.j.}\, \beta_j + \sum_{k=1}^{p} q_{..k}\, \beta_k \right)$$

where q, $\hat{q}$ and p of $I(q:\hat{q})$ and $I(q:p)$ stand for the arrays $[q_{ijk}]$, $[\hat{q}_{ijk}]$ and $[p_{ijk}]$, respectively.

10 (*Industry-wide information balance sheet*)   Consider an industry consisting of N firms and write w_c for the total assets of the cth company measured as a fraction of the total assets of the industry at the same point in time. [This w_c is, of course, also the ratio of the firm's total liabilities to those of the industry.] Write q_{i1c} for any asset ($i = 1$, current and $i = 2$, fixed) of the cth company, measured as a fraction of this company's total assets plus total liabilities, and define q_{i2c} analogously in terms of liabilities. Next define

$$p_{ij} = \sum_{c=1}^{N} w_c\, q_{ijc}$$

and prove that this is the ith asset (for $j = 1$) or the ith liability (for $j = 2$) of the industry, measured as a fraction of total assets plus total liabilities of the industry. Prove that the expression

$$\sum_{i=1}^{2} \sum_{j=1}^{2} q_{ijc} \log \frac{q_{ijc}}{p_{ij}} \qquad\qquad c = 1, \ldots, N$$

is an information expectation which measures the extent to which the four balance sheet proportions of the industry differ from the corresponding proportions of the cth company. Finally, take a weighted average of these information expectations,

$$I(q : p) = \sum_{c=1}^{N} w_c \sum_{i=1}^{2} \sum_{j=1}^{2} q_{ijc} \log \frac{q_{ijc}}{p_{ij}}$$

to be called the industry-wide balance sheet information, and show that it measures the degree to which the relative positions of the balance sheet items differ among the companies of the industry. Note that this is a cross-section comparison, which is in contrast to the time series analysis of one single firm in Section 3.5.

11 (*Continuation*) Apply the two decompositions described in Section 3.5 to obtain an industry-wide information balance sheet. Interpret each item of this balance sheet.

12 For $H_S(V)$ and $H_{PS}(V)$ defined in (7.7) and (7.9), respectively, prove that the latter never exceeds the former. Prove also that the two are equal if and only if, for each triple (p, s, v), the conditional probability of the vth position, given the pth party and the sth state, is independent of p.

13 Use (7.12) to prove $H_P(V) - H_{PS}(V) = H_P(S) - H_{PV}(S)$; that is, the partial entropy reduction given P is symmetric in the two other variables. Compare this with the second right-hand factor in (7.15) and prove that this expression has the same property.

14 (*Continuation of Problem 10*) Express the four assets and liabilities of each firm as fractions of total assets plus total liabilities of the industry:

$$r_{i1c} = \frac{i^{th} \text{ asset of } c^{th} \text{ company}}{\text{total assets} + \text{total liabilities of industry}}$$

$$r_{i2c} = \frac{i^{th} \text{ liability of } c^{th} \text{ company}}{\text{total assets} + \text{total liabilities of industry}}$$

Prove that the sum of r_{ijc} over i, j and c is equal to one and conclude that the r's may be regarded as the proportions of a three-dimensional distribution. Next define the joint unconditional entropy of the balance sheet items,

$$H(I, J) = \sum_{i=1}^{2} \sum_{j=1}^{2} r_{ij.} \log \frac{1}{r_{ij.}}$$

and the average conditional entropy of these items, given the separate companies,

$$H_C(I, J) = \sum_{i=1}^{2} \sum_{j=1}^{2} \sum_{c=1}^{N} r_{ijc} \log \frac{r_{..c}}{r_{ijc}}$$

Prove that the industry-wide balance sheet information defined in Problem 10 satisfies

$$I(q:p) = H(I, J) - H_C(I, J)$$

Finally, prove directly that the difference in the right-hand side vanishes when the balance sheets of all companies are identical except for a scale factor, and that it is positive otherwise.

15 Below are shown, for the 81st through the 90th Congress, the average conditional entropies of the vote (as a percentage of one bit) for all Democrats, for all Southern Democrats, and for all other Democrats. Draw your conclusions.

Congress	81	82	83	84	85	86	87	88	89	90
All Democrats	56	59	58	49	59	58	47	47	52	54
South*	46	57	52	46	53	52	55	56	55	52
North	39	38	43	36	43	41	27	26	40	42

* Alabama, Arkansas, Florida, Georgia, Louisiana, Mississippi, North Carolina, South Carolina, Texas, Virginia.

CHAPTER 4

DECOMPOSITIONS AND THEIR DETERMINING FACTORS

In the three previous chapters we analyzed and compared various distributions, but in most cases we did not consider in any detail the processes which generate them. In this chapter we develop a class of models for such processes. An illustration of the kinds of problems to be examined is given in Table 4.1, taken from STOUFFER et al. (1949, p. 528). The table deals with

TABLE 4.1

PREFERENCE FOR A COMBAT OUTFIT DETERMINED BY ATTITUDE TOWARD RACIAL SEPARATION, REGION OF ORIGIN, AND EDUCATION

Education	Not against racial separation		Against racial separation	
	South	North	South	North
Grade school only	2051	518	1050	600
Some high school	382	320	349	489
High school completed	351	245	478	609
Grade school only	.09	.14	.13	.19
Some high school	.15	.25	.16	.30
High school completed	.17	.28	.21	.31

a survey among black American soldiers in March 1943 in which they were asked "If it were up to you, what kind of an outfit would you rather be in?" These soldiers were classified by education, region of origin (North-South), and attitude toward racial separation (against or not against). The first three lines of the table contain the numbers of observations and the last three the proportions of those who state a preference to be in a combat outfit. Thus, 9 per cent of the 2051 Southern soldiers with grade school only who are not against racial separation prefer a combat outfit, and 91 per cent prefer not to be in such an outfit.

Table 4.1 presents 12 such dichotomies, one for each combination of the level of education, region of origin, and attitude toward racial separation.

Each dichotomy represents the decomposition of the relevant group of soldiers into two groups (for or against a combat outfit), and the problem to be considered is the following: Is it possible to describe the effect of the level of education, the region of origin, and the attitude toward racial separation more systematically? The figures of the three last lines of the table suggest that this is indeed possible. More education leads to a greater frequency of preference to be in a combat outfit; this appears to be true for each of the four combinations of origin and attitude toward racial separation. Northerners have larger proportions of combat outfit preference than Southerners for each of the six combinations of the level of education and the attitude toward racial separation. Those who are against racial separation have larger proportions than those who are not against, for each eduction-origin combination.

The main objective of this chapter is to pursue systematically the dependence of such proportions on the determining factors, of which there are three in the case of Table 4.1 (education, origin, and attitude toward racial separation). The first five sections are largely based on THEIL (1970a).[1]

4.1. Logits and Linear Logit Relations

If the object of the analysis is the dependence of a proportion on certain determining factors, we have to face the fact that proportions are constrained to be nonnegative and not to exceed unity. Such constraints are frequently awkward. The reason is that if the dependence of the proportion is formalized by means of a function that has the determining factors as arguments, this function has to be chosen in such a way that it is constrained to the interval (0, 1) for whatever values of the arguments. This excludes many functions that could otherwise be very useful. A more attractive approach is to transform the proportion so that the constraints disappear. One simple transformation is described in this section.

The Logit

Consider Table 4.1 and write X for the attitude towards racial separation, Y for the region of origin, and Z for education. The variable X takes two values, X_1 = not against separation and X_2 = against separation. Similarly, Y takes two values (Y_1 = South and Y_2 = North) and Z three (Z_1 = grade

---

[1] Reference should be made to COLEMAN (1964, Chapter 6), who also analyzed the data of Tables 4.1, 4.2 and 4.6 but in a different manner.

school only, Z_2 = some high school, Z_3 = high school completed). Write p_{ijk} for the conditional probability of a positive response under the condition that the determining factors (X, Y, Z) take the values $X = X_i$, $Y = Y_j$, and $Z = Z_k$. Thus p_{123} is the conditional probability that a soldier prefers to be in a combat outfit when he is not against racial separation $(X = X_1)$ and when he comes from the North $(Y = Y_2)$ and when he is a high school graduate $(Z = Z_3)$. The observed relative frequency corresponding to p_{123} is .28; note that this figure is not identical with p_{123}, for p_{123} is the theoretical value determined by the model that will now be described.

The objective is to develop a theoretical model, preferably involving few parameters, which describes p_{ijk} in terms of its three determining factors. Consider the ratio $p_{ijk}/(1 - p_{ijk})$, the odds in favor of a positive response (as "the odds are 4 to 1" when the probability is .8). In particular, consider the logarithm of this ratio,

$$(1.1) \qquad L_{ijk} = \log \frac{p_{ijk}}{1 - p_{ijk}}$$

which is known as the *logit* or the *log-odds* corresponding to the proportion p_{ijk}.[1] When this proportion varies between 0 and 1, the odds vary between 0 and ∞, and the logit between $-\infty$ and ∞. The logit as a function of the corresponding probability is illustrated in Figure 4.1; it is a monotonically increasing function and it is not bounded by finite upper and lower limits as is the proportion. There is therefore no need to worry about such limits when the analyst selects a function for the behavior of the logit.[2]

Linear Logit Functions

The simplest function, which will play a prominent role in the sequel, is

$$(1.2) \qquad \log \frac{p_{ijk}}{1 - p_{ijk}} = \alpha + \beta_i + \gamma_j + \delta_k$$

The right-hand side is linear in the parameters, which is the reason why this function is called a linear logit function. In the case of Table 4.1 there are eight such parameters: the constant term α, the coefficients β_1 and β_2 which describe the attitude toward racial separation (β_1 for "not against" and β_2 for "against"), γ_1 and γ_2 for the effect of the region of origin, and $\delta_1, \delta_2, \delta_3$

---

[1] The term logit is due to BERKSON, who contributed extensively to the subject (1944, 1946, 1949, 1953, 1955, 1968).

[2] For a table which transforms proportions into logits see THEIL (1967, pp. 458–462).

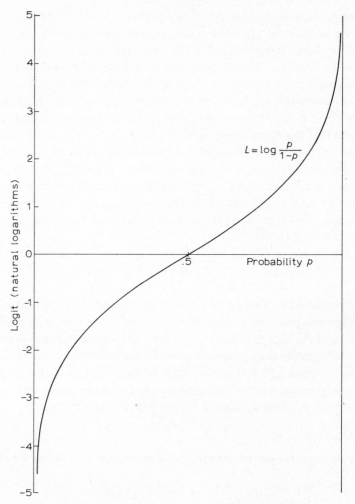

Fig. 4.1.   The logit L as a function of the probability p

for the effect of education. Thus, using the logit notation (1.1), we may conclude from the model (1.2) that the effect on the logit of having high school completed rather than having just grade school is $L_{ij3} - L_{ij1} = \delta_3 - \delta_1$. Hence the model (1.2) states that this effect is the same for all four pairs (X_i, Y_j). It is not self-evident that this constraint is satisfied; this is a matter to be examined for each application.

A convenient property of the linear logit function is that the corresponding function for the complementary event is the same except that the signs of the coefficients are reversed:

$$\log \frac{1-p_{ijk}}{p_{ijk}} = -\alpha - \beta_i - \gamma_j - \delta_k$$

We shall use natural logarithms throughout this chapter, so that (1.1) implies $p_{ijk}/(1-p_{ijk}) = e^{L_{ijk}}$. This enables us to express the probabilities explicitly in terms of the parameters of the model (1.2):

$$(1.3) \qquad p_{ijk} = (1+e^{-L_{ijk}})^{-1} = [1+\exp(-\alpha - \beta_i - \gamma_j - \delta_k)]^{-1}$$

where $\exp(z)$ stands for e^z.

The Behavior of the Logit

 Figure 4.1 shows that the logit vanishes when the probability is $\frac{1}{2}$. The derivative with respect to the probability is

$$(1.4) \qquad \frac{dL}{dp} = \frac{d}{dp}\log p - \frac{d}{dp}\log(1-p) = \frac{1}{p(1-p)}$$

This derivative takes the smallest value at $p = \frac{1}{2}$, and this value is 4. The logit has therefore an inflection point at $p = \frac{1}{2}$, so that the linear Taylor expansion around $p = \frac{1}{2}$,

$$(1.5) \qquad\qquad\qquad L \approx 4(p-\tfrac{1}{2})$$

has an approximation error of the third order of smallness. But Figure 4.1 clearly shows that this approximation becomes highly inaccurate when p approaches 0 or 1. Variations of p in these two areas are accompanied by very substantial changes in the logit. Conversely, any given change in the logit has much less impact on the corresponding p when p is close to 0 or to 1 than when it is around $\frac{1}{2}$.

 It is this particular feature that is highly plausible with respect to logit functions such as (1.2). We shall illustrate this for the data shown in Table 4.2; its proportions exhibit more variation than those of Table 4.1, which facilitates the argument. The new table, which is taken from STOUFFER et al. (1949, p. 553), is based on a World War II survey among American soldiers in which they are asked their preference concerning the location of their military camp. Three determining factors are distinguished: region of origin (North-South), race (black or white), and location of the camp to which the soldier is presently assigned (North-South). The relevant numbers are shown in the first two lines of the table. The figures in the last two lines are the proportions of those who state a preference for a camp in the South

TABLE 4.2

PREFERENCE FOR A SOUTHERN CAMP DETERMINED BY REGION OF ORIGIN, RACE, AND THE
LOCATION OF THE PRESENT CAMP

Present camp	Northern men		Southern men	
	Black	White	Black	White
North	423	1117	653	280
South	1126	1384	2093	961
North	.085	.145	.414	.628
South	.222	.369	.819	.905

(including a preference to stay in the present camp if located in the South). The soldiers who were undecided or who did not name a camp are eliminated.

Table 4.2 has thus the same format as Table 4.1 but the proportions of positive response vary much more widely, from less than 10 to more than 90 per cent. Consider then the Southern men who are presently in a Northern camp. The observed frequency of preference for a Southern camp is 41.4 per cent for blacks and 62.8 per cent for whites. Hence, being white rather than black induces $62.8 - 41.4 = 21.4$ per cent of the soldiers to prefer the South to the North. But such a change would be impossible for Southern men who are presently in a Southern camp, since the preference frequency for the South is as high as 81.9 per cent among blacks and $81.9 + 21.4$ exceeds 100. Still, such a shift would be needed if one were to attempt to express the probability p_{ijk} linearly in terms of the race variable. The actual increase is obviously much smaller, from 81.9 to 90.5 per cent. This is in accordance with the linear logit equation (1.2) when the subscript i is regarded as referring to the region of origin in this case, and j to race and k to the location of the present camp. This equation then implies that when the logit is large and becomes still larger (as is the case when we shift from Southern blacks in Southern camps to Southern whites in Southern camps), this does raise the probability but it does so by a moderate amount.

The Relation Between Logit and Entropy

The logit L corresponding to the probability p of event E may be regarded as minus the excess of the information received from the message which states that E occurred over the information received from the complementary message:

(1.6)
$$-L = \log \frac{1}{p} - \log \frac{1}{1-p}$$

An even more interesting link between the logit and informational measures is obtained by differentiating the entropy with respect to p:

(1.7)
$$\frac{dH}{dp} = \frac{d}{dp}\left[-p \log p - (1-p) \log (1-p)\right]$$
$$= -\log p - 1 + \log (1-p) + 1$$
$$= -L$$

Thus, when natural logarithms (nits) are used, the logit is minus the derivative of the entropy with respect to the probability. The reader is invited to compare Figure 4.1 with Figure 1.2 in Section 1.1 for a visual verification. The result (1.7) may be interpreted in the sense that the logit measures the sensitivity of uncertainty for variations in the probability.

Other Transformations

It is appropriate to stress that the logit is not the only device for transforming proportions to the range from $-\infty$ to ∞. However, it is a particularly simple device, which is a great advantage. Another attractive feature is the fact that it can be interpreted straightforwardly in terms of the odds favoring the event, since such odds have a great intuitive appeal for the description of the likelihood of an event. We shall therefore confine ourselves to the logit transformation in this chapter.

Another well-known transformation is the probit, which is based on the cumulated normal distribution and which leads to a picture very close to that of Figure 4.1. At the empirical level, there is little difference between logit analysis and probit analysis. For details on the latter, see FINNEY (1964).

A third transformation is shown in Figure 4.2. It is concerned with sales by German retailers in the period 1950–1957. A large number of retailers provide reports on whether their monthly sales were higher than the previous month's, at the same level, or lower. The horizontal variable in the figure, denoted by x, is the proportion of those reporting an increase minus the proportion of those reporting a decrease. Hence x is constrained to the interval $(-1, 1)$. The vertical variable is the change in the natural logarithm of the aggregate money value of retail sales in Germany in the same period, denoted by y, which is not restricted to a finite interval. The curve that goes through the observations is

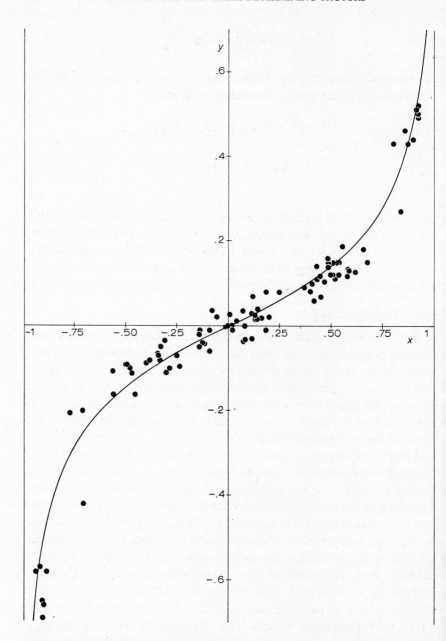

Fig. 4.2.   The relation between the net change x of the survey reports by German retailers (the proportion of those reporting an increase minus the proportion of those reporting a decrease) and the log-change y in the money value of aggregate retail sales, 1950–1957

(1.8)
$$y = \frac{\frac{1}{4}x}{\sqrt{1-x^2}}$$

The fit is evidently rather good, which means that it is possible to use the survey reports to predict the change in aggregate sales with some degree of confidence. [The survey is available several weeks before the data on sales are published, so that this prediction has practical importance.] Basically, the transformation used in (1.8) is that of the tangent: write $x = \sin \phi$, then $y = \frac{1}{4} \sin \phi / \cos \phi = \frac{1}{4} \tan \phi$. For further details, see THEIL (1966, Section 11.5).

4.2. Weighted Least-Squares Estimation of Linear Logit Relations

The objective of this section is to test and to estimate the linear logit relation (1.2) for the data of Table 4.1. The estimation method is weighted least squares and the test is a χ^2 test.

A Normalization

The right-hand side of (1.2) involves eight unknown parameters: α, β_1, β_2, γ_1, γ_2, δ_1, δ_2 and δ_3. However, this number exaggerates what is really unknown. Suppose that we add an arbitrary real number A to α, B to β_1 and β_2, C to γ_1 and γ_2, and subtract $A+B+C$ from each of the δ's. Then the right-hand side of (1.2) becomes

$$\alpha+A+\beta_i+B+\gamma_j+C+\delta_k-(A+B+C) = \alpha+\beta_i+\gamma_j+\delta_k$$

This shows that the eight parameters of (1.2) are subject to a three-dimensional indeterminacy (A, B and C). We may therefore impose the following normalizations without any loss of generality:

(2.1) $\beta_1 = \gamma_1 = \delta_1 = 0$

in which case there are only five unknown parameters: α, β_2, γ_2, δ_2 and δ_3. By substituting $i = j = k = 1$ in (1.2), we conclude that the normalization (2.1) implies that the constant term α is equal to the logit of the preference to be in a combat outfit among Southern soldiers with grade school only who are not against racial separation. Similarly, $\alpha+\beta_2$ is the logit among Southern soldiers with grade school only who are against racial separation, $\alpha+\beta_2+\gamma_2$ is the logit among Northern soldiers with grade school only who are against racial separation, and so on.

Logits Expressed in Terms of Dummy Variables

The left-hand variable of (1.2) involves the probability p_{ijk}, which is unknown. We do know the observed relative frequencies, to be written f_{ijk}, which are given in the lower half of Table 4.1. So we rewrite (1.2) as

$$(2.2) \quad \log \frac{f_{ijk}}{1-f_{ijk}} = \alpha + \beta_i + \gamma_j + \delta_k + \left(\log \frac{f_{ijk}}{1-f_{ijk}} - \log \frac{p_{ijk}}{1-p_{ijk}} \right)$$

which expresses the logit corresponding to the observed relative frequency linearly in terms of the unknown parameters and an unobservable error term (the term in parentheses).

Write l_{ijk} for the logit in the left-hand side of (2.2):

$$(2.3) \quad l_{ijk} = \log \frac{f_{ijk}}{1-f_{ijk}}$$

Since there are 12 combinations of values of the subscripts i, j and k, there are also 12 equations (2.2). The following are the three corresponding to $i = j = 1$, written so that they contain all five parameters:

$$
\begin{aligned}
l_{111} &= \alpha + \beta_2 \times 0 + \gamma_2 \times 0 + \delta_2 \times 0 + \delta_3 \times 0 + (l_{111} - L_{111}) \\
(2.4) \quad l_{112} &= \alpha + \beta_2 \times 0 + \gamma_2 \times 0 + \delta_2 \times 1 + \delta_3 \times 0 + (l_{112} - L_{112}) \\
l_{113} &= \alpha + \beta_2 \times 0 + \gamma_2 \times 0 + \delta_2 \times 0 + \delta_3 \times 1 + (l_{113} - L_{113})
\end{aligned}
$$

Each of the three equations has a constant term (α) and in each case the parameters β_2, γ_2, δ_2 and δ_3 are multiplied by a variable which is either zero or one. Such a variable is called a *dummy variable*. The "behavior" of these variables for the 12 triples (i, j, k) is shown in Table 4.3. Note that the constant term is regarded as the coefficient of a dummy variable which takes the unit value for each observation.

The observed logits l_{ijk} are thus linear functions of dummy variables, and the unknown parameters are the coefficients of these variables. An obvious method of estimating these parameters is the least-squares regression of the observed logit on the dummy variables. But is it true that the standard conditions of the least-squares method are satisfied in this case?

A Weighted Least-Squares Regression

The method of least squares is known to have optimum properties under the following conditions: (1) the error terms $l_{ijk} - L_{ijk}$ all have zero expectation, (2) they all have the same variance, and (3) they are pairwise uncorrelated. Condition (3) does not lead to any difficulties when we assume

TABLE 4.3

DUMMY VARIABLES OF THE LOGIT RELATION (2.2)

	α	β_2	γ_2	δ_2	δ_3
l_{111}	1	0	0	0	0
l_{112}	1	0	0	1	0
l_{113}	1	0	0	0	1
l_{121}	1	0	1	0	0
l_{122}	1	0	1	1	0
l_{123}	1	0	1	0	1
l_{211}	1	1	0	0	0
l_{212}	1	1	0	1	0
l_{213}	1	1	0	0	1
l_{221}	1	1	1	0	0
l_{222}	1	1	1	1	0
l_{223}	1	1	1	0	1

that the 12 relative frequencies are obtained by independent random drawings from 12 different populations. To handle the other two conditions we assume that these populations are binomial. This is pursued in more detail in the next subsection, the result of which may be summarized as follows. Write n_{ijk} for the number of observations on which f_{ijk} is based (the relevant number in the upper half of Table 4.1). Then, if n_{ijk} is sufficiently large, the error term of (2.2) has approximately zero expectation. Hence condition (1) does not lead to difficulties either, provided that n_{ijk} is indeed large. [In our case the n_{ijk}'s are of the order of several hundreds.] However, it is not true that the errors all have the same variance. It appears that for large n_{ijk} the variance of the error term is approximately equal to the reciprocal of $n_{ijk}f_{ijk}(1-f_{ijk})$.

This result enables us to transform eq. (2.2) so that the constant-variance condition is better satisfied. We have the well-known result that if a random variable X has variance σ^2, a multiple k of X has variance $k^2\sigma^2$. By choosing $k = 1/\sigma$ we obtain a random variable with unit variance. Thus, when we take $1/n_{ijk}f_{ijk}(1-f_{ijk})$ as the variance of the error term of (2.2), the expression

$$(2.5) \qquad \sqrt{n_{ijk}f_{ijk}(1-f_{ijk})}\ (l_{ijk}-L_{ijk})$$

has unit variance for each triple (i, j, k).

Combining this result with (2.2), we conclude that multiplication of both sides of the latter equation by the square root of $n_{ijk}f_{ijk}(1-f_{ijk})$ is sufficient to guarantee the applicability of the standard least-squares procedure, at least when the n_{ijk}'s are sufficiently large.[1] This multiplication amounts to weighting the 12 observations (i, j, k) with different weights, and the method is therefore called weighted least squares. The weights are intuitively plausible. Given the value of f_{ijk}, more weight is attached to the observation (i, j, k) when it is based on a larger number of observations (n_{ijk}). Given n_{ijk}, the weight is small when f_{ijk} is close to 0 or to 1 and even zero when f_{ijk} is equal to either of these limits. This is highly desirable, because when $f_{ijk} = 0$ or 1, the left-hand side of (2.2) takes an infinite value and cannot be used for the computations. When f_{ijk} is not equal but close to either of these limits, the corresponding logit takes large (negative or positive) values and it is highly sensitive to small changes in f_{ijk}. It stands to reason that little weight should be given to observations that are highly unstable.

*Derivation of the Weights**

Under the assumption that f_{ijk} is obtained from a sample consisting of n_{ijk} random drawings from a binomial population with probability p_{ijk}, the distribution of f_{ijk} has an expectation equal to p_{ijk} and the following variance:

$$(2.6) \qquad \operatorname{var} f_{ijk} = \frac{1}{n_{ijk}} p_{ijk}(1 - p_{ijk})$$

As n_{ijk} increases indefinitely, this variance converges to zero, so that in the limit the distribution of f_{ijk} becomes degenerate with all its mass concentrated at the expectation p_{ijk}.

To evaluate the distribution of the error term of (2.2) we assume that n_{ijk} is large, so that the distribution of f_{ijk} is concentrated closely around p_{ijk} and a linear Taylor expansion suffices. Then go back to (1.4) which states that the derivative of the logit with respect to the probability p is $1/p(1-p)$. Hence:

$$(2.7) \qquad \log \frac{f_{ijk}}{1 - f_{ijk}} - \log \frac{p_{ijk}}{1 - p_{ijk}} \approx \frac{f_{ijk} - p_{ijk}}{p_{ijk}(1 - p_{ijk})}$$

By taking the expectation of both sides we find that the error term of (2.2) has approximately zero expectation. By squaring both sides and then taking

---

[1] In fact, however, the large-sample distribution of the logit estimator is approximated closely even when n_{ijk} is rather small; see LINDLEY (1964). Also, this large-sample distribution is normal, which is convenient for testing procedures.

the expectation we obtain the second moment of the error term on the left, which is approximately equal to the variance because the expectation is approximately zero. The right-hand side becomes the variance of f_{ijk} divided by the square of $p_{ijk}(1-p_{ijk})$. In view of (2.6), this is equal to

$$(2.8) \qquad \frac{\dfrac{1}{n_{ijk}} p_{ijk}(1-p_{ijk})}{p_{ijk}^2(1-p_{ijk})^2} = \frac{1}{n_{ijk}\, p_{ijk}(1-p_{ijk})}$$

In the previous subsection we replaced p_{ijk} in (2.8) by f_{ijk}, which is asymptotically $(n_{ijk}\to\infty)$ correct. For a more rigorous derivation see THEIL (1970a, Appendix).

Discussion of the Estimates

The procedure to be applied to the data of Table 4.1 is thus a weighted least-squares regression of the observed logit on the dummy variables of Table 4.3, with weights equal to the relevant square root which is shown in (2.5) as the multiplier of $l_{ijk}-L_{ijk}$. It is readily verified that this is equivalent to an ordinary least-squares regression of

$$l_{ijk}\sqrt{n_{ijk}f_{ijk}(1-f_{ijk})}$$

on five modified dummy variables. The modification implies that when the original dummy variable takes the unit value for the $(i,j,k)^{\text{th}}$ observation, this value is replaced by the square root mentioned above.

The resulting parameter estimates are shown below, with their standard errors in parentheses.

$\hat{\alpha}\ =\ -2.29$ (.06)   the logit estimate of an expressed preference to be in a combat outfit among Southern men with grade school only who are not against racial separation;

$\hat{\beta}_2 =$ .28 (.07)   the estimated effect on the logit of being against instead of not against racial separation;

$\hat{\gamma}_2 =$ .57 (.07)   the estimated effect of coming from the North instead of the South;

$\hat{\delta}_2 =$ .54 (.08)   the estimated effect of having some high school rather than just grade school;

$\hat{\delta}_3 =$ .68 (.08)   the estimated effect of having completed high school rather than having just grade school.

The point estimates indicate that the effect of the region of origin is about twice as large as that of the attitude towards racial separation, and about equally large as that of having some high school rather than just grade school. Having completed high school raises the logit still further $(\hat{\delta}_3 > \hat{\delta}_2)$, but the effect is not large.

The Implied Estimates of the Probabilities

Once estimates of the parameters α, β_i, γ_j and δ_k of the logit equation (1.2) have been obtained, we can substitute these in (1.3) to obtain the implied estimates of the probabilities, to be written $\hat{p}_{ijk}$. They are shown in the middle part of Table 4.4 along with the observed relative frequencies of

TABLE 4.4

ESTIMATED PROBABILITIES FOR THE DATA OF TABLE 4.1

Education	Not against racial separation		Against racial separation	
	South	North	South	North
	Observed relative frequencies			
Grade school only	.09	.14	.13	.19
Some high school	.15	.25	.16	.30
High school completed	.17	.28	.21	.31
	Estimated probabilities			
Grade school only	.092	.152	.119	.193
Some high school	.149	.236	.188	.291
High school completed	.167	.261	.210	.320
	Discrepancies			
Grade school only	−.002	−.012	.011	−.003
Some high school	.001	.014	−.028	.009
High school completed	.003	.019	.000	−.010

Table 4.1 on top. The three last lines of the table contain the discrepancies $f_{ijk} - \hat{p}_{ijk}$. They are generally small; six out of 12 discrepancies are less than 1 per cent in absolute value, and only one exceeds 2 per cent.[1]

---

[1] It should be noted that the observed relative frequencies are available to only two decimal places; if there had been more, this would have affected the values of the discrepancies. In general, the best procedure is to publish the original (absolute) numbers in addition to the frequency percentages, so that analysts who want to use such figures as basic data for further analysis can do so without loss of accuracy.

Testing the Validity of a Logit Specification

Although the small values of the discrepancies are promising, it should be stressed that an appraisal of the validity of the linear logit model requires that the numbers of observations (n_{ijk}) be taken into account. The discrepancies concern exclusively differences between proportions and do not, therefore, involve these numbers of observations explicitly. Below is a description of a simple χ^2 test which satisfies this requirement.

To test the null hypothesis that an observed relative frequency f is obtained from n independent random drawings with probability p, one may compute

$$(2.9) \qquad \frac{n(f-p)^2}{p} + \frac{n[1-f-(1-p)]^2}{1-p} = \frac{n(f-p)^2}{p(1-p)}$$

which is approximately distributed as $\chi^2(1)$ – one degree of freedom – if the null hypothesis is true; the approximation is better when the sample size (n) is larger. In the case of Tables 4.1 and 4.4 we have 12 probabilities p_{ijk} and 12 relative frequencies f_{ijk}. Since the f's with different subscript combinations are independent by assumption, the sum of the 12 ratios (2.9),

$$(2.10) \qquad \sum_{i=1}^{2} \sum_{j=1}^{2} \sum_{k=1}^{3} \frac{n_{ijk}(f_{ijk}-p_{ijk})^2}{p_{ijk}(1-p_{ijk})}$$

is asymptotically $(n_{ijk} \to \infty)$ distributed as $\chi^2(12)$ under the null hypothesis.

This result is valid when the 12 values of the probabilities p_{ijk} are specified independently of the sample. This is not the case when we substitute $\hat{p}_{ijk}$ for p_{ijk} in (2.10) to test the validity of the logit model, because $\hat{p}_{ijk}$ has been derived from the sample. It can be shown that for sufficiently large n_{ijk}'s, the expression (2.10) with p_{ijk} replaced by $\hat{p}_{ijk}$ is approximately distributed as χ^2 with a number of degrees of freedom equal to the number of cells (12) minus the number of parameters adjusted (5); for details, see THEIL (1970a, Appendix). This result holds under the null hypothesis that the logit model (1.2) is true for some (unspecified) values of its parameters α, β_i, γ_j and δ_k. The value of this χ^2 for our sample is 5.02, which is not nearly significant for $\chi^2(7)$ at any reasonable statistical standard, so that we may consider the model (1.2) as acceptable for the data of Table 4.1.

4.3. Logit Relations with Interaction Terms

A Linear Logit Function for the Preference for a Southern Camp

We proceed to apply the same procedure to the data of Table 4.2 on page

170 and write X for the region of origin (X_1 = North and X_2 = South), Y for race (Y_1 = black and Y_2 = white), and Z for the location of the present camp (Z_1 = North and Z_2 = South). Under the normalization (2.1) we obtain:

$\hat{\alpha}$ = -2.74 (.08) the logit estimate of an expressed preference for a Southern camp among Northern blacks who are presently in a Northern camp;

$\hat{\beta}_2$ = 2.60 (.06) the estimated effect on the logit of coming from the South rather than the North;

$\hat{\gamma}_2$ = $.76$ (.06) the estimated effect of being white rather than black;

$\hat{\delta}_2$ = 1.54 (.06) the estimated effect of being presently in a Southern rather than a Northern camp.

Table 4.5 contains the observed relative frequencies of Table 4.2 in the first two lines, followed by the estimated probabilities implied by the above parameter estimates as well as the associated discrepancies. It is seen that most of the discrepancies are much larger than those of Table 4.4, the

TABLE 4.5

ESTIMATED PROBABILITIES FOR THE DATA OF TABLE 4.2

Present camp	Northern men		Southern men	
	Black	White	Black	White
Observed relative frequencies				
North	.085	.145	.414	.628
South	.222	.369	.819	.905
Estimated probabilities (no interaction)				
North	.061	.121	.467	.651
South	.232	.391	.803	.897
Discrepancies				
North	.024	.024	−.053	−.023
South	−.010	−.022	.016	.008
Estimated probabilities (with interaction)				
North	.077	.148	.423	.606
South	.220	.371	.819	.905
Discrepancies				
North	.008	−.003	−.009	.022
South	.002	−.002	.000	.000

majority exceeding .02 in absolute value. The χ^2 discussed at the end of the previous section is 25.7 for the present data. The number of degrees of freedom is $8-4 = 4$, for which the value 25.7 is highly significant. We must therefore reject the logit model (1.2) for this body of data.

Interaction

The discrepancies shown in the middle part of Table 4.5 are not only large but they also exhibit regularity. They are positive for Northern men in Northern camps and for Southern men in Southern camps, and negative in all cases in which men are in camps located in an area other than that of their origin. To analyze the implications of this result, consider the logits corresponding to the observed relative frequencies in the first two lines of Table 4.5, to be written l_{ijk} in accordance with (2.3). The logit difference $l_{ij2}-l_{ij1}$ describes the effect of being presently in a Southern rather than a Northern camp. Under the model (1.2) this difference is a constant (independent of i and j) apart from sampling errors. The actual values of these logit differences for Northern men $(i = 1)$ are

(3.1) $l_{112}-l_{111} = 1.12$ (blacks) $l_{122}-l_{121} = 1.24$ (whites)

and for Southern men $(i = 2)$:

(3.2) $l_{212}-l_{211} = 1.86$ (blacks) $l_{222}-l_{221} = 1.73$ (whites)

This means that the effect on the logit of being presently in a Southern rather than a Northern camp is about 1.2 for Northern men and about 1.8 for Southern men. The model (1.2) postulates that the effect is the same for the two groups, and the estimated effect $(\hat{\delta}_2 = 1.54)$ is about halfway between these two figures, which should cause no surprise. However, the present results suggest that it is appropriate to acknowledge the possibility of interaction between the region of origin (X) and the location of the present camp (Z).

A Logit Relation with an Interaction Term

Consider the following logit equation:

(3.3) $$\log \frac{p_{ijk}}{1-p_{ijk}} = \alpha + \beta_{ik} + \gamma_j$$

where β_{ik} is a parameter that measures the combined effect of (X_i, Z_k) on the logit. We normalize as follows:

(3.4) $$\beta_{11} = \gamma_1 = 0$$

so that α stands (as before) for the logit of an expressed preference for a Southern camp among Northern blacks who are presently in a Northern camp. There are five unknown parameters $(\alpha, \beta_{12}, \beta_{21}, \beta_{22}, \gamma_2)$ and their estimation is a straightforward extension of the procedure of the previous section. The estimate of α is raised algebraically from -2.74 to -2.49 and the new standard error is .09.[1] The estimate of γ_2 is lowered slightly from .76 to .74 with standard error .06. For the β's we obtain the following values:

$\hat{\beta}_{12} = 1.22$ (.09)   the estimated effect on the logit, for Northern men only, of being presently in a Southern rather than a Northern camp;

$\hat{\beta}_{21} = 2.18$ (.11)   the estimated effect, for men presently in a Northern camp only, of coming from the South instead of the North;

$\hat{\beta}_{22} = 4.00$ (.10)   the estimated combined effect of coming from the South instead of the North and of being presently in a Southern instead of a Northern camp.

The value of $\hat{\beta}_{12}$ agrees satisfactorily with the logit differences based on observed frequencies that are given in (3.1). The effect of presently being in a Southern rather than a Northern camp for Southerners is $L_{2j2} - L_{2j1} = \beta_{22} - \beta_{21}$. The estimate is $\hat{\beta}_{22} - \hat{\beta}_{21} = 1.82$ with a standard error of .08,[2] which is in good agreement with the logit differences given in (3.2). This effect exceeds the corresponding effect for Northerners by $\beta_{22} - \beta_{21} - \beta_{12}$, which is estimated as .60 with a standard error of .12,[2] so that the excess may be regarded as significantly positive.

The estimated probabilities based on (3.3) and the corresponding discrepancies are given in the last four lines of Table 4.5. They indicate that the interaction specification leads to a considerably better fit. Its χ^2 is only 1.37. Although the number of degrees of freedom is reduced from 4 to $8 - 5 = 3$, this χ^2 is not nearly significant and the interaction equation (3.3) is therefore acceptable.

---

[1] An algebraically larger value of α raises the probability of a positive response under condition (X_1, Y_1, Z_1). Table 4.5 shows that this is desirable from the standpoint of fit, given that the estimated probability under no-interaction (.061) is below the observed proportion (.085).

[2] This standard error is derived from the asymptotic covariance matrix of the coefficient estimates; see THEIL (1970a) for details.

A Geometric Picture of Interaction

Figure 4.3 gives a three-dimensional picture of the dependence of the logit on the region of origin and the location of the present camp. The latter variables take two values each, North (N) and South (S), so that there are four pairs of values: (N, N), (N, S), (S, N), (S, S), where the first N or S refers to the origin and the second to the camp location. These two variables are measured along the horizontal axes and the logit is measured vertically. There are four points implied by the estimates of the previous subsection, indicated by black dots, with the one corresponding to (N, N) shown in the origin. The two points above the horizontal axes correspond to the cases in which either the region of origin or the location of the present camp is South but not both. The plane drawn through these three points intersects the vertical line that goes through (S, S) at a point which is $2.18 + 1.22 = 3.40$ above the horizontal plane. That point would coincide with the black dot at (S, S) if the logit relation were linear without interaction. However, the dot is actually .60 higher, thus implying that there is interaction between these two determining factors.

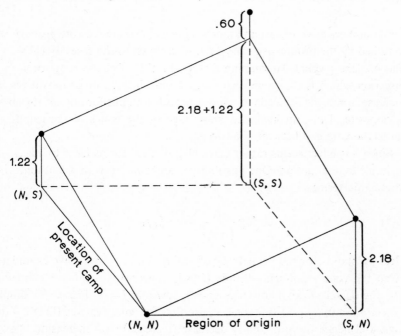

Fig. 4.3. The interaction of the region of origin and the location of the present camp with respect to the logit of a preference for a Southern camp

A Multiplicative Interaction Term

Table 4.6 is concerned with the vote for the progressive candidate in the election of the president of a printers' union; it is taken from COLEMAN (1964, p. 227). The voters are classified by their political attitude (liberal or conservative) and by the question of whether they are low or high in knowledge of the issues of the campaign. The figures in the first two lines are the

TABLE 4.6

VOTES FOR PROGRESSIVE CANDIDATE DETERMINED BY POLITICAL ATTITUDE AND DEGREE OF
KNOWLEDGE

Knowledge	Conservatives	Liberals
Low	87	59
High	36	80
Low	.667	.746
High	.389	.888

total numbers of votes cast and those in the last two are the vote proportions obtained by the progressive candidate. In contrast to the cases of Tables 4.1 and 4.2, the present determining factors do not affect the proportion in a direction which is the same under all circumstances. For conservatives an increase in knowledge leads to a lower proportion, but for liberals the effect is opposite. Thus, an increased knowledge of the issues of the campaign raises the vote gap between the two groups.

Since this effect seems rather plausible, we shall formalize it by means of a simple logit equation. One possibility is an equation with a multiplicative interaction term:

$$(3.5) \qquad \log \frac{p_{ij}}{1-p_{ij}} = \alpha + \beta_i \gamma_j$$

Here p_{ij} stands for the probability of voting for the progressive candidate, given the voter's political attitude ($i = 1$, conservative and $i = 2$, liberal) and the degree of his knowledge ($j = 1$, low and $j = 2$, high). We should expect $\beta_1 < 0, \beta_2 > 0, 0 < \gamma_1 < \gamma_2$, so that for conservatives (liberals) the logit and hence the probability decrease (increase) with increasing knowledge. Since one can raise $\beta_i \gamma_j$ for each pair (i, j) by a constant and subtract this constant from α without affecting the right-hand side of (3.5), we normalize by specifying

(3.6) $\gamma_2 = 1$

There are thus four unknown parameters: α, β_1, β_2 and γ_1. This number is as large as that of the cells in Table 4.6, so that there are zero degrees of freedom. It is therefore impossible to test the validity of the model (3.5) and the estimation of its parameters is a matter of plotting four logits in a diagram and drawing straight lines through the four points (see Figure 4.4).

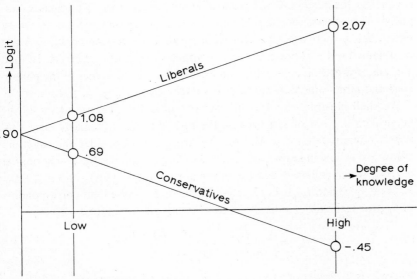

Fig. 4.4. A logit picture of the vote proportions for a progressive candidate

These points are indicated by small circles in the figure; the two nonvertical lines through them serve to describe the effect of knowledge on the logit under the condition that this effect is linear for both conservatives and liberals, as (3.5) specifies.

Numbers of Observations, of Cells, of Parameters, and of Degrees of Freedom

The numbers of *observations* in the various cells (n_{ijk} for Tables 4.1 and 4.2 and n_{ij} for the figures in the first two lines of Table 4.6) play a role in the analysis to the extent that (1) they should be sufficiently large for the large-sample results to be applicable and (2) they have an important effect on the χ^2 statistic. The number of *cells* is the number of triples (i, j, k) in the case of Tables 4.1 and 4.2 and the number of pairs (i, j) in that of Table 4.6. This number is the upper limit for the number of *parameters* (α, β's, γ's, δ's). The excess of the number of cells over the number of parameters is the number of *degrees of freedom*, which is thus always nonnegative and which should be strictly positive if the model is to be tested.

It is of considerable interest to compare this with the normal distribution theory of least-squares regression applied to variables that take real values. Here we have no cells, only a number of observations and a number of parameters adjusted. The number of degrees of freedom of the regression is equal to the *number of observations* minus the number of parameters adjusted. This excess, too, should be positive in order that the model can be tested. When there are zero degrees of freedom, regression coefficients can be obtained but it is not possible to compute their standard errors. In logit analysis, however, it is possible to obtain both point estimates of the parameters and large-sample standard errors under zero degrees of freedom.

We shall illustrate this for the data of Table 4.6. [The result should be taken with a grain of salt because the n_{ij}'s are not particularly large, but this is obviously not essential for the argument.] Consider the question, "How low is 'low in knowledge' relative to 'high in knowledge'?" The answer is γ_1/γ_2, which equals γ_1 because of the normalization (3.6). Since $L_{21}-L_{11} = (\beta_2-\beta_1)\gamma_1$ and $L_{22}-L_{12} = \beta_2-\beta_1$, where L_{ij} is the logit corresponding to p_{ij}, the estimate of γ_1 is the ratio of two logit differences:

$$(3.7) \qquad \hat{\gamma}_1 = \frac{l_{21}-l_{11}}{l_{22}-l_{12}} = \frac{1.08-.69}{2.07-(-.45)} = .15$$

where l_{ij} is the logit corresponding to the observed proportion f_{ij}. The large-sample standard error of $\hat{\gamma}_1$ can be derived along the lines of eq. (2.7) and ff. This is pursued in Problems 7 and 8; the result is .15. This is on the high side, which is the obvious consequence of the fact that the n_{ij}'s of Table 4.6 take modest values.

4.4. Conditional Logit Relations

The previous developments are limited to the dichotomous case in which the response is either Yes or No. In this section we extend the approach to the multiple response case.

Evaluation of Military Policemen

Table 4.7 describes the evaluation of military policemen (MPs) by black soldiers in World War II; it is taken from STOUFFER et al. (1949, p. 560). The first two lines deal with black MPs and contain four cells, each of which consists of four numbers. The number before the parentheses is the number of observations and those within the parentheses are successively the proportion of those who regard the MPs "unfair most of the time", of those

TABLE 4.7

EVALUATION OF MILITARY POLICEMEN BY BLACK SOLDIERS

Camp	Northern men		Southern men	
	Evaluation of black MPs			
North	464	(.078, .511, .411)	801	(.076, .413, .511)
South	1279	(.163, .554, .283)	2392	(.102, .455, .443)
	Evaluation of white MPs			
North	459	(.292, .450, .258)	766	(.261, .409, .330)
South	1237	(.438, .416, .146)	2419	(.314, .416, .270)

who regard them as "about half fair, half unfair", and of those who regard the MPs as "usually fair". The cell upper left thus indicates that there were 464 Northern men in Northern camps who gave a verdict on black MPs, which was "unfair" in 7.8 per cent of the 464 cases, "fair" in 41.1 per cent, and "halfway" in the remaining 51.1 per cent. The last two lines contain similar data on the evaluation of white MPs. Soldiers who were undecided are eliminated.

Table 4.7 thus displays the evaluation of MPs by black soldiers as a function of two characteristics of these soldiers: their region of origin (North/South) and the location of their camp (same). This is analogous to the cases considered in earlier sections of this chapter, but there is a difference in that the evaluation takes the form of three proportions. Our objective is to extend the logit model for such cases in which the number of possible responses is larger than two.[1]

Conditional Logits

We shall indicate the three relative frequencies of each cell in Table 4.7 by $f_{ij}(r)$, where r refers to the verdict ($r = 1$, usually unfair; $r = 2$, halfway;

---

[1] See also BOCK (1971) for an alternative procedure which uses a logistic response function for ordered response categories.

$r = 3$, usually fair) and the subscripts i and j to the determining factors. These are the region of origin X (with subscript $i = 1$ for North and $i = 2$ for South) and the location of the camp Y (with subscript $j = 1$ for North, $j = 2$ for South). The corresponding number of observations will be denoted by n_{ij}.

The observed relative frequency $f_{ij}(r)$ is the sample counterpart of the conditional probability $p_{ij}(r)$ of the rth response, given $X = X_i$ and $Y = Y_j$. These probabilities and frequencies obviously satisfy

$$(4.1) \qquad \sum_{r=1}^{3} p_{ij}(r) = \sum_{r=1}^{3} f_{ij}(r) = 1 \quad \text{for each pair } (i, j)$$

One possible model is a linear logit equation for each response r. This implies that the logarithm of the ratio of $p_{ij}(r)$ to $1 - p_{ij}(r)$ is written as a linear function of unknown parameters. Note, however, that (1.3) implies that $p_{ij}(r)$ is then a nonlinear function of these parameters. Since (4.1) states that summation of $p_{ij}(r)$ over r gives 1, this leads to nonlinear constraints on the parameters.

A more promising approach is to look at pairs of responses, say the rth and the sth ($r \neq s$). Under the condition that the response is either the rth or the sth, the odds favoring the rth are of the form $p_{ij}(r)/p_{ij}(s)$. The logarithm of this ratio is called the conditional logit favoring the rth response relative to the sth, the condition being the one just mentioned (plus, of course, the condition $X = X_i$, $Y = Y_j$). The approach is then to formulate a set of equations, one for each pair (r, s), $r \neq s$. Since such equations determine only ratios of probabilities, they can never be in conflict with (4.1); in fact, that equation will enable us to obtain the individual values of the probabilities once their ratios are determined. This difficulty thus disappears, but we will have to face others, since the equations for different pairs (r, s) must be formulated so that they are not in conflict with each other.

A Linear Model for Conditional Logits

A linear equation for a conditional logit is of the form

$$(4.2) \qquad \log \frac{p_{ij}(r)}{p_{ij}(s)} = A(r, s) + B_i(r, s) + C_j(r, s)$$

This specification describes the effects of the determining factors X and Y linearly without interaction. Next consider the same equation for the conditional odds $p_{ij}(s)/p_{ij}(t)$:

$$\log \frac{p_{ij}(s)}{p_{ij}(t)} = A(s, t) + B_i(s, t) + C_j(s, t)$$

and add this equation to (4.2):

$$(4.3) \quad \log \frac{p_{ij}(r)}{p_{ij}(s)} + \log \frac{p_{ij}(s)}{p_{ij}(t)}$$

$$= [A(r, s) + A(s, t)] + [B_i(r, s) + B_i(s, t)] + [C_j(r, s) + C_j(s, t)]$$

The left-hand side of (4.3) is the logarithm of the odds $p_{ij}(r)/p_{ij}(t)$, for which the equation is

$$(4.4) \qquad\qquad \log \frac{p_{ij}(r)}{p_{ij}(t)} = A(r, t) + B_i(r, t) + C_j(r, t)$$

Since the right-hand sides of (4.3) and (4.4) must be equal for all values of the determining factors X and Y, we have the following constraints:

$$A(r, s) + A(s, t) = A(r, t)$$
$$(4.5) \qquad B_i(r, s) + B_i(s, t) = B_i(r, t)$$
$$C_j(r, s) + C_j(s, t) = C_j(r, t)$$

These are circularity conditions which imply that $A(r, s)$ can be written in the form $\alpha_r - \alpha_s$ for appropriate values of the α's, and similarly $B_i(r, s) = \beta_{ir} - \beta_{is}$ and $C_j(r, s) = \gamma_{jr} - \gamma_{js}$. We can therefore write (4.2) in the form

$$(4.6) \qquad\qquad \log \frac{p_{ij}(r)}{p_{ij}(s)} = (\alpha_r - \alpha_s) + (\beta_{ir} - \beta_{is}) + (\gamma_{jr} - \gamma_{js})$$

It is easily verified that it is sufficient to consider eq. (4.6) for only one value of s (say, $s = 1$) and for all values of r different from this s, since the equations for other (r, s) pairs can be obtained from these by linear combination. Also, the right-hand side of (4.6) shows that only the differences between the α's matter, and similarly for the β's for each i and the γ's for each j. We may therefore normalize as follows:

$$(4.7) \qquad\qquad \alpha_1 = \beta_{i1} = \gamma_{j1} = 0 \quad \text{for each } i \text{ and } j$$

The Linear Conditional Logit Specification for the Evaluation of MPs

For the case of Table 4.7 we have two equations of the form (4.6):

$$(4.8) \qquad\qquad \log \frac{p_{ij}(2)}{p_{ij}(1)} = \alpha_2 + \beta_{i2} + \gamma_{j2}$$

(4.9)
$$\log \frac{p_{ij}(3)}{p_{ij}(1)} = \alpha_3 + \beta_{i3} + \gamma_{j3}$$

These equations correspond to $s = 1$ and $r = 2$ and 3 in (4.6); note that the normalization (4.7) has been applied. Equation (4.8) relates the probability of a "halfway" verdict to that of "usually unfair", and (4.9) compares "usually fair" with "usually unfair". By subtracting (4.9) from (4.8) we obtain the logarithm of $p_{ij}(2)/p_{ij}(3)$ on the left, and the resulting equation thus compares "halfway" with "usually fair".

For three possible responses we have two logit equations, (4.8) and (4.9), instead of the single logit equation of the dichotomous case. As in the latter case we may apply the additional normalization

(4.10)
$$\beta_{12} = \gamma_{12} = \beta_{13} = \gamma_{13} = 0$$

because raising α_2 by A and β_{i2} for each i by B and subtracting $A + B$ from γ_{j2} for each j leaves the right-hand side of (4.8) unaffected, while (4.9) has a similar property.

The total number of unknown parameters is thus six: α_2, α_3, β_{22}, β_{23}, γ_{22}, γ_{23}. Table 4.7 supplies us with three observed proportions in each of the four cells, but one of the three can be derived from the other two, so that there are $4 \times 2 = 8$ independent relative frequencies and hence $8 - 6 = 2$ degrees of freedom. These numbers (6 parameters, 8 cell frequencies, 2 degrees of freedom) are all twice as large as the corresponding numbers for the dichotomous case with two determining factors that take two values each. See Problems 9 and 10 for a generalization of this result.

Least Squares after a Transformation

To simplify the notation we shall write

(4.11)
$$L_{ij}(r, s) = \log \frac{p_{ij}(r)}{p_{ij}(s)} \quad \text{and} \quad l_{ij}(r, s) = \log \frac{f_{ij}(r)}{f_{ij}(s)}$$

for, respectively, the theoretical value of the conditional logit and for the value based on the observed relative frequencies. We can then write eqs. (4.8) and (4.9) with the latter logits in the left-hand sides:

(4.12)
$$l_{ij}(2, 1) = \alpha_2 + \beta_{i2} + \gamma_{j2} + [l_{ij}(2, 1) - L_{ij}(2, 1)]$$

(4.13)
$$l_{ij}(3, 1) = \alpha_3 + \beta_{i3} + \gamma_{j3} + [l_{ij}(3, 1) - L_{ij}(3, 1)]$$

These equations are completely analogous to eq. (2.2). Again, we should ask whether the error terms have zero expectation and constant variance and whether they are uncorrelated. This question will be answered under the assumption that the observed data have been obtained by independent random drawings from four trinomial populations with probabilities $p_{ij}(1)$, $p_{ij}(2)$, and $p_{ij}(3)$, where (i, j) takes the four values $(1, 1)$, $(1, 2)$, $(2, 1)$, and $(2, 2)$.

The present case differs from that of Section 4.2 in that the error terms of (4.12) and (4.13) for the same pair (i, j) are correlated. This means that these two equations have to be transformed linearly in order that the error terms have the desired properties. The matter is pursued in Problems 11 to 13; the result is that the left-hand sides of the equations after the transformation are

(4.14) $$\sqrt{n_{ij} f_{ij}(2)}\, [l_{ij}(2, 1) - a_{ij}]$$

(4.15) $$\sqrt{n_{ij} f_{ij}(3)}\, [l_{ij}(3, 1) - a_{ij}]$$

where

(4.16) $$a_{ij} = \frac{1}{1 - \sqrt{f_{ij}(1)}} [f_{ij}(2) l_{ij}(2, 1) - f_{ij}(3) l_{ij}(3)]$$

This transformation is similar to the weighted least-squares method of Section 4.2 in that the number of observations enters in square-root form. Furthermore, the logit $l_{ij}(2, 1)$ has a zero weight in (4.14) when $f_{ij}(2) = 0$, which is also analogous to the earlier case. When $f_{ij}(2)$ approaches unity, and hence $f_{ij}(1)$ and $f_{ij}(3)$ both approach zero, a_{ij} becomes effectively equal to $l_{ij}(2, 1)$. Since a_{ij} is subtracted from $l_{ij}(2, 1)$ in (4.14), this logit thus disappears from the transformed least-squares computations when $f_{ij}(2) = 1$, which is also in agreement with the procedure of Section 4.2.

Discussion of the Estimates

The estimates obtained from the procedure described above are shown in the upper left part of Table 4.8. The parameter α_2 is the conditional logit in favor of "half fair, half unfair" relative to "unfair most of the time" for Northern men in Northern camps. Its value is much smaller for white than for black MPs, which indicates that the former are less popular than the latter. The same conclusion may also be drawn from the estimates of α_3, the conditional logit in favor of "fair most of the time" relative to "unfair most of the time" for the same group of soldiers. The parameters β_{22} and β_{23} measure the effect on these logits of a Southern instead of a Northern origin. They are positive in all four cases, which means that Southerners look at MPs more favorably than Northerners do. The γ's measure the effect

TABLE 4.8

PARAMETER ESTIMATES OF ALTERNATIVE CONDITIONAL LOGIT SPECIFICATIONS FOR SOLDIERS'
EVALUATION OF MPS

	Black MPs	White MPs	Black MPs	White MPs	
	Unconstrained estimates (*no interaction*)		*Unconstrained estimates* *with interaction*		
α_2	1.64 (.12)	.28 (.08)	1.72 (.13)	.35 (.08)	α_2
α_3	1.32 (.13)	−.39 (.09)	1.47 (.14)	−.27 (.10)	α_3
β_{22}	.20 (.10)	.27 (.07)	.10 (.10)	.18 (.07)	β_{22}
β_{23}	.78 (.10)	.78 (.08)	.62 (.12)	.65 (.09)	β_{23}
γ_{22}	−.37 (.12)	−.30 (.08)	−.41 (.12)	−.32 (.08)	γ_{22}
γ_{23}	−.68 (.12)	−.59 (.09)	−.76 (.13)	−.68 (.09)	γ_{23}
δ	.	.	.07 (.03)	.07 (.02)	δ
	Constrained estimates (*no interaction*)		*Constrained estimates* *with interaction*		
α_2	1.57 (.05)	.32 (.03)	1.57 (.05)	.32 (.03)	α_2
α_3	1.33 (.05)	−.31 (.04)	1.32 (.05)	−.34 (.04)	α_3

of a Southern instead of a Northern camp. Their negative signs imply that MPs in Southern camps are less popular than in the North.

A pairwise comparison of the parameter estimates for black and white MPs shows that the constant terms (α_2 and α_3) are quite different, but that those which measure the effects of origin and camp location are very close to each other. In fact, the following rounded figures seem to give an adequate picture of the β's and γ's for both black and white MPs:

$$(4.17) \qquad \begin{aligned} \beta_{22} &= \tfrac{1}{4} & \gamma_{22} &= -\tfrac{1}{3} \\ \beta_{23} &= \tfrac{3}{4} & \gamma_{23} &= -\tfrac{2}{3} \end{aligned}$$

If the hypothesis of pairwise equal β's and γ's for the two groups of MPs is correct, this has the important implication that, although the levels of the evaluation of black and white MPs as measured by the α's are different, the extent to which this evaluation is affected by the region of origin and the location of the camp is the same for the two groups.

When the specification (4.17) is accepted, the only free parameters of the model are α_2 and α_3. They can be re-estimated subject to (4.17), and the result is shown in the lower left part of Table 4.8. The point estimates are close to those obtained when (4.17) is not imposed, but the standard errors are reduced substantially.

Discussion of the Fit

To test the hypothesis that $f_{ij}(1)$, $f_{ij}(2)$, $f_{ij}(3)$ is the result of n_{ij} independent random drawings from a trinomial population with probabilities $p_{ij}(1)$, $p_{ij}(2)$, $p_{ij}(3)$ we extend the expression in the left-hand side of (2.9) to

$$(4.18) \qquad n_{ij} \sum_{r=1}^{3} \frac{[f_{ij}(r) - p_{ij}(r)]^2}{p_{ij}(r)}$$

which is asymptotically $(n_{ij} \to \infty)$ distributed as $\chi^2(2)$ if the null hypothesis is true. By computing the sum of the expressions (4.18) over the four values taken by the pair (i, j) we obtain a random variable with distribution $\chi^2(8)$. If we then replace $p_{ij}(r)$ by $\hat{p}_{ij}(r)$, the probability estimate implied by the conditional logit model,[1] this random variable becomes

$$(4.19) \qquad \sum_{i=1}^{2} \sum_{j=1}^{2} n_{ij} \sum_{r=1}^{3} \frac{[f_{ij}(r) - \hat{p}_{ij}(r)]^2}{\hat{p}_{ij}(r)}.$$

Its distribution is χ^2 with a number of degrees of freedom equal to 8 minus the number of parameters adjusted. This is $8 - 2 = 6$ for the fit based on (4.17), and the χ^2's are 9.3 for black MPs and 11.1 for white MPs, neither of which is significant at the 5 per cent levels. This suggests that the conditional logit model combined with (4.17) is an acceptable hypothesis for the data of Table 4.7.

Several qualifications must be made, however. First, the 5 per cent point of $\chi^2(6)$ is 12.6, so that the above χ^2's are on the high side even though they are not significant at that level.[2] Second, when we do not impose (4.17) and hence use the estimates of the upper left part of Table 4.8, we obtain χ^2's of 7.8 for black MPs and 10.0 for white MPs. These figures are below the χ^2's mentioned in the previous paragraph, but they are nevertheless significant at the 5 per cent level because the six adjusted coefficients imply that there are only two degrees of freedom in each case.

These considerations suggest that an analysis of the discrepancies between the probability estimates and the observed relative frequencies can shed

---

[1] See Problem 15 for an expression of these probability estimates in terms of the parameter estimates of the conditional logit model.

[2] Note that the two χ^2's are not independent, so that it is not permissible to treat their sum as a χ^2 with 12 degrees of freedom (which would give a significant result at the 5 per cent level). The reason is that each soldier was asked to evaluate both black and white MPs, and it is likely the answers are dependent in the sense that, if a man passes a favorable (unfavorable) verdict on one group of MPs, this raises the probability that he also passes a favorable (unfavorable) verdict on the other group.

TABLE 4.9

DISCREPANCIES BETWEEN ESTIMATED PROBABILITIES AND OBSERVED RELATIVE FREQUENCIES
FOR THE DATA OF TABLE 4.7 (NO INTERACTION)

Camp	Northern men			Southern men		
	Unfair	Halfway	Fair	Unfair	Halfway	Fair
Black MPs, no constraint						
North	−.023	−.009	.032	.011	.007	−.018
South	.007	.004	−.012	−.004	−.002	.006
Black MPs, constraint (4.17)						
North	−.026	.009	.017	.010	.005	−.016
South	.007	.014	−.020	−.003	−.010	.013
White MPs, no constraint						
North	−.041	.008	.033	.023	−.003	−.020
South	.015	−.002	−.013	−.008	.001	.006
White MPs, constraint (4.17)						
North	−.029	.006	.023	.030	−.001	−.028
South	.015	−.002	−.013	−.012	.001	.011

some further light on our problem. Table 4.9 contains $f_{ij}(r) - \hat{p}_{ij}(r)$ for the estimates both with and without constraint (4.17). It appears that the discrepancies for $r = 2$ ("halfway") are mostly close to zero but that those corresponding to $r = 1$ and $r = 3$ are frequently large. Moreover, the latter discrepancies have a very definite sign pattern. Among soldiers whose camp is in their own area (Northern men in Northern camps and Southern men in Southern camps), the discrepancies are negative for $r = 1$ ("unfair") and positive for $r = 3$ ("fair"). Among soldiers whose camp is in an area other than that of their origin (Northern men in Southern camps and Southern men in Northern camps), the signs of the discrepancies are reversed: positive for $r = 1$, negative for $r = 3$.

This means that the conditional logit model predicts too much "unfair" and too little "fair" for men in camps in their own region, and too little "unfair" and too much "fair" for men in camps in a region other than their own. In other words, when men are in camps in their own region, they enjoy a better relationship with their MPs than the conditional logit model indicates, and the situation is exactly the opposite for men in camps outside their region of origin.

A Conditional Logit Model with Interaction

Since the conclusion drawn above does not seem to be a priori unreasonable, it is appropriate to introduce a term describing the interaction between region of origin and location of camp. However, we face the difficulty that there are not enough degrees of freedom available for the introduction of double-subscript terms [such as β_{ik} in (3.3)]. An approach which economizes on the number of unknown parameters is therefore in order.

Consider the conditional odds $p_{ij}(1)/p_{ij}(2)$ and $p_{ij}(3)/p_{ij}(2)$, with the "halfway" case in the denominator, and the following equations for their logarithms:

$$(4.20) \qquad \log \frac{p_{ij}(1)}{p_{ij}(2)} = (\alpha_1 - \alpha_2) + (\beta_{i1} - \beta_{i2}) + (\gamma_{j1} - \gamma_{j2}) - \delta(-1)^{i+j}$$

$$(4.21) \qquad \log \frac{p_{ij}(3)}{p_{ij}(2)} = (\alpha_3 - \alpha_2) + (\beta_{i3} - \beta_{i2}) + (\gamma_{j3} - \gamma_{j2}) + \delta(-1)^{i+j}$$

This specification is identical with (4.6) except for the last term, which represents the interaction effect. For Northern men in Northern camps we have $i+j = 2$, and for Southern men in Southern camps $i+j = 4$. In both cases $i+j$ is even and hence $(-1)^{i+j} = 1$. Therefore, when men are in camps in their own region, we have $-\delta$ in (4.20) and $+\delta$ in (4.21). For men in camps outside their region $i+j$ equals 3 and hence $(-1)^{i+j} = -1$, so that the signs of δ are reversed. Thus, when δ takes a positive value, the probability of "unfair" is reduced relative to that of "halfway", and the probability of "fair" is raised relative to that of "halfway" for all men in camps in their own region. For the others the effect works in the opposite way. Note further that by subtracting (4.21) from (4.20) we obtain

$$(4.22) \qquad \log \frac{p_{ij}(1)}{p_{ij}(3)} = (\alpha_1 - \alpha_3) + (\beta_{i1} - \beta_{i3}) + (\gamma_{j1} - \gamma_{j3}) - 2\delta(-1)^{i+j}$$

This shows that in the conditional logit comparison of "unfair" and "fair", the interaction parameter is twice as large as in (4.20) and (4.21).

The numerical results for this specification are shown in the upper right part of Table 4.8. The point estimate of δ is .07 for both black and white MPs. The estimates of the β's are somewhat smaller than those of the no-interaction specification, whereas those of the γ's have become a little larger in absolute value. However, they are not far from the numerical specification (4.17) when one takes the size of the standard errors into account. A natural procedure is then to re-estimate the model (4.20)–(4.21) for the β's and γ's equal to these rounded values and for δ also equal to a rounded value, for which we shall take .05. The resulting estimates and their standard errors are given in the lower right part of Table 4.8, and it is seen that they are close to those of the no-interaction specification in the lower left part. The implied probability estimates along with the observed relative frequencies and the discrepancies are shown in Table 4.10. These discrepancies are reduced rather considerably relative to the corresponding values of Table 4.9, which is confirmed by the modest values of the new χ^2's, 3.23 for black MPs and 1.69 for white MPs.

TABLE 4.10

PROBABILITY ESTIMATES FOR THE DATA OF TABLE 4.7 UNDER CONDITIONS OF INTERACTION

Camp	Northern men			Southern men		
	Unfair	Halfway	Fair	Unfair	Halfway	Fair
Black MPs: observed relative frequencies						
North	.078	.511	.411	.076	.413	.511
South	.163	.554	.283	.102	.455	.443
Black MPs: probability estimates						
North	.098	.497	.405	.071	.419	.509
South	.166	.546	.288	.099	.460	.442
Black MPs: discrepancies						
North	−.020	.014	.006	.005	−.006	.002
South	−.003	.008	−.005	.003	−.005	.001
White MPs: observed relative frequencies						
North	.292	.450	.258	.261	.409	.330
South	.438	.416	.146	.314	.416	.270
White MPs: probability estimates						
North	.309	.446	.244	.247	.414	.339
South	.441	.413	.147	.314	.417	.270
White MPs: discrepancies						
North	−.017	.004	.014	.014	−.005	−.009
South	−.003	.003	−.001	.000	−.001	.000

4.5. The Explanatory Power of Factors Determining Decompositions

In the previous sections we developed methods to assess the influence of determining factors on qualitative variables. To a large extent, these methods are comparable with the computation of regression coefficients which measure the influence of the independent variables of a regression on the dependent variable. This section is devoted to another extension of least-squares theory, viz., the multiple and partial correlation coefficients which serve as measures of the explanatory power of the determining variables. The exposition is a continuation both of the earlier sections of this chapter and also of Section 3.7.

Correlation Coefficients and Average Conditional Entropies

We start by considering the simple case of two real-valued random variables x and y which follow a bivariate normal distribution with correlation coefficient ρ. It is well known that the conditional distribution of y, given x, is normal with a mean equal to a linear function of x and a variance independent of x, and that this constant variance of y given x is a fraction $1 - \rho^2$ of the unconditional variance of y. Consequently, there is zero variance of y given x, and hence no uncertainty of y given x, in the limiting case $|\rho| = 1$. Conversely, there is a maximum variance of y given x in the other limiting case $\rho = 0$, which is the case of stochastic independence of x and y.

Now go back to Table 4.1 on page 165. For the sake of simplicity, consider the first column only, so that we confine ourselves to Southern soldiers who are not against racial separation. The only two variables are then the preference for a combat outfit (Yes or No) and the level of education, and the question is how we can measure the uncertainty of the former variable, given the latter. There is, obviously, a minimum of uncertainty when the probability of combat outfit preference is either 0 or 1 for every value of the education variable. This is the case of a zero average conditional entropy of the preference for a combat outfit, given education, and it corresponds to the limiting case $|\rho| = 1$ of the previous paragraph. There is a maximum of uncertainty as to the preference for a combat outfit, given education, when the two variables are stochastically independent. This is the case in which the average conditional entropy of combat outfit preference, given education, is equal to the unconditional entropy of the former variable. It corresponds to the other limiting case $\rho = 0$ discussed above.

These considerations suggest that a comparison of unconditional and average conditional entropies can provide adequate measures for the explanatory power of factors determining qualitative variables, in much the same way that we used the average conditional vote entropy, given the legislator's state and party affiliation, for a similar purpose in Section 3.7. Of course, we did not attempt to formulate a logit model or any other type of model to describe the effects of state and party on the legislator's vote, neither with nor without interaction. We were only interested in the average uncertainty of the legislator's vote, given these two factors. However, this subtle distinction is entirely comparable with that between correlation and regression analysis. We may be interested in knowing how highly two variables are correlated without running a regression of one on the other, because when the correlation is known we also know (under conditions of bivariate normality) by how much the variance of one variable is reduced when the other takes a given value. That corresponds to what we did in Section 3.7. But we may also be interested in the counterpart for qualitative variables of *both* regression *and* correlation. The counterpart of regression was the subject of Sections 4.1 to 4.4, and that of correlation is the subject of the present section.

Application to Three Sets of Data

In the case of Tables 4.1 and 4.2 we have three determining factors, denoted by X, Y and Z, and a dependent variable which will be written D. This D is the preference for a combat outfit in Table 4.1 and the preference for a Southern camp in Table 4.2; the variable takes two values in both cases, D_1 (Yes) and D_2 (No). We will write p_{rijk} for the joint probability of $D = D_r$, $X = X_i$, $Y = Y_j$, and $Z = Z_k$, and we will indicate by dots in the relevant place that there is summation over a subscript. The unconditional entropy of the dependent variable is then

$$(5.1) \qquad\qquad H(D) = \sum_r p_{r...} \log \frac{1}{p_{r...}}$$

and its average conditional entropy, given X, Y and Z, is

$$(5.2) \qquad\qquad H_{XYZ}(D) = \sum_r \sum_i \sum_j \sum_k p_{rijk} \log \frac{p_{.ijk}}{p_{rijk}}$$

It is readily verified that $H_{XYZ}(D)$ is indeed a weighted average of the conditional entropies of D, given $X = X_i$, $Y = Y_j$, $Z = Z_k$, with weights equal to the probabilities of the conditions. Note that all summations, both in (5.1) and in (5.2) and in the sequel of this section, are over the entire range of the relevant subscript.

To evaluate these entropies we must specify the probabilities p_{rijk} numerically. We will do so in the simplest possible manner by dividing the observed number of cases by the relevant total. For example, the number of cases corresponding to p_{1111} and p_{2111} in Table 4.1 are $2051 \times (.09)$ and $2051 \times (.91)$, respectively, and to obtain these two probabilities we divide these numbers by the sum of the 12 numbers in the upper half of the table. The above entropies (in nits) for Table 4.1 are then

$$(5.3) \qquad\qquad H(D) = .456 \qquad H_{XYZ}(D) = .437$$

and for Table 4.2:

$$(5.4) \qquad\qquad H(D) = .693 \qquad H_{XYZ}(D) = .499$$

For the MPs of Table 4.7 we have only two conditioning factors, X and Y, so that in (5.1) and (5.2) the fourth subscript and the summation over k are deleted. The result for black MPs is

$$(5.5) \qquad\qquad H(D) = .962 \qquad H_{XY}(D) = .947$$

and for white MPs:

$$(5.6) \qquad\qquad H(D) = 1.076 \qquad H_{XY}(D) = 1.062$$

The average uncertainty reduction due to knowledge of the determining factors, defined as the excess of $H(D)$ over the relevant average conditional entropy of D, is thus about .2 nit in (5.4) but only about 1 or 2 per cent of a nit in the three other cases. The last figure seems incredibly low. How should we interpret this result?

The Magnitude of Average Uncertainty Reductions

In the case of Table 4.1 we basically ask this question. If we know the soldier's attitude toward racial separation, and where he comes from, and the level of his education, to what extent does this enable us to predict whether this man prefers to be in a combat outfit? In particular, to what degree can we make such a prediction with more confidence (less uncertainty) than when such knowledge is not available? The probability $p_{1...}$ of combat outfit preference prior to this knowledge is a little below 20 per cent, which is modified to values ranging from 9 to 31 per cent when this knowledge becomes available. If the probability becomes .09, there is less uncertainty than before; if it becomes .31, there is more uncertainty. Consequently, although there is on the average less uncertainty when we know the values of the three determining factors, this average reduction of uncertainty may take very modest values. It is only in the limiting case in which all conditional probabilities are either 0 or 1 (for any values taken by the determining factors) that the uncertainty is removed completely. The data of Table 4.1 show that this is not nearly the case, and the entropy reduction $H(D) - H_{XYZ}(D)$ therefore takes a small value.

To obtain an intuitive idea of the order of magnitude of entropy reductions, consider the following example from probabilistic weather prediction. The Weather Bureau is able to announce on August 9 whether the chance of a sunny August 10 in a particular area is $\frac{1}{4}$, $\frac{1}{2}$, or $\frac{3}{4}$. In a long series of August 9s these three predictions are made equally frequently. To insure consistency we assume that the climatological chance of a sunny August 10 is $\frac{1}{3}(\frac{1}{4}+\frac{1}{2}+\frac{3}{4}) = \frac{1}{2}$. The unconditional entropy of a sunny August 10 is thus $\log 2 = .6931$ nit; it measures the uncertainty which prevails before the forecast is made. The three possible conditional entropies, given the three possible forecasts, are

$$-\tfrac{1}{4}\log\tfrac{1}{4}-\tfrac{3}{4}\log\tfrac{3}{4} = .5623 \text{ nit}$$
$$-\tfrac{1}{2}\log\tfrac{1}{2}-\tfrac{1}{2}\log\tfrac{1}{2} = .6931 \text{ nit}$$
$$-\tfrac{3}{4}\log\tfrac{3}{4}-\tfrac{1}{4}\log\tfrac{1}{4} = .5623 \text{ nit}$$

The average conditional entropy, given the Weather Bureau's forecast, is obtained by weighting these three values equally, which gives .6059 nit, and the entropy reduction is therefore .0872 nit. This is larger than the corresponding values of Tables 4.1 and 4.7 but smaller than that of Table 4.2.

Indeed, in the case of Table 4.2 we have a relatively large average uncertainty reduction due to the knowledge of the determining factors. The unconditional probability of a preference for a Southern camp is close to $\frac{1}{2}$, which follows from the fact that $H(D)$ of (5.4) agrees in three decimal places with the maximum value for two possible outcomes. But when it is known that the soldier is a Northern black in a Northern camp or a Southern white in a Southern camp, it is nearly certain (the odds are about 10 to 1) what his preference will be. In addition, the odds are better than 3 to 1 for three other groups of soldiers. These five groups form a substantial majority of the sample, which leads to a comparatively large difference between $H(D)$ and $H_{XYZ}(D)$.

Partial Entropy Reductions

As a direct extension of the definition given in eq. (7.12) of Section 3.7, we define the partial entropy reduction of D due to X, given Y and Z, as a difference of two average conditional entropies:

$$(5.7) \quad H_{YZ}(D) - H_{XYZ}(D)$$

$$= \sum_r \sum_j \sum_k p_{r.jk} \log \frac{p_{..jk}}{p_{r.jk}} - \sum_r \sum_i \sum_j \sum_k p_{rijk} \log \frac{p_{.ijk}}{p_{rijk}}$$

$$= \sum_r \sum_i \sum_j \sum_k p_{rijk} \log \frac{p_{rijk}}{p_{r.jk} \, p_{.ijk}/p_{..jk}}$$

It is readily verified that the expression in the last line is the expected information of the message which transforms prior probabilities of the form $p_{r.jk} p_{.ijk}/p_{..jk}$ into corresponding posterior probabilities p_{rijk}. This information expectation is positive except when

$$(5.8) \qquad \frac{p_{rijk}}{p_{.ijk}} = \frac{p_{r.jk}}{p_{..jk}} \quad \text{for each } (r, i, j, k)$$

in which case the partial entropy reduction (5.7) vanishes. Condition (5.8)

TABLE 4.11

ENTROPY REDUCTIONS

Table 4.1 (combat outfit)		Table 4.2 (Southern camp)		Table 4.7 (black MPs)		Table 4.7 (white MPs)	
Unconditional entropy of dependent variable							
	.4558		.6931		.9625		1.0763
Partial entropy reductions							
Separation*:	.0015	Origin:	.1424	Origin:	.0112	Origin:	.0103
Origin:	.0053	Race	.0094	Camp:	.0051	Camp:	.0056
Education:	.0064	Camp:	.0431				
Total partial reduction							
	.0132		.1949		.0164		.0160
Dependence effect							
	.0060		−.0010		−.0011		−.0015
Joint entropy reduction due to all determining factors							
	.0192		.1939		.0153		.0144
Remaining average conditional entropy							
	.4366		.4992		.9472		1.0619

* Attitude toward racial separation.

implies that the distribution of D given X, Y, and Z is completely independent of X. In the special case of the logit model (1.2) this would amount to zero values of the β's.

These partial entropy reductions are shown in Table 4.11 for the data considered earlier in this chapter. It appears that in the case of Table 4.1 the partial entropy reductions due to the region of origin and to education are of the same order of magnitude, whereas that due to the attitude toward racial separation is much smaller. This is, at least qualitatively, in agreement with the corresponding coefficient estimates of the logit equation of Section 4.2. In the case of Table 4.2 the largest partial entropy reduction is that due to region of origin, followed by that due to location of the camp, while the third (race) trails far behind. The picture of the partial reductions for black and white MPs is nearly equal. This is not at all surprising, given our earlier conclusion that the dependence of the soldiers' evaluation of these two groups of MPs on the determining factors (origin and camp location) is at least approximately the same.

Do the Partial Entropy Reductions Add up to the Joint Entropy Reduction?

By adding the partial entropy reductions of all determining factors we obtain the total partial entropy reduction, and the question naturally arises whether this total partial reduction is equal to the total entropy reduction of all factors jointly. We shall consider this problem here for the two-factor case.

The total partial entropy reduction in the case of two factors is

$$[H_Y(D) - H_{XY}(D)] + [H_X(D) - H_{XY}(D)]$$

and the joint reduction is $H(D) - H_{XY}(D)$. Its excess over the total partial reduction is therefore

$$(5.9) \qquad H(D) - H_X(D) - H_Y(D) + H_{XY}(D)$$

It is a matter of straightforward algebra to verify that this excess can be written as

$$(5.10) \quad \sum_r \sum_i \sum_j p_{rij} \left(\log \frac{p_{.ij}}{p_{.i.} p_{..j}} - \log \frac{p_{rij} \, p_{r..}}{p_{ri.} \, p_{r.j}} \right)$$

$$= \sum_i \sum_j p_{.ij} \log \frac{p_{.ij}}{p_{.i.} p_{..j}} - \sum_r p_{r..} \sum_i \sum_j \frac{p_{rij}}{p_{r..}} \log \frac{p_{rij}/p_{r..}}{\dfrac{p_{ri.}}{p_{r..}} \dfrac{p_{r.j}}{p_{r..}}}$$

The first expression in the second line is the expected mutual information of X and Y:

$$(5.11) \qquad J(X, Y) = \sum_i \sum_j p_{.ij} \log \frac{p_{.ij}}{p_{.i.} p_{..j}}$$

The second expression in (5.10) may be regarded as a weighted average of the expected mutual informations of X and Y in their joint conditional distributions given $D = D_r$, with weights equal to the probabilities of the conditions:

$$(5.12) \qquad J_{D_r}(X, Y) = \sum_i \sum_j \frac{p_{rij}}{p_{r..}} \log \frac{p_{rij}/p_{r..}}{\dfrac{p_{ri.}}{p_{r..}} \dfrac{p_{r.j}}{p_{r..}}}$$

We may thus write the excess (5.9) in the form

$$(5.13) \qquad H(D) - H_X(D) - H_Y(D) + H_{XY}(D) = J(X, Y) - J_D(X, Y)$$

where

$$(5.14) \qquad J_D(X, Y) = \sum_r p_{r..} J_{D_r}(X, Y)$$

It thus appears that the excess of the joint entropy reduction over the total partial entropy reduction is equal to the excess of $J(X, Y)$, the expected mutual information of the two determining factors, over $J_D(X, Y)$, which is the average conditional value of their expected mutual informations, given the dependent variable. Since the expected mutual information is a measure of dependence, we may conclude that the joint entropy reduction is larger (smaller) than the total partial reduction when there is more (less) dependence in the joint marginal distribution of the determining factors than in their joint conditional distributions (given the dependent variable) on the average. It appears from Problems 17 to 19 that this result also holds for any larger number of determining factors than two under a suitable multivariate generalization of the expected mutual information concept.

Since the right-hand side of (5.13) concerns the degree to which the determining factors are dependent in their marginal and various conditional distributions, we shall refer to it as the *dependence effect* on the entropy reductions.[1] These effects are shown in Table 4.11 for the data considered

---

[1] This dependence effect bears some resemblance to the multicollinearity effect in product-moment correlation theory, which may be described as follows. Write $R^2 - R_h^2$ for the incremental contribution of the hth independent variable: the increase in the squared

there. It appears that they take values close to zero in the last three columns, but that the effect accounts for about 30 per cent of the joint entropy reduction in the case of Table 4.1. Notice that the dependence effect may be of either sign; there may be either less or more dependence in the joint marginal distribution of the determining factors than in their joint conditional distributions on the average.

4.6. The Cube Law on Party Legislative Representation

The cube law was referred to earlier in Sections 1.8 and 2.5. It is concerned with a two-party system in which representatives are elected according to a single-member district system, and it states that the ratio of the numbers of representatives elected is approximately proportional to the third power of the ratio of the national votes obtained by the two parties. KENDALL and STUART (1950, 1952) considered this law for British election data and mentioned that it goes back to the first decade of this century. MARCH (1957–58) compared the law with certain American data. The objective of this section is to formulate a simple logit model, described more extensively by THEIL (1970b), which predicts the mathematical form of the relationship described by the cube law, and to compare this model with data on British and American elections.

A Logit Model for the Votes of a District

Let there be N districts and write p_{it} for the proportion of the valid votes cast for Party 1 in the ith district at the tth election, so that $1 - p_{it}$ is the corresponding proportion of Party 2. Our starting point is the assumption that, for most of the districts, the changes in these proportions from one election to the next are in the same direction and of comparable magnitude. One way of formalizing this is by means of a linear equation, $p_{it} = a_i + b_t$, where a_i is a district parameter and b_t an election parameter. This specification is not attractive, however, for reasons similar to those given in the discussion of Table 4.2 in Section 4.1. First, the right-hand side of the equation

---

multiple correlation coefficient which is caused by the addition of this variable to the other independent variables. The sum of all incremental contributions is equal to the contribution R^2 of all independent variables jointly when all these variables are uncorrelated, and the excess of R^2 over the sum of the incremental contributions may be of either sign when the variables are correlated. This excess is known as the multicollinearity effect; see THEIL (1971a, Section 4.4). It comes as no surprise that in linear regression 'uncorrelated' takes the place of 'independent'.

may take values outside the range from zero to one. Second, the specification neglects the fact that it is typically much harder to convince hard-core partisans to vote for the other party than to sway those who are less committed. As an example, take two districts, the ith and the jth, with $a_i = .5$ and $a_j = .7$, so that the jth district leans more toward Party 1 than the ith does. Take $b_t = .2$, so that $p_{it} = .7$ and $p_{jt} = .9$. Suppose that at the next election $b_{t+1} = .25$, with $p_{i,t+1} = .75$ and $p_{j,t+1} = .95$. Assume, for simplicity's sake, that the same voters participated in both elections and that no voters shifted from Party 1 to Party 2. In the ith district we then have 5 out of every 30 Party 2 voters at the tth election who shifted to Party 1 at the $(t+1)^{st}$, whereas it is 5 out of every 10 in the jth district. This does not seem plausible. The 10 per cent Party 2 voters of the jth district at the tth election are at least as likely to be hard-core as the 30 per cent of the ith district, yet one-half of the former group changes its alliance and only one-sixth of the latter.

These objections are avoided when we replace $p_{it} = a_i + b_t$ by the linear logit model:

$$(6.1) \qquad \log \frac{p_t}{1 - p_{it}} = \alpha_i + \beta_t$$

where α_i and β_t are parameters which characterize the ith district and the tth election, respectively. When we invert the roles of the two parties by replacing p_{it} by $1 - p_{it}$, these parameters remain unchanged except for their signs.

The National Vote

Write w_{it} for the proportion of the ith district in the national vote at the tth election. The national proportion of the votes obtained by Party 1 is then

$$(6.2) \qquad p_t = \sum_{i=1}^{N} w_{it} p_{it}$$

and the corresponding proportion for Party 2 is $\sum_i w_{it}(1 - p_{it}) = 1 - p_t$.

One could express p_t in terms of the parameters $\alpha_1, \ldots, \alpha_N, \beta_t$, using eq. (1.3) for the relation between p_{it} and the logit parameters, but the resulting expression is not really convenient. Instead, we shall make use of the fact that in a considerable majority of the districts the political distribution is not very far from 50-50, so that a Taylor approximation around $p_{it} = \frac{1}{2}$ leads to a sufficiently accurate result. Then go back to Figure 4.1 in Section 4.1, which shows that the logit as a function of the proportion has an inflection point at $p = \frac{1}{2}$, and to eq. (1.5) which states that the logit L equals $4(p-\frac{1}{2})$ around $p = \frac{1}{2}$ apart from third-order error terms. This is equivalent to $p \approx \frac{1}{2}+\frac{1}{4}L$ or, applied to (6.1),

$$(6.3) \qquad p_{it} \approx \tfrac{1}{2}+\tfrac{1}{4}(\alpha_i+\beta_t)$$

again except for approximation errors of the third order of smallness. Then combine (6.2) and (6.3):

$$(6.4) \qquad p_t \approx \tfrac{1}{2}+\tfrac{1}{4}\sum_{i=1}^{N} w_{it}\,\alpha_i+\tfrac{1}{4}\beta_t$$

Note that in (6.1) one may raise the α's of all districts by an arbitrary constant and reduce the β's of all elections by the same constant without affecting the right-hand side of (6.1) for any pair (i, t). This calls for a normalization, for which we choose

$$(6.5) \qquad \sum_{i=1}^{N} \bar{w}_i \alpha_i = 0$$

where $\bar{w}_i$ is the average of the district proportions w_{it} over t (over all elections under consideration). Equation (6.5) implies that the term involving the α's in (6.4) can be written as

$$(6.6) \qquad \tfrac{1}{4}\sum_{i=1}^{N} (w_{it}-\bar{w}_i)\alpha_i$$

When the district shares w_{it} do not change much over time, the expression (6.6) will be small. If we neglect it, (6.4) is simplified to $p_t \approx \frac{1}{2}+\frac{1}{4}\beta_t$. Consider then the logit of the national vote on the basis of this approximation:

$$(6.7) \qquad \log\frac{p_t}{1-p_t} \approx \log\frac{\frac{1}{2}+\frac{1}{4}\beta_t}{\frac{1}{2}-\frac{1}{4}\beta_t} = \log\frac{1+\frac{1}{2}\beta_t}{1-\frac{1}{2}\beta_t}$$

Since p_t is typically not far from $\frac{1}{2}$, β_t will not be far from zero. We therefore approximate the logarithm in the third member by its Taylor expansion, neglecting third and higher powers of β_t:

$$\log(1+\tfrac{1}{2}\beta_t)-\log(1-\tfrac{1}{2}\beta_t) \approx \tfrac{1}{2}\beta_t-\tfrac{1}{2}(\tfrac{1}{2}\beta_t)^2-(-\tfrac{1}{2}\beta_t)+\tfrac{1}{2}(-\tfrac{1}{2}\beta_t)^2 = \beta_t$$

Combining this with (6.7), we conclude

$$(6.8) \qquad \log\frac{p_t}{1-p_t} \approx \beta_t$$

which states that to our degree of approximation, the election parameter β_t may be identified with the logit of the national vote at the tth election.

The Representatives Elected

The Party 1 candidate of the ith district is elected if and only if $p_{it} > \frac{1}{2}$, that is, if and only if the logit (6.1) is positive, which is equivalent to $\alpha_i > -\beta_t$. Arrange the districts so that the α's are in ascending order, $\alpha_1 \leqq \alpha_2 \leqq \ldots \leqq \alpha_N$; hence the districts that are Party 2 oriented have low values of the subscript and those which are Party 1 oriented have large subscript values. Write $F(\ )$ for the cumulated distribution function of the α's. Since the Party 1 candidate is elected in each district for which $\alpha_i > -\beta_t$, and the Party 2 candidate in each district for which $\alpha_i < -\beta_t$, the proportions of Party 1 and Party 2 candidates elected at the tth election are $1 - F(-\beta_t)$ and $F(-\beta_t)$, respectively. Hence the logit of the representatives elected (the legislative logit) is

$$(6.9) \qquad \log \frac{1 - F(-\beta_t)}{F(-\beta_t)}$$

To evaluate the expression (6.9) we approximate the discrete cumulative distribution function $F(\ )$ by a function with continuous derivatives. Write f for the first and f' for the second derivative, both evaluated at zero. A quadratic Taylor approximation of $F(-\beta_t)$ around zero then gives

$$(6.10) \qquad F(-\beta_t) \approx F(0) - f\beta_t + \tfrac{1}{2}f'\beta_t^2$$

For the interpretation of $F(0)$ we go back to (6.5), which shows that the argument 0 is simply the weighted mean of the α's. Typically, this weighted mean will not be very far from the median of the α's, and it will be advantageous to express this as follows:

$$(6.11) \qquad F(0) = \tfrac{1}{2}(1 - \eta)$$

If the weighted mean coincides with the median, we have $\eta = 0$; in general, η will be a number small compared with 1 in absolute value. Using (6.10) and (6.11), we can thus write the logit (6.9) as

$$(6.12) \qquad \log \frac{1 - F(-\beta_t)}{F(-\beta_t)} \approx \log \frac{1 + \eta + 2f\beta_t - f'\beta_t^2}{1 - \eta - 2f\beta_t + f'\beta_t^2}$$

The Cube Law

Equation (6.8) states that the logit of the national vote is approximately equal to β_t. Equation (6.12) expresses the legislative logit in terms of the same β_t. Suppose now that the median of the α's is so close to their weighted mean that $\eta \approx 0$. Suppose also that the distribution of the α's is unimodal and that the mode is close to the weighted mean. At the mode the second-order derivative of $F(\ )$ vanishes; hence, under this condition we have a small value for the second-order derivative at the weighted mean, and so we approximate $f' \approx 0$. Combining this and $\eta \approx 0$ with (6.12), we find that the legislative logit can be simplified to

$$(6.13) \qquad \log \frac{1-F(-\beta_t)}{F(-\beta_t)} \approx \log \frac{1+2f\beta_t}{1-2f\beta_t} \approx 4f\beta_t$$

and hence, using (6.8),

$$(6.14) \qquad \log \frac{1-F(-\beta_t)}{F(-\beta_t)} \approx 4f \log \frac{p_t}{1-p_t}$$

which connects the legislative logit with the logit of the national vote.

The cube law states that the ratio of the representatives elected is equal to the cube of the national vote ratio or, equivalently, that the legislative logit is three times the logit of the national vote. These two logits both occur in (6.14), and this equation shows that the model developed here does imply an approximate proportionality relation between them. The cube law is more specific and states that the proportionality constant is 3, which amounts to

$$(6.15) \qquad\qquad f = \tfrac{3}{4}$$

Recall that f is the rate of change of the cumulated distribution function of the α's at their weighted mean. This is a characteristic of the central part of their distribution, and it is the only characteristic that matters for the relation between votes and representatives elected under the conditions of our model.

Description of the British Data

The British elections to be examined are those of 1950, 1951, 1955, 1959, and 1964. Prior to the redistricting of 1954, there were 625 seats in the House of Commons. This redistricting abolished 30 districts and created 35 new districts, thus raising the number of seats to 630. There were therefore 595 districts in continued existence during the entire period, but 143 of them had major boundary changes owing to the redistricting. These districts will be disregarded, reducing the available number to 452. Also, since we are interested in a two-party system, we shall delete the four districts in which a candidate ran unopposed in any of the five elections, and the eight districts in which there was a split in either major party (Conservatives or Labour). This reduces the number further to 440. Finally, again to restrict the analysis to a two-party system, we will delete all districts in which a third party finished in either first or second position in any of the five elections; this costs us 72 districts in addition to the earlier deletions. The number of districts to be examined is therefore 368. This is more than 40 per cent below the total number, which is a restriction that should be kept in mind when we speak about the "national" vote.[1]

Description of the American Data

The American data refer to the five congressional elections in the period 1952–1960. This period is chosen because it encompassed relatively few cases of redistricting. The total number of districts is 437, which includes those of Alaska and Hawaii. Eleven districts are deleted because of redistricting (in Kentucky and Washington), four because states (New Mexico and North Dakota) each had two candidates elected at large from the state as a whole, and 134 (mostly Southern) because a candidate ran unopposed in one or several elections.[2] The number of districts considered is therefore 288, which is about one third below the total number.

Verification of the Logit Model for Districts

Multiplying both sides of (6.1) by $\bar{w}_i$ and summing over i, we obtain $\sum \bar{w}_i \alpha_i$ for the first term on the right, which vanishes because of the normalization (6.5). This shows that β_t can be estimated by

$$(6.16) \qquad \hat{\beta}_t = \sum_{i=1}^{N} \bar{w}_i \log \frac{p_{it}}{1 - p_{it}}$$

where the "hat" above β indicates that this equation provides an estimate

---

[1] The source used is B. R. MITCHELL and K. BOEHM, *British Parliamentary Election Results 1950–1964* (Cambridge University Press, 1966). The districts that were subject to minor redistricting were not deleted.

[2] The South accounts for 98 of these 134 districts and California for 17. The state-by-state breakdown for the South is Alabama (9), Arkansas (6), Florida (7), Georgia (10), Louisiana (8), Mississippi (6), North Carolina (7), South Carolina (6), Tennessee (8), Texas (22), and Virginia (9). The states outside the South and California account for the following missing districts: Massachusetts (7), Missouri (2), New York (2), Ohio (2), and one each for Illinois, Iowa, Maryland, Oklahoma, West Virginia, and Wisconsin. The source used is *America Votes 4*, edited by R. M. SCAMMON (Pittsburgh: University of Pittsburgh Press, 1962).

which varies with the set of elections included in the sample. Substitution of $\hat{\beta}_t$ in (6.1) gives a value of α_i for each t. Our estimate of α_i is the average of these values, averaged over $t = 1, \ldots, 5$:

$$(6.17) \qquad \hat{\alpha}_i = \tfrac{1}{5} \sum_{t=1}^{5} \left(\log \frac{p_{it}}{1 - p_{it}} - \hat{\beta}_t \right)$$

The proportion $\hat{p}_{it}$ implied by the estimates $\hat{\alpha}_i$ and $\hat{\beta}_t$ can then be derived along the lines of (1.3), using eq. (6.1), and the average information inaccuracy over all N districts,

$$(6.18) \qquad \bar{I}_t = \sum_{i=1}^{N} w_{it} \left[p_{it} \log \frac{p_{it}}{\hat{p}_{it}} + (1 - p_{it}) \log \frac{1 - p_{it}}{1 - \hat{p}_{it}} \right]$$

may be used to measure the fit of the logit model for the outcomes of the tth election.

TABLE 4.12

RESULTS FOR THE LOGIT MODEL APPLIED TO BRITISH AND AMERICAN ELECTIONS

	Election				
	1	2	3	4	5
	British				
$\log [p_t/(1-p_t)]$	−.107	−.050	.016	.058	−.076
$\hat{\beta}_t$	−.115	−.058	.005	.057	−.092
$\Sigma_i(w_{it}-\bar{w}_i)\hat{\alpha}_i$	−.008	−.001	.006	−.001	.004
$100\,\bar{I}_t$	.090	.046	.047	.065	.141
	American				
$\log [p_t/(1-p_t)]$	.196	.043	.149	−.106	−.013
$\hat{\beta}_t$	.216	.047	.152	−.137	−.038
$\Sigma_i(w_{it}-\bar{w}_i)\hat{\alpha}_i$	−.019	−.009	−.001	.013	.015
$100\,\bar{I}_t$	.378	.204	.256	.289	.419

Table 4.12 gives a summary of the results for the five British and the five American elections. Party 1 is interpreted as the Conservatives or the Republicans; hence a positive value of the logarithm of $p_t/(1-p_t)$ indicates that either of these parties obtained the majority of all votes in the set of districts considered here. These logits of the national votes are shown in the first lines of the upper and lower halves of the table, followed by the estimated elec-

tion parameters on the next line. Equation (6.8) states that they are approximately equal; the figures confirm this, although the approximation is not very close. The third line gives one of the expressions that have been neglected in the derivation leading to (6.8);[1] the figures indicate that in the five cases in which $\hat{\beta}_t$ deviates from the logit of the national vote by more than .01, it accounts for at least part of the discrepancy. It is interesting to observe that this expression increases uninterruptedly for the successive American elections. Given that districts with algebraically large α values are Republican oriented, this means that among the 288 congressional districts considered here, the predominantly Republican districts had on the average a more rapid increase in the number of voters than those which lean toward the Democratic Party.

But by far the most interesting feature of Table 4.12 is the difference between the British and American outcomes with respect to the fit of the model. All five American information inaccuracies exceed all five British inaccuracies. The average American and British inaccuracies are .00309 nit and .00078 nit, respectively. By applying the approximation procedure of Section 2.4, eq. (4.8) and ff., we find that these figures correspond to root-mean-square errors of the order of 4 and 2 per cent, respectively.[2] We conclude that the logit model is much more accurate for the British elections than for the American ones. This is not entirely surprising for two main reasons. First, Britain is politically more homogeneous than the United States, partly because it is smaller. Second, the American congressman has a more independent power base than his British counterpart. The latter's source of power is the party rather than the district (in which he is not required to live).

We shall not go into the problem of statistically testing the validity of the logit model on the basis of the election data. This model will be regarded

---

[1] Using (6.5), we can write (6.4) as

$$p_t \approx \tfrac{1}{2} + \tfrac{1}{4}[\beta_t + \sum_{i=1}^{N} (w_{it} - \bar{w}_i)\alpha_i]$$

which shows the nature of this approximation more clearly.

[2] Interpret p of eq. (4.8) of Section 2.4 as $\hat{p}_{it}$ and q as p_{it}, so that this equation states that the squared error is approximately equal to the information inaccuracy multiplied by $2p_{it}(1-p_{it})$. This factor is between .48 and .50 for $.4 \leq p_{it} \leq .6$, and between .42 and .50 for $.3 \leq p_{it} \leq .7$. Hence the mean square error is about equal to the average information inaccuracy multiplied by a factor which is just a little below $\tfrac{1}{2}$. This gives mean square errors of about .0015 (American) and .0004 (British), from which the root-mean-square errors mentioned in the text are derived.

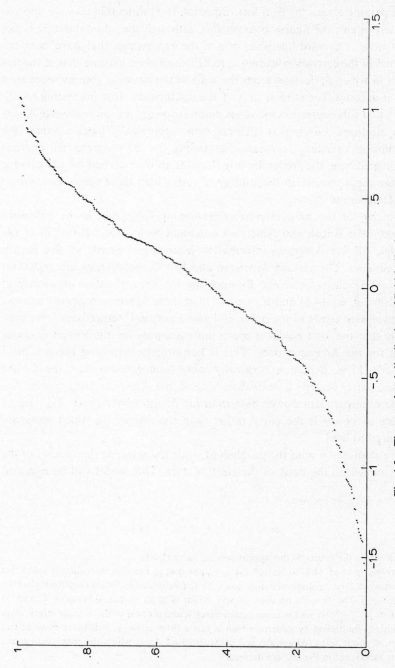

Fig. 4.5. The cumulated distribution of British district parameters

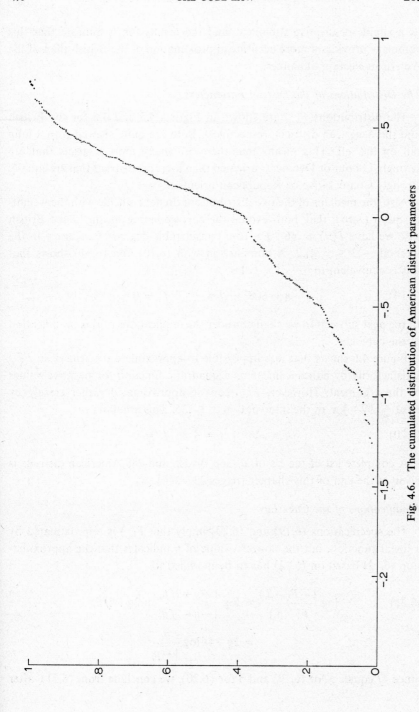

Fig. 4.6. The cumulated distribution of American district parameters

as a simple descriptive summary, and the results for $\bar{I}_t$ indicate that this summary provides a more accurate approximation of the British than of the American election outcomes.

The Distributions of the District Parameters

The distributions $F(\ )$ are shown in Figures 4.5 and 4.6 for the British and the American districts, respectively. Both are quite skewed with a long tail on the left. This means that there are many more districts that are strongly Labour or Democrat oriented than there are districts that are equally strongly Conservative or Republican oriented.

Also, the medians of the two distributions do not coincide with the weighted mean (zero); they both exceed the corresponding mean. In the British case we have $F(x) \approx .46 + \frac{3}{4} x$ to a considerable degree of accuracy in the interval $-.2 \leq x \leq .2$. A comparison with (6.10) and (6.11) shows that this is equivalent to

$$(6.19) \qquad \eta = .08 \qquad f = \tfrac{3}{4} \qquad f' = 0$$

In the next subsection we shall consider the implications of this modification of the cube law.

Figure 4.6 shows that it is impossible to approximate the American $F(\ )$ satisfactorily by either a linear or a quadratic function for negative values of the argument. However, $F(\ )$ can be approximated rather closely by $F(x) = .37 + \frac{5}{4} x$ in the interval $0 \leq x \leq .35$. This amounts to

$$(6.20) \qquad \eta = .26 \qquad f = \tfrac{5}{4} \qquad f' = 0$$

A complete list of the α's of all 368 British and 288 American districts is given at the end of this chapter (pages 237–244).

Modifications of the Cube Law

The specifications (6.19) and (6.20) imply that $F(\ )$ is approximated by a linear function, but the nonzero value of η indicates that the approximation (6.13) based on (6.12) has to be modified to

$$(6.21) \qquad \log \frac{1-F(-\beta_t)}{F(-\beta_t)} \approx \log \frac{1+\eta+2f\beta_t}{1-\eta-2f\beta_t} \approx 2\eta+4f\beta_t$$

$$= 2\eta+4f \log \frac{p_t}{1-p_t}$$

Since $4f$ equals 3 for (6.19) and 5 for (6.20), we conclude from (6.21), after taking antilogs, that our specifications amount to a cube law for the British elections and to a fifth power law for the American elections. However, these laws are to be modified to the extent that the third or fifth power of the ratio of the national votes is to be multiplied by $e^{2\eta}$, which is about 1.17 for the British and 1.68 for the American specification. Moreover, there is a difference between the two cases as regards the validity of the linear approximation of $F(\ )$. Equation (6.21) shows that the relevant argument of this function is $-\beta_t$, which is approximately equal to minus the logit of the national vote. The range of validity in the British case is $(-.2, .2)$, which covers all five elections (see the first line of Table 4.12). In the American case this range is $(-.35, 0)$,[1] which covers only the last two elections. Finally, we have to take into consideration that the logit model itself provides a more accurate approximation for the British than for the American election results.

TABLE 4.13

THE PERFORMANCE OF THE CUBE LAW AND ITS MODIFICATIONS AT THE LEVEL OF PARLIAMENT
SEATS

Proportion of seats	Election				
	1	2	3	4	5
	British				
Observed	.465	.516	.541	.573	.476
Error cube law	−.045	−.053	−.029	−.030	−.032
Error of (6.19)	−.005	−.013	.011	.010	.008
	American				
Observed	.688	.628	.625	.472	.542
Error of (6.20)	.130	.048	.155	.025	.070

Table 4.13 summarizes the performance of the cube law and its modifications. The first line contains the actual proportion q_t of seats obtained by the Conservatives (out of the total of 368). The second line gives $\hat{q}_t - q_t$, where $\hat{q}_t$ is the prediction implied by the cube law:

$$(6.22) \qquad \log \frac{\hat{q}_t}{1 - \hat{q}_t} = 3 \log \frac{p_t}{1 - p_t}$$

---

[1] The linear approximation of $F(x)$ applies to the range $0 \leq x \leq .35$, but x is identified here as *minus* the logit of the national vote.

The prediction errors $\hat{q}_t - q_t$ are all negative and of the order of 3 to 5 per cent. The addition of $2\eta = .16$ to the right-hand side of (6.22) improves the predictions substantially. This is shown in the third line of the table, which contains errors of the order of 1 per cent.

As could be expected, the performance of the fifth power law (6.20) is poor for elections that were good for the Republicans. The fourth election is the worst for the Republicans and, not surprisingly, the best from the standpoint of the fifth power law. However, the last election also has a negative logit of the national vote, but nevertheless a substantial prediction error. This is due to the poor fit of the logit model for that election; see the $\bar{I}_t$ in the lower right-hand corner of Table 4.12.[1]

Conclusions

A modified cube law thus appears to provide, in the British case, a reasonable approximation to the relation between the national vote and the representatives elected. It should be noted that it is quite possible that the original law without any modification applies to the set of all British districts, because the specification (6.19) is not invariant under changes in the set of districts included in the analysis. So it is conceivable that $\eta = 0, f = \frac{3}{4}, f' = 0$ holds when all districts are considered, but to verify this one would need a sufficient number of successive elections which are not disturbed by redistrictings.

---

[1] A straightforward way of measuring the performance of the logit model with respect to the seats obtained in the elections is by means of a double dichotomy that describes which party is predicted to win ($\alpha_i + \beta_t \gtrless 0$) and which party actually wins ($p_{it} \gtrless \frac{1}{2}$). For all $5 \times 368 = 1840$ British cases this dichotomy is as follows:

	$p_{it} > \frac{1}{2}$	$p_{it} < \frac{1}{2}$
$\alpha_i + \beta_t > 0$	913	37
$\alpha_i + \beta_t < 0$	33	857

Hence the model predicts correctly in $913 + 857$ cases, but there are 37 cases in which the Conservatives are erroneously predicted to win and 33 cases in which Labour is erroneously predicted to win. The American double dichotomy for all $5 \times 288 = 1440$ cases is

	810	63
	41	526

The error fraction is $(63 + 41)/1440 = .072$ for the American elections, which exceeds $(37 + 33)/1840 = .038$ of the British elections. For the fifth American election there are 21 incorrect victory predictions for the Republicans and only 8 incorrect victory predictions for the Democrats. This accounts for a net fraction $(21 - 8)/288 = .045$ at the level of the predicted seat proportion $\hat{q}_t$ for the Republicans, which in turn accounts for more than 60 per cent of the error (.070) shown in the last line of Table 4.13.

The American data clearly indicate that the law, even when it is modified to a fifth power law, does not satisfactorily approximate the relation between the national vote and the representatives elected. First, the logit model provides a comparatively poor fit. It is conceivable that the fit is improved when other determining factors are taken into consideration, such as the number of terms served by the incumbent if he decides to run again, but this is beyond the scope of this book. Second, the cube law and its modifications require that the cumulated distributions function of the district parameters be linear around the weighted mean, and the available evidence does not corroborate this for the American case.

The logit model can also be applied to the districts of each of the American states separately. This is pursued in Problems 21 and 22, where it appears that the average information inaccuracies are of the order of 25 to 50 per cent below the corresponding values of Table 4.12. Although this suggests that the model is more accurate at the level of individual states, it must be kept in mind that this result is at least to some extent spurious because of the much larger number of parameters adjusted in the state-by-state analysis (one set of β's for each state).

4.7. Miscellaneous Applications of the Logit

The logit owes its name to the logistic curve, which is frequently used as a growth curve. The equation of the logistic is

$$(7.1) \qquad x_t = \frac{1}{1 + e^{-a-bt}} \qquad (b > 0)$$

As t (time) goes from $-\infty$ to ∞, x_t increases from 0 to 1. The ratio of x_t to $1 - x_t$ equals e^{a+bt}, so that the logit corresponding to x_t is a linear function of t. Sometimes the numerator 1 is replaced by a constant $c \leqq 1$, in which case c is the limit towards which x_t converges as $t \to \infty$. An interesting example of this version of the logistic is GRILICHES' (1957) analysis of the acceptance of hybrid corn in the United States. He interpreted x_t as the proportion of the total corn acreage in a certain region which is planted with hybrid seed in year t; he adjusted the parameters a, b and c for each region, and subsequently described the parameter values in terms of economic characteristics of the region.

There are many cases in which the logit appears rather unexpectedly. The main objective of this section is to provide some examples from various areas. At the end we will generalize the conditional logit model of Section 4.4.

The Effect of Grouping on Correlation Coefficients

Consider the least-squares regression of a variable y on a variable x,

$$(7.2) \qquad\qquad y_i = a + bx_i + e_i \qquad\qquad i = 1, \ldots, n$$

where a and b are regression coefficients and e_i is the ith residual. It is well known that the squared correlation coefficient of the two variables can be written in the form

$$r^2 = 1 - \frac{\sum e_i^2}{\sum (y_i - \bar{y})^2} = \frac{b^2 \sum (x_i - \bar{x})^2}{b^2 \sum (x_i - x)^2 + \sum e_i^2}$$

where $\bar{x}$ and $\bar{y}$ are the means of the x_i's and the y_i's, respectively, and all summations are over i from 1 through n. The following equivalent result will prove to be more convenient in the sequel:

$$(7.3) \qquad\qquad \frac{r^2}{1 - r^2} = \frac{b^2 \sum (x_i - \bar{x})^2}{\sum e_i^2}$$

Following CRAMER (1964), we now assume that the n observations are divided into G groups, $S_1, \ldots, S_G$, containing $n_1, \ldots, n_G$ observations each $(\sum n_g = n)$. The underlying theoretical relationship can then be written as

$$(7.4) \qquad\qquad y_{gj} = \alpha + \beta x_{gj} + \varepsilon_{gj}$$

where α and β are the unknown parameters and (x_{gj}, y_{gj}) is the jth observation of S_g. Equation (7.2) is the least-squares estimate of (7.4) when all observations of each group are used individually. Suppose, however, that the analyst decides to use group averages,

$$(7.5) \qquad\qquad \bar{x}_g = \frac{1}{n_g} \sum_j x_{gj} \qquad \bar{y}_g = \frac{1}{n_g} \sum_j y_{gj} \qquad g = 1, \ldots, G$$

and to run a weighted regression based on these group averages with weights equal to $\sqrt{n_1}, \ldots, \sqrt{n_G}$. This amounts to minimizing the sum of the squares of $e_1', \ldots, e_G'$ in

$$(7.6) \qquad\qquad \bar{y}_g \sqrt{n_g} = a' \sqrt{n_g} + b' \bar{x}_g \sqrt{n_g} + e_g' \qquad\qquad g = 1, \ldots, G$$

where primes are attached to the coefficients and the residuals to distinguish them from those of (7.2). For this new regression we have a new correlation coefficient, to be written r', for which an equation similar to (7.3) can be derived:

$$(7.7) \qquad\qquad \frac{r'^2}{1 - r'^2} = \frac{b'^2 \sum n_g (\bar{x}_g - \bar{x})^2}{\sum e_g'^2}$$

The problem to be considered is what can be said about the relation between the r of the individual observations and the r' of the group averages. For that purpose we take the logs of (7.3) and (7.7) and subtract:

$$(7.8) \quad \log \frac{r'^2}{1-r'^2} - \log \frac{r^2}{1-r^2} = \log \left(\frac{b'}{b}\right)^2 + \log \frac{\sum n_g(\bar{x}_g - \bar{x})^2}{\sum (x_i - \bar{x})^2} - \log \frac{\sum e_g'^2}{\sum e_i^2}$$

The logarithm of $r^2/(1-r^2)$ may be regarded as the logit corresponding to the squared correlation coefficient. Hence the left-hand side of (7.8) is the effect on this logit of using group averages instead of individual observations, and the equation states that this effect is equal to the sum of three terms, one dealing with the two estimators of β, the second with the behavior of the independent variable, and the third with sums of squares of residuals.

To evaluate these three terms we consider the following sum-of-squares decomposition from the analysis of variance:

$$(7.9) \quad \sum_{g=1}^{G} \sum_{j} (x_{gj} - \bar{x})^2 = \sum_{g=1}^{G} n_g(\bar{x}_g - \bar{x})^2 + \sum_{g=1}^{G} \sum_{j} (x_{gj} - \bar{x}_g)^2$$

The expression on the left is simply $\sum (x_i - x)^2$ in the notation of (7.3). It follows that the second right-hand term in (7.8) is negative and thus contributes to a lower value of r'^2 relative to r^2 except when all x's within each group are equal. However, this term is typically small when the grouping takes place according to increasing values of the independent variable, because most of the variation among the x values is then between the groups (the first term in the sum-of-squares decomposition) rather than within the groups (the second term). We shall confine ourselves to this kind of grouping in what follows.

Assume furthermore that the ε's of (7.4) are uncorrelated random variables with zero mean and variance σ^2. The first right-hand term in (7.8) is then also small (see Problem 25), so that what remains is the third, dealing with sums of squares of residuals. When n is sufficiently large, $\sum e_i^2$ will be of the same order of magnitude as the sum of squares of the corresponding ε's, the expectation of which is $n\sigma^2$. For $\sum e_g'^2$ the analogous expectation is $G\sigma^2$.[1] Using these values as approximations, we obtain $-\log (G/n) = \log n - \log G$ for the third term in (7.8). This is a large positive value when the number of observations is large relative to the number of groups, which

---

[1] It follows from (7.6) that the expression in the ε's corresponding to e_g' is the sum of ε_{gj} over j divided by $\sqrt{n_g}$. The square of this ratio has expectation $n_g\sigma^2/(\sqrt{n_g})^2 = \sigma^2$, which becomes $G\sigma^2$ after summation over g.

explains why correlations are typically "improved" by grouping. Needless to say, the logit difference in the left-hand side of (7.8) is not really a constant determined by n and G, because the residual sums of squares may deviate rather substantially from the expectations of the corresponding expressions in the ε's. For further elaborations see CRAMER (1964).

Prior and Posterior Odds

When deriving the cube law and its modifications in Section 4.6, we expressed the legislative logit as a linear function of the logit of the national vote. Equation (7.8) is similar in that the logits corresponding to two squared correlations are also linearly related. There are more examples of linear relations between logits as we shall shortly see.

Write $P[E]$ for the probability of an event E, and O for a random sample of observations. Consider the various joint, marginal, and conditional probabilities involving E and O, which are connected by

$$(7.10) \qquad \begin{aligned} P[E \text{ and } O] &= P[E]P[O|E] \\ &= P[O]P[E|O] \end{aligned}$$

We may call $P[E]$ the prior probability of E and $P[E|O]$ its posterior probability (after the observations become available). Furthermore, $P[O|E]$ is the likelihood of the observations, given that E occurs.

From (7.10) we derive

$$P[E|O] = \frac{P[E]P[O|E]}{P[O]}$$

and similarly $P[\bar{E}|O] = P[\bar{E}]P[O|\bar{E}]/P[O]$, where $\bar{E}$ means "E does not occur". Taking the ratio of the two equations, we obtain

$$(7.11) \qquad \frac{P[E|O]}{P[\bar{E}|O]} = \frac{P[E]}{P[\bar{E}]}\frac{P[O|E]}{P[O|\bar{E}]}$$

The left-hand side is a ratio of probabilities which measures the posterior odds favoring E, and the first factor on the right describes the prior odds. The second factor is the likelihood ratio. We take logarithms,

$$(7.12) \qquad \log\frac{P[E|O]}{P[\bar{E}|O]} = \log\frac{P[E]}{P[\bar{E}]} + \log\frac{P[O|E]}{P[O|\bar{E}]}$$

which is a simple linear equation stating that the posterior logit exceeds the prior logit by the logarithmic likelihood ratio.

When we obtain new observations O' after O was received, we can similarly derive

$$(7.13) \qquad \log \frac{P[E|O \text{ and } O']}{P[\bar{E}|O \text{ and } O']} = \log \frac{P[E|O]}{P[\bar{E}|O]} + \log \frac{P[O'|E \text{ and } O]}{P[O'|\bar{E} \text{ and } O]}$$

Since the first term on the right is identical with the left-hand side of (7.12), this result shows that each new posterior logit can be obtained from its predecessor by adding the most recent log-likelihood ratio.

See also Problem 26 on the value of a random experiment defined in terms of the average reduction of the entropy of the posterior distribution below that of the prior distribution.

"Psychological" Probabilities

PRESTON and BARATTA (1948) were the first to measure subjective probability experimentally. In their experiments subjects were run in groups of two and more, using play money to bid for gambles in an auction game. The successful bidder was permitted to roll a set of dice after the bidding was completed, and the probability of winning with the dice was identical with the probability stated on the card that was presented at the auction. Thus, subjects might bid for a prize of 250 points with probability $\frac{1}{4}$ of winning. If the average successful bid was 50, Preston and Baratta computed the "psychological probability" to be 50/250 or $\frac{1}{5}$.[1] They introduced several different numerical values for the probability of winning (p) and found that it was exceeded by the psychological probability (q) when $p < .2$ but that $q < p$ when $p > .2$. Their results are indicated by circles in Figure 4.7.

LUCE and SUPPES (1965, Section 4.3) report that similar results, based on betting data for horse races, were obtained by other authors. It is therefore of some interest to know whether there is a simple function which adequately represents the dependence of q on p as exhibited by the circles of Figure 4.7. Again, a linear relation between the logits is a simple solution. The smooth curve in the figure corresponds to the equation

$$(7.14) \qquad \log \frac{q}{1-q} = \theta \log \frac{p}{1-p} + (1-\theta) \log \frac{.2}{.8}$$

---

[1] It is presently more customary to use concepts from a theory which is based on a simultaneous axiomatization of utility and probability; in the language of this theory, the Preston-Baratta method of computing psychological probabilities assumes that the utility of play money is a linear function of the value assigned to the money. See LUCE and SUPPES (1965).

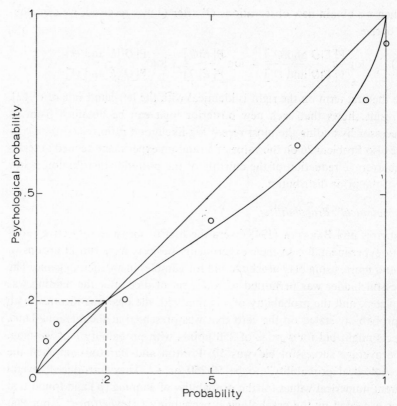

Fig. 4.7.   The Preston-Baratta measurements of psychological probability

where θ is specified as .7. This curve intersects the line $q = p$ at $p = .2$ and it is above (below) this line for smaller (larger) values of p.

A Problem of Personnel Assignment

Consider the following problem, from KING (1965). There are n jobs to be performed and n persons, one for each job. Which person should do which job? It is known that if individual i is assigned job j, the probability is $p(i, j)$ that he will perform satisfactorily. A complete set of assignments amounts to the selection of a permutation $\sigma = \{\sigma_1, \ldots, \sigma_n\}$ of the first n positive integers in such a way that individual i is assigned job σ_i, $i = 1, \ldots, n$. The n^2 probabilities $p(i, j)$ are the only data available. The problem is to find a permutation σ such that an appropriate function (the objective function) of the probabilities $p(1, \sigma_1), \ldots, p(n, \sigma_n)$ is maximized.

The specification of the objective function is thus the preliminary problem. King considers two possibilities. One is the product over i of $p(i, \sigma_i)$, which amounts to the maximization of the joint probability of successful performance of all n individuals. This is appropriate when failure in one job makes all others worthless, but this special assumption will not be made here. The second criterion is the sum over i of $p(i, \sigma_i)$, which is equivalent to maximizing the expected number of successful assignments. Given the central place of expectations in probability theory, this criterion will probably appeal to many. However, WEIL (1967) tends to prefer to maximize the average logit of successful performance:

$$(7.15) \qquad \frac{1}{n} \sum_{i=1}^{n} \log \frac{p(i, \sigma_i)}{1 - p(i, \sigma_i)}$$

The argument is that the criterion of the expected number of assignments is insufficiently sensitive to changes in probabilities close to zero and one, and too sensitive to changes around $\frac{1}{2}$. For example, suppose that for some pair (i, j), $p(i, j)$ takes two alternative values, .4 and .6. In the former case individual i has a slightly less than even chance of performing job j satisfactorily, in the latter he has a slightly better than even chance. There is a difference, of course, but not really very much. If, however, the alternative values are .05 and .25, the difference is felt to be much larger. If $p(i, j) = .05$, the person will succeed with only 5 per cent probability; if it is .25, the probability of success is five times larger. Other things being equal, one might guess that the man who is in charge of the assignments would be very reluctant to assign individual i to job j if $p(i, j) = .05$, and that this reluctance would diminish sharply if that probability is .25. The criterion of the expected number of successful assignments simply states that there is a .2 difference between .4 and .6 and also a .2 difference between .05 and .25. The logit criterion, on the other hand, states that the distance between $p = .4$ and $p = .6$ is .81 and that the distance between $p = .05$ and $p = .25$ is 1.85 or more than twice as large.[1]

It was on the basis of these considerations that Weil argued in favor of the logit criterion. Another consideration is the following. Suppose that the man in charge of the assignments does not have any real data from which the probabilities $p(i, j)$ can be derived, but that these are subjective prob-

---

[1] The logit based on natural logs corresponding to a .6 probability is .405, that of a .4 probability $-.405$, hence the distance is .81. The logits corresponding to $p = .25$ and $p = .05$ are -1.099 and -2.944, respectively.

abilities reflecting his willingness to bet on the individuals' success, similar to the auctions and horse bets of the previous subsection. Furthermore, imagine that these subjective probabilities are related to the observed frequencies of successful performance as Figure 4.7 indicates; in principle, it is possible to verify this on the basis of a large number of assignments. It is quite conceivable that the person in charge of the assignments would have preferred to forget about his subjective probabilities and to replace them by the relevant observed frequencies. How would this have affected the assignments under the logit criterion, and those based on the expected number of successful assignments?

The answer is that the assignments would have been the same under the logit criterion, whereas this is not true for the other criterion. This is clearly an advantage of the former criterion over the latter. The transformation (7.14) implies that the logit corresponding to $p(i, \sigma_i)$ is replaced by

$$(7.16) \qquad c_0 + c \log \frac{p(i, \sigma_i)}{1 - p(i, \sigma_i)} \qquad\qquad c > 0$$

where c_0 and c are constants determined by those of (7.14).[1] Hence the average logit is an increasing linear function of (7.15). This establishes the invariance of the optimal assignment under the logit criterion, because we obtain the same permutation σ when we maximize (7.15) as when we maximize this function. See Problem 27 for the criterion of the expected number of successful assignments.

Extension of the Conditional Logit Model

Let there be three forms of transportation to downtown from the surrounding areas: bus (D_1), train (D_2), and private car (D_3). We are interested in the proportions of people who use these different modes of transportation and assume that family income (x) and the time needed to reach the destination $(y_1, y_2, y_3$ for the three alternatives) are the determining factors. More specifically, consider the following conditional logit model, from Theil (1969b):

$$(7.17) \qquad \log \frac{P[D_r | x, y_1, y_2, y_3]}{P[D_s | x, y_1, y_2, y_3]} = \alpha_{rs} + \beta_{rs} \log x + \gamma_{rs} \log \frac{y_r}{y_s}$$

where $P[D_r | x, y_1, y_2, y_3]$ is the probability that a person decides to use the

---

[1] The relation is $c = 1/\theta$, $c_0 = (1 - 1/\theta) \log (.2/.8)$. Actually, c_0 and c may take arbitrary values subject only to $c > 0$.

r^{th} mode of transportation, given that his income is x and that the times needed to arrive downtown are y_1, y_2 and y_3. The left-hand side of (7.17) is the conditional logit favoring the rth alternative relative to the sth, and β_{rs} is the income elasticity of the corresponding conditional odds. Note that these odds are postulated to depend only on the ratio of the travel times of the two alternatives that are compared (y_r and y_s), and hence that they are assumed to be independent of the third travel time.

As in the case of Section 4.4, the parameters of (7.17) are subject to constraints. By adding to (7.17) the same equation for D_s and D_t we obtain on the right

$$(7.18) \qquad (\alpha_{rs}+\alpha_{st})+(\beta_{rs}+\beta_{st})\log x+\gamma_{rs}\log\frac{y_r}{y_s}+\gamma_{st}\log\frac{y_s}{y_t}$$

On the left we obtain the conditional logit favoring the rth alternative relative to the tth, which is equal to

$$(7.19) \qquad \alpha_{rt}+\beta_{rt}\log x+\gamma_{rt}\log\frac{y_r}{y_t}$$

A term by term comparison shows that α_{rs} and β_{rs} should be of the forms $\alpha_r-\alpha_s$ and $\beta_r-\beta_s$, respectively, which is analogous to the result obtained in (4.6). As to the γ's, note first that γ_{rs} is symmetric in its subscripts; this is proved by interchanging the roles of r and s in (7.17). Second, note that (7.19) does not involve y_s, so that we must have $\gamma_{rs}=\gamma_{st}$ in (7.18). This is equivalent to $\gamma_{rs}=\gamma_{ts}$ because of the symmetry, which means that the γ's are independent of their first subscript. Given the same symmetry, they must then also be independent of their second subscript. Hence we can simplify (7.17) to

$$(7.20) \quad \log\frac{P[D_r|x,y_1,y_2,y_3]}{P[D_s|x,y_1,y_2,y_3]}=(\alpha_r-\alpha_s)+(\beta_r-\beta_s)\log x+\gamma\log\frac{y_r}{y_s}$$

The parameter γ is the elasticity of any conditional odds with respect to the ratio of the corresponding transportation times. See Problem 28 for an extension of this result to the case of a larger number of determining factors.

The Effect of Small Changes in the Extended Logit Model

The specification (7.20) combined with the restriction that the P's add up to one provides only an implicit description of the way in which these P's depend on income and travel times. It is possible, however, to obtain an explicit expression for infinitesimal changes. Suppose first that x is subject to a change dx, the y's remaining constant, so that (7.20) implies

$$(7.21) \qquad d\left(\log \frac{P[D_r|x, y_1, y_2, y_3]}{P[D_s|x, y_1, y_2, y_3]}\right) = (\beta_r - \beta_s)d(\log x)$$

Using the abbreviation

$$(7.22) \qquad P_r = P[D_r|x, y_1, y_2, y_3]$$

we conclude that the left-hand side of (7.21) is equal to $dP_r/P_r - dP_s/P_s$. Thus, by multiplying both sides of (7.21) by P_s we obtain

$$P_s \frac{dP_r}{P_r} - dP_s = P_s(\beta_r - \beta_s)d(\log x)$$

and after summation over s:

$$(7.23) \qquad d(\log P_r) = (\beta_r - \sum_s P_s \beta_s)d(\log x)$$

where use is made of $\sum dP_s = 0$. The result (7.23) shows that the income elasticity of the rth proportion is equal to the excess of its income coefficient (β_r) over a weighted average of all income coefficients, with weights equal to the corresponding proportions. Note that these weights are not constant.

Next suppose that y_1 changes by dy_1, while x, y_2 and y_3 all remain constant. It follows from (7.20) that the ratios P_r/P_s with $r \ne 1 \ne s$ are not affected, and that

$$(7.24) \qquad d(\log P_r) - d(\log P_1) = -\gamma d(\log y_1) \qquad\qquad r \ne 1$$

This is equivalent to $dP_r - P_r(dP_1/P_1) = -\gamma P_r d(\log y_1)$, which gives after summation over $r \ne 1$

$$-dP_1 - (1 - P_1)\frac{dP_1}{P_1} = -\gamma(1 - P_1)d(\log y_1)$$

which can be simplified to

$$(7.25) \qquad d(\log P_1) = \gamma(1 - P_1)d(\log y_1)$$

Combining this with (7.24), we obtain

$$(7.26) \qquad d(\log P_r) = -\gamma P_1 d(\log y_1) \qquad\qquad r \ne 1$$

We conclude from (7.25) and (7.26) that the elasticity of the first proportion with respect to the corresponding travel time is of the form $\gamma(1 - P_1)$, and that of the rth proportion with respect to the same travel time is $-\gamma P_1$. The selection of the subscript 1 in these derivations is of course arbitrary, and it is readily verified that the general result is

$$(7.27) \qquad \frac{\partial(\log P_r)}{\partial(\log y_s)} = \gamma(1-P_s) \quad \text{if } r = s$$
$$-\gamma P_s \quad \text{if } r \neq s$$

from which we can derive the effect on P_r of infinitesimal changes in all distances:

$$(7.28) \qquad d(\log P_r) = \sum_s \frac{\partial(\log P_r)}{\partial(\log y_s)} d(\log y_s)$$
$$= \gamma[d(\log y_r) - \sum_s P_s d(\log y_s)]$$

A combination of (7.28) and (7.23) gives the effect on P_r of infinitesimal changes in all determining factors:

$$(7.29) \quad d(\log P_r) = (\beta_r - \sum_s P_s \beta_s)d(\log x) + \gamma[d(\log y_r) - \sum_s P_s d(\log y_s)]$$

The logarithmic change in the rth proportion is thus the sum of an income effect and a distance effect. The income effect is equal to the logarithmic income change multiplied by the excess of the rth income coefficient over a weighted average of all income coefficients. The distance effect is a multiple γ of the logarithmic change in the deflated travel time of the rth alternative, where "deflated" means that this travel time is measured relative to a weighted average of all travel times. Note that the weights of these two averages are the same. See Problems 29 to 31 for further developments.

PROBLEMS

1 Consider (1.4) and prove that the next two derivatives of L with respect to p are

$$\frac{d^2L}{dp^2} = -\frac{1}{p^2} + \frac{1}{(1-p)^2} \quad \text{and} \quad \frac{d^3L}{dp^3} = \frac{2}{p^3} + \frac{2}{(1-p)^3}$$

Use this result to prove that the third-order Taylor approximation of L around $p = \frac{1}{2}$ is

$$L \approx 4(p-\tfrac{1}{2}) + \tfrac{16}{3}(p-\tfrac{1}{2})^3$$

Evaluate the accuracy of this approximation and of (1.5) at $p = .6, .7, .8$ and $.9$.

2 Consider a linear logit relation (1.2) for three determining factors, the first of which takes m values and the second n and the third p. How many free parameters are to be adjusted? Assuming that an observed relative frequency f_{ijk} is available for each triple (i, j, k), how many degrees of freedom do you have for the estimation of these parameters? Generalize your results for the case of K determining factors, the first of which takes N_1 values, the second N_2, and so on.

3 Write the interaction equation (3.3) in the form (2.4) for $j = 1$. Introduce the relevant dummy variables for this equation, and display their values in the form of Table 4.3.

4 Consider a linear logit equation with a double-subscript term for the interaction of two factors. Prove that the number of degrees of freedom is positive only if there are at least three determining factors. Also, formulate an equation containing a triple-subscript term for the interaction of three factors, and discuss the conditions under which the number of degrees of freedom is positive.

5 (*Continuation*) A two-factor linear logit equation has a double-subscript interaction term. Are the parameters estimable?

6 Interpret the number $.90$ on the vertical axis of Figure 4.4 (page 185) in terms of the parameters of (3.5). Also, use this figure to estimate the sensitivity of liberals and of conservatives to variations in the degree of knowledge with respect to the logit of the vote for the progressive candidate.

7 Write n_{ij} for the numbers of observations in the upper half of Table 4.6 (page 184). Use the large-sample theory discussed between eqs. (2.6) and (2.8) to prove that, under appropriate conditions, the four l_{ij}'s which occur in (3.7) are independent and have approximately zero mean and a variance equal to the reciprocal of $n_{ij}p_{ij}(1 - p_{ij})$. State these conditions.

8 (*Continuation*) Prove the following linear Taylor expansion of $\hat{\gamma}_1$ at the point of the true logits L_{ij}:

$$\hat{\gamma}_1 - \gamma_1 \approx -c(l_{11} - L_{11}) + c(l_{21} - L_{21}) + c^2(L_{21} - L_{11})(l_{12} - L_{12})$$

$$- c^2(L_{21} - L_{11})(l_{22} - L_{22})$$

where $c = 1/(L_{22} - L_{12})$. Square both sides and take the expectation to conclude that the large-sample variance of $\hat{\gamma}_1$ is equal to

$$\frac{c^2}{n_{11}\,p_{11}(1-p_{11})} + \frac{c^2}{n_{21}\,p_{21}(1-p_{21})} + \frac{c^4(L_{21}-L_{11})^2}{n_{12}\,p_{12}(1-p_{12})} + \frac{c^4(L_{21}-L_{11})^2}{n_{22}\,p_{22}(1-p_{22})}$$

When f's and l's are substituted for the p's and L's in this expression, we obtain .023; the large-sample standard error mentioned in the text below (3.7) is the square root of this number.

9 Consider a conditional logit model with R possible responses and two determining factors. Prove that this amounts to $R-1$ equations,

$$\log \frac{p_{ij}(r)}{p_{ij}(1)} = \alpha_r + \beta_{ir} + \gamma_{jr} \qquad\qquad r = 2, \ldots, R$$

when the normalization (4.7) is used. Generalize the additional normalization (4.10) for this case and prove that the total number of free parameters and the number of degrees of freedom are $3(R-1)$ and $R-1$, respectively, when the two determining factors take two values each.

10 (*Continuation*) Generalize the above result for the case of K determining factors, the first of which takes N_1 values, the second N_2, and so on, by proving that the total number of free parameters is

$$(R-1)(\sum_{h=1}^{K} N_h - K + 1)$$

and that the degrees of freedom are obtained by subtracting this number from $(R-1)N_1 N_2 \ldots N_K$.

11 Prove that the error terms $l_{ij}(r, s) - L_{ij}(r, s)$ of (4.12) and (4.13) can be written as

$$\log \frac{f_{ij}(r)}{p_{ij}(r)} - \log \frac{f_{ij}(s)}{p_{ij}(s)} \approx \frac{f_{ij}(r) - p_{ij}(r)}{p_{ij}(r)} - \frac{f_{ij}(s) - p_{ij}(s)}{p_{ij}(s)}$$

When the f's are obtained from a random sample of size n_{ij} from a trinomial population with probabilities $p_{ij}(1)$, $p_{ij}(2)$ and $p_{ij}(3)$, the variance of $f_{ij}(r)$ and the covariance of $f_{ij}(r)$ and $f_{ij}(s)$ for $r \neq s$ are equal to

$$\frac{1}{n_{ij}}\,p_{ij}(r)[1-p_{ij}(r)] \quad \text{and} \quad -\frac{1}{n_{ij}}\,p_{ij}(r)p_{ij}(s)$$

respectively. Use this property to prove that the large-sample variance of $l_{ij}(r, s)$ is

$$\frac{1}{n_{ij}}\left[\frac{1}{p_{ij}(r)} + \frac{1}{p_{ij}(s)}\right]$$

and that the large sample covariance of $l_{ij}(2, 1)$ and $l_{ij}(3, 1)$ is equal to $1/n_{ij}p_{ij}(1)$.

12 (*Continuation*) Define:

$$A_{ij} = \frac{1}{1-\sqrt{p_{ij}(1)}} \left[p_{ij}(2)l_{ij}(2, 1) + p_{ij}(3)l_{ij}(3, 1) \right]$$

and prove that the large-sample variance of A_{ij} and the large-sample covariance of A_{ij} and $l_{ij}(2, 1)$ are equal to

$$\frac{1+\sqrt{p_{ij}(1)}}{n_{ij}\, p_{ij}(1)[1-\sqrt{p_{ij}(1)}]} \quad \text{and} \quad \frac{1}{n_{ij}\, p_{ij}(1)[1-\sqrt{p_{ij}(1)}]}$$

respectively. Use this to prove that $\sqrt{n_{ij}p_{ij}(2)}\,[l_{ij}(2, 1)-A_{ij}]$ has a large-sample variance equal to unity, and note that this random variable is asymptotically equivalent to (4.14).

13 (*Continuation*) Prove that the random variables

$$\sqrt{n_{ij}}\,[l_{ij}(2, 1)-A_{ij}] \quad \text{and} \quad \sqrt{n_{ij}}\,[l_{ij}(3, 1)-A_{ij}]$$

have a zero large-sample covariance. Draw your own conclusions as to the correlation of the random variables (4.14) and (4.15) for large n_{ij}.

14 The conditional logit comparison of "halfway" and "fair", based on (4.8) and (4.9) is

$$\log \frac{p_{ij}(2)}{p_{ij}(3)} = (\alpha_2 - \alpha_3) + (\beta_{i2} - \beta_{i3}) + (\gamma_{j2} - \gamma_{j3})$$

Consider the estimates of $\alpha_2 - \alpha_3$ under the constraint (4.17), shown in Table 4.8, and verify that they are positive for both black and white MPs, but smaller for the former than for the latter. Describe what this means in terms of the popularity of these two groups of MPs among Northern men in Northern camps. Also, consider the parameters $\beta_{22} - \beta_{23}$ and $\gamma_{22} - \gamma_{23}$ of this equation as implied by the values (4.17), and describe their implications for the region of origin and the location of the camp as determinants of the popularity of the MPs.

15 Use eq. (4.11) to prove $p_{ij}(1) = B_{ij}$ and

$$p_{ij}(2) = B_{ij} \exp\{L_{ij}(2, 1)\} \quad \text{and} \quad p_{ij}(3) = B_{ij} \exp\{L_{ij}(3, 1)\}$$

where

$$B_{ij} = [1 + \exp\{L_{ij}(2, 1)\} + \exp\{L_{ij}(3, 1)\}]^{-1}$$

Apply this result to describe how probability estimates can be obtained from the parameter estimates of a conditional logit model.

16 Consider three variables, D, X and Y which take two values each. Take first the case $p_{111} = p_{222} = \frac{1}{2}$; prove that $J_D(X, Y)$ defined in (5.14) vanishes and that $J(X, Y) = \log 2$. Next consider the case $p_{111} = p_{122} = p_{212} = p_{221} = \frac{1}{4}$; prove that $J(X, Y)$ vanishes and that $J_D(X,Y) = \log 2$. This shows that dependence effects may be of either sign.

17 Define the expected mutual information of an n-variate distribution as

$$J(X_1, \ldots, X_n) = H(X_2, X_3, \ldots, X_n) + H(X_1, X_3, \ldots, X_n) + \ldots$$
$$+ H(X_1, X_2, \ldots, X_{n-1}) - (n-1)H(X_1, \ldots, X_n)$$

Prove that this includes, as a special case for $n = 2$, the expected mutual information defined in Section 3.3. Also prove that its value is zero when $X_1, \ldots, X_n$ are mutually independent.

18 (*Continuation*) Consider the following n equations:

$$H(X_1, \ldots, X_n) - H(X_2, X_3, \ldots, X_n) = H_{X_2 X_3 \ldots X_n}(X_1)$$
$$H(X_1, \ldots, X_n) - H(X_1, X_3, \ldots, X_n) = H_{X_1 X_3 \ldots X_n}(X_2)$$
$$\vdots$$
$$H(X_1, \ldots, X_n) - H(X_1, X_2, \ldots, X_{n-1}) = H_{X_1 X_2 \ldots X_{n-1}}(X_n)$$

Prove that the sum of the first $n-1$ of these equations can be written as shown below, and verify the steps thereafter.

$$-J(X_1, \ldots, X_n) + H(X_1, X_2, \ldots, X_{n-1})$$
$$= H_{X_2 X_3 \ldots X_n}(X_1) + H_{X_1 X_3 \ldots X_n}(X_2) + \ldots + H_{X_1 \ldots X_{n-2} X_n}(X_{n-1})$$
$$\leqq H_{X_2 X_3 \ldots X_{n-1}}(X_1) + H_{X_1 X_3 \ldots X_{n-1}}(X_2) + \ldots + H_{X_1 X_2 \ldots X_{n-2}}(X_{n-1})$$
$$= (n-1)H(X_1, \ldots, X_{n-1}) - H(X_2, X_3, \ldots, X_{n-1})$$
$$- H(X_1, X_3, \ldots, X_{n-1}) - \ldots - H(X_1, X_2, \ldots, X_{n-2})$$

Prove that this is equivalent to

$$J(X_1, \ldots, X_n) \geqq J(X_1, \ldots, X_{n-1})$$

or, in words, that there cannot be less dependence in an n-dimensional distribution than in any of its marginal distributions, whatever the dimension. Note that this also implies that the multivariate expected mutual information is nonnegative.

19 (*Continuation*) Let there be a dependent variable D with n determining factors, $X_1, \ldots, X_n$. Prove that the joint entropy reduction of D due to all n factors can be written as

$$H(D) + H(X_1, \ldots, X_n) - H(D, X_1, \ldots, X_n)$$

TABLE 4.14

AVERAGE INFORMATION INACCURACIES OF THE LOGIT MODEL APPLIED TO AMERICAN STATES
(in 10^{-2} nit)

State	Number of districts	1952	1954	1956	1958	1960	Arithmetic average
California	13	.449	.225	.091	.290	.475	.306
Connecticut	6	.031	.030	.036	.129	.025	.050
Illinois	24	.204	.098	.142	.145	.127	.143
Indiana	11	.041	.010	.080	.075	.074	.056
Iowa	7	.188	.106	.033	.106	.196	.126
Kansas	6	.770	.239	.134	.072	.688	.380
Maryland	6	.097	.181	.110	.475	.237	.220
Massachusetts	7	.186	.328	.049	.141	.662	.273
Michigan	18	.139	.061	.040	.084	.163	.097
Minnesota	9	.302	.010	.107	.214	.137	.154
Missouri	9	.093	.041	.133	.167	.053	.097
New Jersey	14	.164	.205	.243	.130	.300	.209
New York	41	.461	.261	.167	.166	.408	.293
North Carolina	5	.069	.132	.095	.135	.078	.102
Ohio	21	.405	.182	.207	.334	.385	.303
Oklahoma	5	.144	.170	.357	.691	.294	.331
Pennsylvania	30	.094	.226	.047	.081	.327	.155
West Virginia	5	.265	.076	.103	.198	.403	.209
Wisconsin	9	.264	.158	.096	.170	.177	.173
Weighted average		.247	.158	.120	.175	.280	.196

and the total partial entropy reduction as

$$nH(X_1, \ldots, X_n) - H(X_2, X_3, \ldots, X_n) - \ldots - H(X_1, X_2, \ldots, X_{n-1})$$
$$- nH(D, X_1, \ldots, X_n) + H(D, X_2, X_3, \ldots, X_n) + \ldots$$
$$+ H(D, X_1, X_2, \ldots, X_{n-1})$$

Next prove that the excess of the joint entropy reduction over the total partial reduction is equal to the sum of

$$-(n-1)H(X_1, \ldots, X_n) + H(X_2, X_3, \ldots, X_n) + \ldots$$
$$+ H(X_1, X_2, \ldots, X_{n-1}) = J(X_1, \ldots, X_n)$$

and

$$H(D) + (n-1)H(D, X_1, \ldots, X_n) - H(D, X_2, X_3, \ldots, X_n)$$
$$- \ldots - H(D, X_1, X_2, \ldots, X_{n-1})$$
$$= (n-1)H_D(X_1, \ldots, X_n) - H_D(X_2, X_3, \ldots, X_n) - \ldots$$
$$- H_D(X_1, X_2, \ldots, X_{n-1})$$

Write $-J_D(X_1, \ldots, X_n)$ for the expression in the last two lines, and interpret this expression. Draw your conclusions.

20 In the discussion of Table 4.12 on page 211 it was stated that the figures in the second line from the bottom indicate that, on the average, the predominantly Republican districts had a more rapid increase in the number of voters than those which lean to the other party. Explain this statement.

21 In Table 4.14 the logit model (6.1) is applied to each of the states that have at least five congressional districts in the analysis of Section 4.6.[1] The figures shown in the successive columns of the table are the number of districts used, the average information inaccuracy $\bar{I}_t$ for each t, and the average of $\bar{I}_t$ over t, in all cases for each state separately. The last row contains weighted averages with weights proportional to the number of voters included in each election. Make your comments on these results.

22 (*Continuation*) Write β_{st} for the election parameter of the sth state and the tth election. Prove that, for each t, these parameters are not comparable across states when the normalization rule (6.5) is used, but that their successive differences $(\beta_{st} - \beta_{s,t-1})$ are independent of the normalization rule. These successive differences are shown in Table 4.15. The last three lines of the table contain weighted averages and standard deviations, μ_t and σ_t defined as follows:

$$\mu_t = \sum_s W_{st}^*(\beta_{st} - \beta_{s,t-1}) \quad \text{where} \quad W_{st}^* = \frac{W_{st} + W_{s,t-1}}{2}$$

$$\sigma_t^2 = \sum_s W_{st}^*(\beta_{st} - \beta_{s,t-1} - \mu_t)^2$$

and also the successive differences of the national election parameters taken from Table 4.12 (page 210). In the above equation, W_{st} is the number of voters of the sth state at the tth election measured as a fraction of the total number of voters of all districts of the nation that are considered here. Give your comments on the figures shown in this table, and also on the weighting procedure used for μ_t and σ_t.

23 Consider Griliches' application of the logistic curve, described in the opening paragraph of Section 4.7, with c instead of 1 in the right-hand numerator of (7.1), where $0 < c \leq 1$. Prove that the equation implies that the logit corresponding to a conditional probability is a linear func-

---

[1] This reduces the total number of districts included from 288 to 246.

TABLE 4.15

SUCCESSIVE DIFFERENCES OF ELECTION PARAMETERS FOR SEPARATE STATES

State	1952–54	1954–56	1956–58	1958–60
California	.051	.061	−.272	.184
Connecticut	−.140	.411	−.644	.043
Illinois	−.203	.154	−.348	.083
Indiana	−.167	.130	−.389	.210
Iowa	−.248	−.172	−.170	.169
Kansas	−.126	−.139	−.139	.188
Maryland	−.192	.007	−.590	.254
Massachusetts	−.162	.045	−.247	.070
Michigan	−.198	.074	−.180	.092
Minnesota	−.288	.067	−.053	.094
Missouri	−.187	.008	−.350	.316
New Jersey	−.275	.317	−.379	.057
New York	−.188	.175	−.275	−.084
North Carolina	−.045	.120	−.379	.393
Ohio	.004	.085	−.321	.216
Oklahoma	−.158	.090	−.577	.808
Pennsylvania	−.131	.130	−.168	−.047
West Virginia	−.166	.175	−.230	.094
Wisconsin	−.415	.077	−.379	.178
Mean (μ_t)	−.165	.129	−.303	.098
Standard deviation (σ_t)	.096	.113	.131	.147
$\hat{\beta}_t - \hat{\beta}_{t-1}$	−.169	.106	−.290	.099

tion of t, and that this is the probability of finding an acre planted with hybrid seed in year t, given that it will ultimately be planted with that seed.

24 In eqs. (7.3) and (7.7) the same average $\bar{x}$ is used in the denominator of the right-hand side. Verify that this is indeed correct.

25 Prove that the β estimators b and b' occurring in (7.2) and (7.6), respectively, have the following sampling errors:

$$b - \beta = \frac{\sum (x_i - \bar{x}) \, \varepsilon_i}{\sum (x_i - \bar{x})^2} \quad \text{and} \quad b' - \beta = \frac{\sum n_g (\bar{x}_g - \bar{x}) \, \bar{\varepsilon}_g}{\sum n_g (\bar{x}_g - \bar{x})^2}$$

where ε_i is the disturbance corresponding to the residual e_i and $\bar{\varepsilon}_g$ is the average of the n_g disturbances that fall under S_g. Next prove, under the condition that all disturbances are uncorrelated random variables with zero expectation and variance σ^2, that b and b' are both unbiased estimators of β with variances

$$\operatorname{var} b = \frac{\sigma^2}{\sum (x_i - \bar{x})^2} \quad \text{and} \quad \operatorname{var} b' = \frac{\sigma^2}{\sum n_g(\bar{x}_g - \bar{x})^2}$$

and covariance

$$\operatorname{cov}(b, b') = \frac{\sigma^2}{\sum (x_i - \bar{x})^2}$$

Define η as follows:

$$\sum n_g(\bar{x}_g - \bar{x})^2 = (1 - \eta) \sum (x_i - \bar{x})^2$$

so that η is a small fraction when the first right-hand term in (7.9) dominates the second. Use the above results to prove that $b - b'$ has zero expectation and variance

$$\operatorname{var}(b - b') = \frac{\sigma^2}{\sum (x_i - \bar{x})^2} \frac{\eta}{1 - \eta}$$

and draw your own conclusions as to the magnitude of the first right-hand term of (7.8) when η is small.

26 Write $\theta_1, \theta_2, \ldots$ for the possible values of a parameter θ and $p(\theta)$ for the prior probability distribution of θ.[1] Measure the prior uncertainty of θ by the entropy of this distribution,

$$\sum_i p(\theta_i) \log \frac{1}{p(\theta_i)}$$

Write x for a random sample of observations from the population described by the parameter θ; this x takes the values $x_1, x_2, \ldots$. Write $p(\theta_i | x_h)$ for the posterior probability of $\theta = \theta_i$, given $x = x_h$, and formulate the corresponding posterior entropy. Prove that the average posterior entropy of θ, obtained by weighting with the probabilities of the conditions, is equal to

$$\sum_h \sum_i p(x_h, \theta_i) \log \frac{1}{p(\theta_i | x_h)}$$

where $p(x_h, \theta_i)$ is the joint probability of $x = x_h$ and $\theta = \theta_i$, and that

---

[1] A discrete probability formulation is chosen here for reasons of simplicity; see LINDLEY (1956) for a more general formulation.

the prior entropy of θ exceeds its average posterior entropy by

(1)
$$\sum_h \sum_i p(x_h, \theta_i) \log \frac{p(x_h, \theta_i)}{p(x_h)p(\theta_i)}$$

where $p(x_h)$ is the probability that the sample takes the value x_h. Interpret expression (1) in terms of concepts from two-dimensional information theory and show that it is a measure for the degree to which the observations shed light on the value of the parameter.

27 Suppose that (7.15) is replaced by the criterion of the expected number of successful assignments, $\sum p(i, \sigma_i)$. Suppose also that the person in charge of the assignments wants to correct the probabilities $p(i, j)$ on the basis of the results shown in Figure 4.7, reducing values smaller than .2 and raising values larger than .2. Prove that the only transformation of $p(i, j)$ which guarantees the selection of the same permutation σ under this criterion is the increasing linear transformation, but that it is not feasible in this case because it leads to transformed probabilities outside the range from zero to one.

28 Consider the following equation for a pair of proportions (P_r, P_s):

$$\frac{P_r}{P_s} = e^{\alpha_r - \alpha_s} \prod_{i=1}^{n} x_i^{\beta_{ir} - \beta_{is}} \prod_{i=1}^{n'} \left(\frac{y_{ir}}{y_{is}}\right)^{\gamma_i}$$

where $r, s = 1, \ldots, R$. Prove that this is an extension of (7.20) for the case of n variables $x_1, \ldots, x_n$ which are analogous to income in (7.20) and for n' variables corresponding to the travel time. Prove also that the total number of parameters is

$$(R-1)(n+1)+n'$$

29 Prove that the market share equations (8.5) and (8.9) of Section 1.8 fall under the model (7.20) when appropriate modifications are made. For both cases, describe these modifications.

30 Define $H = -\sum P_r \log P_r$, in nits. Prove:

$$dH = \sum_r P_r \log \frac{1}{P_r} d(\log P_r)$$

and use (7.29) to prove

$$dH = d(\log x) \sum_r P_r (\beta_r - \sum_s P_s \beta_s) \log \frac{1}{P_r}$$

$$+ \gamma \sum_r P_r [d(\log y_r) - \sum_s P_s d(\log y_s)] \log \frac{1}{P_r}$$

Compare this with eqs. (8.8) and (8.10) of Section 1.8 to conclude that the entropy change may be regarded as a weighted sum of two covariances. Interpret these covariances.

31 Use (7.29) and Problem 17 of Chapter 2 to prove that the expected information of the message which transforms the proportions $P_1, P_2, \ldots$ into $P_1 + dP_1, P_2 + dP_2, \ldots$ is equal to

$$\tfrac{1}{2}[d(\log x)]^2 \sum_r P_r(\beta_r - \sum_s P_s \beta_s)^2 + \tfrac{1}{2}\gamma^2 \sum_r P_r [d(\log y_r) - \sum_s P_s d(\log y_s)]^2$$

$$+ \gamma d(\log x) \sum_r P_r(\beta_r - \sum_s P_s \beta_s)[d(\log y_r) - \sum_s P_s d(\log y_s)]$$

Prove that this is a weighted sum of two variances and a covariance, and discuss each term.

BRITISH AND AMERICAN DISTRICT PARAMETERS

Below are listed the 368 British constituencies and the 288 American congressional districts that are considered in Section 4.6. They are arranged in the order of increasing values of the district parameters.

British			
−1.80	Abertillery	−1.07	Dagenham
−1.57	Aberdare	−1.03	Blyth
−1.54	Bedwellty	−1.00	Aberavon
−1.42	Ebbw Vale	−.97	Normanton
−1.41	London: Bermondsey	−.97	Don Valley
−1.40	London: Stepney	−.92	Ince
−1.38	London: Poplar	−.91	Pontypridd
−1.36	Easington	−.89	Morpeth
−1.34	Merthyr Tydfil	−.88	Barking
−1.31	Bolsover	−.88	London: Battersea N.
−1.29	Dearne Valley	−.87	London: Southwark
−1.24	Neath	−.85	Fife W.
−1.24	Caerphilly	−.78	Hamilton
−1.17	Ogmore	−.76	Consett
−1.14	Pontypool	−.75	Durham N-W.
−1.13	Chester-1e-Street	−.73	Liverpool: Scotland
−1.12	Pontefract	−.71	London: Islington S-W.
−1.11	Houghton-1e-Spring	−.71	Wigan
−1.09	Gower	−.70	Stoke-on-Trent N.
−1.08	Swansea E.	−.70	London: Peckham
−1.07	Rother Valley	−.68	Durham
		−.68	Aberdeen N.

−.63	Middlesbrough	−.31	Burnley
−.62	London: Deptford	−.30	Gloucestershire W.
−.60	Glasgow: Maryhill	−.28	Swindon
−.59	Derbyshire N-E.	−.28	Motherwell
−.59	Rotherham	−.28	Leyton
−.59	London: Vauxhall	−.27	Bilston
−.58	London: Woolwich E.	−.27	London: Lewisham S.
−.58	Rowley Regis & Tipton	−.26	Leicester N-E.
−.57	East Ham S.	−.26	Leicester S-W.
−.57	Wrexham	−.25	Newcastle-under-Lyme
−.57	Thurrock	−.24	Coatbridge & Airdrie
−.56	St. Helens	−.23	Salford E.
−.55	Leigh	−.23	Bosworth
−.53	Stoke-on-Trent S.	−.23	Brecon & Radnor
−.53	Stoke-on-Trent C.	−.23	Smethwick
−.52	Chesterfield	−.22	Stirlingshire W.
−.51	Norwich N.	−.22	Bothwell
−.50	Kilmarnock	−.22	Brigg
−.50	Willesden W.	−.21	Stockton-on-Tees
−.47	Ayrshire S.	−.21	Edmonton
−.47	South Shields	−.21	Newport
−.46	Kirkcaldy	−.21	Belper
−.44	Glasgow: Shettleston	−.21	Barrow-in-Furness
−.44	Tottenham	−.21	Coventry N.
−.43	Hayes & Harlington	−.20	Southall
−.43	Westhoughton	−.20	London: Brixton
−.42	Bishop Auckland	−.20	Loughborough
−.42	Goole	−.19	Oldham W.
−.42	Dunfermline	−.19	Leicester N-W.
−.41	Workington	−.18	Oldbury & Halesowen
−.41	Enfield E.	−.18	Cardiff W.
−.41	Stirlingshire E. & Clackmannan	−.18	Lincoln
−.40	West Bromwich	−.18	Kettering
−.40	London: Islington E.	−.17	Wood Green
−.40	Sedgefield	−.17	Birkenhead
−.38	Farnworth	−.16	Edinburgh: Leith
−.38	Batley & Morley	−.16	Huyton
−.38	London: Greenwich	−.15	London: Paddington N.
−.37	London: St. Pancras N.	−.14	Cardiff S-E.
−.37	Coventry E.	−.13	Dundee E.
−.37	London: Islington N.	−.13	Grimsby
−.37	East Ham N.	−.13	Edinburgh E.
−.34	Newton	−.13	Birmingham: Perry Barr
−.34	Dudley	−.12	Flintshire E.
−.33	Lanarkshire N.	−.12	Northampton
−.32	Whitehaven	−.12	London: Kensington N.
−.32	Wallsend	−.12	Eccles

—.12	Dunbartonshire E.
—.11	Widnes
—.11	Keighley
—.11	Salford W.
—.10	Accrington
—.10	Nelson & Colne
—.10	Stirling & Falkirk
—.10	Sowerby
—.09	Dunbartonshire W.
—.09	Ipswich
—.08	Cleveland
—.08	Wellingborough
—.08	Falmouth & Camborne
—.08	Rossendale
—.07	Eton & Slough
—.06	Ayrshire C.
—.06	Coventry S.
—.06	The Hartlepools
—.04	Leek
—.04	Swansea W.
—.03	London: Holborn & St. Pancras S.
—.03	Acton
—.02	Stalybridge & Hyde
—.02	Faversham
—.01	Halifax
—.01	Oldham E.
—.01	Willesden E.
—.00	Norfolk N.
.01	Sunderland S.
.01	Rochester & Chatham
.01	Uxbridge
.02	Lowestoft
.02	London: Wandsworth
.03	Brierley Hill
.03	London: Clapham
.03	Darlington
.03	Lanark
.03	Bolton E.
.03	Rugby
.04	Rutherglen
.04	Buckingham
.04	Norfolk S-W.
.04	London: Dulwich
.05	London: Battersea S.
.05	Watford
.05	The Wrekin
.05	Ealing N.

.06	Maldon
.07	Preston S.
.07	Doncaster
.08	King's Lynn
.08	Hornchurch
.09	London: Woolwich W.
.09	York
.10	Walthamstow E.
.10	Bedfordshire S.
.10	Yarmouth
.10	Berwick & East Lothian
.11	Bury & Radcliffe
.13	Norwich S.
.13	Preston N.
.13	Stockport S.
.13	Dover
.13	Peterborough
.13	Heywood & Royton
.13	Brentford & Chiswick
.14	Manchester: Blackley
.15	Luton
.15	Epping
.16	Portsmouth W.
.16	Liverpool: Toxteth
.16	Burton
.16	Renfrewshire W.
.16	Middlesbrough W.
.17	Stockport N.
.17	London: Lewisham N.
.17	Devizes
.18	Norfolk S.
.18	Somerset N.
.19	Bexley
.20	London: Lewisham W.
.20	Conway
.20	Hendon N.
.20	London: Norwood
.21	Shipley
.22	Barry
.22	Brighton: Kemptown
.22	London: Putney
.22	Northamptonshire S.
.22	Bromsgrove
.23	Banbury
.23	Yeovil
.23	Bedford
.23	Colchester

.23	Bedfordshire Mid.		.39	Macclesfield
.24	Dorset S.		.39	Hertfordshire S-W.
.24	Exeter		.40	Louth
.24	Grantham		.40	Middleton & Prestwich
.24	Westbury		.41	Cheltenham
.24	Lancaster		.41	Dumfriesshire
.25	Pudsey		.42	Henley
.25	Carlton		.42	Salisbury
.25	High Peak		.43	Hornsey
.25	Rutland & Stamford		.43	Melton
.26	Ilford S.		.44	Huntingdonshire
.26	Taunton		.46	Chertsey
.27	Cambridgeshire		.46	Chester
.27	Mitcham		.46	Poole
.27	Merton & Morden		.47	Shrewsbury
.27	Wycombe		.47	Ilford N.
.27	Cambridge		.47	Flintshire W.
.27	Oxford		.48	Skipton
.27	Bury St. Edmunds		.48	Carshalton
.27	Monmouth		.48	Ludlow
.28	Gillingham		.48	Isle of Thanet
.28	Clitheroe		.49	Ashford
.28	Truro		.50	London: Paddington S.
.29	Bath		.50	Dorset W.
.29	Bebington		.51	London: Hampstead
.30	Wells		.51	Manchester: Moss Side
.31	Ayr		.52	Newcastle-upon-Tyne N.
.31	Worcester		.52	Warwick & Leamington
.32	Isle of Ely		.52	Harwich
.32	Stretford		.54	Isle of Wight
.32	Norfolk C.		.54	Wallasey
.32	Cardiff N.		.55	Gosport & Fareham
.33	Gainsborough		.55	Wembley N.
.34	Hemel Hempstead		.56	Sevenoaks
.35	Kidderminster		.56	Ayrshire N. & Bute
.35	Wembley S.		.56	Moray & Nairn
.36	Barkston Ash		.56	Reigate
.36	Abingdon		.56	Portsmouth: Langstone
.36	Saffron Walden		.56	Runcorn
.37	Aberdeen S.		.57	Horsham
.37	Stafford & Stone		.57	Aldershot
.37	Sudbury & Woodbridge		.58	Belfast E.
.37	Aylesbury		.58	Hendon S.
.38	Maidstone		.59	Oswestry
.38	Holland with Boston		.59	Windsor
.38	Tynemouth		.61	Ealing S.
.39	Bridgwater		.61	Guildford

.62	Totnes	*American*[1]	
.62	Twickenham	−2.03	Michigan 1
.62	Belfast N.	−1.54	Oklahoma 3
.64	Richmond (Surrey)	−1.46	New York 11
.65	Blackpool S.	−1.43	New York 23
.65	London: Streatham	−1.26	Illinois 7
.66	Folkestone & Hythe	−1.24	North Carolina 3
.66	Woking	−1.15	New York 10
.67	Ruislip-Northwood	−1.15	New York 13
.68	Sutton & Cheam	−1.14	New York 22
.68	Glasgow: Cathcart	−1.13	Michigan 15
.68	Canterbury	−1.10	Ohio 21
.69	Portsmouth S.	−1.04	Illinois 1
.70	Renfrewshire E.	−.98	Missouri 3
.70	Wirral	−.97	New York 19
.71	Stratford-upon-Avon	−.96	Pennsylvania 4
.71	Bournemouth W.	−.95	New York 8
.72	Birmingham: Edgbaston	−.93	Minnesota 8
.74	Altrincham & Sale	−.91	Illinois 24
.75	Argyll	−.88	Illinois 5
.76	Honiton	−.87	Wisconsin 4
.78	Bromley	−.87	Ohio 20
.80	Brighton: Pavilion	−.87	Ohio 19
.81	Edinburgh S.	−.86	New York 14
.82	Dorking	−.86	Michigan 13
.83	Morecambe & Lonsdale	−.84	Oklahoma 5
.84	Banff	−.84	Missouri 1
.84	London: St. Marylebone	−.83	New York 9
.84	London: Cities of London &	−.83	Illinois 6
	Westminster	−.76	Pennsylvania 1
.85	Beckenham	−.73	Michigan 16
.86	Thirsk & Malton	−.71	Illinois 8
.86	North Fylde	−.69	Pennsylvania 30
.86	Blackpool N.	−.68	New York 20
.88	Arundel & Shoreham	−.67	California 17
.89	Fife E.	−.66	New York 24
.93	Esher	−.66	Pennsylvania 2
.96	Perth & Perthshire E.	−.66	Oklahoma 2
.97	Solihull	−.62	Oklahoma 6
1.00	London: Chelsea	−.62	New Jersey 13
1.00	Bournemouth E. & Christchurch	−.62	New York 21
1.04	Hove	−.60	Pennsylvania 28
1.05	Richmond (Yorks)	−.58	Pennsylvania 26
1.25	Belfast S.	−.56	Alaska A.L.

[1] The number after the state is that of the relevant district in that state. The addition A.L. means 'at large'.

—.54	Ohio 18		—.22	Pennsylvania 25
—.52	New Jersey 10		—.22	Michigan 17
—.52	Pennsylvania 3		—.21	Connecticut 1
—.51	Minnesota 4		—.20	Missouri 4
—.49	Maryland 7		—.18	Illinois 25
—.49	Illinois 2		—.18	Illinois 3
—.49	Maryland 4		—.17	Indiana 8
—.49	Missouri 5		—.16	Ohio 6
—.49	West Virginia 6		—.16	Missouri 11
—.48	Indiana 1		—.15	Illinois 12
—.46	Rhode Island 2		—.14	Pennsylvania 6
—.45	Massachusetts 4		—.14	Wisconsin 9
—.45	Maryland 5		—.14	Oregon 2
—.45	Rhode Island 1		—.11	Minnesota 3
—.44	New York 30		—.06	Delaware A.L.
—.44	Colorado 4		—.05	Indiana 3
—.42	Arizona 2		—.04	West Virginia 4
—.42	Michigan 14		—.03	Montana 2
—.41	Minnesota 6		—.01	Connecticut 3
—.41	Illinois 9		—.01	Illinois 11
—.41	North Carolina 8		.00	Maryland 2
—.39	Montana 1		.01	Pennsylvania 19
—.39	Colorado 1		.01	Connecticut A.L.
—.38	New York 6		.02	Ohio 15
—.38	New Jersey 4		.02	Kentucky 3
—.37	Oregon 3		.03	West Virginia 1
—.37	Massachusetts 8		.03	Minnesota 9
—.36	Pennsylvania 15		.03	Maine 2
—.36	New Jersey 14		.04	Iowa 5
—.35	North Carolina 21		.04	Michigan 6
—.35	Missouri 8		.05	Illinois 23
—.34	Pennsylvania 21		.05	Indiana 9
—.34	Wisconsin 5		.05	Connecticut 2
—.34	New Jersey 11		.05	Massachusetts 13
—.33	Ohio 9		.05	Connecticut 5
—.32	West Virginia 3		.06	Michigan 7
—.32	Idaho 1		.06	Colorado 3
—.32	Pennsylvania 11		.06	California 6
—.31	New York 7		.06	Indiana 5
—.31	Hawaii A.L.		.06	Indiana 6
—.31	West Virginia 2		.07	Maryland 6
—.28	Pennsylvania 5		.07	Pennsylvania 10
—.27	North Carolina 9		.08	Utah 2
—.26	Pennsylvania 14		.08	Maine 1
—.24	Nevada 1		.08	Oregon 4
—.24	Illinois 21		.08	Missouri 7
—.23	Missouri 6		.09	Wisconsin 2

.09	New York 5		.22	New Hampshire 1
.10	Iowa 6		.23	New York 4
.10	Maryland 1		.23	New Jersey 8
.10	Kansas 2		.24	Nebraska 3
.10	Massachusetts 10		.24	California 13
.10	New Jersey 6		.24	California 21
.11	New York 12		.25	California 9
.11	Virginia 10		.26	Massachusetts 9
.11	Kansas 3		.26	New York 42
.12	Iowa 2		.26	Ohio 16
.13	Pennsylvania 24		.26	Michigan 9
.13	Kansas 1		.26	North Carolina 10
.13	Missouri 2		.26	Connecticut 4
.14	Wisconsin 1		.26	Michigan 12
.14	Iowa 4		.27	Minnesota 5
.14	New York 17		.27	Oklahoma 1
.14	New Jersey 12		.28	Illinois 18
.14	Florida 1		.28	New York 27
.15	Illinois 19		.28	Iowa 7
.16	Kansas 4		.29	Idaho 2
.16	Colorado 2		.30	Iowa 1
.16	New York 15		.30	New York 25
.16	Michigan 18		.30	Oregon 4
.16	Pennsylvania 22		.30	Ohio 2
.16	Indiana 11		.30	Pennsylvania 17
.16	New Jersey 1		.31	Ohio 14
.16	South Dakota 1		.31	California 16
.16	Illinois 4		.31	Illinois 15
.17	Kansas 6		.32	Nebraska 2
.17	Pennsylvania 8		.32	Illinois 20
.17	Minnesota 7		.32	California 10
.17	Ohio 3		.32	Indiana 2
.17	New York 41		.33	Ohio 22
.17	Michigan 11		.33	Indiana 4
.18	Kansas 5		.33	Pennsylvania 7
.18	Utah 1		.33	Iowa 3
.19	Indiana 10		.33	New York 3
.19	Pennsylvania 12		.34	New Jersey 3
.20	Wyoming A.L.		.34	New York 1
.20	Arizona 1		.34	California 25
.20	Oregon 5		.34	Pennsylvania 18
.21	Ohio 11		.35	Illinois 10
.22	Oregon 3		.36	Ohio 13
.22	New York 32		.36	California 18
.22	California 22		.36	Ohio 12
.22	New York 34		.36	New Jersey 5
.22	Indiana 7		.37	Pennsylvania 16

.37	California 30		.48	Pennsylvania 20
.37	Ohio 17		.49	New York 26
.39	South Dakota 2		.49	Illinois 17
.39	New York 35		.51	Wisconsin 8
.39	New York 40		.51	Michigan 10
.39	Minnesota 2		.52	Michigan 8
.40	California 4		.52	Maine 3
.40	Michigan 2		.53	Pennsylvania 23
.41	New Jersey 2		.54	Wisconsin 7
.41	Wisconsin 3		.55	Pennsylvania 13
.41	Oregon 1		.56	New York 2
.41	Ohio 1		.57	Ohio 8
.41	Ohio 5		.58	New Jersey 7
.42	Michigan 3		.58	Pennsylvania 9
.42	Vermont A.L.		.58	New York 36
.42	Nebraska 1		.58	New York 39
.43	Massachusetts 14		.59	Michigan 5
.43	Illinois 22		.62	New York 38
.44	Minnesota 1		.63	Ohio 4
.44	Pennsylvania 29		.63	New York 29
.45	Nebraska 4		.64	New York 43
.45	Wisconsin 6		.66	Ohio 23
.45	New Jersey 9		.66	New York 31
.46	Massachusetts 1		.67	Tennessee 1
.46	New Hampshire 2		.71	New York 33
.47	California 28		.73	New York 37
.47	Michigan 4		.73	Illinois 14
.48	New York 28		.75	Illinois 13
.48	Pennsylvania 27			

CHAPTER 5

SOCIAL MOBILITY AND SOCIAL DISTANCE:
A MARKOV CHAIN APPROACH

This chapter differs from its predecessors in that its main subject is not a set of tools which are subsequently applied in several different areas. Rather, it is concerned with one particular substantive area, intergenerational occupational mobility, which is approached by means of tools from decomposition analysis. Each occupation is allocated to one of n occupational categories, such as nonmanual, skilled manual, and unskilled manual, so that any group of economically active persons is characterized by an occupational distribution consisting of n nonnegative proportions that add up to one. Among the problems to be examined are how this distribution changes from one generation to the next, and how the occupation of a person affects those of his descendants. A Markov chain model is used for the solution of these problems.

5.1. A Markov Chain Model for Social Mobility

In an article published in the *American Journal of Sociology*, LIEBERSON and FUGUITT (1967) considered the occupational distributions of American whites and blacks in successive generations. They distinguished between 10 occupational categories, listed in the first column of Table 5.1. The 1960 figures on the occupational distributions are quite different for the two races. As we shall see later (Table 5.2 on page 250), 13 per cent of the whites are in the professional and technical category and 14 per cent are managers and officials, whereas these percentages are only 4 and 2, respectively, for blacks. On the other hand, as many as 22 per cent of the blacks and only 5 per cent of the whites are nonfarm laborers.

The problem examined by Lieberson and Fuguitt is the development of these occupational distributions in successive generations under certain conditions, to be stated later in this section. For this purpose they used the so-called *matrix of transition probabilities* (or *transition matrix*) which is shown in Table 5.1. Each row of this table deals with one of the 10 occu-

TABLE 5.1

MATRIX OF TRANSITION PROBABILITIES

Father's occupation (i of p_{ij})	Subject's occupation (j of p_{ij})									
	1	2	3	4	5	6	7	8	9	10
1. Professional and technical	.410	.175	.090	.069	.087	.103	.031	.019	.012	.004
2. Managers and officials	.216	.341	.091	.071	.139	.085	.025	.019	.010	.003
3. Sales workers	.195	.300	.150	.062	.119	.104	.032	.020	.017	.001
4. Clerical workers	.281	.178	.078	.097	.169	.092	.061	.030	.014	.000
5. Craftsmen and foremen	.130	.165	.047	.078	.294	.175	.051	.048	.008	.004
6. Operatives	.117	.122	.044	.066	.239	.259	.059	.076	.009	.009
7. Service workers*	.101	.142	.057	.095	.210	.209	.111	.063	.010	.002
8. Laborers (nonfarm)	.059	.080	.036	.080	.226	.263	.091	.142	.012	.011
9. Farmers	.053	.115	.025	.047	.197	.205	.052	.085	.178	.043
10. Farm laborers	.023	.075	.020	.038	.205	.260	.081	.134	.062	.102

* Including private households.

pational categories. Under the condition that the father's occupation is as specified on the left, the figures of the row are the probabilities that his son will end up in any of the 10 categories. Thus, the table states that there is a 41 per cent chance that the son of a person in the professional and technical category will be in the same category, and a chance of less than 2 per cent that he will be a nonfarm laborer. The elements of each row should of course add up to one. Note that in most of the columns of the table the element in the diagonal takes the largest value. This means that entrance into such an occupational category has the largest probability when the father was in that category.

The Markov Chain Model

We shall treat the problem described above by means of a Markov chain model. This model is a stochastic process which moves through a number of states (occupational categories in our case) and for which the probability of entering a certain state depends only on the last state occupied. Thus the probability that a person will be in the jth occupational category should depend exclusively on that of his father (the last state occupied); we will denote such a probability by p_{ij}, where the first subscript refers to the occupational category of the father (the conditioning factor) and the second to that of the person under consideration. In particular, the occupation of the grandfather should have no direct effect; the model does recognize the indirect effect via the father's occupation. It is certainly possible that this is unrealistic in particular cases. For example, it may be that among fathers with nonagricultural occupations a larger percentage of sons go into farming when the grandfather was a farmer than among those fathers whose nonagricultural backgrounds extend over a larger number of generations. The Markov chain model does not take such a possibility into account.

It is quite conceivable that the probability of entering an occupational category depends on factors other than the father's occupation, which would seem to invalidate the model. However, this is not necessarily true. Suppose that the probability of entering the jth category depends on two things, the father's occupational category and the son's years of formal education. This conditional probability may be written as

(1.1) $$P[M \in j | F \in i, M_k]$$

where $M \in j$ stands for "the person is in the jth occupational category", $F \in i$ for "the father is in the ith category", and M_k for "the person has k years of formal education". Suppose further that the probability of obtaining k years of formal education is determined by the father's occupational category. Then, by multiplying this probability, $P[M_k|F \in i]$, by the probability (1.1) and summing over k we obtain the conditional probability of $M \in j$ given $F \in i$ only:

$$(1.2) \qquad \sum_k P[M \in j|F \in i, M_k]P[M_k|F \in i] = P[M \in j|F \in i]$$

The right-hand side is nothing but p_{ij} defined in the previous paragraph, so that the Markov chain model is applicable in spite of our initial denial that the father's occupation is the sole determinant of the probability that the son will enter the jth occupational category. Basically, what is needed in this case is an appropriate interpretation of the probability p_{ij}; it is conditional on the father's occupation and not conditional on the son's education. See Problem 1 for an extension of this result.

In spite of this it remains true that the use of the Markov chain model implies severe restrictions, particularly when it is assumed that the transition probabilities remain constant generation after generation. It is conceivable, for example, that changes in economic conditions affect these probabilities, and we shall indeed find some evidence of this in Section 5.6 (page 296). Also, when the figures used for the transition probabilities are observed proportions based on a sample, we shall have to face the problem of sampling errors. In addition to all this, we have the difficulty that the occupational category of a person may change when he grows older, so that a rather arbitrary decision has to be made as to the age at which the occupation is to be recorded. But it is equally true, despite these limitations, that the Markov chain model can provide interesting and valuable insight into the mechanism of intergenerational mobility as long as its results are interpreted carefully.[1]

Occupational Distributions of Successive Generations

Write q_{0i} for the proportion of persons of the present (initial) generation who are in the ith occupational category. Disregarding those who have no sons, consider the eldest (or only) sons, Given that the relevant transition probabilities are $p_{i1}, \ldots, p_{in}$, the ith category of the initial generation supplies a proportion $q_{0i}p_{ij}$ to the jth occupational category. The total propor-

---

[1] The idea of using a Markov chain model for the analysis of intergenerational mobility originated with PRAIS (1955). For more recent contributions, see MATRAS (1967) and the articles quoted by him.

tion of the jth category in the new generation is thus

(1.3)
$$q_{1j} = \sum_{i=1}^{n} q_{0i} p_{ij} \qquad j = 1, \ldots, n$$

or, equivalently,

(1.4)
$$\mathbf{q}_1' = \mathbf{q}_0' \mathbf{P}$$

where $\mathbf{P} = [p_{ij}]$ is the transition matrix and $\mathbf{q}_t$ (for $t = 0$ and $t = 1$) is the n-element column vector whose jth element is q_{tj}. [Primes attached to vectors or matrices indicate transposition.] We shall call $\mathbf{q}_t$ the occupational distribution of the tth generation or, for short, the tth occupational distribution.

If we take $\mathbf{q}_1$ instead of $\mathbf{q}_0$ as our starting point, the same line of argument leads to $\mathbf{q}_2' = \mathbf{q}_1' \mathbf{P}$ for the second occupational distribution, which implies $\mathbf{q}_2' = \mathbf{q}_0' \mathbf{P}^2$ because $\mathbf{q}_1' \mathbf{P} = \mathbf{q}_0' \mathbf{P}^2$ follows from (1.4). Repeated application of this procedure gives

(1.5)
$$\mathbf{q}_t' = \mathbf{q}_0' \mathbf{P}^t \qquad t = 1, 2, \ldots$$

Hence the occupational distribution of any generation after the initial one can be found from the latter by multiplication by the appropriate power of the transition matrix.

Lieberson and Fuguitt used this device to analyze the development of the occupational distributions of blacks and of whites under the condition of nondiscrimination. This condition was formalized by the use of the same transition matrix (shown in Table 5.1) for the two groups. The result is given in Table 5.2; the initial distribution ($t = 0$) is based on data for 1960. It shows that although the distributions for low values of t are quite different for black and white, they ultimately converge to exactly the same distribution, to be called the *limit distribution* (at $t = \infty$). This is a result of considerable importance; the discussion from here until the end of Section 5.2 is devoted to it. Note that the development is not monotonic; for example, at $t = 0$ there are 13 per cent craftsmen and foremen among the blacks, which increases to slightly over 22 per cent at $t = 1$, after which the direction of change is reversed until it stabilizes at a value just below 18 per cent. Therefore, there is a convergence even though the development is not necessarily monotonic. The large number of decimal places of the figures in Table 5.2 serves to illustrate the convergence more clearly; the practical significance of the fourth place is, of course, nil.

It is not difficult to criticize the procedure described here. We confined

TABLE 5.2

OCCUPATIONAL DISTRIBUTIONS IN SUCCESSIVE GENERATIONS

Generation (t)	Occupational category									
	1. Professional and technical	2. Managers and officials	3. Sales workers	4. Clerical workers	5. Craftsmen and foremen	6. Operatives	7. Service workers	8. Laborers (nonfarm)	9. Farmers	10. Farm laborers
	Occupational distributions of whites									
0	.13	.14	.07	.07	.24	.20	.04	.05	.05	.01
1	.1813	.1841	.0660	.0725	.2009	.1672	.0505	.0506	.0194	.0076
2	.2023	.1948	.0708	.0735	.1879	.1561	.0487	.0458	.0143	.0059
3	.2107	.1988	.0729	.0734	.1827	.1515	.0475	.0436	.0135	.0054
4	.2139	.2004	.0737	.0734	.1806	.1497	.0469	.0428	.0133	.0053
5	.2150	.2010	.0740	.0733	.1797	.1490	.0467	.0425	.0133	.0053
6	.2155	.2012	.0741	.0733	.1794	.1488	.0467	.0424	.0133	.0053
∞	.2157	.2014	.0742	.0733	.1793	.1486	.0466	.0423	.0133	.0053
	Occupational distributions of blacks									
0	.04	.02	.01	.06	.13	.30	.13	.22	.04	.05
1	.1209	.1300	.0482	.0743	.2227	.2191	.0706	.0817	.0196	.0130
2	.1758	.1764	.0636	.0743	.2045	.1747	.0547	.0547	.0143	.0070
3	.2001	.1926	.0701	.0738	.1899	.1582	.0495	.0467	.0134	.0057
4	.2099	.1982	.0726	.0735	.1834	.1521	.0477	.0439	.0133	.0054
5	.2136	.2002	.0736	.0734	.1808	.1499	.0470	.0429	.0133	.0053
6	.2149	.2010	.0740	.0734	.1798	.1491	.0468	.0425	.0133	.0053
∞	.2157	.2014	.0742	.0733	.1793	.1486	.0466	.0423	.0133	.0053

ourselves to eldest or only sons, but in every generation of males there are younger sons. An alternative justification is on the basis of a hypothetical society in which each person in each generation has exactly one son. Since the number of children per family is on the average not far above two and since the sex composition is about 50-50, this assumption is not too unrealistic on the average, but this does not mean that the rather sizable deviations from this average cannot affect the results shown in Table 5.2 significantly. It is also possible that whites have their children at an earlier (or later) age than blacks on the average, so that $t = 3$ for whites may not correspond in calendar time with $t = 3$ for blacks. These problems can be solved only by the introduction of explicit demographic models, but they are beyond the scope of this book.[1]

A Historical Example

In a pioneering study on intergenerational mobility, ROGOFF (1953) collected data on occupations from marriage license applications for Marion County, Indiana. These documents describe the occupations of both the applicant and his father. The data collected refer to two time periods – 1905 to 1912 and 1938 through the first half of 1941 – which will be indicated briefly as 1910 and 1940, respectively. We can thus compare the transition matrices of two different time periods, which makes this example particularly interesting. Following KEMENY and SNELL (1960, pp. 198-199), we distinguish here only three broad occupational categories, (1) nonmanual nonfarm, (2) manual nonfarm, and (3) farming. The 1910 and 1940 transition matrices are, respectively,

$$\mathbf{P}_1 = \begin{bmatrix} .594 & .396 & .009 \\ .211 & .782 & .007 \\ .252 & .641 & .108 \end{bmatrix} \text{ and } \mathbf{P}_2 = \begin{bmatrix} .622 & .375 & .003 \\ .274 & .721 & .005 \\ .265 & .694 & .042 \end{bmatrix}$$

These matrices are fairly close to each other, but the probabilities of transition to the nonmanual category (first column) have all increased in 1940 relative to the 1910 level, whereas those to farming (third column) have all decreased.

Considering the 1910 situation first, its observed occupational distribution is (.310, .656, .034). Postmultiplying this row by $\mathbf{P}_1$, we obtain (.331, .658, .011) for the distribution of the next generation. The limit distribution is

---

[1] Lieberson and Fuguitt also examine the effect of education on the occupational developments of the two groups. This aspect will not be explored here.

(.343, .648, .009). This suggests that there will be a considerable reduction of the farm population from 1910 onward and a modest increase of the proportion of those engaged in nonmanual activities.

These predictions are confirmed – at least qualitatively – by the observed occupational distribution of 1940, which is (.373, .616, .011). The new limit distribution is (.420, .576, .004), which indicates that there will be an additional decrease of the farming proportion and a further increase of the nonmanual category, even beyond the levels predicted by the limit distribution of 1910. Given the differences of the first and third columns of $\mathbf{P}_1$ and $\mathbf{P}_2$, the latter result should cause no surprise.

Absorbing and Regular Markov Chains

We return to Table 5.2 and observe that the convergence of $\mathbf{q}_t$ has nothing to do with the initial occupational distributions of whites and of blacks.[1] As will be shown below, this is exclusively a property of the transition matrix of Table 5.1. Not every transition matrix has the property that it ultimately leads to a limit distribution with strictly positive proportions. A simple counterexample is

$$(1.6) \qquad \mathbf{P} = \begin{bmatrix} \frac{1}{2} & \frac{1}{2} \\ 0 & 1 \end{bmatrix}$$

If the system is presently in state 1 (first row of $\mathbf{P}$), it is equally likely to be in state 1 or in state 2 in the next step. But if the system is in state 2 (second row), it is bound to stay there. Such a state is called *absorbing*. The second and third powers of this $\mathbf{P}$ are

$$(1.7) \qquad \mathbf{P}^2 = \begin{bmatrix} \frac{1}{4} & \frac{3}{4} \\ 0 & 1 \end{bmatrix} \qquad \mathbf{P}^3 = \begin{bmatrix} \frac{1}{8} & \frac{7}{8} \\ 0 & 1 \end{bmatrix}$$

When t increases indefinitely, $\mathbf{P}^t$ converges to a 2×2 matrix with a first column consisting of zeros and a second consisting of ones. This in conjunction with (1.5) implies that the first element of $\mathbf{q}_t$ converges to 0 and the second to 1 as $t \rightarrow \infty$. Hence there is a limit distribution, but not all of its proportions are positive; the first state disappears in the limit.

An absorbing occupational category is not plausible in the context of intergenerational mobility, because it would imply that once a person is in

---

[1] It is true that the blacks need more generations to get close to the limit distribution, given that their initial distribution is so far from it, but that is a different matter which will be considered in the next section.

such a category, the queue of his descendants will stay there forever with unit probability. It is much more realistic to assume that any category can be reached from any category with nonzero probability, not necessarily in one step but possibly in several steps. This is the case of a *regular Markov chain*, to which we shall confine ourselves in the rest of this chapter. A sufficient condition for regularity is that the transition matrix $\mathbf{P}$ consist exclusively of nonzero elements; any state can then be reached from any state in just one step. A necessary and sufficient condition is that $\mathbf{P}^t$ for some t consist exclusively of nonzero elements; then any transition can be made in at most t steps. The transition matrix of Table 5.1 consists of positive elements with the exception of $p_{4,10}$. However, it is possible to move from state 4 to state 10 in two generations, for example, via state 6 ($p_{46} = .092$, $p_{6,10} = .009$), so that this matrix does satisfy the regularity condition.

The Limit Distribution of a Regular Markov Chain

If some positive power of $\mathbf{P}$ consists of exclusively positive elements, then no matter what initial distribution $\mathbf{q}_0$, there is always convergence to the same limit distribution $\boldsymbol{\pi}$ with proportions $\pi_1, \ldots, \pi_n$:

(1.8) $$\lim_{t \to \infty} \mathbf{q}_0' \mathbf{P}^t = \boldsymbol{\pi}'$$

and these proportions add up to one and are all positive:

(1.9) $$\sum_{i=1}^{n} \pi_i = 1 \quad \text{and} \quad \pi_i > 0 \quad \text{for} \quad i = 1, \ldots, n$$

In the next subsection we prove a lemma which enables us to derive this result in a straightforward manner. For simplicity, we confine ourselves there to a matrix $\mathbf{P}$ with positive elements; see Problem 3 for an extension to general regular transition matrices.

When the limit (1.8) has been attained, the system will stay there. Consequently, the limit distribution has the property that it reproduces itself on the basis of its transition matrix $\mathbf{P}$:

(1.10) $$\boldsymbol{\pi}' = \boldsymbol{\pi}' \mathbf{P}$$

This means that if a generation has this $\boldsymbol{\pi}$ as its occupational distribution, the next generation has exactly the same distribution, and so on forever, which is frequently expressed by referring to $\boldsymbol{\pi}$ as the "steady-state distribution".[1] This is an alternative interpretation of π, which has nothing to do with the concept of a limit as time elapses indefinitely; it is the unique "fixed" vector of $\mathbf{P}$,[2] fixed in the sense that it remains unchanged when multiplied by $\mathbf{P}$.

This particular property will appear to be very useful for the measurement of the relative size of occupational categories. One way of solving this measurement problem is by using the present observed distribution of persons over occupations. In the empirical analysis of intergenerational occupational mobility a sample of such persons is drawn and each is asked to report the occupation of his father. Since the Markov chain approach postulates that the occupational distribution of the fathers determines that of their sons, the former distribution may be regarded as an alternative solution to the above measurement problem. It is awkward, however, to have two almost equally plausible solutions to the same problem. We obtain a unique solution by using the proportions $\pi_1, \ldots, \pi_n$ of the fixed vector, because these proportions apply to every generation once the system is in equilibrium. Also, these proportions are determined exclusively by the transition matrix $\mathbf{P}$ and are hence independent of the occupational distribution of any particular observed generation. Since most of the analysis that follows is concerned with the matrix $\mathbf{P}$, this property will prove to be convenient.

A Lemma

Let the $n \times n$ matrix $\mathbf{P}$ consist exclusively of positive elements and write ε for the value of its smallest element. Consider any n-element column vector $\mathbf{x}$ and also the product vector $\mathbf{Px}$. Write m_0 for the (algebraically) smallest element of $\mathbf{x}$ and M_0 for its largest element. Write m_1 and M_1 for the smallest and largest elements, respectively, of $\mathbf{Px}$. The lemma, formulated by KEMENY and SNELL (1960, p. 69), states

(1.11) $M_1 \leqq M_0 \quad \text{and} \quad m_1 \geqq m_0$

(1.12) $M_1 - m_1 \leqq (1 - 2\varepsilon)(M_0 - m_0)$

To prove this lemma we introduce the vector $\mathbf{x}^*$ which is obtained from $\mathbf{x}$ by replacing all elements, except one m_0 element,[3] by M_0. For example,

---

[1] This does *not* mean that every person's occupation is the same as that of his father. There are still changes from one generation to the next, but these cancel each other out as far as the proportions of the successive occupational distributions are concerned.

[2] The uniqueness will be proved in the last subsection of this section.

[3] It is possible that several elements of $\mathbf{x}$ are equal to m_0. In $\mathbf{x}^*$ we replace all of them by M_0 with only one exception.

if the first element of $\mathbf{x}$ is the smallest and the last the largest, we have

$$(1.13) \qquad \mathbf{x} = \begin{bmatrix} m_0 \\ x_2 \\ \vdots \\ x_{n-1} \\ M_0 \end{bmatrix} \quad \text{and} \quad \mathbf{x}^* = \begin{bmatrix} m_0 \\ M_0 \\ \vdots \\ M_0 \\ M_0 \end{bmatrix}$$

where $m_0 \leqq x_2, \ldots, x_{n-1} \leqq M_0$. Each element of $\mathbf{x}^*$ exceeds the corresponding element of $\mathbf{x}$ by a nonnegative amount, which we indicates as follows:

$$(1.14) \qquad \mathbf{x} \leqq \mathbf{x}^*$$

In the case (1.13), the ith element of the vector $\mathbf{Px}^*$ is

$$p_{i1} m_0 + \sum_{j=2}^{n} p_{ij} M_0 = p_{i1} m_0 + (1 - p_{i1}) M_0$$

because $p_{i1} + \ldots + p_{in} = 1$. The ith element of $\mathbf{Px}^*$ can thus be written $M_0 - p_{i1}(M_0 - m_0)$, which is $\leqq M_0 - \varepsilon(M_0 - m_0)$ because $p_{i1} \geqq \varepsilon$. It is readily verified that in the general case, not only (1.13), each element of $\mathbf{Px}^*$ is equal to M_0 minus the difference $M_0 - m_0$ multiplied by an appropriate transition probability. Since each such probability is $\geqq \varepsilon$, each element of $\mathbf{Px}^*$ is $\leqq M_0 - \varepsilon(M_0 - m_0)$. It will be proved in the next paragraph that each element of $\mathbf{Px}$ is at most equal to the corresponding element of $\mathbf{Px}^*$. Hence, given the definition of M_1 as the largest element of $\mathbf{Px}$,

$$(1.15) \qquad M_1 \leqq M_0 - \varepsilon(M_0 - m_0)$$

which proves the first inequality of (1.11).

To establish that the ith element of $\mathbf{Px}$ does not exceed the corresponding element of $\mathbf{Px}^*$, $i = 1, \ldots, n$, we consider their difference,

$$(1.16) \qquad \sum_{j=1}^{n} p_{ij} x_j - \sum_{j=1}^{n} p_{ij} x_j^* = \sum_{j=1}^{n} p_{ij}(x_j - x_j^*)$$

where x_j and x_j^* are the jth elements of $\mathbf{x}$ and $\mathbf{x}^*$ respectively. The nonpositive sign of the difference (1.16) then follows from (1.14) and from the positive signs of the p_{ij}'s.

Next replace $\mathbf{x}$ by $-\mathbf{x}$ and hence $\mathbf{Px}$ by $\mathbf{P}(-\mathbf{x}) = -\mathbf{Px}$. The largest element of $-\mathbf{x}$ is $-m_0$ and the smallest $-M_0$. Similarly, the largest element of $-\mathbf{P}\mathbf{x}$ is $-m_1$ and the smallest $-M_1$. Inequality (1.15) thus becomes

$$(1.17) \qquad\qquad -m_1 \leqq -m_0 - \varepsilon(-m_0 + M_0)$$

which is equivalent to $m_1 \geqq m_0 + \varepsilon(M_0 - m_0)$. This proves the second inequality of (1.11). Adding (1.15) and (1.17) gives

$$M_1 - m_1 \leqq M_0 - m_0 - 2\varepsilon(M_0 - m_0)$$
$$= (1 - 2\varepsilon)(M_0 - m_0)$$

which proves (1.12).

Proof of the Convergence to the Limit Distribution

In this subsection we prove that if $\mathbf{P}$ has no zero elements, the matrix $\mathbf{P}^t$ converges as $t \to \infty$ to a matrix whose rows are all identical with the limit distribution:

$$(1.18) \qquad \lim_{t \to \infty} \mathbf{P}^t = \begin{bmatrix} \pi_1 & \pi_2 & \cdots & \pi_n \\ \pi_1 & \pi_2 & \cdots & \pi_n \\ \cdot & \cdot & & \cdot \\ \cdot & \cdot & & \cdot \\ \cdot & \cdot & & \cdot \\ \pi_1 & \pi_2 & \cdots & \pi_n \end{bmatrix} = \begin{bmatrix} \boldsymbol{\pi}' \\ \boldsymbol{\pi}' \\ \cdot \\ \cdot \\ \cdot \\ \boldsymbol{\pi}' \end{bmatrix} = \boldsymbol{\iota}\boldsymbol{\pi}'$$

where $\boldsymbol{\iota}$ is a column vector consisting of n elements all equal to 1. We also prove that each π_i is positive.

Write $\mathbf{i}_j$ for the n-element column vector whose j^{th} element is 1 and all others are 0. Then $\mathbf{A}\mathbf{i}_j$ is the jth column of $\mathbf{A}$, for any matrix $\mathbf{A}$ consisting of n columns. To prove (1.18) it is sufficient to show that $\mathbf{P}^t\mathbf{i}_j$ converges to a column with all elements equal to π_j. Consider then the sequence of vectors $\mathbf{i}_j, \mathbf{P}\mathbf{i}_j, \ldots, \mathbf{P}^t\mathbf{i}_j, \ldots$ and write $M_0, M_1, \ldots, M_t, \ldots$ for the largest elements of these vectors and $m_0, m_1, \ldots, m_t, \ldots$ for their smallest elements. Since $\mathbf{P}^t\mathbf{i}_j = \mathbf{P}(\mathbf{P}^{t-1}\mathbf{i}_j)$, we can use the lemma to conclude that $M_0 \geqq M_1 \geqq M_2 \geqq \ldots$ and $m_0 \leqq m_1 \leqq m_2 \leqq \ldots$ and

$$(1.19) \qquad M_t - m_t \leqq (1 - 2\varepsilon)(M_{t-1} - m_{t-1}) \quad \text{for} \quad t \geqq 1$$

Write $d_t = M_t - m_t$, so that (1.19) implies

$$(1.20) \qquad d_t \leqq (1 - 2\varepsilon)^t d_0 = (1 - 2\varepsilon)^t$$

because d_0 is the difference between the largest and the smallest element of $\mathbf{i}_j$, which is 1. We conclude from (1.20) that d_t converges to zero as $t \to \infty$, so that M_t and m_t approach the same limit. Since M_t is the largest element of the jth column of $\mathbf{P}^t$ and m_t the smallest element, all elements of this column must converge to the same limit, which is written π_j in (1.18).

To prove that this limit π_j is positive we use the fact that it is equal to the limit of m_t and that $m_1 \leqq m_2 \leqq \ldots$. Hence it is sufficient to prove $m_1 > 0$. This m_1 is equal to the smallest element of the vector $\mathbf{P}\mathbf{i}_j$, that is, the smallest of the transition probabilities $p_{1j}, \ldots, p_{nj}$. Each of these is $\geqq \varepsilon > 0$, which completes the proof.

By premultiplying $\mathbf{P}^t$ by $\mathbf{q}_0'$ and taking the limit we obtain

$$(1.21) \qquad\qquad \lim_{t \to \infty} \mathbf{q}_0' \mathbf{P}^t = \mathbf{q}_0' \boldsymbol{\iota} \boldsymbol{\pi}' = \boldsymbol{\pi}'$$

where use is made of $\mathbf{q}_0' \boldsymbol{\iota} = 1$, the sum of the proportions of the initial occupational distribution. This proves (1.8). Note that (1.21) holds for any initial distribution $\mathbf{q}_0$, which verifies the statement (page 252) that the convergence has nothing to do with the initial distribution. Furthermore, using the same $\boldsymbol{\iota}$ notation, we have

$$(1.22) \qquad\qquad \mathbf{P}\boldsymbol{\iota} = \boldsymbol{\iota} \quad \text{and} \quad \boldsymbol{\pi}'\boldsymbol{\iota} = 1$$

which states that the n rows of the transition matrix and the proportions of the limit distribution all add up to 1.

Proof of the Uniqueness of the Limit Distribution

To prove that there is only one fixed vector $\boldsymbol{\pi}$ satisfying (1.10) we suppose that there is some other vector $\mathbf{z}$ so that $\mathbf{z}' = \mathbf{z}'\mathbf{P}$ and $\mathbf{z}'\boldsymbol{\iota} = 1$. It follows from (1.21) that $\mathbf{z}'\mathbf{P}^t$ converges to $\boldsymbol{\pi}'$ for any $\mathbf{z}$. Compare this with

$$\mathbf{z}'\mathbf{P}^t = (\mathbf{z}'\mathbf{P})\mathbf{P}^{t-1} = \mathbf{z}'\mathbf{P}^{t-1} = (\mathbf{z}'\mathbf{P})\mathbf{P}^{t-2} = \mathbf{z}'\mathbf{P}^{t-2}$$

$$= \ldots = \mathbf{z}'\mathbf{P}^2 = (\mathbf{z}'\mathbf{P})\mathbf{P} = \mathbf{z}'\mathbf{P} = \mathbf{z}'$$

This is evidently compatible with a convergence of $\mathbf{z}'\mathbf{P}^t$ to $\boldsymbol{\pi}'$ only if $\mathbf{z}$ is identical with $\boldsymbol{\pi}$, which proves the uniqueness.

5.2. The Rate of Convergence Toward the Limit Distribution

The limit vector $\boldsymbol{\pi}$ describes the occupational distribution as it will ultimately emerge. Table 5.2 shows that for most of the occupational categories, the whites have presently ($t = 0$) proportions that are a great deal closer to the limit proportions than are those of the blacks. In this section we address ourselves to the problem of measuring the distance of occupational distributions from the limit distribution and the rate of convergence toward the limit distribution.

An Informational Measure for the Distance from the Limit Distribution

Since we are concerned with sets of proportions and since the limit distribution is the one that will eventually emerge, a natural distance measure is the expected information of the message which transforms the proportions of the tth occupational distribution into those of the limit distribution:

$$(2.1) \qquad I_t = \sum_{i=1}^n \pi_i \log \frac{\pi_i}{q_{ti}}$$

One of the attractive features of this measure is the simplicity of its decompositions.[1] This is particularly true since occupational categories can be ranked reasonably well according to the prestige which they command, provided that the agricultural occupations are deleted. [It is difficult to compare the farmers' position with those of nonagricultural occupations.] This suggests as one possibility to make the farm/nonfarm distinction and to analyze separately the development in successive generations of the occupations on the farm (farmers and farm laborers in Table 5.2) and that of the nonfarm occupations (the first eight categories). So we introduce

$$(2.2) \qquad q_{tF} = q_{t9} + q_{t,10} \qquad \pi_F = \pi_9 + \pi_{10}$$

which are the combined farm proportions of the tth occupational distribution and of the limit distribution, respectively. The information expectation,

$$(2.3) \qquad I_{0t} = \pi_F \log \frac{\pi_F}{q_{tF}} + (1-\pi_F) \log \frac{1-\pi_F}{1-q_{tF}}$$

describes the extent to which the farm/nonfarm dichotomy of the tth distribution differs from that of the limit distribution. Furthermore, the expression

$$(2.4) \qquad I_{Ft} = \frac{\pi_9}{\pi_F} \log \frac{\pi_9/\pi_F}{q_{t9}/q_{tF}} + \frac{\pi_{10}}{\pi_F} \log \frac{\pi_{10}/\pi_F}{q_{t,10}/q_{tF}}$$

is the on-the-farm information expectation which measures the difference between the farmer/farm laborer dichotomy of the tth distribution and that of the limit distribution, and

$$(2.5) \qquad I_{Nt} = \sum_{i=1}^8 \frac{\pi_i}{1-\pi_F} \log \frac{\pi_i/(1-\pi_F)}{q_{ti}/(1-q_{tF})}$$

---

[1] Lieberson and Fuguitt use the dissimilarity index as a distance measure. This index was discussed in the last two subsections of Section 2.2, and the objections raised there apply here also, particularly the aggregation complications arising from the use of absolute differences.

measures the distance between the tth distribution and the limit distribution as far as the eight nonagricultural categories are concerned. The four I's are related by

$$(2.6) \qquad I_t = I_{0t} + \pi_F I_{Ft} + (1 - \pi_F) I_{Nt}$$

These informational measures (in nits) are shown in columns (2), (4), (5) and (6) of Table 5.3. [Column (3) will be discussed in the next subsection.] In each column there is a substantial decline in successive generations, both for whites and for blacks, but the black I_t is about ten times the white I_t in each generation. For the initial generation of the whites, there is a substantial difference between its farm/nonfarm dichotomy and that of the limit distribution, the I_{0t} accounting for more than 25 per cent of I_t at $t = 0$. However, this proportion declines rapidly in later generations. The I_{Ft} for occupations on the farm and I_{Nt} for those not on the farm decrease in successive generations approximately as fast as I_t, particularly for larger values of t.

TABLE 5.3

INFORMATIONAL MEASURES FOR THE CONVERGENCE TOWARD THE LIMIT DISTRIBUTION*

t (1)	I_t (2)	I_t/I_{t-1} (3)	I_{0t} (4)	I_{Ft} (5)	I_{Nt} (6)
			Whites		
0	.0728		.0205	.0421	.0525
1	.0²894	.123	.0²149	.0⁴104	.0²760
2	.0²126	.141	.0⁴671	.0³224	.0²121
3	.0³180	.142	.0⁵247	.0⁴550	.0³179
4	.0⁴250	.139	†	.0⁵845	.0⁴253
5	.0⁵343	.137	†	.0⁵117	.0⁵347
6	.0⁶464	.135	†	.0⁶159	.0⁶469
			Blacks		
0	.801		.0448	.152	.768
1	.0904	.113	.0²364	.0288	.0879
2	.0129	.142	.0³186	.0²462	.0128
3	.0²182	.142	.0⁵724	.0³656	.0²184
4	.0³252	.138	†	.0⁴891	.0³255
5	.0⁴344	.136	†	.0⁴119	.0⁴348
6	.0⁵463	.135	†	.0⁵160	.0⁵469

* The number of zeros after the decimal point is indicated by an exponent. For example, .0²894 stands for .00894.

† Less than 10^{-6}.

The Rate of Convergence

Column (3) of Table 5.3 contains the ratios I_t/I_{t-1} which are measures for the rate of convergence toward the limit distribution during the transition from the $(t-1)^{st}$ generation to the tth. These ratios show that in the beginning (until about $t = 3$) the distance of each occupational distribution from the limit distribution is a proportion of the corresponding distance for the previous distribution which fluctuates between 11 and a little over 14 per cent, and that for later distributions this proportion seems to converge to a value of about $13\frac{1}{2}$ per cent. This holds both for whites and for blacks. Figure 5.1 illustrates this development for whites (indicated by circles) and for blacks (dots). The vertical axis measures I_t logarithmically. The horizontal axis gives time measured in generations, but note that the black time scale is lagged relative to the white time scale by a little over 1.1 generations.

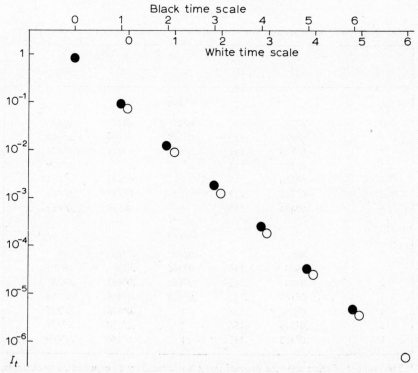

Fig. 5.1. The development of I_t in successive generations for whites (circles) and for blacks (dots)

The figure shows that this arrangement insures that the dots and the circles are all located on the same downward sloping straight line, at least approximately.

These results suggest that once one I_t has been found, regardless of whether it refers to whites or to blacks, all subsequent distance values can be approximated by moving along this straight line, so that the only knowledge needed is the slope. It is shown in the next two subsections that this slope is determined by the second largest latent root of the transition matrix. Note that this is again a characteristic of that matrix only, independent of the initial occupational distribution $\mathbf{q}_0$, just as the limit vector $\boldsymbol{\pi}$. Therefore both the limit distribution and the rate of convergence toward that distribution are the same for blacks and for whites (and for any other initial distribution as well).

The Spectral Decomposition of a Transition Matrix

The clue to the rate of convergence toward the limit distribution is the spectral decomposition of the transition matrix, which may be explained as follows. For any $n \times n$ matrix such as $\mathbf{P}$ there are n numbers $\lambda_1, \ldots, \lambda_n$, called the latent roots of the matrix, such that

$$(2.7) \qquad (\mathbf{P} - \lambda_i \mathbf{I})\mathbf{u}_i = \mathbf{0} \quad \text{and} \quad \mathbf{v}'_i(\mathbf{P} - \lambda_i \mathbf{I}) = \mathbf{0}$$

where $\mathbf{I}$ is the $n \times n$ unit matrix and $\mathbf{u}_i$ and $\mathbf{v}'_i$ are the characteristic column and row, respectively, corresponding to the ith latent root of $\mathbf{P}$. These characteristic vectors are nonzero, so that (2.7) implies that $\mathbf{P} - \lambda_i \mathbf{I}$ is a singular $n \times n$ matrix. Hence the determinant of $\mathbf{P} - \lambda_i \mathbf{I}$ vanishes. Since this determinant can be written as an nth degree polynomial, this result confirms that there are n latent roots. It is assumed that these roots are all distinct, but they need not be real.

We proceed to arrange the characteristic columns and vectors into two $n \times n$ matrices and introduce a diagonal $n \times n$ matrix $\boldsymbol{\Lambda}$ with the roots $\lambda_1, \ldots, \lambda_n$ on the diagonal:

$$(2.8) \qquad \mathbf{U} = [\mathbf{u}_1 \quad \mathbf{u}_2 \ldots \mathbf{u}_n] \quad \mathbf{V}' = \begin{bmatrix} \mathbf{v}'_1 \\ \mathbf{v}'_2 \\ \vdots \\ \mathbf{v}'_n \end{bmatrix} \quad \boldsymbol{\Lambda} = \begin{bmatrix} \lambda_1 & 0 & \ldots & 0 \\ 0 & \lambda_2 & \ldots & 0 \\ \vdots & \vdots & & \vdots \\ 0 & 0 & \ldots & \lambda_n \end{bmatrix}$$

If the roots are all distinct, we have $v_i'u_j = 0$ whenever $i \neq j$.[1] In addition, we can normalize so that $v_i'u_i = 1$ for each i, because (2.7) shows that the characteristic vectors are subject to a multiplicative degree of freedom. These two results can be combined in the form $V'U = I$, which means that U is the inverse of V'. Also, we can write the first equation of (2.7) for $i = 1,\dots, n$ as

$$P[\mathbf{u}_1 \quad \mathbf{u}_2 \dots \mathbf{u}_n] = [\mathbf{u}_1 \quad \mathbf{u}_2 \dots \mathbf{u}_n] \begin{bmatrix} \lambda_1 & 0 & \dots & 0 \\ 0 & \lambda_2 & \dots & 0 \\ \vdots & \vdots & & \vdots \\ 0 & 0 & \dots & \lambda_n \end{bmatrix}$$

or, more briefly, as $PU = U\Lambda$. Postmultiplication by V' gives $PUV' = U\Lambda V'$ or, given that U is the inverse of V',

$$(2.9) \qquad P = U\Lambda V' = \sum_{i=1}^{n} \lambda_i \mathbf{u}_i \mathbf{v}_i'$$

which is the spectral decomposition of the matrix P. For the square of P we obtain

$$P^2 = U\Lambda V'U\Lambda V' = U\Lambda I\Lambda V' = U\Lambda^2 V'$$

and, more generally, for every positive integer t,

$$(2.10) \qquad P^t = U\Lambda^t V' = \sum_{i=1}^{n} \lambda_i^t \mathbf{u}_i \mathbf{v}_i'$$

so that P^t has the same characteristic vectors as P and latent roots equal to the tth powers of those of P.

For the 10×10 transition matrix of Table 5.1 we have the roots shown below. They are all distinct and include one conjugate complex pair.

$$
\begin{aligned}
&\lambda_1 = 1 & \lambda_6, \lambda_7 &= .0703 \pm .0051i \\
&\lambda_2 = .3649 & \lambda_8 &= .0537 \\
(2.11) \quad &\lambda_3 = .1973 & \lambda_9 &= .0372 \\
&\lambda_4 = .1826 & \lambda_{10} &= .0065 \\
&\lambda_5 = .1012
\end{aligned}
$$

---

[1] *Proof.* Postmultiply the second equation of (2.7) by $\mathbf{u}_j$ to obtain $v_i'P\mathbf{u}_j = \lambda_i v_i'\mathbf{u}_j$. Next, replace i by j in the first equation of (2.7) and premultiply by v_i' to obtain $v_i'P\mathbf{u}_j = \lambda_j v_i'\mathbf{u}_j$. Subtraction of the latter equation from the former gives $0 = (\lambda_i - \lambda_j)v_i'\mathbf{u}_j$, which implies $v_i'\mathbf{u}_j = 0$ when $\lambda_i \neq \lambda_j$.

It is easily proved that the largest latent root of a transition matrix $\mathbf{P}$ is always a unit root. This largest root cannot exceed 1 in absolute value, because (2.10) shows that $\mathbf{P}^t$ would then "explode" as $t \to \infty$, and we know that $\mathbf{P}^t$ actually has a finite limit. Furthermore, we have $(\mathbf{P} - \mathbf{I})\iota = \mathbf{0}$ from (1.22) and $\pi'(\mathbf{P} - \mathbf{I}) = \mathbf{0}$ from (1.10), which shows that ι is a characteristic column of $\mathbf{P}$ and π' a characteristic row, both corresponding to root $\lambda = 1$.[1] Hence the spectral decomposition of $\mathbf{P}$ is

$$(2.12) \qquad \mathbf{P} = \iota\pi' + \lambda_2 \mathbf{u}_2 \mathbf{v}_2' + \ldots + \lambda_n \mathbf{u}_n \mathbf{v}_n'$$

and that of its tth power:

$$(2.13) \qquad \mathbf{P}^t = \iota\pi' + \lambda_2^t \mathbf{u}_2 \mathbf{v}_2' + \ldots + \lambda_n^t \mathbf{u}_n \mathbf{v}_n'$$

The Second Largest Latent Root and the Rate of Convergence

The latent roots shown in (2.11) are listed in the order of decreasing absolute values.[2] Since the largest root is 1, all others have absolute values less than 1, so that λ_i^t converges to 0 as $t \to \infty$ for $i = 2, \ldots, n$. Hence we may conclude from (2.13):

$$(2.14) \qquad \lim_{t \to \infty} \mathbf{P}^t = \iota\pi'$$

Thus, if we premultiply $\mathbf{P}^t$ by any initial occupational vector $\mathbf{q}_0'$ and then take the limit, we obtain $(\mathbf{q}_0'\iota)\pi' = \pi'$, which is in agreement with (1.21).

For any initial distribution $\mathbf{q}_0$ we have $\mathbf{q}_t' = \mathbf{q}_0'\mathbf{P}^t$ and hence, in view of (2.13),

$$(2.15) \qquad \begin{aligned} \mathbf{q}_t' &= \mathbf{q}_0' \iota\pi' + \lambda_2^t \mathbf{q}_0' \mathbf{u}_2 \mathbf{v}_2' + \ldots + \lambda_n^t \mathbf{q}_0' \mathbf{u}_n \mathbf{v}_n' \\ &= \pi' + \lambda_2^t (\mathbf{q}_0' \mathbf{u}_2) \mathbf{v}_2' + \ldots + \lambda_n^t (\mathbf{q}_0' \mathbf{u}_n) \mathbf{v}_n' \end{aligned}$$

The tth occupational distribution measured as a deviation from the fixed vector is thus of the form

$$(2.16) \qquad \mathbf{q}_t' - \pi' = \lambda_2^t (\mathbf{q}_0' \mathbf{u}_2) \mathbf{v}_2' + \ldots + \lambda_n^t (\mathbf{q}_0' \mathbf{u}_n) \mathbf{v}_n' \approx \lambda_2^t (\mathbf{q}_0' \mathbf{u}_2) \mathbf{v}_2'$$

---

[1] Note that the normalization $\mathbf{v}_i'\mathbf{u}_i = 1$ for $i = 1$ thus amounts to $\pi'\iota = 1$, which is in agreement with (1.22).

[2] For complex roots, $a \pm bi$, the absolute value is defined as the positive square root of $a^2 + b^2$. If the second largest latent root λ_2 is complex, the convergence toward the limit distribution is of the damped oscillatory type. We shall not pursue this here because our λ_2 is real, but we should mention that if λ_2 is complex, it is to be replaced by its absolute value as defined above in eq. (2.19) below.

where the approximation is based on the fact that $|\lambda_i| < |\lambda_2|$ for $i \geq 3$, so that the approximation error converges to zero as t increases. The leading term of this error is λ_3^t multiplied by a constant, so that the relative error is of the order $(\lambda_3/\lambda_2)^t$. This is evidently more satisfactory for any given t when λ_3 is smaller relative to λ_2 in absolute value. In the case (2.11) we have $\lambda_3/\lambda_2 = .54$.

Now return to the informational distance measure (2.1). The simplest way to handle it is by means of the quadratic approximation given in eq. (1.12) of Section 2.1:[1]

$$(2.17) \qquad I_t \approx \tfrac{1}{2} \sum_{i=1}^{n} \frac{(q_{ti} - \pi_i)^2}{\pi_i}$$

The sum in the right-hand side can be written as

$$\begin{bmatrix} q_{t1} - \pi_1 & q_{t2} - \pi_2 & \dots & q_{tn} - \pi_n \end{bmatrix} \begin{bmatrix} 1/\pi_1 & 0 & \dots & 0 \\ 0 & 1/\pi_2 & \dots & 0 \\ \vdots & \vdots & & \vdots \\ 0 & 0 & \dots & 1/\pi_n \end{bmatrix} \begin{bmatrix} q_{t1} - \pi_1 \\ q_{t2} - \pi_2 \\ \vdots \\ q_{tn} - \pi_n \end{bmatrix}$$

Hence (2.17) in matrix form becomes

$$(2.18) \qquad I_t \approx \tfrac{1}{2}(\mathbf{q}_t - \boldsymbol{\pi})' \boldsymbol{\Delta}^{-1} (\mathbf{q}_t - \boldsymbol{\pi})$$

where $\boldsymbol{\Delta}$ is the diagonal matrix which contains the successive limit proportions $\pi_1, \dots, \pi_n$ in the diagonal. On substituting the approximation (2.16) in (2.18), we obtain

$$(2.19) \qquad I_t \approx \tfrac{1}{2}\lambda_2^{2t}(\mathbf{q}_0' \mathbf{u}_2)^2 \mathbf{v}_2' \boldsymbol{\Delta}^{-1} \mathbf{v}_2$$
$$= k\lambda_2^{2t} \quad \text{where} \quad k = \tfrac{1}{2}(\mathbf{q}_0' \mathbf{u}_2)^2 \mathbf{v}_2' \boldsymbol{\Delta}^{-1} \mathbf{v}_2$$

Thus, I_t is approximately equal to λ_2^{2t} multiplied by a positive constant, and the rate of convergence I_t/I_{t-1} to $\lambda_2^{2t}/\lambda_2^{2(t-1)} = \lambda_2^2$. Using the relevant root of (2.11), we obtain $(.3649)^2 = .1332$, which is in close agreement with the figures of column (3) of Table 5.3.

In summary, the largest latent root of a transition matrix is a unit root; the limit vector is a characteristic row corresponding to this root; the square of the second largest latent root is the limit of the ratio I_t/I_{t-1} when t in-

---

[1] This approximation is not very good for the figures of Table 5.2 at $t = 0$, but the error at $t = 1$ is only 3 per cent for whites and a little over 1 per cent for blacks. Thereafter it reduces to smaller and smaller fractions of 1 per cent.

creases indefinitely; and the ratio of the absolute values of the third and the second largest roots determines the accuracy of the square of the latter root as an approximation of I_t/I_{t-1} for lower values of t.

Perfect Mobility and Imperfect Mobility

Perfect social mobility is generally defined as the situation in which the probability of entering the jth occupational category is independent of the father's occupation, for $j = 1, \ldots, n$. This is an extreme case which is unlikely to occur in the real world, but since it is important to know how imperfect actual occupational mobility is, the perfect-mobility case is useful as a standard of reference. We shall use it frequently for this purpose in the sequel.

When there is perfect mobility, the transition probability p_{ij} for each pair (i, j) is independent of i, so that every column of $\mathbf{P}$ consists of identical elements. Write z_j for the common value of the elements of the jth column of $\mathbf{P}$ and $\mathbf{z}$ for the column vector of z_j's; obviously we have $\iota' \mathbf{z} = 1$. The transition matrix is then of the form $\mathbf{P} = \iota \mathbf{z}'$, which implies $\mathbf{P}^t = \iota \mathbf{z}'$ for any $t \geqq 1$. This, however, is compatible with the earlier result (1.18) if and only if $\mathbf{z} = \boldsymbol{\pi}$. So we have proved that the transition matrix in this case is of the simple form

$$(2.20) \qquad \mathbf{P} = \iota \boldsymbol{\pi}' \quad \text{for perfect mobility}$$

which in conjunction with (2.12) shows that the leading (unit) latent root of this $\mathbf{P}$ is the only nonzero root. What distinguishes the general transition matrix from this particular one is the presence of $n-1$ other terms in the spectral decomposition besides the term $\iota \boldsymbol{\pi}'$.

In the case of perfect mobility we thus have $\lambda_2 = 0$. The limit distribution is then reached immediately at $t = 1$, for whatever initial distribution $\mathbf{q}_0$. Hence the latter distribution exerts no influence whatever on the occupational distributions of later generations. But there is such an influence when $\lambda_2 \neq 0$, and it is larger when λ_2^2 is larger. Therefore, we may regard λ_2^2 (a nonnegative number less than 1) as a measure for the imperfection of intergenerational social mobility. Again note that it is determined completely by the transition matrix.

The Descendance Effects of Individual Occupational Categories

Consider a large group of persons all of whom are in the ith occupational category. The occupational distribution of their first descendants is $p_{i1}, \ldots, p_{in}$ and that of their second descendants is $p_{i1}^{(2)}, \ldots, p_{in}^{(2)}$, where $p_{ij}^{(t)}$ stands for the $(i, j)^{\text{th}}$ element of the matrix $\mathbf{P}^t$. We are interested in the question of how fast the distributions of these successive generations – all descendants of members of the ith occupational category – move toward the limit distribution.

The distance measure (2.1) for this case is

$$(2.21) \qquad\qquad I_{it} = \sum_{j=1}^{n} \pi_j \log \frac{\pi_j}{p_{ij}^{(t)}}$$

Equation (2.13) implies $\mathbf{P}^t - \boldsymbol{\iota}\boldsymbol{\pi}' \approx \lambda_2^t \mathbf{u}_2 \mathbf{v}_2'$ for t not too small, and hence $p_{ij}^{(t)} - \pi_j \approx \lambda_2^t u_{2i} v_{2j}$, where u_{2i} is the ith element of $\mathbf{u}_2$ and v_{2j} the jth element of $\mathbf{v}_2$. Approximating I_{it} by its leading quadratic term, we obtain

$$(2.22) \qquad\qquad I_{it} \approx \frac{1}{2} \sum_{j=1}^{n} \frac{(p_{ij}^{(t)} - \pi_j)^2}{\pi_j} \approx \frac{1}{2} \lambda_2^{2t} u_{2i}^2 \sum_{j=1}^{n} \frac{v_{2j}^2}{\pi_j}$$

$$= c_i \lambda_2^{2t} \quad \text{where} \quad c_i = \frac{1}{2} u_{2i}^2 \sum_{j=1}^{n} \frac{v_{2j}^2}{\pi_j}$$

This is again proportional to λ_2^{2t} but the proportionality constant c_i is specific for the occupational origin of the series of successive generations. When c_i is large, the tth generation of descendants of the ith category have an occupational distribution that differs more from the limit distribution than when c_i is small. We therefore call c_i the *descendance effect* of the ith occupational category. These c_i's are shown in Table 5.4 for the transition matrix of Table 5.1. The effects are particularly large for the two agricultural

TABLE 5.4

DESCENDANCE EFFECTS OF 10 OCCUPATIONAL CATEGORIES

	Occupational category	c_i
1.	Professional and technical	.60
2.	Managers and officials	.46
3.	Sales workers	.33
4.	Clerical workers	.11
5.	Craftsmen and foremen	.26
6.	Operatives	.89
7.	Service workers	.53
8.	Laborers (nonfarm)	2.26
9.	Farmers	4.96
10.	Farm laborers	6.19

categories, which is not surprising. As far as the nonagricultural occupations
are concerned, the descendance effects are on the high side for those categories which typically require either much or very little formal education,
while the categories requiring a moderate amount of education (sales and
clerical workers and craftsmen and foremen) have small descendance effects.
This is not surprising either, because it usually takes a rather large number
of generations before the descendants of an extreme occupational category
(either high or low) are spread out all over the scale.

5.3. Mean First Passage Times

In the rest of this chapter we shall be concerned exclusively with occupational categories that can be ranked according to social prestige. To indicate this more explicitly, we will call them *status categories*. The ranking of
such categories implies the existence of an ordinal scale in the sense that,
for example, the "social distance" between the first and the second categories
is smaller than that between the first and the third. This is a much weaker
statement than "the distance between the first and second status categories
is one-quarter of the distance between the first and the third". The latter
statement implies the existence of a cardinal scale. That such a cardinal scale
is appropriate is not self-evident at this stage, but it is worthwhile to find
out. In fact, this is the main objective of the rest of this chapter.

Status Categories for British, Danish, and American Mobility Data

Five status categories are distinguished in Table 5.5: top professional and
top business, semi-professional and middle business, clerical and sales workers, skilled manual workers, and semi-skilled and unskilled workers. The
table contains transition matrices for these categories based on four sets of
data. The matrix on top goes back to GLASS and HALL (1954) and is based
on a sample of British males drawn in 1949. The second matrix is Danish
and was constructed by SVALASTOGA (1959); the underlying data are also
from the postwar period. The third and fourth matrices are from ROGOFF
(1953); they refer to Marion County, Indiana as described in Section 5.1
but the present occupational categories are different.[1]

---

[1] The farming category was excluded from Rogoff's data. The first status category of
Table 5.5 corresponds to her professional category, the second to her semi-professional
and proprietors/managers/officials categories, the third to her clerical/sales group, the
fourth to her skilled and protective service groups, and the fifth to her semi-skilled, un-

We mentioned in the second opening paragraph of Section 5.1 (page 247) that in most columns of Table 5.1 the element on the diagonal takes the largest value. The transition matrices of Table 5.5 have the same property

TABLE 5.5

FOUR TRANSITION MATRICES

Father's status category	Subject's status category				
	1	2	3	4	5
British					
1. Top professional and top business	.388	.146	.264	.141	.062
2. Semi-professional and middle business	.107	.267	.347	.206	.073
3. Clerical and sales workers	.027	.064	.347	.401	.161
4. Skilled manual workers	.009	.024	.198	.473	.296
5. Semi-skilled and unskilled workers	.000	.011	.124	.379	.486
Danish					
1. Top professional and top business	.419	.259	.161	.129	.032
2. Semi-professional and middle business	.051	.309	.303	.239	.098
3. Clerical and sales workers	.021	.128	.360	.333	.158
4. Skilled manual workers	.009	.038	.207	.453	.293
5. Semi-skilled and unskilled workers	.006	.022	.134	.368	.470
American 1910					
1. Top professional and top business	.216	.164	.250	.225	.145
2. Semi-professional and middle business	.075	.261	.290	.209	.165
3. Clerical and sales workers	.059	.108	.455	.229	.149
4. Skilled manual workers	.020	.059	.160	.509	.251
5. Semi-skilled and unskilled workers	.016	.044	.127	.304	.509
American 1940					
1. Top professional and top business	.290	.143	.286	.158	.123
2. Semi-professional and middle business	.087	.221	.308	.158	.226
3. Clerical and sales workers	.080	.133	.437	.156	.194
4. Skilled manual workers	.035	.076	.203	.342	.345
5. Semi-skilled and unskilled workers	.026	.060	.171	.187	.557

skilled, and personal service categories. For the Danish data, the first status category corresponds to the upper class and the upper middle class of Svalastoga's classification, the second to the middle middle class, the third to the lower middle class, the fourth to the upper working class, and the fifth to the middle and lower working classes. For the British data, see the second subsection of Section 5.7 below (pages 304–305).

but exhibit even more regularity. The elements of each column tend to decline monotonically when we move away from the diagonal element in either an upward or a downward direction. This means that a person is less and less likely to enter the jth status category when his father is in successively higher status categories $(i = j-1, j-2, \ldots, 1)$ and also when his father is in successively lower categories $(i = j+1, \ldots, 5)$. There are some exceptions to this general rule, but by and large it seems to hold rather well. One of the objectives of the remainder of this chapter is to present a model which formalizes such regularities.

First Passage Times

Consider a randomly selected individual from the ith status category and let us ask: How many generations are needed before his first descendant enters the jth category? This number of generations is known as the first passage time from the ith status category to the jth. If this person's son enters the jth category, the first passage time is 1; if it is not his son but his grandson, it is 2, and so on. The first passage time is always a random variable simply because the Markov chain model describes the mobility process stochastically.

It will be intuitively clear that the probability distribution of the first passage times from the ith status category to the jth has something to do with the degree of difficulty of moving from the former category to the latter, and hence with the distance between the two categories as described in intuitive terms in the opening paragraph of this section. As a summary statistic we shall use the mean of this distribution, known as the *mean first passage time* and denoted by m_{ij}. The expressions for this mean are simple. For $i = j$ we have

$$(3.1) \qquad\qquad m_{ii} = \frac{1}{\pi_i}$$

and otherwise

$$(3.2) \qquad\qquad m_{ij} = \frac{z_{jj} - z_{ij}}{\pi_j} \quad \text{if} \quad i \neq j$$

where z_{ij} is the $(i, j)^{\text{th}}$ element of the so-called fundamental matrix $\mathbf{Z}$ associated with the transition matrix $\mathbf{P}$, defined as

$$(3.3) \qquad\qquad \mathbf{Z} = (\mathbf{I} - \mathbf{P} + \iota\pi')^{-1}$$

These results are derived in the remainder of this section after some numerical values are discussed in the next subsection. At this stage it is appropriate to stress the difference between the expressions for m_{ii} and for m_{ij} with $i \neq j$. The former is known as a *mean recurrence time* (the expected number of generations needed to return to the ith status category for the first time). Equation (3.1) states that it is simply equal to the reciprocal of the corresponding limit proportion. Mean first passage times with $i \neq j$ involve the transition matrix in a more extensive manner, via Z as shown in (3.3). This difference should cause no real surprise, given that the latter mean first passage time must have something to do with the distance between i and j, whereas there should be no distance between i and itself.

Mean First Passage Times for Four Transition Matrices

Table 5.6 contains the limit distributions and the mean first passage times corresponding to the four transition matrices of Table 5.5. They are taken from BESHERS and LAUMANN (1967), who were the first to propose their use for the measurement of distances between status groups. These authors are also responsible for the grouping of the occupational categories of the original sources so that these are approximately comparable for the three countries.

The four matrices of mean first passage times are all far from symmetric. For example, in each case the mean first passage time from the first status category to any other is considerably smaller than the corresponding passage time from the latter to the first ($m_{1j} < m_{j1}$ for $j > 1$). It is clear, therefore, that the matrix $[m_{ij}]$ in its raw form cannot serve as a distance matrix, since the distance concept requires that the distance between i to j be equal to that between j to i. However, the matrices do exhibit regularity, similar to that of the transition matrices discussed in the first subsection. Typically, the smallest element of the jth column of $[m_{ij}]$ is the diagonal element m_{jj} (the mean recurrence time of the jth category) and the elements tend to increase monotonically when the origin is of successively higher status ($i < j$) or of successively lower status ($i > j$).

The large values of some of the m_{ij}'s may cause some surprise. What is the meaning of $m_{51} \approx 75$ generations for the British transition matrix? Does it mean that an English unskilled worker from the time of the Roman Empire could have expected his first top professional or business descendant around this time? Some of the mean recurrence times are very large too, such as $m_{11} \approx 44$ for the same matrix. How can this large expected number of generations needed to return to the first status category be reconciled

TABLE 5.6

LIMIT DISTRIBUTIONS AND MEAN FIRST PASSAGE TIMES FOR FOUR TRANSITION MATRICES

Origin (i of m_{ij})	Destination (j of m_{ij})					Limit distribution
	1	2	3	4	5	
British						
1. Top professional and top business	44.00	26.39	4.57	3.89	6.01	.023
2. Semi-professional and middle business	63.26	24.18	4.24	3.47	5.68	.041
3. Clerical and sales workers	71.34	31.61	4.66	2.69	4.84	.215
4. Skilled manual workers	73.57	33.45	5.65	2.44	4.08	.410
5. Semi-skilled and unskilled workers	74.76	34.24	6.20	2.67	3.21	.311
Danish						
1. Top professional and top business	41.37	11.00	5.25	4.32	6.62	.024
2. Semi-professional and middle business	67.41	12.33	4.52	3.54	5.67	.081
3. Clerical and sales workers	70.32	15.65	4.40	3.12	5.14	.227
4. Skilled manual workers	71.89	17.72	5.37	2.66	4.28	.376
5. Semi-skilled and unskilled workers	72.38	18.27	5.86	2.87	3.43	.292
American 1910						
1. Top professional and top business	24.47	12.49	5.33	4.12	5.50	.041
2. Semi-professional and middle business	28.54	11.33	5.11	4.18	5.39	.088
3. Clerical and sales workers	29.10	13.39	4.26	4.09	5.47	.235
4. Skilled manual workers	31.02	14.57	6.21	2.89	4.70	.346
5. Semi-skilled and unskilled workers	31.32	14.93	6.51	3.60	3.45	.290
American 1940						
1. Top professional and top business	15.03	10.09	4.26	6.04	4.93	.066
2. Semi-professional and middle business	19.09	9.46	4.26	6.01	4.37	.106
3. Clerical and sales workers	19.17	10.33	3.68	6.03	4.53	.272
4. Skilled manual workers	20.56	11.30	4.94	4.87	3.68	.205
5. Semi-skilled and unskilled workers	20.87	11.58	5.16	5.74	2.85	.351

with the fact that it takes only one generation in almost 40 per cent of all cases? [See the leading element of the first transition matrix of Table 5.5.]

The answer to these questions is that first passage times typically have distributions with a very long tail for large values. This implies that the mean can take values that are considerably larger than, say, the median or the mode. Actually, the variance of these distributions is usually substantial, so that it is not advisable to use the mean or any other measure of central tendency as an approximation for individual first passage times. We shall indeed not use the m_{ij}'s for that purpose. Rather, we will compare these m_{ij}'s for different values of the subscripts, and we will use the regularity of the pattern of these means to make inferences about distances between status categories.

Properties of the Fundamental Matrix

The matrix $\mathbf{Z}$ defined in (3.3) has the following properties which we will use in the sequel:

$$(3.4) \qquad\qquad \mathbf{Z}\iota = \iota$$

$$(3.5) \qquad\qquad \pi'\mathbf{Z} = \pi'$$

$$(3.6) \qquad\qquad (\mathbf{I}-\mathbf{P})\mathbf{Z} = \mathbf{I}-\iota\pi'$$

Equation (3.4) states that the sum of the n columns of $\mathbf{Z}$ is equal to a column consisting of n unit elements. It is similar to the property $\mathbf{P}\iota = \iota$ of (1.22), and (3.5) is similar to $\pi'\mathbf{P} = \pi'$ of (1.10).

To prove (3.4) we premultiply both sides by $\mathbf{Z}^{-1}$, which gives the equivalent equation $\iota = \mathbf{Z}^{-1}\iota$. This is verified straightforwardly on the basis of the $\mathbf{Z}$ definition (3.3):

$$\mathbf{Z}^{-1}\iota = (\mathbf{I}-\mathbf{P}+\iota\pi')\iota = \iota-\mathbf{P}\iota+\iota(\pi'\iota) = \iota-\iota+\iota = \iota$$

For (3.5) we proceed in the same way:

$$\pi'\mathbf{Z}^{-1} = \pi'(\mathbf{I}-\mathbf{P}+\iota\pi') = \pi'-\pi'\mathbf{P}+(\pi'\iota)\pi' = \pi'-\pi'+\pi' = \pi'$$

and for (3.6) also:

$$(\mathbf{I}-\iota\pi')\mathbf{Z}^{-1} = (\mathbf{I}-\iota\pi')(\mathbf{I}-\mathbf{P}+\iota\pi') = \mathbf{I}-\mathbf{P}$$

Derivation of the Mean Recurrence Time

The first passage time from i to j is 1 when this move is made immediately, and its conditional mean, given that the first move is to $k \neq j$, is

$m_{kj}+1$. We can then derive m_{ij} as the mean of the conditional means, given the outcome of the first step:

$$m_{ij} = p_{ij} \times 1 + \sum_{k \neq j} p_{ik}(m_{kj}+1)$$

$$= p_{ij} + \sum_{k \neq j} p_{ik} m_{kj} + 1 - p_{ij}$$

which may be written as

$$(3.7) \qquad m_{ij} = \sum_{k=1}^{n} p_{ik} m_{kj} - p_{ij} m_{jj} + 1 \qquad\qquad i, j = 1, \dots, n$$

Next multiply both sides by π_i and sum over i:

$$\sum_{i=1}^{n} \pi_i m_{ij} = \sum_{k=1}^{n} \left(\sum_{i=1}^{n} \pi_i p_{ik} \right) m_{kj} - \left(\sum_{i=1}^{n} \pi_i p_{ij} \right) m_{jj} + \sum_{i=1}^{n} \pi_i$$

$$= \sum_{k=1}^{n} \pi_k m_{kj} - \pi_j m_{jj} + 1$$

where the second equality sign is based on $\boldsymbol{\pi}'\mathbf{P} = \boldsymbol{\pi}'$. Since the first term in the second line is identical with the expression on the left, we have $\pi_j m_{jj} = 1$, from which (3.1) follows immediately.

Derivation of Other Mean First Passage Times

Equation (3.6) implies $z_{ij} - \sum_k p_{ik} z_{kj} = -\pi_j$ for $i \neq j$. This is equivalent to

$$\frac{z_{ij}}{\pi_j} = \sum_{k=1}^{n} p_{ik} \frac{z_{kj}}{\pi_j} - 1$$

and also to

$$(3.8) \qquad \frac{z_{jj} - z_{ij}}{\pi_j} = \sum_{k=1}^{n} p_{ik} \frac{z_{jj} - z_{kj}}{\pi_j} + 1$$

The term corresponding to $k = j$ in the right-hand sum vanishes; we may therefore restrict the summation to the $n-1$ values of $k \neq j$. The m_{ij} specification (3.2) then implies that (3.8) can be written as $m_{ij} = \sum_{k \neq j} p_{ik} m_{kj} + 1$, which is identical with (3.7). This means that (3.2) is a solution of (3.7).

What remains to be shown is that (3.2) is the only solution. Write m_{ij} and $\overline{m}_{ij}$ for two solutions of (3.7). We know from the previous subsection that $m_{ii} = \overline{m}_{ii} = 1/\pi_i$. Hence (3.7) implies

$$m_{ij} - \overline{m}_{ij} = \sum_{k=1}^{n} p_{ik}(m_{kj} - \overline{m}_{kj})$$

This can be written as $(\mathbf{P}-\mathbf{I})[m_{ij}-\bar{m}_{ij}] = \mathbf{0}$, which means that each column of $[m_{ij}-\bar{m}_{ij}]$ is a characteristic column vector of $\mathbf{P}$ corresponding to the unit root. We know that this column is equal to ι multiplied by some scalar (we chose 1 for this scalar in the previous section). Since the diagonal of $[m_{ij}-\bar{m}_{ij}]$ consists of zeros, this scalar must be zero. Hence all columns of this matrix are zero columns, so that $m_{ij} = \bar{m}_{ij}$ for each pair (i, j). This proves that (3.7) has at most one solution, and hence that (3.2) is the unique solution.

5.4. Waiting Times and Travel Times

Mean First Passage Times under Conditions of Perfect Social Mobility

Equation (2.20) states that the transition matrix $\mathbf{P}$ is equal to $\iota\pi'$ in the case of perfect mobility, so that the associated fundamental matrix $\mathbf{Z}$ as defined in (3.3) is the $n \times n$ unit matrix. It follows from (3.2) that the mean first passage time m_{ij} for $i \neq j$ is then simply $1/\pi_j$. Hence, applying (3.1) also, we have

$$(4.1) \qquad m_{ij} = m_{jj} = \frac{1}{\pi_j} \quad \text{for perfect mobility}$$

This means that each column of the matrix $[m_{ij}]$ of mean first passage times consists of identical elements, so that the expected number of generations needed to enter the jth status category is independent of the point of departure (the occupational origin of the series of successive generations).

Waiting Times

The mean first passage time matrices of Table 5.6 do not have columns consisting of constant elements, because their elements tend to increase when we move away from the diagonal element in either direction. This increase in conjunction with the result (4.1) for perfect mobility suggests that $1/\pi_j$ must be regarded as the lower limit of the expected number of generations needed to enter the jth status category. The limit is thus attained (1) when this status category is also the point of departure ($m_{jj} = 1/\pi_j$) and (2) when there is perfect mobility, for any point of departure. In both cases there is no real "distance" to be covered as far as intergenerational mobility is concerned. This is obvious for (1) but it is also true for (2) since perfect mobility denies that there is any effect of the father's category. Thus, this line of reasoning suggests that each mean first passage time m_{ij} has a component, equal to $1/\pi_j$, which has nothing to do with "distance" at all.

The fact that this component is a decreasing function of π_j has considerable appeal for the following reason. Even when there is no "distance" to be covered, there is still the problem of obtaining *entrance* into the jth category, and intuition suggests that entrance is more time-consuming when the category is of smaller size. This is precisely what the component $1/\pi_j$ performs under the condition that the limit proportion π_j is an adequate measure of the size of the jth status category. We shall therefore interpret

$$(4.2) \qquad\qquad \omega_j = \frac{1}{\pi_j}$$

as the *waiting time*, measured in generations, which is on the average needed to enter the jth status category once the distance has been overcome.

Travel Times

We thus have $m_{ij} = \omega_j$ whenever $i = j$ and also when there is perfect mobility (for any i in that case). The results shown in Table 5.6 indicate that, typically, $m_{ij} > \omega_j$ for $i \neq j$. This suggests the following decomposition of mean first passage times:

$$(4.3) \qquad\qquad m_{ij} = \tau_{ij} + \omega_j \qquad\qquad i, j = 1, \ldots, n$$

where τ_{ij} is the *travel time*, measured in generations, which is on the average needed to move from the ith status category to the gate of the jth ("to the gate of" means excluding the waiting time):

$$(4.4) \qquad\qquad \begin{aligned} \tau_{ij} &= 0 \qquad\qquad &\text{if} \quad i = j \\[2mm] &\frac{z_{jj} - z_{ij} - 1}{\pi_j} \qquad\qquad &\text{if} \quad i \neq j \end{aligned}$$

The matrix of travel times, $[\tau_{ij}]$, is the $n \times n$ zero matrix when there is perfect mobility. For the data of Table 5.6 we can compute such a matrix straightforwardly by subtracting from each element of a column the corresponding diagonal element. For example, we have $\tau_{12} = 2.21$ and $\tau_{21} = 19.26$ for the British data. This shows that $[\tau_{ij}]$ is not, in general, a symmetric matrix; which is the reason why we prefer to speak about travel times rather than about distances.[1]

---

[1] We obtain a negative τ_{ij} in some of those cases in which m_{jj} is not the smallest element of the jth column. However, there are only few such cases and the negative values are rather small absolutely, and it should also be borne in mind that the figures of Table 5.6 are subject to sampling errors. See further footnote 1 on page 295 below.

Travel Times from the Limit Distribution

The mean first passage time m_{ij} is the expected number of generations needed to enter the jth status category for the first time, given that the ith category is the point of departure. Suppose now that the system is in equilibrium, so that the proportions presently in the n categories are $\pi_1, \ldots, \pi_n$. Let us take this complete set of individuals as our starting point and ask: How many generations does it take, averaged over all these persons, before their first descendants enter the jth category? The answer, obviously, is the left-hand side of

$$(4.5) \qquad \pi_1 m_{1j} + \ldots + \pi_n m_{nj} = \frac{z_{jj}}{\pi_j}$$

which may be called the mean first passage time *from the limit distribution* to the jth status category. The equality sign in (4.5) is verified as follows:

$$\sum_{i=1}^{n} \pi_i m_{ij} = \pi_j m_{jj} + \sum_{i \neq j} \pi_i m_{ij} = 1 + \frac{1}{\pi_j} \sum_{i \neq j} \pi_i (z_{jj} - z_{ij})$$

$$= 1 + \frac{1}{\pi_j} \sum_{i=1}^{n} \pi_i (z_{jj} - z_{ij}) = 1 + \frac{z_{jj}}{\pi_j} - \frac{1}{\pi_j} \sum_{i=1}^{n} \pi_i z_{ij} = \frac{z_{jj}}{\pi_j}$$

the last step of which is based on (3.5).

The decomposition (4.3) can be applied to this mean first passage time also. Its waiting time component is ω_j, since the jth status category is the destination in each case. The travel time from the limit distribution to the jth category is therefore

$$(4.6) \qquad \frac{z_{jj}}{\pi_j} - \omega_j = \frac{z_{jj} - 1}{\pi_j}$$

which may also be verified directly by weighting $\tau_{1j}, \ldots, \tau_{nj}$ as defined in (4.4) by $\pi_1, \ldots, \pi_n$.

Travel Times to the Limit Distribution

We now invert the role of the limit distribution by making it the destination rather than the point of departure. The latter point is now one particular status category, say the ith. So consider a large number of persons presently in the ith category and divide them at random into n subsets of relative sizes $\pi_1, \ldots, \pi_n$. Our interest is in the number of generations which the jth subset needs, on the average, to enter the jth status category for the first time, and particularly in the grand average over $j = 1, \ldots, n$. This grand average is the left-hand side of

(4.7) $$\pi_1 m_{i1} + \ldots + \pi_n m_{in} = \sum_{j=1}^{n} z_{jj}$$

and it may be called the mean first passage time from the ith status category *to the limit distribution*. The right-hand side indicates that this mean first passage time is completely independent of the point of departure (the ith category). The equality sign may be verified as follows:

$$\sum_{j=1}^{n} \pi_j m_{ij} = \pi_i m_{ii} + \sum_{j \neq i} \pi_j m_{ij} = 1 + \sum_{j \neq i} (z_{jj} - z_{ij})$$

$$= 1 + \sum_{j=1}^{n} (z_{jj} - z_{ij}) = \sum_{j=1}^{n} z_{jj}$$

The last step is based on (3.4).

This mean first passage time can also be divided into a travel time and a waiting time component. Since a fraction π_j enters the jth status category, the average waiting time is

(4.8) $$\sum_{j=1}^{n} \pi_j \omega_j = n$$

which is even completely independent of the transition matrix. By subtracting this from (4.7) we obtain

(4.9) $$\sum_{j=1}^{n} z_{jj} - n = \sum_{j=1}^{n} (z_{jj} - 1)$$

which is the travel time from the ith status category to the limit distribution. This is independent of i, so that the expected number of generations needed to travel from any status category to the limit distribution is the same whatever the origin.

Moreover, this constant travel time (constant in the sense that it applies to any origin) is equal to the weighted average, with the π's as weights, of the travel times (4.6) that correspond to the passage from rather than to the limit distribution:

(4.10) $$\sum_{j=1}^{n} \pi_j \frac{z_{jj} - 1}{\pi_j} = \sum_{j=1}^{n} (z_{jj} - 1)$$

In summary, τ_{ij} is the expected number of generations needed for the journey from i to j, and the expression (4.6) performs the same role when the ith status category is replaced by the limit distribution as the point of departure. These are measures for "how long on the average" a queue of descendants has to travel to arrive at the jth status category (excluding waiting time), given the relevant point of departure. Furthermore, there is the travel time (4.9) describing the average number of generations needed to move from any status category to the limit distribution, and the result (4.10) indicates that this measure also describes how much there is to be traveled on the average in the system as a whole. Note finally that in the case of perfect mobility all travel times are zero, including those which involve the limit distribution as origin or destination.

Travel Times to and from Limit Distributions for Four Transition Matrices

The $n^2 = 25$ travel times τ_{ij} for each of the four transition matrices of Table 5.5 will be examined in the next section. Here we confine ourselves to the travel times (4.6) and (4.9) from and to each limit distribution, respectively. These are shown in Table 5.7. In all four cases we have the smallest travel time (4.6) at $j = 4$, skilled manual workers. Also, in all cases

TABLE 5.7

TRAVEL TIMES TO AND FROM LIMIT DISTRIBUTIONS

	Travel time from limit distribution to status category:					Travel time to limit distribution
	1	2	3	4	5	
British	28.4	8.6	.87	.20	.87	1.54
Danish	29.2	4.5	.82	.28	.97	1.64
American 1910	5.7	2.7	1.44	.65	1.16	1.37
American 1940	4.7	1.4	.88	.82	.93	1.19

these travel times take roughly equal values for the adjacent categories $j = 3$ and $j = 5$, and they increase further at $j = 2$ and $j = 1$. However, there is a considerable difference as to the numerical values. In the British and Danish cases the minimum travel time (at $j = 4$) is only 20 or 30 per cent of a generation, but the increase from the minimum is so fast that the largest value (at $j = 1$) is more than 100 times larger. For the American 1910 case the value of the minimum is more than twice as large as those of the British and Danish data, but the maximum is about five times smaller than those of the latter data. As a result, the ratio of the maximum to the minimum is about 9, so that the "curve" is much flatter. This effect is even more pro-

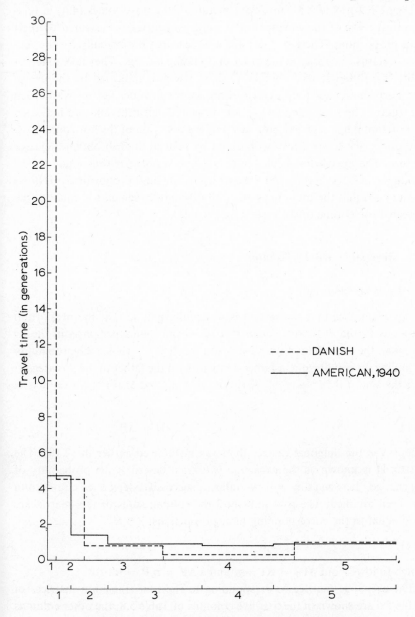

Fig. 5.2.   Travel times from and to the limit distribution

nounced for the American 1940 data, the ratio of its maximum to its minimum being less than 6.

Figure 5.2 provides a convenient picture of the travel times (4.6) in relation to the size of the corresponding status categories as measured by their limit proportions. These proportions are measured horizontally for the successive status categories in the order of declining prestige. They take different values for different sets of mobility data, which is indicated by the use of two horizontal axes; only two cases are shown in order not to overburden the figure. The travel times (4.6) are measured vertically and are indicated by horizontal line segments above the relevant section of the horizontal axis. Successive line segments are connected by vertical lines to obtain a clearer picture. The area below each horizontal line segment is thus equal to the product of the travel time and the corresponding limit proportion. It follows from (4.10) that the total area under all $n = 5$ line segments is equal to the expected travel time in the system as a whole.

5.5. Reversible Markov Chains

The Exchange Matrix

Again suppose that the system is in equilibrium, so that the proportion presently in the ith status category is π_i. Given that a person is in the ith category, the probability that his son is in the jth is p_{ij}. Hence the probability of finding, in equilibrium, a father-son pair with the father in the ith category and the son in the jth is $\pi_i p_{ij}$. Write $\pi_{ij} = \pi_i p_{ij}$ and Π for the $n \times n$ matrix $[\pi_{ij}]$:

$$(5.1) \qquad \pi_{ij} = \pi_i p_{ij} \qquad\qquad \Pi = \Delta P$$

where Δ is the diagonal matrix that was introduced earlier in (2.18). The matrix Π is known as the *exchange matrix*; it describes the probability of "exchange" between any pair of states in successive steps once equilibrium has been attained. The row sums and the column sums of this matrix are both equal to the corresponding limit proportions:

$$(5.2) \qquad \Pi \iota = \pi \qquad\qquad \iota' \Pi = \pi'$$

which follows from $\Delta P \iota = \Delta \iota = \pi$ and $\iota' \Delta P = \pi' P = \pi'$.

The exchange matrices corresponding to the four transition matrices of Table 5.5 are shown in the first five columns of Table 5.8; the other columns contain adjusted values that will be discussed in the next section. The figures

TABLE 5.8

OBSERVED AND ADJUSTED EXCHANGE MATRICES FOR FOUR TRANSITION MATRICES

Father's status category	Subject's status category					Subject's status category				
	1	2	3	4	5	1	2	3	4	5
					British					
1	.009	.003	.006	.003	.001	.0088	.0040	.0042	.0037	.0020
2	.004	.011	.014	.009	.003	.0040	.0108	.0112	.0100	.0054
3	.006	.014	.074	.086	.035	.0042	.0112	.0836	.0752	.0405
4	.004	.010	.081	.194	.121	.0037	.0100	.0752	.2086	.1123
5	.000	.003	.039	.118	.151	.0020	.0054	.0405	.1123	.1514
					Danish					
1	.010	.006	.004	.003	.001	.0101	.0048	.0042	.0033	.0018
2	.004	.025	.025	.019	.008	.0048	.0259	.0227	.0177	.0100
3	.005	.029	.082	.076	.036	.0042	.0227	.0903	.0702	.0398
4	.003	.014	.078	.170	.110	.0033	.0177	.0702	.1818	.1030
5	.002	.006	.039	.107	.137	.0018	.0100	.0398	.1030	.1369
					American 1910					
1	.009	.007	.010	.009	.006	.0085	.0073	.0106	.0082	.0063
2	.007	.023	.026	.018	.015	.0073	.0225	.0272	.0183	.0130
3	.014	.025	.107	.054	.035	.0106	.0272	.1056	.0551	.0363
4	.007	.020	.055	.176	.087	.0082	.0183	.0551	.1773	.0873
5	.005	.013	.037	.088	.147	.0063	.0130	.0363	.0873	.1470
					American 1940					
1	.019	.010	.019	.011	.008	.0186	.0100	.0178	.0085	.0116
2	.009	.023	.033	.017	.024	.0100	.0231	.0371	.0157	.0197
3	.022	.036	.119	.042	.053	.0178	.0371	.1178	.0447	.0543
4	.007	.016	.042	.070	.071	.0085	.0157	.0447	.0663	.0702
5	.009	.021	.060	.066	.195	.0116	.0197	.0543	.0702	.1950

indicate that the four matrices differ rather substantially from each other but that they do have one feature in common: they are all very close to symmetry.[1] If Π is symmetric, the probability of being in status category i

---

[1] BERGER and SNELL (1957) observed this symmetry for the British data although at a higher level of aggregation (three instead of five status categories). They did not suggest that symmetry is a more universal property, but the present results seem to point in this direction.

now and in status category j in the next generation is in equilibrium equal to the probability of being in j now and in i next, for all pairs (i, j). The system is then said to be "in equal exchange". This is a very strong equilibrium property which goes far beyond the stability of the proportions $\pi_1, \ldots, \pi_n$. The stability of the π's is fully compatible with an asymmetric exchange matrix. An example is

$$(5.3) \qquad \mathbf{\Pi} = \begin{bmatrix} .1 & .15 & .05 \\ .1 & .2 & .1 \\ .1 & .05 & .15 \end{bmatrix}$$

corresponding to $\pi' = [.3 \ .4 \ .3]$.

Given that the exchange matrices of Table 5.8 are so close to symmetry, it is worthwhile to explore the implications of this property.

Reverse Markov Chains

We return to the notation of (1.1) and (1.2) by writing $M \in j$ and $F \in i$ for "a person is in the jth status category" and "this person's father is in the ith category". Applying the familiar rule on conditional probabilities, we have

$$P[F \in i \text{ and } M \in j] = P[F \in i]P[M \in j | F \in i] = P[M \in j]P[F \in i | M \in j]$$

from which we conclude

$$(5.4) \qquad P[F \in i | M \in j] = \frac{P[F \in i]P[M \in j | F \in i]}{P[M \in j]}$$

The right-hand side is equal to $\pi_i p_{ij}/\pi_j$ if the system is in equilibrium. The probability on the left is a probability of the *reverse Markov chain* which describes the status category of the father given the occupation of his son. Note that this is indeed a Markov chain when there is equilibrium, because $\pi_i p_{ij}/\pi_j$ does not involve the occupation of the grandson or later descendants.

Write $\mathbf{P}_R$ for the transition matrix of the reverse Markov chain. The left-hand probability in (5.4) is the $(i, j)^{\text{th}}$ element of the transpose of $\mathbf{P}_R$, so that the $(i, j)^{\text{th}}$ element of $\mathbf{P}_R$ itself is equal to $\pi_j p_{ji}/\pi_i$, which is the $(i, j)^{\text{th}}$ element of $\mathbf{\Delta}^{-1}\mathbf{P}'\mathbf{\Delta}$:

$$(5.5) \qquad \mathbf{P}_R = \mathbf{\Delta}^{-1}\mathbf{P}'\mathbf{\Delta}$$

This $\mathbf{P}_R$ has ι and π' as characteristic column and row, respectively, corresponding to the unit root:

$$(5.6) \qquad \mathbf{P}_R \boldsymbol{\iota} = \boldsymbol{\Delta}^{-1}\mathbf{P}'\boldsymbol{\Delta}\boldsymbol{\iota} = \boldsymbol{\Delta}^{-1}\mathbf{P}'\boldsymbol{\pi} = \boldsymbol{\Delta}^{-1}\boldsymbol{\pi} = \boldsymbol{\iota}$$

$$(5.7) \qquad \boldsymbol{\pi}'\mathbf{P}_R = \boldsymbol{\pi}'\boldsymbol{\Delta}^{-1}\mathbf{P}'\boldsymbol{\Delta} = \boldsymbol{\iota}'\mathbf{P}'\boldsymbol{\Delta} = \boldsymbol{\iota}'\boldsymbol{\Delta} = \boldsymbol{\pi}'$$

Equation (5.5) can be written in the equivalent form

$$(5.8) \qquad \boldsymbol{\Delta}\mathbf{P}_R = (\boldsymbol{\Delta}\mathbf{P})'$$

But $\boldsymbol{\Delta}\mathbf{P} = \boldsymbol{\Pi}$ is the exchange matrix corresponding to the original (forward) Markov chain, and $\boldsymbol{\Delta}\mathbf{P}_R$ must be the exchange matrix corresponding to the reverse chain because $\boldsymbol{\Delta}$ (the diagonal matrix with the limit proportions on the diagonal) applies equally to $\mathbf{P}$ and $\mathbf{P}_R$ in view of (5.7). Thus, (5.8) implies that the exchange matrices corresponding to the forward and the reverse chains are equal if and only if $\boldsymbol{\Pi}$ is symmetric – which is precisely the property discussed at the end of the previous subsection. Since the transition matrix can be obtained uniquely from the exchange matrix (by dividing the elements of each row by the row sum, $p_{ij} = \pi_{ij}/\pi_i$), we have thus proved that symmetry of the exchange matrix is a necessary and sufficient condition in order that the transition matrices of the forward and reverse Markov chains be identical, in which case the Markov chain is said to be *reversible*.

Decomposition of Travel Times for Reversible Markov Chains

Consider the fundamental matrix $\mathbf{Z}$ defined in (3.3) and postmultiply it by $\boldsymbol{\Delta}^{-1}$:

$$(5.9) \qquad \begin{aligned} \mathbf{Z}\boldsymbol{\Delta}^{-1} &= (\mathbf{I}-\mathbf{P}+\boldsymbol{\iota}\boldsymbol{\pi}')^{-1}\boldsymbol{\Delta}^{-1} \\ &= [\boldsymbol{\Delta}(\mathbf{I}-\mathbf{P}+\boldsymbol{\iota}\boldsymbol{\pi}')]^{-1} \\ &= (\boldsymbol{\Delta}-\boldsymbol{\Pi}+\boldsymbol{\pi}\boldsymbol{\pi}')^{-1} = -\mathbf{S} \quad (\text{say}) \end{aligned}$$

In the expression on the last line both $\boldsymbol{\Delta}$ and $\boldsymbol{\pi}\boldsymbol{\pi}'$ are always symmetric, and $\boldsymbol{\Pi}$ is symmetric if and only if the Markov chain is reversible. Hence $\mathbf{S} = -\mathbf{Z}\boldsymbol{\Delta}^{-1}$ is a symmetric matrix under this condition. The $(i, j)^{\text{th}}$ element of this matrix is

$$(5.10) \qquad s_{ij} = -\frac{z_{ij}}{\pi_j}$$

Combining this with the travel time definition (4.4), we decompose τ_{ij} as follows:

$$(5.11) \qquad \tau_{ij} = s_{ij} + \frac{z_{jj}-1}{\pi_j} \quad \text{if} \quad i \neq j$$

The symmetry of s_{ij} in the origin (i) and the destination (j) suggests that it may be regarded as the *distance effect* on the travel time τ_{ij}. The second term in the right-hand side of (5.11) involves j only, which suggests that it describes the *destination effect*.

When we combine this with the earlier decomposition (4.3), we thus have the following expression for the mean first passage time m_{ij} with $i \neq j$:

$$
(5.12) \qquad
\begin{aligned}
m_{ij} &= s_{ij} && \text{distance effect} && \left.\begin{array}{c} \\ \\ \end{array}\right\} \\
&\quad + (z_{jj}-1)/\pi_j && \text{destination effect} && \text{travel time } \tau_{ij} \\
&\quad + \omega_j && \text{waiting time}
\end{aligned}
$$

The waiting time is the only nonzero component of m_{ij} when there is perfect mobility.[1] Both the waiting time and the destination effect depend exclusively on the destination. The waiting time $\omega_j = 1/\pi_j$ is concerned with the likelihood of obtaining entrance once the distance has been overcome. The distance effect describes how far apart origin and destination are, and the destination effect how slowly one travels on the average when the jth status category is the destination. The latter statement is confirmed by the fact that this destination effect is identical with the travel time (4.6) from the limit distribution to the jth category. Indeed, the figures of Table 5.7 indicate that the speed is at its maximum when the skilled manual category is the destination, and that it decreases monotonically both for successively higher and for lower destinations. It seems natural to ascribe the speed reduction for higher destinations to their increasing demands and that for lower destinations to an increased resistance to move to the bottom of society.

Decompositions for Four Transition Matrices

Table 5.9 gives the decomposition (5.12) for our four transition matrices. The figures are based on symmetric exchange matrices, obtained by replacing $\mathbf{\Pi}$ of Table 5.8 by $\frac{1}{2}(\mathbf{\Pi}+\mathbf{\Pi}')$. The first five columns contain the distance effects, the sixth the destination effects, and the last the waiting times. For example, in the British case the average number of generations needed to move from the second status category to the first is obtained by adding three numbers in the first row of the table:

$$
\begin{aligned}
-7.7 &\quad \text{for the distance effect} \\
28.4 &\quad \text{for the destination effect} \\
44.0 &\quad \text{for the waiting time.}
\end{aligned}
$$

---

[1] The destination effect vanishes in the case of perfect mobility because $\mathbf{Z} = \mathbf{I}$ implies $z_{jj} = 1$ for each j. The distance effect is also zero, because $s_{ij} = 0$ for $i \neq j$ follows from the fact that $\mathbf{Z} = \mathbf{I}$ and hence also $\mathbf{S} = -\mathbf{Z}\mathbf{\Delta}^{-1}$ are diagonal matrices.

TABLE 5.9

DECOMPOSITION OF MEAN FIRST PASSAGE TIMES FOR FOUR TRANSITION MATRICES

Destination	Distance effect from origin:					Destination effect	Waiting time
	1	2	3	4	5		
			British				
1	.	−7.7	−1.0	1.2	2.2	28.4	44.0
2	−7.7	.	−1.2	.8	1.5	8.6	24.2
3	−1.0	−1.2	.	.1	.7	.9	4.7
4	1.2	.8	.1	.	.0	.2	2.4
5	2.2	1.5	.7	.0	.	.9	3.2
			Danish				
1	.	−4.5	−.1	1.4	2.0	29.3	41.4
2	−4.5	.	−.9	.8	1.4	4.5	12.3
3	−.1	−.9	.	.2	.7	.8	4.4
4	1.4	.8	.2	.	−.1	.3	2.7
5	2.0	1.4	.7	−.1	.	1.0	3.4
			American 1910				
1	.	−1.6	−.7	.7	1.0	5.7	24.5
2	−1.6	.	−.6	.6	.8	2.7	11.3
3	−.7	−.6	.	.5	.8	1.4	4.3
4	.7	.6	.5	.	.1	.7	2.9
5	1.0	.8	.8	.1	.	1.2	3.4
			American 1940				
1	.	−.7	−.5	.6	1.1	4.7	15.0
3	−.7	.	−.4	.4	.7	1.4	9.5
3	−.5	−.4	.	.4	.7	.9	3.7
4	.6	.4	.4	.	−.0	.8	4.9
5	1.1	.7	.7	−.0	.	.9	2.8

The figures show that the total travel time from the second status category to the first is much larger than that from the first to the second ($-7.7+28.4$ versus $-7.7+8.6$). It is only the distance effect which is symmetric, and the difference is caused by the destination effects which are indeed quite different.[1]

---

[1] Although the destination effects and the corresponding travel times from the limit distribution are theoretically equal there are some (but very minor) discrepancies between the former as shown in Table 5.9 and the latter as shown in Table 5.7. This is due to the fact that Table 5.9 is based on the symmetrized version, $\frac{1}{2}(\mathbf{\Pi}+\mathbf{\Pi}')$, of the exchange matrix.

One of the most interesting features of Table 5.9 is the regular behavior of the distance effects. In each row and each column of their matrix, the elements tend to increase algebraically when we move away from the diagonal. The plausibility of this result suggests that it is worthwhile to see whether the distance effects on the travel times can be used to provide acceptable measures for the distance between status categories.

Distance Effects and Distances

An adequate distance definition requires (1) that the distance between i and i be zero, (2) that the distance between i and j be equal to that between j and i, and (3) that the distance between i and j plus that between j and k be at least equal to the distance between i and k directly. It follows from (1) and (3) that all distances are then nonnegative.

Here we confine ourselves to the first two conditions and note that the second is satisfied by the distance effect when the Markov chain is reversible. Regarding (1), the dots in the diagonal elements of Table 5.9 indicate that these elements are not defined. To provide an adequate definition, note that the diagonal elements are concerned with mean first passage times from the jth status category to itself. These are the mean recurrence times which are equal to the waiting times, $m_{jj} = \omega_j$. Hence, if we want to interpret the decomposition of the mean first passage times for all pairs (i, j) in exactly the same way, including the cases in which $i = j$, we should replace the dots of Table 5.9 by minus the destination effects. For the British case $i = j = 1$ we then obtain the following decomposition:

$$-28.4 \quad \text{for the distance effect} \ (\equiv \text{minus the destination effect})$$
$$28.4 \quad \text{for the destination effect}$$
$$44.0 \quad \text{waiting time,}$$

which adds up (trivially) to 44.0, as it should.

We thus use the sixth column of Table 5.9, multiplied by -1, as the main diagonal of the matrix of distance effects. This matrix is then of the form s_{ij} for $i \neq j$ and $-(z_{ii}-1)/\pi_i$ for $i = j$. This is not a distance matrix, because it has negative elements in the diagonal (and in several nondiagonal positions also). To obtain distances we have to transform this matrix so that it has zeros on the diagonal. Given that our decompositions are all additive, it seems natural to transform in an additive manner. Also, to retain the symmetry of the matrix – condition (2) – we should transform in a way which is symmetric in i and j. The following is a simple transformation which satisfies these requirements and which has an attractive interpretation in terms of travel times from i to j and from j to i as will be shown in the next subsection: we subtract from each row and each column of the matrix one-half of its diagonal element. This leads to a distance matrix $[d_{ij}]$ with a zero diagonal and off-diagonal elements of the form

(5.13)
$$d_{ij} = s_{ij} + \frac{1}{2}\left(\frac{z_{ii}-1}{\pi_i} + \frac{z_{jj}-1}{\pi_j}\right)$$

$$= s_{ij} - \frac{1}{2}\left(s_{ii} + \frac{1}{\pi_i}\right) - \frac{1}{2}\left(s_{jj} + \frac{1}{\pi_j}\right) \quad \text{if} \quad i \neq j$$

These distances all vanish in the case of perfect mobility, as they should, because $\mathbf{Z} = \mathbf{I}$ implies that $z_{ii} = 1$ for each i and that $\mathbf{S} = -\mathbf{Z}\boldsymbol{\Delta}^{-1}$ is a

TABLE 5.10

DISTANCES BASED ON MEAN FIRST PASSAGE TIMES

Status category	Status category				Status category			
	2	3	4	5	2	3	4	5
British								
1	10.8	13.7	15.5	16.8	10.47	14.39	15.28	15.94
2		3.5	5.2	6.3		3.92	4.81	5.48
3			.6	1.6			.89	1.55
4				.6				.66
Danish								
1	12.4	14.9	16.1	17.2	12.82	15.00	15.96	16.59
2		1.7	3.2	4.1		2.17	3.13	3.76
3			.7	1.6			.96	1.59
4				.5				.63
American 1910								
1	2.6	2.9	3.9	4.5	2.21	2.90	3.70	4.09
2		1.5	2.3	2.8		1.30	2.33	2.80
3			1.6	2.1			1.56	2.10
4				1.0				.99
American 1940								
1	2.3	2.4	3.4	4.0	2.07	2.43	3.12	3.55
2		.7	1.5	1.8		.60	1.49	1.99
3			1.2	1.6			1.08	1.61
4				.9				.76

diagonal matrix. It will be shown in the last subsection that, when the Markov chain is reversible, $d_{ij} = 0$ for all pairs (i, j) is a necessary and sufficient condition for social mobility to be perfect.

The first four columns of Table 5.10 contain the d_{ij}'s for $i < j$ for our four transition matrices; the other columns of the table will be discussed in the next section. These d_{ij}'s, which are based on the figures of Table 5.9, indicate that the distances in each row increase monotonically as one moves to the right and also in each column as one moves upward. The large distances from the first status category in the British and Danish cases are particularly striking.

Distances and Round-Trip Travel Times

Consider τ_{ij} as specified in (5.11) and add to it the travel time τ_{ji} corresponding to the same pair (i, j) but in opposite direction:

$$\tau_{ij} + \tau_{ji} = s_{ij} + s_{ji} + \frac{z_{ii} - 1}{\pi_i} + \frac{z_{jj} - 1}{\pi_j}$$

Comparing this with the first line of (5.13) and taking account of the symmetry of $[s_{ij}]$, we conclude

$$(5.14) \qquad\qquad d_{ij} = \frac{\tau_{ij} + \tau_{ji}}{2}$$

This means that the distance definition (5.13) amounts to equating each distance to the average of the two corresponding travel times. In other words, by making a round trip between i and j the same distance is covered twice. The plausibility of this result should contribute to the appeal of the distance definition (5.13), particularly since it will appear in the next subsection that a similarly attractive result can be obtained for travel times to and from the limit distribution in relation to average distances from the status categories. Note that (5.14) also holds for $i = j$ because we defined both τ_{ii} and d_{ii} as zero.

Average Distances and the Distance Between a Status Category and the Limit Distribution

Define $\bar{d}_i$ as the average distance from the ith status category – the average of the distances between i and all n categories – and $\bar{d}$ as the average distance in the system as a whole, using the limit proportions as weights:

$$(5.15) \qquad \bar{d}_i = \sum_{j=1}^{n} \pi_j d_{ij} \qquad \bar{d} = \sum_{i=1}^{n} \pi_i \bar{d}_i = \sum_{i=1}^{n} \sum_{j=1}^{n} \pi_i \pi_j d_{ij}$$

It is shown in the next paragraph that $\bar{d}$ is identical with the travel time (4.9) from any status category to the limit distribution,

$$(5.16) \qquad \bar{d} = \sum_{j=1}^{n} (z_{jj} - 1)$$

and that $\bar{d}_i$ is equal to the arithmetic average of the overall average $\bar{d}$ and the destination effect on the travel time to the ith category:

$$(5.17) \qquad \bar{d}_i = \frac{1}{2} \left(\bar{d} + \frac{z_{ii} - 1}{\pi_i} \right)$$

Recall that this destination effect is identical with the travel time from the limit distribution to the ith category. Hence the average distance from the ith status category is equal to the average of the two travel times between this category and the limit distribution. Comparing this result with (5.14), we may conclude by analogy that the average distance $\bar{d}_i$ from the ith status category can be interpreted as the *distance between this category and the limit distribution*.

To prove (5.16) and (5.17) consider d_{ij} as specified in the second line of (5.13). Multiply both sides by π_i and sum over $i \neq j$:

$$(5.18) \qquad \sum_{i \neq j} \pi_i d_{ij} = \sum_{i \neq j} \pi_i s_{ij} - \frac{1}{2} \sum_{i \neq j} \pi_i s_{ii} - \frac{1}{2}(n-1) - \frac{1}{2}(1 - \pi_j)s_{jj} - \frac{1 - \pi_j}{2\pi_j}$$

The left-hand side is equal to $\bar{d}_j$ because $d_{ij} = d_{ji}$ and $d_{jj} = 0$. The first term on the right is the jth element of the vector $\boldsymbol{\pi}'\mathbf{S}$ minus $\pi_j s_{jj}$. Since $\mathbf{S} = -\mathbf{Z}\boldsymbol{\Lambda}^{-1}$ and $\boldsymbol{\pi}'\mathbf{Z} = \boldsymbol{\pi}'$, we have $\boldsymbol{\pi}'\mathbf{S} = -\boldsymbol{\pi}'\mathbf{Z}\boldsymbol{\Lambda}^{-1} = -\boldsymbol{\pi}'\boldsymbol{\Lambda}^{-1} = -\boldsymbol{\iota}'$, the jth element of which is -1. So we can simplify (5.18) to

$$(5.19) \qquad \bar{d}_j = -1 - \pi_j s_{jj} - \frac{1}{2}\left(\sum_{i=1}^{n} \pi_i s_{ii} - \pi_j s_{jj} \right) - \frac{1}{2}(n-1) - \frac{1}{2}(1 - \pi_j)s_{jj} - \frac{1 - \pi_j}{2\pi_j}$$

$$= -\frac{1}{2}s_{jj} - \frac{1}{2}\sum_{i=1}^{n} \pi_i s_{ii} - \frac{1}{2}n - \frac{1}{2\pi_j}$$

Next multiply both sides of this equation by π_j and sum over j:

$$(5.20) \qquad \bar{d} = -\sum_{i=1}^{n} \pi_i s_{ii} - n$$

Applying $s_{ii} = -z_{ii}/\pi_i$, we conclude that (5.16) is true. Finally, substitute (5.20) in (5.19):

(5.21) $$\bar{d}_j = -\tfrac{1}{2}s_{jj} + \tfrac{1}{2}\bar{d} - \frac{1}{2\pi_j}$$

which leads directly to (5.17).

Distance Effects Expressed in Terms of Distances

Combining (5.13) with (5.21), we find for $i \neq j$,

$$s_{ij} = d_{ij} + \frac{1}{2}\left(s_{ii} + \frac{1}{\pi_i}\right) + \frac{1}{2}\left(s_{jj} + \frac{1}{\pi_j}\right)$$
$$= d_{ij} - \bar{d}_i + \tfrac{1}{2}\bar{d} - \bar{d}_j + \tfrac{1}{2}\bar{d}$$

which can be written as

(5.22) $$s_{ij} = (d_{ij} - \bar{d}) - (\bar{d}_i - \bar{d}) - (\bar{d}_j - \bar{d}) \quad \text{if} \quad i \neq j$$

This shows that the distance effect on the travel time from the ith status category to the jth (and also, in view of the symmetry, from the jth to the ith) is equal to the excess of their distance d_{ij} over the sum of the average distances from these two categories ($\bar{d}_i$ and $\bar{d}_j$) with the understanding that these three d's are all measured as deviations from the overall average distance $\bar{d}$. Note that this accounts for the negative sign of the distance effects in the upper left-hand corners of Table 5.9, because for that set of status categories the sum of $\bar{d}_i - \bar{d}$ and $\bar{d}_j - \bar{d}$ exceeds $d_{ij} - \bar{d}$.

Travel Times Expressed in Terms of Distances

The travel time τ_{ij} is equal to the distance effect s_{ij}, for which we substitute the right-hand side of (5.22), plus the destination effect which is equal to $2\bar{d}_j - \bar{d}$ according to (5.17). This gives

(5.23) $$\tau_{ij} = d_{ij} - \bar{d}_i + \bar{d}_j \qquad\qquad i,j = 1,\ldots,n$$

which shows that the excess of the travel time τ_{ij} over the corresponding distance d_{ij} is equal to the excess of the distance between the destination and the limit distribution over the distance between the origin and the limit distribution. Note that (5.23) also holds for $i = j$, whereas (5.22) is only applicable to $i \neq j$.

It was shown below eq. (5.13) that perfect mobility implies $d_{ij} = 0$ for all pairs (i, j). Conversely, if all d_{ij}'s vanish, all travel times are also zero because of (5.23) and hence $m_{ij} = \omega_j = 1/\pi_j$ for each (i, j) in view of (4.3). It then follows from (3.2) that $z_{jj} - z_{ij} = 1$ whenever $i \neq j$. Next go to (3.8) and multiply both sides by π_j, which gives $1 = \sum_{k \neq j} p_{ik} + \pi_j$ or $1 = 1 - p_{ij} + \pi_j$ for each $i \neq j$. Hence $p_{ij} = \pi_j$ for each $i \neq j$. Since $p_{i1} + \ldots + p_{in} = \pi_1 + \ldots + \pi_n = 1$, we also have $p_{ii} = \pi_i$ for each i. We conclude that zero values of all distances are both necessary and sufficient for perfect social mobility, at least under the condition that the Markov chain is reversible.

5.6. A Distance Model for Social Mobility

It was stated on page 286 that an adequate distance measure must satisfy three conditions, but only the first two were discussed there explicitly. The third condition specifies that the distance between i and j plus that between j and k be at least equal to that between i and k directly, for any triple (i, j, k). An inspection of the distances displayed in Table 5.10 for the British and Danish data suggests that this condition is met, approximately at least, in strict equality form:

$$d_{13} = d_{12} + d_{23}$$

$$d_{14} = d_{13} + d_{34} = d_{12} + d_{23} + d_{34}$$

and so on. The general formulation is

(6.1) $$d_{ij} = d_{i, i+1} + \ldots + d_{j-1, j} \quad \text{if} \quad i < j$$

This equation implies that all distances can be expressed as sums of distances between adjacent status categories, $d_{12}, d_{23}, \ldots$, to be called the *successive distances*. The objective of this section is to develop a model for transition matrices based on these successive distances.

A Linear Distance Model for the British and Danish Transition Matrices

To verify the extent to which the linear model (6.1) is acceptable, we shall proceed conditionally on the limit distribution. This may be justified by the consideration that such a distribution describes the size of the status categories in equilibrium, whereas our main interest is in the intergenerational transitions from any category to any category.

Under the hypothesis (6.1) we can derive all distances from the successive distances. We then use (5.15) to determine the average distances (given the limit distribution), next (5.22) for the distance effects on the travel times, and finally (5.9) to determine the exchange matrix $\mathbf{\Pi}$ from $\mathbf{S} = [s_{ij}]$:

(6.2) $$\mathbf{\Pi} = \Delta + \pi\pi' + \mathbf{S}^{-1}$$

Let us write $\hat{\mathbf{\Pi}} = [\hat{\pi}_{ij}]$ for the adjusted exchange matrix thus obtained, which is obviously a function of the values chosen for the four successive distances d_{12}, d_{23}, d_{34} and d_{45}. Our objective will be to minimize the information inaccuracy,

$$(6.3) \qquad I = \sum_{i=1}^{n} \sum_{j=1}^{n} \pi_{ij} \log \frac{\pi_{ij}}{\hat{\pi}_{ij}}$$

where π_{ij} is the $(i, j)^{\text{th}}$ element of the observed exchange matrix shown in the first five columns of Table 5.8. The distances are all zero in the case of perfect mobility and the exchange matrix is then $\mathbf{\Pi} = \mathbf{\Delta P} = \mathbf{\Delta \iota \pi'} = \mathbf{\pi \pi'}$, so that the function (6.3) for zero adjusted distances becomes

$$(6.4) \qquad I_0 = \sum_{i=1}^{n} \sum_{j=1}^{n} \pi_{ij} \log \frac{\pi_{ij}}{\pi_i \pi_j}$$

Since π_i is both the ith row sum and the ith column sum of $\mathbf{\Pi}$, this I_0 is nothing but the expected mutual information of the exchange matrix. The extent to which the minimum value of I is smaller than I_0 is a natural measure of the fit obtained by the selection of adequate positive values for the successive distances.

The procedure for adjusting these distances to minimize (6.3) is described at the end of this section. The values of I_0 are .105 for the British data and .117 for the Danish data (natural logarithms). The minimum of I is .0076 (British) and .0049 (Danish), which amounts to 7 and 4 per cent, respectively, of the corresponding I_0. In both cases we have a 5×5 table whose marginal proportions (the limit distribution) are taken as given, so that there are 16 degrees of freedom. The adjustment of only four successive distances thus reduces the information inaccuracy (6.3) to a level which is between 93 and 96 per cent below that of the perfect mobility assumption.

The adjusted distances are shown in the last four columns of Table 5.10 and the implied exchange matrices in the last five columns of Table 5.8. The results indicate that the $\hat{\pi}_{ij}$'s are mostly rather close to the corresponding π_{ij}'s. The model predicts lower values for the (3, 4) and (4, 3) combinations than the observations indicate ($\hat{\pi}_{34} < \pi_{34}$, $\hat{\pi}_{43} < \pi_{43}$) and a higher probability that father and son are both in either of these categories ($\hat{\pi}_{33} > \pi_{33}$, $\hat{\pi}_{44} > \pi_{44}$). Apart from this, however, the fit seems rather good.

A Picture of Distances and Travel Times

The linear distance model (6.1) permits a simple picture of distances and travel times simultaneously. The status categories $1, \ldots, 5$ are indicated along the horizontal axes of the two diagrams of Figure 5.3 at the successive

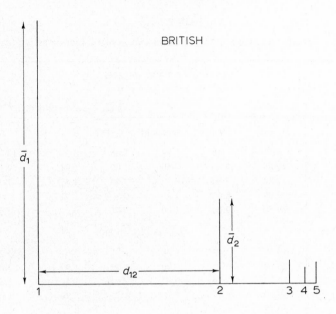

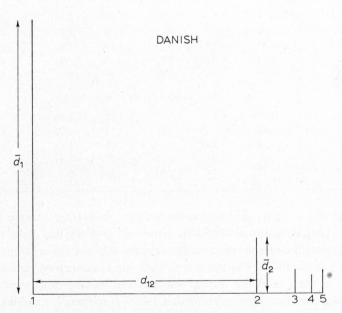

Fig. 5.3.   Distances between status categories and travel times according to the distance model for British and Danish occupational data

TABLE 5.11

ADJUSTED VALUES OF TRAVEL TIMES AND AVERAGE DISTANCES

Status category	Travel time to status category					d_t
	1	2	3	4	5	
British ($d = 1.578$)						
1	0	.48	.98	1.48	2.39	14.75
2	20.46	0	.50	1.00	1.91	4.76
3	27.80	7.34	0	.50	1.41	1.34
4	29.09	8.63	1.29	0	.91	.94
5	29.50	9.04	1.70	.41	0	1.19
Danish ($d = 1.701$)						
1	0	.62	1.08	1.71	2.61	15.28
2	25.03	0	.46	1.09	1.99	3.08
3	28.92	3.89	0	.64	1.53	1.36
4	30.20	5.17	1.28	0	.90	1.04
5	30.57	5.54	1.65	.37	0	1.31
American 1910 ($d = 1.350$)						
1	0	.88	.94	1.37	2.00	3.35
2	3.54	0	.67	1.33	2.03	2.01
3	4.87	1.93	0	1.19	1.96	1.38
4	6.04	3.34	1.93	0	1.22	1.01
5	6.19	3.56	2.23	.75	0	1.25
American 1940 ($d = 1.151$)						
1	0	.61	.67	1.28	1.82	2.76
2	3.53	0	.31	1.11	1.72	1.30
3	4.18	.89	0	.99	1.64	1.01
4	4.96	1.87	1.17	0	.87	.92
5	5.27	2.25	1.59	.64	0	1.04

distances $d_{12}, \ldots, d_{45}$. For each status category, the average distance $\bar{d}_i$ from that category is measured vertically. [One may also say that these vertical line segments indicate the distance between the relevant status category and the limit distribution.] The travel time from i to j can then be visualized by starting at the top of the vertical line at i and moving downward to the horizontal axis, next moving along that axis to j, and finally climbing to the top of the vertical line at j. Equation (5.23) shows that to compute this travel time, one must count the horizontal and upward portions of this trip positively and the downward portion negatively. The figure also shows immediately which of the two travel times, from i to j or from j to i, is larger; this is the one whose destination has a longer vertical line (or, equivalently, whose destination is farther from the limit distribution).

The relevant travel times and average distances, computed from the adjusted d_{ij}'s of Table 5.10 and the limit distribution, are shown in the upper half of Table 5.11. The lower half deals with the American transition matrices and will be discussed in the next subsection.[1]

A Generalized Distance Model for the American Transition Matrices

The simple model (6.1) is not adequate for the American data. Table 5.10 (first four columns) shows that $d_{13} < d_{12} + d_{23}$ holds both for 1910 and for 1940 and, more generally, that d_{ij} with $|i-j| > 1$ is smaller than the sum of the corresponding successive distances. This suggests that there are "shortcuts" in the American society for moving from any status category to any nonadjacent category, both upward and downward. It is then no longer true that any distance can be computed from the corresponding successive distances without further knowledge, but the regular pattern of the American d_{ij}'s of Table 5.10 indicates that it is worthwhile to try a generalization of the linear distance model. A simple generalization is

$$(6.5) \qquad d_{ij}^r = d_{i,i+1}^r + \ldots + d_{j-1,j}^r \quad \text{if} \quad i < j$$

where r is a number not less than 1. The case $r = 1$ is equivalent to (6.1), and $r > 1$ implies that each nonsuccessive distance is less than the sum of the corresponding successive distances. In the case $r = 2$ all nonsuccessive distances can be displayed as hypotenuses of right-angled triangles in an $(n-1)$-dimensional Euclidean space, as is shown in Figure 5.4 for $n = 4$. As $r \to \infty$, the distance d_{ij} converges to the largest successive distance between i and j (see Problem 11).

Our criterion function is (6.3) as before. For any fixed value of $r \geqq 1$, one can determine the nonsuccessive distances from the chosen values of the successive distances, and a systematic search can be designed to find the minimizing values. The result is $r = 1.42$ for 1910 and 1.24 for 1940, and the corresponding distances are shown in the lower right-hand corner of Table 5.10. The $\hat{\pi}_{ij}$'s are given in the last five columns of Table 5.8. They

---

[1] Note that the adjusted travel times of Table 5.11 are all nonnegative. The observed travel times (obtained from Table 5.6) do not have this property; see footnote 1 on page 275.

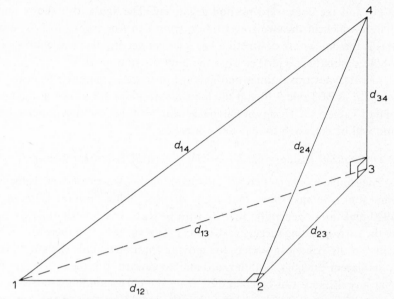

Fig. 5.4. The generalized distance model (6.5) for $r = 2$, $n = 4$

are close to the observed π_{ij}'s, particularly for the 1910 data. This is corroborated by the minimum values of (6.3), which are .0013 for 1910 and .0032 for 1940. The values of I_0 defined in (6.4) are .121 and .104, respectively, which implies that the adjustment of five coefficients (r plus four successive distances) reduces the information inaccuracy to a level between 97 and 99 per cent below that of the naive perfect mobility model. The adjusted values of the travel times and the average distances are shown in the lower half of Table 5.11.

The decline of r from 1.42 to 1.24 is interesting. It suggests that the American society of 1940 had moved almost halfway to the "European" pattern ($r = 1$). The depression of the 1930's is a possible explanation. It stimulated fathers to find jobs for their sons in their own work environment, which may have reduced the number of cases in which the son's status is far from that of his father. The depression may also be responsible for the remarkable increase of the limit proportion of the lowest status category and the equally remarkable decrease of that of the next category (see Table 5.6). When there is little demand for skills, there is little stimulus to acquire them.

Moments of Distances as Functions of Status

The upper part of Figure 5.5, which concerns the British and Danish data,

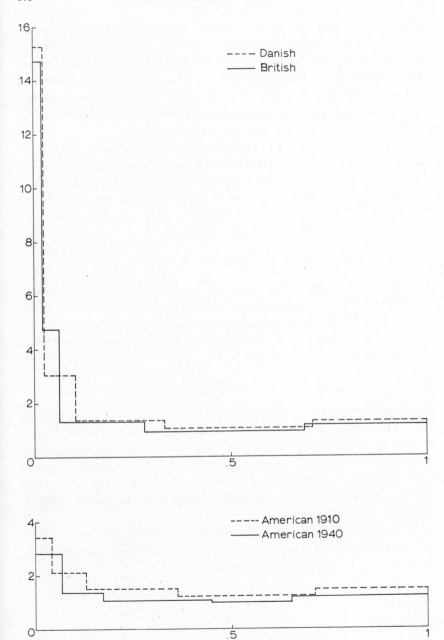

Fig. 5.5.   Moments of distances and status

is similar to Figure 5.2 (p. 279) in that the successive limit proportions $\pi_1, \ldots, \pi_5$ are measured horizontally. However, in the present figure the average distances (the adjusted $\bar{d}_i$'s in the last column of Table 5.11) are measured vertically, whereas we had travel times from the limit distribution in the earlier figure.[1] The area of the rectangle below each horizontal line segment is thus equal to $\pi_i \bar{d}_i$ for some i, so that the total area below all five line segments equals the overall average distance $\bar{d}$.

When we move from left to right (from the society's top to its bottom), we observe that the successive horizontal line segments move downward until the fourth status category is reached, after which they move upward. It is important to note that in both the British and the Danish cases this fourth category is the *median status category* in the sense that it contains the midpoint of the status ranking in equilibrium:

$$\pi_1 + \pi_2 + \pi_3 < \tfrac{1}{2} \quad \text{and} \quad \pi_1 + \pi_2 + \pi_3 + \pi_4 > \tfrac{1}{2}$$

The regularity revealed by the figure is an implication of the linear distance model (6.1). It will be proved in the next paragraph that, under the condition of this model, the difference between the average distances from two adjacent status categories can be expressed in terms of their (successive) distance and the limit proportions:

$$(6.6) \qquad \bar{d}_{i+1} - \bar{d}_i = (\pi_1 + \ldots + \pi_i - \pi_{i+1} - \ldots - \pi_n) d_{i, i+1}$$

Since successive distances are positive, the sign of $\bar{d}_{i+1} - \bar{d}_i$ is the same as that of the expression in parentheses on the right. This expression is negative for small values of i (high status categories); it increases with successively larger i values and it becomes positive when we have passed the median status category. Therefore, when we start at the society's top, the average distances from the successive categories decline until the median category, and they increase thereafter.

To prove that (6.6) is true under condition (6.1) we shall derive a more general result under condition (6.5). We define the rth order moment of the distances $d_{i1}, \ldots, d_{in}$ from the ith category:

$$(6.7) \qquad \mu_{ir} = \sum_{j=1}^{n} \pi_j d_{ij}^r$$

---

[1] Recall from the discussion below eq. (5.17) that d_i is equal to the average of d and the travel time from the limit distribution to the ith status category. Hence the vertical variables of the two figures are linear functions of each other. See also Problem 13.

In particular, consider these moments for two adjacent categories:

$$\mu_{ir} = \sum_{j=1}^{i-1} \pi_j d_{ij}^r + \pi_{i+1} d_{i,i+1}^r + \sum_{j=i+2}^{n} \pi_j d_{ij}^r$$

$$\mu_{i+1,r} = \sum_{j=1}^{i-1} \pi_j d_{i+1,j}^r + \pi_i d_{i,i+1}^r + \sum_{j=i+2}^{n} \pi_j d_{i+1,j}^r$$

and subtract the first equation from the second:

(6.8) $$\mu_{i+1,r} - \mu_{ir} = \sum_{j=1}^{i-1} \pi_j (d_{i+1,j}^r - d_{ij}^r) + (\pi_i - \pi_{i+1}) d_{i,i+1}^r$$

$$+ \sum_{j=i+2}^{n} \pi_j (d_{i+1,j}^r - d_{ij}^r)$$

In the first summation on the right we have $j < i$, so that

$$d_{i+1,j}^r - d_{ij}^r = d_{j,i+1}^r - d_{ji}^r = d_{i,i+1}^r$$

follows from (6.5). Hence the first right-hand term in (6.8) can be simplified to $(\pi_1 + \ldots + \pi_{i-1}) d_{i,i+1}^r$. In the last term we have $j > i+1$ and hence $d_{i+1,j}^r - d_{ij}^r = -d_{i,i+1}^r$, so that the equation may be written in the simpler form

(6.9) $$\mu_{i+1,r} - \mu_{ir} = (\pi_1 + \ldots + \pi_i - \pi_{i+1} - \ldots - \pi_n) d_{i,i+1}^r$$

Since the moment μ_{ir} coincides with the mean $\bar{d}_i$ for $r = 1$, this also proves that (6.6) is true under condition (6.1).

We may apply a reasoning similar to that below (6.6) to conclude that under the generalized distance model (6.5) the rth moment of the distances declines until the median status category and increases thereafter. This is also true for the rth root of this moment, $\mu_{ir}^{1/r}$, which is shown in the lower part of Figure 5.5 for the two sets of American data, because this root is a monotonically increasing function of the moment.[1] The use of the rth root is preferred because it has the same dimension (generations) as the average distances which are shown in the upper part of the figure for the British and Danish data. Note that this root exceeds the corresponding average distance $\bar{d}_i$ when $r > 1$; see Problem 14.

---

[1] These roots (in the order $i = 1, \ldots, 5$) take the following values on the basis of the d_{ij}'s implied by the generalized distance model (6.5):

1910	3.41	2.10	1.51	1.19	1.45
1940	2.81	1.36	1.09	.99	1.16

The Moment Functions as Determinants of the Intergenerational Occupational Mobility Process

Figure 5.5 shows that the pictures of the British and Danish average distances are nearly the same. This is important because (6.6) implies that, given the limit proportions, the successive distances $d_{i,\,i+1}$ are determined by the average distances in the left-hand side of the equation. Since the successive distances determine all distances and thereby the transition matrix, we may conclude that the British and Danish data reveal approximately the same intergenerational occupational mobility process. It is of course true that the Danish $\bar{d}_2$ is much smaller than the British $\bar{d}_2$, but the figure clearly indicates that this is simply due to the fact that the Danish π_2 is much larger than the British π_2. We may be confident that, if we had reduced the size of the second Danish status category by merging its less prestigious occupations with the third, $\bar{d}_2$ would have moved in the direction of the British value.

The lower part of Figure 5.5 shows that the behavior of $\mu_{ir}^{1/r}$ for the two sets of American data is also quite similar except that those of 1910 appear to be consistently a little higher than the corresponding values of 1940. However, the difference between the two is minor compared with that between the lower and the upper part of the figure, so let us neglect them in first approximation. Since (6.9) implies that the successive distances can be determined from these r^{th} roots of rth order moments when r and the limit proportions are given, we may conclude that the American intergenerational occupational mobility process as revealed by these data has remained roughly the same from 1910 to 1940 with the exception of the change in r, which measures the extent to which shortcuts between nonadjacent status categories can be made, and the change in the relative magnitude of the status categories as measured by the limit proportions.

The Implied Values of the Transition Matrices

As in the case of the logit model for election data (Section 4.6) we regard the distance models as simple descriptive devices and we will not, therefore, consider statistical tests for the hypothesis that these models are acceptable on the basis of the four samples. Even so, it is of considerable importance to know whether the fit is good or bad, particularly at the level of the transition matrix. Write $\hat{p}_{ij} = \hat{\pi}_{ij}/\pi_i$ for the $(i, j)^{\text{th}}$ transition probability implied by the distance model. These adjusted values are shown in the first five columns of Table 5.12. To verify how far the ith row of $\hat{\mathbf{P}} = [\hat{p}_{ij}]$ deviates

TABLE 5.12

ADJUSTED VALUES OF TRANSITION PROBABILITIES AND THEIR INFORMATION INACCURACIES

Father's status category	Subject's status category					Information inaccuracy
	1	2	3	4	5	
British						
1	.388	.176	.183	.164	.088	.0249
2	.097	.260	.270	.242	.130	.0286
3	.019	.052	.390	.350	.189	.0107
4	.009	.024	.183	.509	.274	.0027
5	.006	.017	.130	.360	.486	.0080
Danish						
1	.419	.197	.173	.135	.076	.0259
2	.059	.319	.280	.218	.123	.0056
3	.018	.100	.397	.309	.175	.0074
4	.009	.047	.187	.484	.274	.0035
5	.006	.034	.136	.353	.470	.0029
American 1910						
1	.207	.179	.260	.200	.155	.0024
2	.083	.255	.308	.207	.148	.0017
3	.045	.116	.450	.234	.155	.0024
4	.024	.053	.159	.512	.252	.0006
5	.022	.045	.125	.301	.507	.0010
American 1940						
1	.279	.151	.268	.127	.174	.0129
2	.095	.219	.351	.149	.187	.0073
3	.066	.136	.434	.164	.200	.0018
4	.041	.077	.218	.323	.342	.0015
5	.033	.056	.155	.200	.556	.0022

from the corresponding row of Table 5.5 we compute the information inaccuracy,

$$(6.10) \qquad I_i = \sum_{j=1}^{n} p_{ij} \log \frac{p_{ij}}{\hat{p}_{ij}} \qquad\qquad i = 1, \ldots, n$$

This is a measure of the inaccuracy of the distance model (relative to the
observed transition matrix) concerning the probabilities of transition from
the ith status category. The weighted average of these inaccuracies with

$\pi_1, \ldots, \pi_n$ as weights is identical with the information inaccuracy (6.3) that was minimized:

$$\sum_{i=1}^{n} \pi_i \sum_{j=1}^{n} p_{ij} \log \frac{p_{ij}}{\hat{p}_{ij}} = \sum_{i=1}^{n} \sum_{j=1}^{n} \pi_{ij} \log \frac{\pi_{ij}/\pi_i}{\hat{\pi}_{ij}/\pi_i}$$

$$= \sum_{i=1}^{n} \sum_{j=1}^{n} \pi_{ij} \log \frac{\pi_{ij}}{\hat{\pi}_{ij}}$$

The inaccuracies (6.10) are shown in the last column of Table 5.12. They indicate that the fit for $i = 1$ and 2, particularly $i = 1$, tends to be poorer than that of the other categories. This is not at all surprising, because the weights of I_1 and I_2 in the minimization procedure are π_1 and π_2, respectively, which are considerably smaller than the other limit proportions. In fact, the observed p_{ij}'s for $i = 1$ and 2 are frequently based on small samples, which may easily lead to rather large deviations from the corresponding $\hat{p}_{ij}$'s. As an example, take $p_{15} = .062$ for the British matrix of Table 5.5, which is determined as the ratio 8/129, the number of fathers in the first status category being 129.[1] Assume, for simplicity's sake, that the conventional multinomial conditions are satisfied; then the standard error of the estimate .062 is of the order of .02, which is relatively large.[2] The corresponding adjusted value of the probability is .088 (see Table 5.12) and it is based on the entire sample via the distance model, not only on the subsample of 129. Therefore, one should expect that such an adjusted value will typically be a better estimate of the true transition probability when the distance model gives at least a substantially correct description of the mobility process.

Fitting Successive Distances*

The minimization of the criterion function (6.3) with respect to its arguments was performed by means of a technique described by SHANNO (1969); we refer to this article for details. The technique requires an algebraic formulation of the gradient of the criterion function (the vector of its first-order derivatives). The function and its gradient are evaluated at certain initial values (for which zero distances are chosen) and the matrix of second-order derivatives is approximated by an initial estimate (the unit matrix in this

---

[1] See the first row of Table 5.13 below. The number 8 is determined as 6+2, because the lowest categories of Table 5.13 are combined in the present analysis.

[2] This standard error is computed as $\sqrt{(.062)(.938)/129}$.

case). Thereafter a search is made for lower and lower values of the criterion function, based on new values of the gradient as well as improved estimates of the second-order derivatives, until the gradient is sufficiently close to a zero vector.

Finding an algebraic expression for the gradient is the essential element of the technique. This is pursued in Problems 15 to 17, the results of which may be summarized as follows. Consider the generalized distance model (6.5) and write $\alpha = i + \frac{1}{2}$ and $b_\alpha = d^r_{i,i+1}$; hence b_α is the rth power of the distance between the $(\alpha - \frac{1}{2})^{\text{th}}$ and the $(\alpha + \frac{1}{2})^{\text{th}}$ status categories, and these b's are used as the arguments of the criterion function. Equation (6.5) can then be written in the form

$$(6.11) \qquad d_{ij} = \left(\sum_\alpha b_\alpha \right)^{1/r}$$

where the summation range is min $(i, j) < \alpha < \max (i, j)$. [Note that, in contrast to (6.5), the restriction $i < j$ need not be made.] Then, for n status categories, the derivative of (6.3) with respect to b_α is

$$(6.12) \qquad \frac{\partial I}{\partial b_\alpha} = \frac{1}{r} \sum_{h=1}^{n} \sum_{k=1}^{n} \frac{\pi_{hk}}{\hat{\pi}_{hk}} \sum_{i < \alpha} \sum_{j > \alpha} (c_{hi} c_{jk} + c_{hj} c_{ik}) d_{ij}^{1-r}$$

where $\alpha = 1\frac{1}{2}, 2\frac{1}{2}, \ldots, n - \frac{1}{2}$ and

$$(6.13) \qquad c_{ij} = s^{ij} + \pi_i \pi_j$$

with s^{ij} being defined as the $(i, j)^{\text{th}}$ element of $\mathbf{S}^{-1}$. In the case $r = 1$ we have $d_{ij}^{1-r} = 1$ in (6.12); it appears that the derivative can then be simplified to

$$(6.14) \qquad \frac{\partial I}{\partial b_\alpha} = -2 \sum_{h=1}^{n} \sum_{k=1}^{n} \frac{\pi_{hk}}{\hat{\pi}_{hk}} \left(\sum_{i < \alpha} c_{hi} \right) \left(\sum_{i < \alpha} c_{ki} \right)$$

5.7. The Effects of Aggregating Status Categories

The transition matrices considered in the previous sections are all based on status categories that were defined prior to our analysis. However, the problem of grouping occupations into such categories is of sufficient importance for a further analysis. Recall that we considered on p. 300 the possibility that particular occupations are deleted from the second Danish status category and added to the third. We may also ask whether it is appropriate to combine, as was done in Table 5.5, the semi-skilled and the unskilled workers, or whether it is better to keep them as two distinct categories. Even if it is in principle better to choose the latter alternative, one may nevertheless decide in favor of the former on the ground that the available observations do not permit the estimation of a large number of transition probabilities with sufficient precision. The relevant question is then, how serious are the consequences of such a specification error?

When Does Aggregation Lead to a New Markov Chain?

Our starting point is a Markov chain model for intergenerational mobility based on n occupational categories, with transition matrix $\mathbf{P} = [p_{ij}]$. Suppose that we group these categories into $G < n$ sets of categories, $S_1, \ldots, S_G$ in such a way that each category belongs to exactly one S_g, where $g = 1, \ldots, G$. We are interested in the question of whether the Markov chain model is valid at the level of sets of categories for whatever initial occupational distribution $q_{01}, \ldots, q_{0n}$ at the level of the individual categories.

To answer this question we consider two status categories, i and j, with $i \in S_g$ and $j \in S_h$. The transition from i to j is $q_{0i}p_{ij}$ on the basis of the initial distribution $q_{01}, , \ldots, q_{0n}$. The total transition from S_g to S_h is thus

$$\sum_{i \in S_g} q_{0i} \sum_{j \in S_h} p_{ij}$$

If the Markov chain model is valid at the level of $S_1, \ldots, S_G$ with transition matrix $[P_{gh}]$, this expression should be of the form $Q_{0g}P_{gh}$, where Q_{0g} is the sum over $i \in S_g$ of q_{0i}. This clearly requires

$$(7.1) \qquad \sum_{j \in S_h} p_{ij} = P_{gh} \quad \text{for each } i \in S_g \text{ and for each pair } (S_g, S_h)$$

or, in words, the probability of transition from any category of S_g to the set S_h should be the same for all categories of S_g, and this should be true for all pairs of sets S_g and S_h.

Application to a British Transition Matrix for Seven Status Categories

The transition matrix based on British data that was discussed at length in the previous sections is actually a condensation of the original 7×7 matrix published by GLASS and HALL (1954). The number of observed father-son pairs in their sample is shown in the upper half of Table 5.13 and the corresponding transition matrix in the lower half. The seven status categories, in their terminology, are the following:

1. Professional and high administrative
2. Managerial and executive
3. Inspectional, supervisory, and other nonmanual (higher grade)

TABLE 5.13

BASIC DATA ON SEVEN STATUS CATEGORIES

Father's status category	Subject's status category							Total
	1	2	3	4	5	6	7	
	Numbers of observations							
1	50	19	26	8	18	6	2	129
2	16	40	34	18	31	8	3	150
3	12	35	65	66	123	23	21	345
4	11	20	58	110	223	64	32	518
5	14	36	114	185	714	258	189	1510
6	0	6	19	40	179	143	71	458
7	0	3	14	32	141	91	106	387
	Transition matrix							
1	.388	.147	.202	.062	.140	.047	.016	1
2	.107	.267	.227	.120	.207	.053	.020	1
3	.035	.101	.188	.191	.357	.067	.061	1
4	.021	.039	.112	.212	.431	.124	.062	1
5	.009	.024	.075	.123	.473	.171	.125	1
6	.000	.013	.041	.087	.391	.312	.155	1
7	.000	.008	.036	.083	.364	.235	.274	1

4. Same (lower grade)
5. Skilled manual and routine grades of nonmanual
6. Semi-skilled manual
7. Unskilled manual.

The 5×5 matrix shown in Table 5.5 was obtained by combining the categories $(3, 4)$ as well as $(6, 7)$.[1] To verify whether condition (7.1) is satisfied by this aggregation procedure we compute the left-hand side of this equation for each i which is aggregated ($i = 3, 4, 6$ and 7) and for each set S_h. The results are shown in Table 5.14 and indicate the condition is not satisfied. The chance of moving to higher status, $S_h = (1)$ or (2), is

---

[1] There are some minor discrepancies, at most one unit in the third decimal place, between Table 5.5 and the transition matrix of Table 5.13. This is due to the fact that the former table has been derived from the mean first passage times published by Beshers and Laumann and reproduced in Table 5.6 (see Problem 7 for the derivation). This procedure was preferred because it insured uniform treatment of all transition matrices of Table 5.5.

TABLE 5.14

TRANSITION PROBABILITIES FROM STATUS CATEGORIES TO SETS OF CATEGORIES

Father's status (i)	Subject's status (S_h)				
	(1)	(2)	(3, 4)	(5)	(6, 7)
3	.035	.101	.380	.357	.128
4	.021	.039	.324	.431	.185
6	.000	.013	.129	.391	.467
7	.000	.008	.119	.364	.509

consistently larger for a man whose father is in $i = 3$ than for a man whose father is in $i = 4$, and the situation is exactly the opposite for the chance of moving to lower status, $S_h = (5)$ or $(6, 7)$. The picture for $i = 6$ and $i = 7$ is essentially the same.

Basically, the transition matrix of Table 5.13 shows the same regularities as those of Table 5.5. The largest element of each column is typically the diagonal element, and the elements tend to decline monotonically when we move either upward or downward from the diagonal. This suggests that it is preferable to analyze the transition matrix at the 7×7 level. We shall do so in this section, but we shall also examine the degree of distortion caused by aggregation at various levels.[1]

Aggregation to Six and to Five Sets of Categories

Since status categories can be ranked according to prestige, one should combine only adjacent categories. There are then six ways of combining so that $G = 6$ sets of categories are obtained:

$$(1, 2) \quad (3) \quad (4) \quad (5) \quad (6) \quad (7)$$
$$(1) \quad (2, 3) \quad (4) \quad (5) \quad (6) \quad (7)$$

and so on. For brevity's sake, we shall indicate each such grouping by specifying only the sets of categories that contain more than one. The six cases are thus

(7.2)
$$\begin{array}{ll} (1, 2) & (4, 5) \\ (2, 3) & (5, 6) \\ (3, 4) & (6, 7) \end{array}$$

---

[1] For a further mathematical analysis of aggregation in Markov chain models see KEMENY and SNELL (1960, Sections 6.3 and 6.4).

At the level of $G = 5$ sets of categories we have, first, the cases in which three successive categories are combined:

(7.3)

(1, 2, 3)	(4, 5, 6)
(2, 3, 4)	(5, 6, 7)
(3, 4, 5)	

In addition to these five possibilities there are 10 obtained by forming two pairs, listed below. The total number of cases for $G = 5$ sets of categories is thus 15.

(7.4)

(1, 2), (3, 4)	(2, 3), (4, 5)	(3, 4), (5, 6)	(4, 5), (6, 7)
(1, 2), (4, 5)	(2, 3), (5, 6)	(3, 4), (6, 7)	
(1, 2), (5, 6)	(2, 3), (6, 7)		
(1, 2), (6, 7)			

In the remainder of this section we shall make a systematic comparison of the original seven categories and the combinations (7.2) through (7.4) for the main descriptive measures developed in this chapter: the limit distribution, the second largest latent root of the transition matrix, the descendance effects, the degree of symmetry of the exchange matrix, and the distance model and its parameters.

The Limit Distribution

When the number of status categories is reduced from seven to six by combining the first two into one set, $(1, 2)$, the procedure is to add the first two rows of the upper half of Table 5.13 and also to add the first two columns. This leads to a 6×6 matrix, and the transition matrix is then obtained by dividing each element of a row by the row sum. We act as if the Markov chain model is valid at the level of these six sets of status categories by computing the limit distribution,

(7.5)
$$[\pi'_{12} \quad \pi'_3 \quad \pi'_4 \quad \pi'_5 \quad \pi'_6 \quad \pi'_7]$$

as the characteristic row, normalized such that the elements add up to 1, of the 6×6 transition matrix corresponding to the unit root. Primes are attached to the π's to distinguish them from the limit proportions $\pi_1, \ldots, \pi_7$ of the 7×7 matrix; the notation π'_{12} indicates that this proportion refers to the first and second categories jointly.

A comparison of the vector (7.5) with the limit vector of the original 7×7 matrix will reveal two differences. First, the former fails to distinguish between the first two status categories; but this is an obvious effect and it

TABLE 5.15

LIMIT DISTRIBUTIONS AND THEIR INFORMATION INACCURACIES AT DIFFERENT LEVELS OF AGGREGATION

Aggregates	Status category 1	2	3	4	5	6	7	Information inaccuracy ($\times 10^6$)
Seven categories								
none	.0228	.0414	.0879	.1269	.4097	.1820	.1293	—
Six sets of categories								
(1, 2)	←.0661→		.0880	.1265	.4087	.1817	.1290	30
(2, 3)	.0225	←.1285→		.1271	.4102	.1822	.1295	4
(3, 4)	.0227	.0412	←.2146→		.4099	.1822	.1293	0
(4, 5)	.0231	.0417	.0885	←.5371→		.1813	.1284	10
(5, 6)	.0238	.0425	.0902	.1289	←.5876→		.1271	112
(6, 7)	.0228	.0412	.0878	.1268	.4093	←.3121→		1
Five sets of categories: one triple								
(1, 2, 3)	←.1556→			.1262	.4080	.1815	.1287	48
(2, 3, 4)	.0222	←.2548→			.4107	.1826	.1297	13
(3, 4, 5)	.0232	.0420	←.6257→			.1809	.1282	18
(4, 5, 6)	.0245	.0432	.0915	←.7157→			.1252	244
(5, 6, 7)	.0240	.0427	.0906	.1293	←.7134→			154
Five sets of categories: two pairs								
(1, 2), (3, 4)	←.0657→		←.2143→		.4090	.1819	.1291	20
(1, 2), (4, 5)	←.0667→		.0886	←.5357→		.1809	.1281	62
(1, 2), (5, 6)	←.0682→		.0903	.1284	←.5863→		.1268	210
(1, 2), (6, 7)	←.0659→		.0879	.1264	.4084	←.3115→		26
(2, 3), (4, 5)	.0228	←.1295→		←.5377→		.1814	.1286	4
(2, 3), (5, 6)	.0235	←.1319→		.1290	←.5883→		.1273	78
(2, 3), (6, 7)	.0225	←.1283→		.1270	.4098	←.3125→		8
(3, 4), (5, 6)	.0237	.0422	←.2188→		←.5881→		.1272	91
(3, 4), (6, 7)	.0227	.0410	←.2144→		.4095	←.3124→		3
(4, 5), (6, 7)	.0231	.0416	.0883	←.5366→		←.3104→		4

would take place even if condition (7.1) were satisfied for this particular aggregation procedure. Second, the proportions corresponding to the status categories that are not combined are different in the two vectors when (7.1) is not satisfied. This is the distortion of the limit distribution caused by the aggregation.

Table 5.15 presents a picture of this distortion. It appears to be quite small in most cases, usually not more than one or two units in the third decimal place, which is the reason why four decimal places are presented. A simple way of measuring the degree of distortion is by means of the information inaccuracy, which in the case of (7.5) takes the form

$$(7.6) \qquad I_{12} = (\pi_1 + \pi_2) \log \frac{\pi_1 + \pi_2}{\pi'_{12}} + \sum_{i=3}^{7} \pi_i \log \frac{\pi_i}{\pi'_i}$$

where I_{12} stands for the inaccuracy associated with the aggregate $(1, 2)$. These information inaccuracies are given in the last column of Table 5.15. They are all smaller than 70×10^{-6} (natural logs) except for all cases that contain the combination $(5, 6)$. The relatively substantial effect of this particular combination is not really surprising, given that the fifth and sixth categories are the two largest groups and jointly account for almost 60 per cent of the population in the equilibrium situation. However, even the aggregation that leads to the largest inaccuracy – the one containing $(4, 5, 6)$ – is not really far off.

The Rate of Convergence Toward the Limit Distribution

In Section 5.2 we concluded that λ_2^2, the square of the second largest latent root of the transition matrix, is a measure for the rate of convergence of the occupational distributions of successive generations toward the limit distribution, for whatever initial distribution. We also concluded that it is a more accurate measure for later generations than for early generations and that $|\lambda_3|/|\lambda_2|$, where λ_3 is the third largest latent root of the transition matrix, determines the accuracy of λ_2^2 for the rate of convergence during earlier generations.

The roots λ_2 and λ_3 are shown in the first two columns of Table 5.16. They are real and positive without exception. The λ_2 value of the 7×7 case is .500 and those at various levels of aggregation are mostly (but not all) below this value. The differences are small, however, and there are only two cases with $\lambda_2 < .45$. The ratios λ_3/λ_2 vary between about 40 and 55 per cent. We conclude that the rate of convergence is described almost identically at all levels of aggregation considered here.

TABLE 5.16

LATENT ROOTS AND DESCENDANCE EFFECTS AT DIFFERENT LEVELS OF AGGREGATION

Aggregates	Latent roots λ_2	λ_3	Descendance effect of status category 1	2	3	4	5	6	7
			Seven categories						
none	.500	.255	10.2	3.46	.42	.025	.031	.22	.29
			Six sets of categories						
(1, 2)	.491	.212	←5.39→		.50	.025	.034	.23	.32
(2, 3)	.475	.255	12.1	←.98→		.044	.027	.25	.33
(3, 4)	.485	.255	10.6	3.45	←.14→		.031	.23	.31
(4, 5)	.492	.243	10.8	3.44	.36	←.010→		.21	.29
(5, 6)	.491	.237	10.7	3.39	.34	.010	←.069→		.28
(6, 7)	.501	.255	10.2	3.47	.43	.025	.030	←.25→	
			Five sets of categories: one triple						
(1, 2, 3)	.430	.159	←2.23→			.089	.029	.35	.51
(2, 3, 4)	.441	.255	13.5	←.38→			.024	.27	.37
(3, 4, 5)	.453	.230	12.7	3.32	←.000→			.22	.30
(4, 5, 6)	.480	.221	11.4	3.31	.26	←.040→			.26
(5, 6, 7)	.486	.225	11.1	3.39	.31	.004	←.093→		
			Five sets of categories: two pairs						
(1, 2), (3, 4)	.473	.211	←5.49→		←.17→		.034	.25	.35
(1, 2), (4, 5)	.482	.198	←5.60→		.45	←.012→		.23	.32
(1, 2), (5, 6)	.481	.180	←5.56→		.42	.010	←.076→		.31
(1, 2), (6, 7)	.491	.212	←5.40→		.51	.025	.033	←.27→	
(2, 3), (4, 5)	.466	.242	13.1	←.89→		←.006→		.24	.32
(2, 3), (5, 6)	.463	.234	13.0	←.85→		.021	←0.69→		.31
(2, 3), (6, 7)	.475	.255	12.0	←.99→		.044	.026	←.28→	
(3, 4), (5, 6)	.476	.236	11.2	3.37	←.10→		←.071→		.29
(3, 4), (6, 7)	.485	.255	10.6	3.46	←.14→		.030	←.26→	
(4, 5), (6, 7)	.493	.243	10.8	3.45	.37	←.010→		←.24→	

The Descendance Effects

The descendance effects c_i were introduced in eq. (2.22) in the last subsection of Section 5.2. They are shown in the last seven columns of Table 5.16. The figures in the first row, corresponding to all seven status categories, indicate that they decline from the first category to the fourth and then increase again. This behavior is similar to that which we found in Table 5.4

but the present figures show much more regularity, which is not entirely surprising given that we are now dealing with occupations arranged in status categories.

The descendance effects after aggregation are shown in the successive rows of the table after the first. A comparison of these figures with the corresponding ones on top shows that they are usually of the same order of magnitude and that the descendance effects of status categories that are combined are usually between the values before combination. For example, when the first two categories are combined, we obtain descendance effects varying between 5.39 and 5.60, and the descendance effects of these two categories separately are 10.2 and 3.46, respectively, as shown in the first line (before any aggregation). The only exceptions are those obtained by aggregating the fourth and fifth categories, but they are no real exceptions. Recall that the descendance effects decline from the first to the fourth category and increase thereafter. By far the smallest values are those of the fourth and fifth categories. If we imagine that the minimum is somewhere around the borderline between the two, it seems quite plausible that the descendance effect for their combination is lower than that of either category.

It must be admitted, though, that there are some aggregations which lead to rather large discrepancies from the corresponding figures on top. An example is the case $(1, 2, 3)$, for which the descendance effects of the fourth, sixth and seventh categories are substantially larger than those without aggregation. Such discrepancies should be expected for the following reasons. The largest latent root of any transition matrix is a unit root and the corresponding characteristic column is always ι (except for an arbitrary multiplicative scalar). The limit distribution π' is affected by the aggregation, but it is always a characteristic row corresponding to the same root and it always satisfies $\iota'\pi = 1$, so that it should not cause too much surprise when the limit proportions remain substantially unchanged when adjacent categories are combined. But the second largest latent root λ_2 and the corresponding characteristic column and row ($\mathbf{u}_2$ and $\mathbf{v}_2'$) are all affected by the aggregation.[1] The descendance effect c_i defined in (2.22) depends on both this column and this row besides on π, and it does stand to reason that it is more sensitive to aggregation than is the limit distribution.

---

[1] Note that the aggregation $(1, 2, 3)$, mentioned in the beginning of this paragraph as a case of substantial discrepancies of descendance effects, is also the case with the largest discrepancy of the root λ_2.

The Symmetry of the Exchange Matrices

The exchange matrix $\Pi = [\pi_{ij}] = [\pi_i p_{ij}]$ of the 7×7 transition matrix is shown in the upper half of Table 5.17; the lower half contains adjusted values that will be discussed in the next subsection. Again, we conclude that Π is close to symmetry. A simple measure for the discrepancy from symmetry is the expected information of the message that transforms the

TABLE 5.17

OBSERVED AND ADJUSTED EXCHANGE MATRICES FOR THE 7×7 CASE

Father's status category	Subject's status category						
	1	2	3	4	5	6	7
	Observed						
1	.009	.003	.005	.001	.003	.001	.000
2	.004	.011	.009	.005	.009	.002	.001
3	.003	.009	.017	.017	.031	.006	.005
4	.003	.005	.014	.027	.055	.016	.008
5	.004	.010	.031	.050	.194	.070	.051
6	.000	.002	.008	.016	.071	.057	.028
7	.000	.001	.005	.011	.047	.030	.035
	Adjusted						
1	.0088	.0040	.0028	.0019	.0034	.0011	.0007
2	.0040	.0108	.0075	.0051	.0091	.0030	.0019
3	.0028	.0075	.0219	.0149	.0265	.0088	.0055
4	.0019	.0051	.0149	.0281	.0499	.0166	.0104
5	.0034	.0091	.0265	.0499	.2083	.0692	.0433
6	.0011	.0030	.0088	.0166	.0692	.0513	.0321
7	.0007	.0019	.0055	.0104	.0433	.0321	.0354

elements of the symmetrized exchange matrix, $\frac{1}{2}(\Pi + \Pi')$, to the corresponding elements of the original exchange matrix:

$$(7.7) \qquad \sum_{i=1}^{n} \sum_{j=1}^{n} \pi_{ij} \log \frac{2\pi_{ij}}{\pi_{ij} + \pi_{ji}}$$

These expressions are information inaccuracies corresponding to $\frac{1}{2}(\pi_{ij} + \pi_{ji})$ as estimates of π_{ij}. They are shown in the first column of Table 5.18, both for the 7×7 case and at various levels of aggregation. Without aggregation the value of (7.7) is a little over .002 nit, for the 6×6 cases it is between

TABLE 5.18

INFORMATION INACCURACIES FOR SYMMETRY OF THE EXCHANGE MATRIX AND FOR THE
DISTANCE MODEL

Aggregates	Symmetry		Distance model		Expected mutual information
	Direct	Indirect	Direct	Indirect	
Seven categories					
None	.00219		.00891		.117
Six sets of categories					
(1, 2)	.00102	.00096	.00753	.00744	.115
(2, 3)	.00187	.00187	.00802	.00680	.108
(3, 4)	.00147	.00147	.00892	.00687	.109
(4, 5)	.00166	.00164	.00958	.00717	.108
(5, 6)	.00118	.00119	.00635	.00449	.102
(6, 7)	.00183	.00183	.00739	.00737	.114
Five sets of categories: one triple					
(1, 2, 3)	.00052	.00053	.00474	.00481	.099
(2, 3, 4)	.00130	.00133	.00828	.00575	.092
(3, 4, 5)	.00116	.00115	.00764	.00413	.084
(4, 5, 6)	.00067	.00058	.00587	.00351	.087
(5, 6, 7)	.00066	.00064	.00261	.00261	.089
Five sets of categories: two pairs					
(1, 2), (3, 4)	.00050	.00048	.00768	.00564	.106
(1, 2), (4, 5)	.00057	.00050	.00826	.00579	.105
(1, 2), (5, 6)	.00064	.00059	.00573	.00375	.100
(1, 2), (6, 7)	.00067	.00061	.00603	.00591	.111
(2, 3), (4, 5)	.00135	.00133	.00869	.00508	.098
(2, 3), (5, 6)	.00090	.00090	.00544	.00244	.092
(2, 3), (6, 7)	.00155	.00155	.00674	.00552	.104
(3, 4), (5, 6)	.00047	.00050	.00677	.00292	.093
(3, 4), (6, 7)	.00133	.00134	.00773	.00567	.105
(4, 5), (6, 7)	.00149	.00148	.00842	.00597	.104

.001 and .002 nit, and for the 5×5 cases it is between about .0005 and .0015 nit. These results suggest that aggregation leads to exchange matrices that are more symmetric.

This conclusion is premature, however, because we are comparing exchange matrices consisting of 49, 36 and 25 elements, and these are not directly comparable. Less detail is shown in a 6×6 matrix than in a 7×7 matrix, and less again in a 5×5 matrix, which tends to conceal deviations from symmetry.[1] To verify whether there is really less symmetry at the 7×7 level than after aggregation one may proceed as follows. Take the 7×7 matrix shown in the upper half of Table 5.17 and form the $(1, 2)$ aggregate by adding the first two rows of this matrix and also its first two columns. This leads to a 6×6 matrix, and an information inaccuracy similar to (7.7) can then be computed which measures how asymmetric the 7×7 matrix is at the level of this aggregation. Its value $(.00096)$ is shown in the second row and column of Table 5.18. Since it is lower than the value obtained when (7.7) is applied to the 6×6 exchange matrix directly (which is $.00102$), we may conclude that in this case the 7×7 exchange matrix exhibits more, not less, symmetry. A comparison of the first two columns of Table 5.18 indicates that in 10 cases out of 21 the difference between the two information inaccuracies is only one unit or less in the fifth decimal place. When the difference is larger, it is usually not much larger but the "indirect" value is generally smaller than the "direct" value (9 versus 2 cases). The conclusion is that the 7×7 exchange matrix is approximately as symmetric as the exchange matrices after aggregation but that, when there are differences in this regard, the 7×7 matrix is usually more symmetric.

It is also interesting to note that for the particular aggregation used in the previous sections, containing the pairs $(3, 4)$ and $(6, 7)$, the two information inaccuracies are a little over $.0013$, which exceeds a substantial majority of the inaccuracies of other combinations of five sets of status categories. Therefore, if we consider the upper left-hand matrix of Table 5.8 as approximately symmetric, we should certainly be willing to accept most other 5×5 cases as having approximately symmetric exchange matrices.

The Accuracy of the Distance Model

The third column of Table 5.18 contains the minimum values of the information inaccuracy corresponding to the linear distance model (6.1), and the last column specifies the expected mutual information I_0 defined in (6.4). These I_0's are all of the order of one-tenth of a nit. The adjusted 7×7 exchange matrix implied by the distance model is shown in the lower half of Table 5.17.

As in the case of the first column of Table 5.18, the minimum inaccuracy

---

[1] Basically, the point made here is identical with that of footnote 1 on page 83, which is concerned with value share predictions.

of the 7×7 case tends to exceed those of the 6×6 cases, but the figures of the third column indicate that this rule is not without exceptions when it is applied to the distance model. This is pursued in the fourth column, which is similar to the second. The figures of the fourth column are the minimum information inaccuracies in the 6×6 and 5×5 cases that are obtained when the adjustment of the distance model is based on the 7×7 exchange matrix with appropriate rows and columns added, not on the 6×6 or 5×5 exchange matrices. The results indicate that, apart from two minor exceptions, this alternative procedure (via the 7×7 exchange matrix) leads to a lower information inaccuracy. The difference is substantial in several cases, and larger than 50 per cent in two. Our conclusion is that aggregation may lead to a poorer fit of the distance model, and sometimes a considerably poorer fit.

Again note that the information inaccuracy of the aggregation applied in the previous sections, with $(3, 4)$ and $(6, 7)$ as the two pairs, exceeds a substantial majority of the other 5×5 inaccuracies. The conclusion drawn at the end of the previous subsection on symmetry may therefore be extended to the accuracy of the distance model.

Distances at Different Levels of Aggregation

The first row of Table 5.19 contains the adjusted values of all 21 distances d_{ij} $(i < j)$, computed from the linear distance model, at the 7×7 level. The other rows specify the same distances after aggregation insofar as these distances are specified by the particular aggregation procedure. A dot indicates that this is not the case, and the table shows that this occurs frequently. For example, the second row concerns the aggregate $(1, 2)$, for which no distances are specified between any status category and the first, nor between any status category and the second. For six sets of status categories 10 of the 21 distances can be traced; this number drops to six for five sets of status categories obtained by forming a triple, and to only three for five sets obtained by forming two pairs.

Table 5.19 should be read column by column. To facilitate the discussion we consider first the successive distances, starting at the bottom: $d_{67}, d_{56},$ $\ldots, d_{12}$. The figures indicate that d_{67} equals either .52 or .53 and that $d_{56} = .57$ and $d_{45} = .65$. This holds at all relevant levels of aggregation. Furthermore, d_{34} equals 1.18 prior to aggregation and it varies between 1.14 and 1.20 after aggregation; d_{23} is equal to 3.29 when the seven status categories are individually distinguished and it takes values in the interval $(3.10, 3.30)$ after aggregation; and d_{12} equals 10.40 prior to aggregation and is between 9.61 and 10.45 after aggregation. Hence the sensitivity to aggre-

TABLE 5.19

DISTANCES BETWEEN STATUS CATEGORIES AT DIFFERENT LEVELS OF AGGREGATION

Aggregates	d_{12}	d_{13}	d_{14}	d_{15}	d_{16}	d_{17}	d_{23}	d_{24}	d_{25}	d_{26}	d_{27}	d_{34}	d_{35}	d_{36}	d_{37}	d_{45}	d_{46}	d_{47}	d_{56}	d_{57}	d_{67}
None	10.40	13.68	14.86	15.51	16.08	16.60	3.29	4.47	5.11	5.69	6.21	1.18	1.83	2.40	2.92	.65	1.22	1.74	.57	1.09	.52
(1, 2)	.	.	14.06	14.70	15.28	15.79	.	.	.	.	.	1.20	1.84	2.42	2.94	.65	1.22	1.74	.57	1.09	.52
(2, 3)	10.43	13.50	.	15.26	15.83	16.35	.	.	4.82	5.40	5.92	.	.	2.19	2.72	.65	1.22	1.74	.57	1.09	.52
(3, 4)	10.25	13.08	14.23	.	15.69	15.75	3.25	.	.	5.45	5.97	.	.	.	2.66	.	.	.	.57	1.09	.52
(4, 5)	9.91	13.71	14.89	.	.	.	3.18	4.32	.	.	.	1.14	.	.	.	.	.	1.52	.	1.09	.53
(5, 6)	10.41	.	.	15.54	.	.	3.30	4.48	5.13	.	5.84	.	1.83	.	.	.	.	.	.	.	.
(6, 7)	.	.	.	.	.	.	.	.	.	.	.	1.18	.	.	.	.65	.	1.74	.	.	.
(1, 2, 3)	10.19	12.72	.	14.29	14.86	15.38	.	.	.	.	.	.	.	.	.	.65	.	.	.57	1.10	.52
(2, 3, 4)	9.61	12.98	.	.	15.09	15.61	.	.	.	.	.	.	.	.	.	.	.	.	.57	1.09	.52
(3, 4, 5)	9.83	.	.	.	.	15.14	3.10	4.29	.	4.90	5.43	1.14	.	.	2.43	.	.	.	.	.	.53
(4, 5, 6)	.	.	.	.	.	.	3.15	.	.	.	5.53	.	.	.	.	.	.	1.52	.	.	.
(5, 6, 7)	.	.	14.12	.	.	.	.	.	.	.	.	.	.	.	.	.	.	.	.	.	.
(1, 2), (3, 4)	.	.	.	.	.	.	.	.	.	.	.	.	.	2.21	.	.65	1.22	.	.57	1.09	.52
(1, 2), (4, 5)	.	.	.	.	.	.	.	.	.	.	.	.	.	.	2.74	.	.	1.52	.	.	.53
(1, 2), (5, 6)	.	.	.	.	.	.	.	.	.	.	.	.	.	.	2.68	.	.	.	.	.	.
(1, 2), (6, 7)	.	.	.	.	.	.	.	.	.	.	.	1.16	1.85	.	.	.	.	.	.	.	.
(2, 3), (4, 5)	.	.	13.45	.	14.90	15.42	.	.	.	.	.	1.20	.	.	.	.	.	.	.	.	.52
(2, 3), (5, 6)	.	.	14.08	.	.	14.97	.	.	.	.	.	.	.	.	.	.	.	1.52	.	.	.
(2, 3), (6, 7)	.	.	.	14.73	.	.	.	.	.	.	.	.	.	.	.	.65	.	.	.	.	.
(3, 4), (5, 6)	9.95	.	.	.	.	.	.	.	.	.	5.56	.	.	.	.	.	.	.	.	.	.
(3, 4), (6, 7)	10.45	.	15.28	.	.	15.51	3.26	4.84	4.84	.	.	.	.	.	.	.	.	.	.	.	.
(4, 5), (6, 7)	10.26	13.52	.	.	.	.	3.26	.	.	.	.	.	.	.	.	.	.	.	.	.	.

gation increases for successive distances between higher status categories and the effect of aggregation on these distances is predominantly negative.

For the distances between status categories which have only one category in between, $d_{57}, d_{46}, \ldots, d_{13}$, we have a similar picture. There is virtually no aggregation effect for such distances which do not involve the two top categories (d_{57}, d_{46}, d_{35}). For d_{24} we have a value of 4.47 prior to aggregation and values ranging from 4.29 to 4.48 after aggregation, and $d_{13} = 13.68$ at the seven-category level and it takes values between 12.72 and 13.71 after aggregation.

All other distances refer to status categories that have at least two status categories in between, and here it appears to be quite important whether the latter categories are or are not combined. If they are combined, the distance between the former categories is reduced. The effect is clearly noticeable even at the lower status levels for which we found no appreciable aggregation effect in the cases discussed in the two previous paragraphs. Take d_{47}, which is 1.74 in all cases in which the fifth and sixth status categories are not combined but which reduces to 1.52 in all cases that contain (5, 6) as a pair; also d_{36}, which is about 2.4 when there is no pair (4, 5) but which reduces to about 2.2 when this combination is formed; and d_{25}, which is about 5.1 without (3, 4) as a pair but only about 4.8 when this pair is used as a combined status category. For d_{14} we have both this effect and also the increased variability which is associated with the higher status categories. Prior to aggregation we have $d_{14} = 14.86$; the range of d_{14} is from 14.12 to 14.89 when the second and third categories are not combined, and it is from 13.45 to 14.08 when (2, 3) occurs as a pair.

Status categories with three categories in between allow the possibility that these three are merged as one triple, which reduces their distance even more. An example is d_{37}, which is a little over 2.9 when no status categories between the third and the seventh are combined; this distance reduces to about 2.7 when one pair between these limits is formed, and to 2.43 when the triple (4, 5, 6) is formed. For d_{26} we have a similar reduction (from 5.69 to about 5.4 to 4.90) and also for d_{15}, d_{16}, d_{17} and d_{27}. The last three distances have four or more categories in between, which allow the possibilities of two pairs. For d_{17} we have a value of 16.60 prior to aggregation, values ranging from 15.75 to 16.35 when one pair is merged, and from 14.97 to 15.61 when one triple or two pairs are formed. The smallest value (14.97) is just barely larger than $d_{14} = 14.86$ prior to aggregation, which illustrates the tendency of distances to shrink when more and more status categories are aggregated.

Average Distances

If aggregation tends to reduce distances, one would expect that it will also lead to smaller average distances, $\bar{d}_i = \sum_j \pi_j d_{ij}$, from the various status categories. This problem is pursued in Table 5.20. Its first row gives these average distances (adjusted according to the distance model) prior to aggregation. They decrease monotonically from the first to the fifth category and they increase thereafter. This is as it should be, because the fifth is the median status category (see Table 5.15).

TABLE 5.20

AVERAGE DISTANCES AT DIFFERENT LEVELS OF AGGREGATION

Aggregates	d_1	d_2	d_3	d_4	d_5	d_6	d_7	d
	Seven categories							
None	14.95	5.03	2.16	1.34	1.05	1.27	1.65	1.79
	Six sets of categories							
(1, 2)	←——5.95——→		2.02	1.19	.91	1.13	1.51	1.49
(2, 3)	14.26	←——2.30——→		1.23	.94	1.15	1.54	1.57
(3, 4)	14.77	4.81	←——1.37——→		.98	1.20	1.58	1.65
(4, 5)	14.63	4.86	2.03	←——.95——→		1.20	1.59	1.65
(5, 6)	14.20	4.76	2.01	1.22	←——.93——→		1.55	1.62
(6, 7)	14.94	5.00	2.13	1.30	1.01	←——1.26——→		1.71
	Five sets of categories: one triple							
(1, 2, 3)	←———2.28———→			1.00	.72	.93	1.32	1.11
(2, 3, 4)	13.97	←———1.26———→			.82	1.03	1.41	1.34
(3, 4, 5)	14.17	4.46	←———.79———→			1.05	1.44	1.39
(4, 5, 6)	13.67	4.53	1.85	←———.80———→			1.47	1.46
(5, 6, 7)	14.00	4.64	1.91	1.13	←———.83———→			1.44
	Five sets of categories: two pairs							
(1, 2), (3, 4)	←——5.74——→		←——1.23——→		.84	1.05	1.44	1.36
(1, 2), (4, 5)	←——5.77——→		1.89	←——.81——→		1.05	1.45	1.36
(1, 2), (5, 6)	←——5.65——→		1.87	1.08	←——.79——→		1.40	1.33
(1, 2), (6, 7)	←——5.93——→		1.99	1.16	.87	←——1.12——→		1.42
(2, 3), (4, 5)	13.95	←——2.17——→		←——.84——→		1.08	1.47	1.44
(2, 3), (5, 6)	13.54	←——2.14——→		1.11	←——.81——→		1.43	1.41
(2, 3), (6, 7)	14.24	←——2.27——→		1.19	.90	←——1.15——→		1.49
(3, 4), (5, 6)	14.04	4.56	←——1.25——→		←——.86——→		1.47	1.49
(3, 4), (6, 7)	14.76	4.78	←——1.34——→		.94	←——1.19——→		1.57
(4, 5), (6, 7)	14.62	4.83	1.99	←——.91——→		←——1.19——→		1.57

The other rows of Table 5.20 contain the average distances at various levels of aggregation. It appears that in every case $\bar{d}_i$ is smaller than the corresponding figure in the first row, but the relative discrepancies are different for different status categories. When six sets of categories are used, the maximum reduction of $\bar{d}_1$ and $\bar{d}_2$ below the level prior to aggregation is about 5 per cent, but for lower status categories $(\bar{d}_4, \ldots, \bar{d}_7)$ it is of the order of 10 per cent or higher. Aggregation to five sets leads to maximum reductions that are about twice as large. Also, when two adjacent status categories are merged, the average distance from the pair is typically close to the smaller of the two corresponding average distances prior to aggregation. For example, the average distances from the pair $(1, 2)$ vary between 5.65 and 5.95; they are much closer to $\bar{d}_2 = 5.03$ (prior to aggregation) than to $\bar{d}_1 = 14.95$ (same). Similarly, the average distances from $(6, 7)$ are between 1.12 and 1.26, and hence smaller than both $\bar{d}_6 = 1.27$ and $d_7 = 1.65$ but closer to $\bar{d}_6$.

The result of all this is that the overall average distance $\bar{d}$ is affected rather substantially by the aggregation. Its value is almost 1.8 prior to aggregation; its average over the six cases of six sets of status categories is slightly over 1.6, and over the 15 cases of five sets of status categories a little over 1.4. Figure 5.6 provides an illustration; it contains the average distances from the five sets of status categories which were illustrated earlier in Figure 5.5, with $(3, 4)$ and $(6, 7)$ as two pairs, and also the average distances from the original seven categories. The difference between the two cases is minor for the two top categories, but substantial for the lower end of the social scale.

Conclusion

It thus appears that for the data considered here, aggregation has little effect in certain applications of Markov chain theory but serious effects in others. Those which fall under the former category are the limit distribution, the rate of convergence toward that distribution as measured by the square of the second largest latent root of the transition matrix, the descendance effects (although to a lesser degree), and the symmetry of the exchange matrix.

However, aggregation has undesirable effects with respect to the implementation of the distance model. The data analyzed here indicate that aggregation leads to a poorer fit of the model and that it tends to affect the distances in downward direction, thus reducing also the average distances from the various status categories. This suggests that raising the number of status categories above seven will lead to still larger average distances than

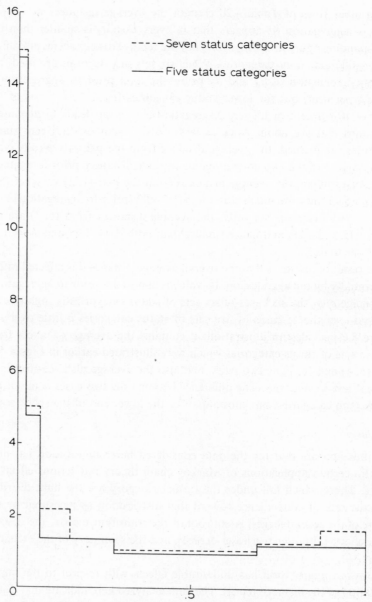

Fig. 5.6. Average distances before and after aggregation

those shown by the broken lines of Figure 5.6. For example, we could introduce an eighth status category by separating from the seventh those un-

skilled workers who are illiterate. It is quite conceivable that the average distance from this eighth category is very large, which could indicate that the average distance as a function of status has a vertical asymptote both at the upper and at the lower end of the social scale.

Indeed, one can imagine that status is measured continuously by means of a real-valued variable x, $0 \leq x \leq 1$, rather than in terms of a finite number of status categories. The average distance will then be a positive function of x with one single minimum at $x = \frac{1}{2}$, and this will be true for the rth moment of the distance under the generalized distance model (6.5). By selecting a particular mathematical form for such a moment function and using (6.9) one can adjust the parameters of this function to a given observed transition matrix.

PROBLEMS

1 Consider the probability (1.1) and the definitions below (1.1). Suppose that the chance of a person having k years of formal education depends on his father's occupation and also on the number of years of his father's education, $P[M_k|F \in i, F_h]$, where F_h stands for "the father has h years of formal education". Prove that the joint conditional probability that a person is in the jth occupational category and has k years of formal education, given that the father is in the ith occupational category and has h years of formal education, is equal to

$$P[M_k|F \in i, F_h]P[M \in j|F \in i, M_k] = p_{hi, kj} \quad \text{say}$$

and conclude that under these conditions the joint education-occupation distribution in successive generations follows a Markov process. Write down the transition matrix and note that its order is $mn \times mn$ when h and i take m and n values, respectively.

2 Apply the initial distributions $\mathbf{q}_0 = [1 \quad 0]'$ and $\mathbf{q}_0 = [0 \quad 1]'$ to the transition matrix (1.6). For both cases, compute $\mathbf{q}_t$ for $t = 1, 2, \ldots$ and illustrate the result graphically.

3 (*Proof of the convergence to the limit distribution for general regular Markov chains*) Prove that when $\mathbf{P}$ has some zero elements, the sequence d_t considered in (1.20) is still nonincreasing although not necessarily decreasing. Suppose that $\mathbf{P}^N$ for some positive integer N has only positive elements, and write ε' for the value of its smallest element. Prove $d_{kN} \leq (1-2\varepsilon')^k$ and conclude that the nonincreasing sequence

d_t has a subsequence which converges to zero, and hence that $d_t \to 0$ as $t \to \infty$. Complete the proof.

4 Generalize (2.3) by assuming that the n occupational categories are combined into G sets of categories in such a way that each category belongs to exactly one set. Write Π_g and Q_{tg} for $\sum \pi_i$ and $\sum q_{ti}$, where the summation is over $i \in S_g$, and prove

$$\sum_{g=1}^{G} \Pi_g \log \frac{\Pi_g}{Q_{tg}} \approx \tfrac{1}{2}\lambda_2^{2t}(\mathbf{q}_0' \mathbf{u}_2)^2 \sum_{g=1}^{G} \frac{V_{2g}^2}{\Pi_g}$$

where V_{2g} is the sum over $i \in S_g$ of v_{2i} [the ith element of the vector $\mathbf{v}_2$ which occurs in (2.16)]. Conclude that the movement of the occupational distribution toward the limit distribution, when confined to sets of categories rather than individual categories, is characterized by the same rate of convergence (λ_2^{2t}).

5 (*Continuation*) Consider the conditional probabilities π_i/Π_g (in equilibrium) and q_{ti}/Q_{tg} (for the tth distribution) that a person belongs to the ith occupational category, given that he falls under S_g. Prove:

(1) $$\sum_{i \in S_g} \frac{\pi_i}{\Pi_g} \log \frac{\pi_i/\Pi_g}{q_{ti}/Q_{tg}} \approx \tfrac{1}{2}\lambda_2^{2t} \frac{(\mathbf{q}_0' \mathbf{u}_2)^2}{\Pi_g} \left[\sum_{i \in S_g} \frac{v_{2i}^2}{\pi_i} - \frac{V_{2g}^2}{\Pi_g} \right]$$

where the left-hand side is the information expectation of the message which transforms the conditional proportions of the tth occupational distribution into those of the limit distribution. Draw your own conclusions as to the rate of convergence at this conditional level.

6 (*Continuation*) The expression in brackets in the right-hand side of (1) is the difference between two positive quantities. It would be awkward if this difference could be negative (why?). Argue that this cannot happen by proving that the expression in brackets is equal to

$$\Pi_g \sum_{i \in S_g} \frac{\pi_i}{\Pi_g} \left(\frac{v_{2i}}{\pi_i} \right)^2 - \Pi_g \left(\sum_{i \in S_g} \frac{\pi_i}{\Pi_g} \frac{v_{2i}}{\pi_i} \right)^2 = \Pi_g \sum_{i \in S_g} \frac{\pi_i}{\Pi_g} \left(\frac{v_{2i}}{\pi_i} - \sum_{j \in S_g} \frac{\pi_j}{\Pi_g} \frac{v_{2j}}{\pi_j} \right)^2$$

Verify that the expression in the right-hand side is a multiple Π_g of the weighted variance of the ratios of the corresponding elements of the characteristic rows of $\mathbf{P}$ that correspond to the second and first roots, with weights proportional to the characteristic row elements corresponding to the latter root.

7 Apply (3.1) to write (3.7) in the form

$$m_{ij} = \sum_{k=1}^{n} p_{ik} m_{kj} - \frac{p_{ij}}{\pi_j} + 1 \qquad\qquad i, j = 1, \ldots, n$$

and prove that this is equivalent to

$$M = PM - P\Delta^{-1} + \iota\iota'$$

where $M = [m_{ij}]$ is the $n \times n$ matrix of mean first passage times, Δ the $n \times n$ diagonal matrix with $\pi_1, \ldots, \pi_n$ on the diagonal, and ι a column vector consisting of n unit elements. Next prove:

$$P = I + (\Delta^{-1} - \iota\iota')(M - \Delta^{-1})^{-1}$$

This shows that the matrix of mean first passage times determines the transition matrix uniquely. Note that the nonzero elements of Δ (the proportions of the limit distribution) can be found from M by taking the reciprocals of its diagonal elements.

8 Multiply the travel time τ_{ij} defined in (4.4) by π_i and sum over i to verify that the result is equal to the right-hand side of (4.6). Also, multiply τ_{ij} by π_j and sum over j to verify that the result is equal to (4.9).

9 Prove that each Markov chain which represents perfect mobility is reversible.

10 (*Continuation*) Prove that the matrix $\Pi - \pi\pi'$ provides the discrepancies between the exchange matrix elements and the values that would prevail if there were perfect mobility. Compute these discrepancy matrices for the Π's shown in the first five columns of Table 5.8, using the limit proportions given in the last column of Table 5.6, and discuss the regularity which you observe.

11 Write eq. (6.5) in the form

$$d_{ij} = (x_1^r + x_2^r + \ldots + x_k^r)^{1/r}$$

where the x's are successive distances (all positive) and $k = j - i$. Suppose that x_1 exceeds all other x's; prove that, as $r \to \infty$, x_1^r dominates x_i^r for each $i > 1$, and use this to prove that d_{ij} converges to x_1 as $r \to \infty$. Next analyze the asymptotic behavior of d_{ij} when $x_1 = x_2$ and when all other x's are smaller than these two.

12 When the generalized distance model (6.5) rather than the linear model (6.1) is applied to the Danish data, a minimum of I equal to .0027 is attained at $r = .87$. For the British data of Section 5.6 the minimum is .0028, attained at $r = .81$. Discuss these figures in relation to the other similar figures obtained for the Danish, British and American data, and consider in particular the implications of these r values for the distances between status categories.

13 Prove that, under the condition of reversibility, the total area below the

Danish horizontal line segments of Figure 5.2 is equal to the analogous total area in Figure 5.5.

14 HARDY, LITTLEWOOD and PÓLYA (1952, p. 26) prove a theorem stating that if a random variable takes positive values which are not all equal, the rth root of its rth moment is an increasing function of r. Use this theorem to prove that the American average distances $\bar{d}_i$ are below the corresponding horizontal line segments in the lower part of Figure 5.5.

15 For the b_α's introduced at the end of Section 5.6, prove that (given fixed limit proportions)

$$(2) \qquad \frac{\partial s_{ij}}{\partial b_\alpha} = \frac{\partial d_{ij}}{\partial b_\alpha} - \frac{\partial \bar{d}_i}{\partial b_\alpha} - \frac{\partial \bar{d}_j}{\partial b_\alpha} + \frac{\partial \bar{d}}{\partial b_\alpha}$$

holds for all pairs (i, j), including the cases $i = j$. Next use this result to prove

$$(3) \qquad \frac{\partial \hat{\pi}_{hk}}{\partial b_\alpha} = - \sum_{i=1}^{n} \sum_{j=1}^{n} s^{hi} s^{jk} \left(\frac{\partial d_{ij}}{\partial b_\alpha} - \frac{\partial \bar{d}_i}{\partial b_\alpha} - \frac{\partial \bar{d}_j}{\partial b_\alpha} + \frac{\partial \bar{d}}{\partial b_\alpha} \right)$$

Furthermore, prove

$$(4) \qquad \sum_{i=1}^{n} \sum_{j=1}^{n} s^{hi} s^{jk} \frac{\partial \bar{d}_i}{\partial b_\alpha} = -\pi_k \sum_{i=1}^{n} \sum_{j=1}^{n} s^{hi} \pi_j \frac{\partial d_{ij}}{\partial b_\alpha}$$

$$(5) \qquad \sum_{i=1}^{n} \sum_{j=1}^{n} s^{hi} s^{jk} \frac{\partial \bar{d}}{\partial b_\alpha} = \pi_h \pi_k \sum_{i=1}^{n} \sum_{j=1}^{n} \pi_i \pi_j \frac{\partial d_{ij}}{\partial b_\alpha}$$

and use this to prove

$$(6) \qquad \frac{\partial \hat{\pi}_{hk}}{\partial b_\alpha} = - \sum_{i=1}^{n} \sum_{j=1}^{n} c_{hi} c_{jk} \frac{\partial d_{ij}}{\partial b_\alpha}$$

the c's being defined in (6.13).

16 (*Continuation*) Use (6.11) to prove

$$\frac{\partial d_{ij}}{\partial b_\alpha} = \frac{1}{r} d_{ij}^{1-r} \quad \text{if } \min (i, j) < \alpha < \max (i, j)$$

$$0 \qquad \text{otherwise}$$

and combine this with (6) to obtain

$$\frac{\partial \hat{\pi}_{hk}}{\partial b_\alpha} = -\frac{1}{r} \sum_{i<\alpha} \sum_{j>\alpha} (c_{hi} c_{jk} + c_{hj} c_{ik}) d_{ij}^{1-r}$$

Then complete the proof of (6.12).

17 (*Continuation*) Prove that (6.12) can be simplified to (6.14) in the case $r = 1$.

BIBLIOGRAPHY

BERGER, J., and J. L. SNELL (1957). "On the Concept of Equal Exchange." *Behavioral Science*, Vol. 2, pp. 111–118.

BERKSON, J. (1944). "Application of the Logistic Function to Bio-assay." *Journal of the American Statistical Association*, Vol. 39, pp. 357–365.

BERKSON, J. (1946). "Approximation of Chi-square by 'Probits' and by 'Logits'." *Journal of the American Statistical Association*, Vol. 41, pp. 70–74.

BERKSON, J. (1949). "Minimum χ^2 and Maximum Likelihood Solution in Terms of a Linear Transform, with Particular Reference to Bio-assay." *Journal of the American Statistical Association*, Vol. 44, pp. 273–278.

BERKSON, J. (1953). "A Statistically Precise and Relatively Simple Method of Estimating the Bio-assay with Quantal Response, Based on the Logistic Function." *Journal of the American Statistical Association*, Vol. 48, pp. 565–599.

BERKSON, J. (1955). "Maximum Likelihood and Minimum χ^2 Estimates of the Logistic Function." *Journal of the American Statistical Association*, Vol. 50, pp. 130–162.

BERKSON, J. (1968). "Application of Minimum Logit χ^2 Estimate to a Problem of Grizzle with a Notation on the Problem of 'No Interaction'." *Biometrics*, Vol. 24, pp. 75–95.

BESHERS, J. M., and E. O. LAUMANN (1967). "Social Distance: A Network Approach." *American Sociological Review*, Vol. 32, pp. 225–236.

BOCK, R. D. (1971). "Estimating Multinomial Response Relations for Ordered Categories." Mimeographed report. Department of Education of The University of Chicago.

COLEMAN, J. S. (1964). *Introduction to Mathematical Sociology*. New York: The Free Press of Glencoe.

CRAMER, J. S. (1964). "Efficient Grouping, Regression and Correlation in Engel Curve Analysis." *Journal of the American Statistical Association*, Vol. 59, pp. 233–250.

DEMING, W. E., and F. F. STEPHAN (1940). "On a Least Squares Adjustment of a Sampled Frequency Table When the Expected Marginal Totals Are Known." *Annals of Mathematical Statistics*, Vol. 11, pp. 427–444.

DOSSER, D. (1963). "Allocating the Burden of International Aid for Underdeveloped Countries." *The Review of Economics and Statistics*, Vol. 45 (1963) , pp. 207–209.

DOSSER, D., and A. T. PEACOCK (1964). "The International Distribution of Income with 'Maximum' Aid." *The Review of Economics and Statistics*, Vol. 46, pp. 432–434.

DUNCAN, O. D., and B. DUNCAN (1955). "A Methodological Analysis of Segregation Indexes." *American Sociological Review*, Vol. 20, pp. 210–217.

FIENBERG, S. E. (1970). "An Iterative Procedure for Estimation in Contingency Tables." *Annals of Mathematical Statistics*, Vol. 41, pp. 907–917.

FINKELSTEIN, M. O., and R. M. FRIEDBERG (1967). "The Application of an Entropy Theory of Concentration to the Clayton Act." *The Yale Law Review*, Vol. 76, pp. 677–717.

FINNEY, D. J. (1964). *Probit Analysis*. Second edition (first edition, 1947). Cambridge University Press.

FRIEDMAN, Y. (1971). "Sources of Division in the U.S. House of Representatives, 1947–1968." Doctoral Dissertation, The University of Chicago.

GLASS, D. V., and J. R. HALL (1954). "Social Mobility in Great Britain: A Study of Inter-Generation Changes in Status." Chapter VIII of *Social Mobility in Britain*, edited by D. V. Glass. Glencoe, Ill.: The Free Press.

GRILICHES, Z. (1957). "Hybrid Corn: An Exploration in Economics of Technological Change." Doctoral Dissertation, The University of Chicago.

GROSFELD, F., (1967). "De kwadratuur van de democratische cirkelgang." *Vrij Nederland*, December 30, 1967, p. 4.

HARDY, G. H., J. E. LITTLEWOOD and G. PÓLYA (1952). *Inequalities*. Second edition (first edition, 1934). Cambridge University Press.

HERFINDAHL, O. C. (1950). "Concentration in the Steel Industry." Doctoral Dissertation, Columbia University.

HILDENBRAND, W., and H. PASCHEN (1964). "Ein axiomatisch begründetes Konzentrationsmass." *Statistical Information*, published by the Statistical Office of the European Communities, No. 3, pp. 53–61.

HIRSCHMAN, A. O. (1945). *National Power and the Structure of Foreign Trade*. Berkeley and Los Angeles: University of California Press.

HOROWITZ, A., and I. HOROWITZ (1968). "Entropy, Markov Processes, and Competition in the Brewing Industry." *Journal of Industrial Economics*, Vol. 16, pp. 196–211.

JOCHEMS, D. B. (1962). "Forecasting the Outcomes of Soccer Matches: A Statistical Appraisal of the Dutch Experience." *Metrika*, Vol. 5, pp. 194–207.

KEMENY, J. G., and J. L. SNELL (1960). *Finite Markov Chains*. Princeton, N. J.: D. Van Nostrand, Inc.

KENDALL, M. G., and A. STUART (1950). "The Law of the Cubic Proportion in Election Results." *British Journal of Sociology*, Vol. 1, pp. 183–196.

KENDALL, M. G., and A. STUART (1952). "La loi du cube dans les élections Britanniques." *Revue Française de Science Politique*, Vol. 2, pp. 270–276.

KESSELMAN, M. (1967). *The Ambiguous Consensus*. New York: Alfred A. Knopf.

KHINCHIN, A. I. (1957). *Mathematical Foundations of Information Theory*. New York: Dover Publications, Inc.

KING, W. R. (1965). "A Stochastic Personnel-Assignment Model." *Operations Research*, Vol. 13, pp. 67–81.

KOOPMAN, B. O., and G. E. KIMBALL (1959). "Information Theory." Chapter 9 of *Notes on Operations Research*. Cambridge, Mass.: The M.I.T. Press.

LEV, B. (1968). "The Aggregation Problem in Financial Statements: An Informational Approach." *Journal of Accounting Research*, Vol. 6, pp. 247–261.

LEV, B. (1969). "An Information Theory Analysis of U.S. Corporate Balance Sheets, 1947–1966." Report 6940 of the Center for Mathematical Studies in Business and Economics, The University of Chicago.

LEV, B. (1970a). "The Informational Approach to Aggregation in Financial Statements: Extensions." *Journal of Accounting Research*, Vol. 8, pp. 78–94.

LEV, B. (1970b). "The RAS Method for Two-dimensional Forecasts." Report 7037 of the Center for Mathematical Studies in Business and Economics, The University of Chicago.

LIEBERSON, S., and G. V. FUGUITT (1967). "Negro-White Occupational Differences in the Absence of Discrimination." *American Journal of Sociology*, Vol. 73, pp. 188–200.

LINDLEY, D. V. (1956). "On a Measure of the Information Provided by an Experiment." *Annals of Mathematical Statistics*, Vol.27, pp. 986–1005.

LINDLEY, D. V. (1964). "The Bayesian Analysis of Contingency Tables." *Annals of Mathematical Statistics*, Vol. 35, pp. 1622–1643.

LUCE, R. D. (1960). "The Theory of Selective Information and Some of Its Behavioral Applications." Part I of *Developments in Mathematical Psychology*, edited by R. D. Luce. Glencoe, Ill.: The Free Press.

LUCE, R. D., and P. SUPPES (1965). "Preference, Utility, and Subjective Probability." Chapter 19 of *Handbook of Mathematical Psychology*, edited by R. D. Luce, R. R. Bush, and E. Galanter. New York: John Wiley and Sons, Inc.

MacRAE, D., JR. (1970). *Issues and Parties in Legislative Voting*. New York: Harper and Row.

MARCH, J. G. (1957–58). "Party Legislative Representation as a Function of Election Results." *Public Opinion Quarterly*, Vol. 21, pp. 521–542.

MATRAS, J. (1967). "Social Mobility and Social Structure: Some Insights from the Linear Model." *American Sociological Review*, Vol. 32, pp. 608–614.

MOSTELLER, F. (1968). "Association and Estimation in Contingency Tables." *Journal of the American Statistical Association*, Vol. 63, pp. 1–28.

PARKS, R. W. (1969). "Systems of Demand Equations: An Empirical Comparison of Alternative Functional Forms." *Econometrica*, Vol. 37, pp. 629–650.

PENROSE, L. S. (1946). "The Elementary Statistics of Majority Voting." *Journal of the Royal Statistical Society*, Vol. 109, pp. 53–57.

PENROSE, L. S. (1952). *On the Objective Study of Crowd Behaviour*. London: H. K. Lewis.

PRAIS, S. J. (1955). "Measuring Social Mobility." *Journal of the Royal Statistical Society*, Vol. 118, pp. 56–66.

PRESTON, M. G., and P. BARATTA (1948). "An Experimental Study of the Auction-Value of an Uncertain Outcome." *American Journal of Psychology*, Vol. 61, pp. 183–193.

RAE, D. W. (1967). *The Political Consequences of Electoral Laws*. New Haven, Conn.: Yale University Press.

RICE, S. R. (1928). *Quantitative Methods in Politics*. New York: Alfred A. Knopf, Inc.

ROGOFF, N. (1953). *Recent Trends in Occupational Mobility*. Glencoe, Ill.: The Free Press.

ROSENSTEIN-RODAN, P. N. (1961). "International Aid for Underdeveloped Countries." *The Review of Economics and Statistics*, Vol. 43 (1961), pp. 107–138.

SHANNO, D. F. (1969). "Inverse Quasi-Newton Methods." Report 6938 of the Center for Mathematical Studies in Business and Economics, The University of Chicago.

SHANNON, C. E. (1948). "A Mathematical Theory of Communication." *Bell System Technical Journal*, Vol. 27, pp. 379–423, 623–656.

STONE, R., and A. BROWN (1964). *A Computable Model of Economic Growth*. London: Chapman and Hall, Ltd.

STOUFFER, S. A., E. A. SUCHMAN, L. C. DeVINNEY, S. A. STAR, and R. M. WILLIAMS, JR. (1949). *The American Soldier*, Volume I. Princeton University Press.

SVALASTOGA, K. (1959). *Prestige, Class and Mobility*. London: William Heinemann, Ltd.

THEIL, H. (1966). *Applied Economic Forecasting*. New York: American Elsevier Company, and Amsterdam: North-Holland Publishing Company.

THEIL, H. (1967). *Economics and Information Theory*. New York: American Elsevier

Company, and Amsterdam: North-Holland Publishing Company.

THEIL, H. (1969a). "How to Worry About Increased Expenditures." *The Accounting Review*, Vol. 44, pp. 27–37.

THEIL, H. (1969b). "A Multinomial Extension of the Linear Logit Model." *International Economic Review*, Vol. 10, pp. 251–259.

THEIL, H. (1969c). "On the Use of Information Theory Concepts in the Analysis of Financial Statements." *Management Science*, Vol. 15, pp. 459–480.

THEIL, H. (1969d). "The Desired Political Entropy." *The American Political Science Review*, Vol. 63, pp. 521–525.

THEIL, H. (1970a). "On the Estimation of Relationships Involving Qualitative Variables." *American Journal of Sociology*, Vol. 76, pp. 103–154.

THEIL, H. (1970b). "The Cube Law Revisited." *Journal of the American Statistical Association*, Vol. 65, pp. 1213–1219.

THEIL, H. (1971a). *Principles of Econometrics*. New York: John Wiley and Sons, Inc., and Amsterdam: North-Holland Publishing Company.

THEIL, H. (1971b). "The Allocation of Power That Minimizes Tension." *Operations Research*, Vol. 19, pp. 977–982.

THEIL, H., and A. J. FINIZZA (1967). "An Informational Approach to the Measurement of Racial Segregation in Schools." Report 6712 of the Center for Mathematical Studies in Business and Economics, The University of Chicago.

THEIL, H., and A. J. FINIZZA (1971). "A Note on the Measurement of Racial Integration of Schools by Means of Informational Concepts." *Journal of Mathematical Sociology*, Vol. 1, pp. 187–193.

THEIL, H., and R. F. KOSOBUD (1968). "How Informative Are Consumer Buying Intentions Surveys?" *The Review of Economics and Statistics*, Vol. 50, pp. 50–59.

TIDEMAN, T. N. (1967). "Graphical Representations of Some Concepts from Information Theory and Its Economic Applications." Report 6708 of the Center for Mathematical Studies in Business and Economics, The University of Chicago.

WEIL, R. L., JR. (1967). "Functional Selection for the Stochastic Assignment Model." *Operations Research*, Vol. 15, pp. 1063–1067.

HINTS FOR SELECTED PROBLEMS

CHAPTER 1

3 The entropy is .161 bit (to three decimal places). The entropy of the distribution (.976, .024) is .163 bit and that of (.977, .023) is .158 bit (also to three decimal places).

5 See the table on pages 330–331.

6 What is special about the industry group S_4?

7 Combining (1, 2) reduces the entropy from 2.23 to 1.95 bits (to two decimal places).

13 Inspect the relevant p's and q's in Figure 1.7.

CHAPTER 2

3 The relative error of the first quadratic approximation is less than one-tenth of 1 per cent; that of the second is almost 30 per cent of the correct value.

4 Prove that $0 < P_r < 1$ holds when $0 < p_j < 1$ is true for some $j \in D_r$.

5 See the table on pages 330–331.

8 At the level of the three proportions, the revision reduces the information inaccuracy by almost two-thirds.

10 To prove (5), use the constraint that the q's add up to one as well as (4).

14 See THEIL (1967, Section 4.2).

17 To prove (11), apply the quadratic approximation to the information expectation. Why is it not really an approximation in this case?

CHAPTER 3

11 See THEIL (1969c).

14 See THEIL (1969c).

BLACK AND WHITE STUDENTS IN THE 23 SCHOOLS OF THE FOURTH DISTRICT OF THE CHICAGO PUBLIC SCHOOL SYSTEM

Year	Bridge		Burbank		Byford		Canty		Canty Branch		Dever	
	Black	White	Black	White	Black	White	Black	White	Black	White	Black	White
1963	0	435	0	287	0	489	0	782	*	*	0	782
1964	0	439	0	312	0	524	0	782	*	*	0	862
1965	0	421	0	330	0	555	0	897	*	*	0	881
1966	0	407	0	371	3	621	0	886	*	*	0	892
1967	0	428	0	393	2	571	0	793	0	75	0	857
1968	48	413	57	393	6	583	0	830	0	76	88	827
1969	54	525	56	396	3	638	0	812	0	62	82	850

	Emmet		Hay		Hay U.G.**		Howe		Key		Key Branch	
	Black	White	Black	White	Black	White	Black	White	Black	White	Black	White
1963	0	1081	0	413	*	*	1	492	0	395	0	88
1964	0	1120	0	440	*	*	1	497	0	384	0	94
1965	0	1086	0	439	*	*	0	564	0	419	1	92
1966	0	1109	0	493	*	*	0	553	0	461	1	94
1967	13	1173	0	437	238	166	1	582	0	508	7	95
1968	294	1154	0	410	349	125	3	586	4	510	9	97

Year	Sayre		Smyser		Spencer		Thorp, O.A.		Young	
1963	0	393	0	546	0	903	0	683	79	631
1964	0	400	0	521	0	971	0	676	85	672
1965	0	421	0	526	112	1004	0	696	94	732
1966	0	433	0	526	694	610	0	734	104	694
1967	0	448	0	564	1091	234	0	765	112	733
1968	53	479	58	558	1474	150	78	774	114	760
1969	63	505	62	570	2015	61	77	772	104	761

Year												
1963	0	575	0	728	0	335	0	511	86	715	7	837
1964	0	582	0	747	0	347	0	534	203	644	6	880
1965	3	623	0	769	0	409	0	544	278	639	11	922
1966	2	661	0	831	0	410	0	556	597	438	14	942
1967	2	669	0	856	0	418	0	616	1308	251	12	981
1968	7	658	97	865	0	421	66	606	1521	65	13	977
1969	6	709	101	851	0	447	67	595	2057	23	21	980

* School is not open in this year.

** Hay Upper Grade.

CHAPTER 4

1 The correct values (to three decimal places) of the logit at $p = .6, .7,$ .8 and .9 are: .405, .847, 1.386 and 2.197.

6 Conservatives are more sensitive than liberals (on the basis of the relevant point estimates).

11 Simplify the notation by writing p_r for $p_{ij}(r)$.

18 An average conditional entropy never becomes smaller when the set of conditioning factors is reduced to a subset.

22 What would you conclude from the upward trend of the standard deviation (σ_t)?

25 To derive the covariance of b and b', separate the summation over i in the numerator of $b-\beta$ into two parts, $i \in S_g$ and $i \in \bar{S}_g$, where $\bar{S}_g$ is the set of observations that do not fall under S_g.

CHAPTER 5

1 Note that the result is also applicable when the probability (1.1) involves the father's education as a conditioning factor.

5 Prove first:

$$\log \frac{\pi_i/\Pi_g}{q_{ti}/Q_{tg}} = -\log \frac{q_{ti}}{\pi_i} + \log \frac{Q_{tg}}{\Pi_g}$$

$$\approx -\left[\frac{q_{ti}-\pi_i}{\pi_i} - \frac{(q_{ti}-\pi_i)^2}{2\pi_i^2}\right] + \left[\frac{Q_{tg}-\Pi_g}{\Pi_g} - \frac{(Q_{tg}-\Pi_g)^2}{2\Pi_g^2}\right]$$

7 Note that $\mathbf{M}-\mathbf{\Delta}^{-1}$ is the matrix of mean first passage times with its diagonal elements (the mean recurrence times) replaced by zero.

8 Use (3.5) and (3.4).

12 Consider condition (3) on page 286.

15 For (2), use (5.21) and (5.22). For (3), use (6.2). For (4) and (5), use $\iota'\mathbf{S}^{-1} = -\boldsymbol{\pi}'$, which follows (prove this!) from (5.9) and (3.5).

17 Prove first:

$$\sum_{j>\alpha} c_{jk} = -\sum_{j<\alpha} c_{jk}$$

INDEX

Below are listed, under four different headings, entries in the Index which apply to the various disciplines discussed in this book.

Economics and Industrial Organization

Concentration ratio; Consumer buying intention survey; Consumer demand; Employment distribution; Employment entropy; Hirschman-Herfindahl index; Income inequality; Industrial concentration; Industrial diversity; Input-output analysis; Lorenz curve; Market entropy; Occupational distribution

Management Science and Accounting

Assets information; Balance sheet; Balance sheet information; Budget score; Compustat firms; Current items information; Expenditure control; Financial diversity; Fixed items information; IFORS; Information balance sheet; Liabilities information; Market entropy; Materiality problem; Personnel assignment; Sales forecasting; Time horizon information

Regional Science and Marketing

Brand loyalty; Camp location (preference for); Concentration ratio; Consumer buying intention survey; Consumer demand; Distance model (regional); Employment distribution; Employment entropy; Income inequality; Industrial concentration; Industrial diversity; Lorenz curve; Market entropy; Sales forecasting

Sociology and Political Science

Camp location (preference for); Coalition cabinet; Combat outfit (preference for); Cube law; Descendance effect; Destination effect; d'Hondt's method; Dissimilarity index; Distance*; Distance effect*; Election results; Exchange matrix; First passage time; Limit distribution; Markov chain model; Mean first passage time; Mean recurrence time; Military policemen (evaluation of); Mobility*; Occupational distribution; Parliament composition; Party loyalty; Political entropy; Printers' union; Racial entropy; Redistricting; Rice's index of cohesion; Roll call; Segregation; Senate of United States; Square-root representation system; Status category; Transition matrix; Travel time*; Waiting time; Weak proportionality axiom

---

* Intergenerational occupational mobility.

333

RENEWALS: 691-4574

DATE DUE

MAY 10